# Contemporary Anthropology:
## AN ANTHOLOGY

# Contemporary Anthropology:
## AN ANTHOLOGY

Daniel G. Bates
and
Susan H. Lees
both of Hunter College,
The City University of New York

Alfred A. Knopf  New York

THIS IS A BORZOI BOOK
PUBLISHED BY ALFRED A. KNOPF, INC.
First Edition

987654321

**Library of Congress Cataloging in Publication Data**

Main entry under title:

Contemporary anthropology.

1. Anthropology–Addresses, essays, lectures. 2. Anthropology–Field
work–Addresses, essays, lectures. I. Bates, Daniel G. II. Lees, Susan H.
GN29.C59    301.2    79–26123
ISBN 0–394–32043–3

Manufactured in the United States of America

(October 28, 1977), pp. 373–378. Copyright © 1977 by the American Association for the Advancement of Science. Reprinted by permission of *Science.*

Susan H. Lees, "Hydraulic Development and Political Response in the Valley of Oaxaca, Mexico," from *Anthropological Quarterly,* Vol. 49, 3 (July 1976), pp. 107–210. Reprinted by permission of the *Anthropological Quarterly* and The Catholic University of America Press.

Elliot Liebow, "A Field Experience in Retrospect," from *Tally's Corner.* Copyright © 1967 by Little, Brown and Company. Reprinted by permission of Little, Brown and Company.

Madeleine Leininger, "Witchcraft Practices and Psychoculture Therapy with Urban U. S. Families," from *Human Organization,* Vol. 32, 1 (1973), pp. 73–83. Reprinted by permission of the Society for Applied Anthropology.

Lorna Marshall, "Sharing, Talking and Giving: Relief of Social Tensions Among !Kung Bushmen," *Africa,* Vol. 31 (1961). Reprinted by permission of the auithor and the International African Institute.

John Middleton, "The End of Fieldwork," from *The Study of the Lugbara: Expectation and Paradox in Anthropological Research.* Copyright © 1970 by Holt, Rinehart and Winston, Inc. Reprinted by permission of Holt, Rinehart, and Winston, Inc.

William E. Mitchell, "New Weapons Stir Up Old Ghosts," Vol. 82, 6 (December 1973), pp. 75–84. Copyright © the American Museum of Natural History, 1973. Reprinted by permission of *Natural History Magazine* (December 1973).

Bernard Neitschmann, "When the Turtle Collapses, the World Ends," Vol. 83, 2 (June 1974), pp. 34–42. Copyright © the American Museum of Natural History, 1974. Reprinted by permission of *Natural History Magazine* (June/July 1974).

Elliot P. Skinner, "Political Conflict and Revolution in an African Town," from *American Anthropologist,* Vol. 74 (1972), pp. 1208–1217. Reprinted by permission of American Anthropological Association.

# Acknowledgments

In preparing this collection of essays the authors benefited from the advice and assistance of many people. We would in particular like to express our appreciation to Francis Conant, Daniel Gross, Rachel Helm, Carol Hirsch, William Irons, Gregory Johnson, Karen Judd, Jim Lemke, and Bahram Tavakolian.

# Contents

Introduction     1

Part I.    **Being an Anthropologist**     9
  1. Doing Fieldwork Among the Yąnomamö     11
     Napoleon A. Chagnon
  2. Kapluna Daughter: Doing Fieldwork Among the Utku
     Eskimos     25
     Jean Briggs
  3. Housekeeping in El Nahra     33
     Elizabeth Fernea


Part II.    **Responding to Environmental Pressures**     47
  4. The Predatory Baboons of Kekopey     49
     Robert S. O. Harding and Shirley C. Strum
  5. When the Turtle Collapses, the World Ends     56
     Bernard Nietschmann
  6. "Development" and the Pastoral People of Karamoja,
     North-Eastern Uganda: An Example of the Treatment of
     Symptoms     66
     Randall Baker
  7. Ecology and Planning     78
     C. S. Holling and M. A. Goldberg


Part III.   **Responding to Technological and
            Economic Change**     95
  8. New Weapons Stir Up Old Ghosts     97
     William E. Mitchell
  9. Hydraulic Development and Political Response in the Valley
     of Oaxaca, Mexico     106
     Susan H. Lees
  10. The Great Sisal Scheme     117
     Daniel R. Gross
  11. Energy Conservation in Amish Agriculture     124
     Warren A. Johnson, Victor Stoltzfus, Peter Craumer

**Part IV. Sources and Consequences of Inequality** 139

12. The Prestige and Influence System 142
    C. W. M. Hart and Arnold R. Pilling
13. Productive Efficiency and Customary Systems of Rewards in Rural South India 157
    Scarlett Epstein
14. Ecological Perception and Economic Adaptation in Jamaica 174
    Allen S. Ehrlich
15. Collectivization, Kinship, and the Status of Women in Rural China 184
    Norma Diamond

**Part V. People in Conflict** 203

16. Sharing, Talking and Giving: Relief of Social Tensions Among !Kung Bushmen 207
    Lorna Marshall
17. Marriage by Kidnapping Among the Yörük of Southeastern Turkey 212
    Daniel G. Bates
18. Political Conflict and Revolution in an African Town 224
    Elliott P. Skinner
19. An Analysis of the Memphis Garbage Strike of 1968 233
    Thomas W. Collins

**Part VI. Turning to the Supernatural** 243

20. Witchcraft Practices and Psychocultural Therapy with Urban U.S. Families 244
    Madeleine Leininger
21. Witchcraft Explains Unfortunate Events 260
    E. E. Evans-Pritchard
22. Cargo Cults 266
    Peter M. Worsley
23. Religious Mass Movements and Social Change in Brazil 273
    Emilio Willems

**Part VII. Perspectives and Retrospectives** 293

24. The End of Fieldwork 294
    John Middleton

25. A Field Experience in Retrospect 309
    Elliot Liebow
26. The Structure of Permanence: The Relevance of
    Self-Subsistence Communities for World Ecosystem
    Management 320
    William C. Clarke

# Contemporary Anthropology:
## AN ANTHOLOGY

# Introduction

In this book we shall use the works of anthropologists and others to introduce students to the field of anthropology, what it means to be an anthropologist, and what it feels like to do anthropological research. Most important, we shall attempt to show what the anthropological perspective can contribute to an understanding of how people behave —that is, to an understanding of ourselves.

Anthropology, more than any other discipline, has long emphasized connections between human beings and human society, on one hand, and the larger web of life, on the other. It is only by appreciating the fact that we are subject to the same laws that affect all living organisms that we can come to understand those many aspects of human behavior that distinguish us from other species.

Human beings are relative newcomers on earth, but by most criteria we are an extremely successful species—certainly the most widespread and numerous "large animal." Human beings are distributed throughout the world and live under the most diverse and extreme conditions. Perhaps our most impressive characteristics are the extreme range of local problems or hazards that we overcome in order to make a living and the remarkable similarity among all of us in physique. Compared with many other animals, we appear a dull bunch, not only lacking in plumage but also decidedly commonplace in terms of virtually every physical attribute. It is said that evolution is the process by which life forms change in response to particular environmental conditions; then what accounts for the biological unity of humankind? What accounts for the success of our species, and what can we conclude about our future?

Such concerns characterize much anthropological research. Most anthropologists agree that the key to the success of the human species and the relative lack of biological commitment to particular climates and ways of life lies in our capacity for learned social behavior. Our species is unique among animals in its commitment to group living, to group solutions to environmental problems, and in the rapidity with which groups and the behavior of their members can change as the situation demands.

Furthermore, our continued survival as a species will quite simply depend entirely on our continued ability to respond, through learning, to problems presented by our environments. Very often the problems facing a local population, whether in the tropical rain forests of Amazonia or North American urban centers, result from conditions created by the people themselves. We are continually adapting to environments shaped in great measure by ourselves, and we are forced to find solutions to problems of human origin that threaten our well-being.

Natural selection, the primary mechanism of evolution, has determined human physical attributes, including the complex neurological systems on which our behavior rests. In this sense culture, or the capacity for learned behavior, has a biological basis. Furthermore, culture is adaptive in that our evolutionary success depends on making use of what we and our forebearers have learned in the past. Culture, or learned behavior, is our principal tool for coping with environmental challenges.

The concept of "adaptation" has served as a central theme in our choice of articles for this collection. In its simplest meaning, it refers to the process by which a population becomes adjusted to its environment —the operation of natural selection on individual organisms. An attribute that contributes to an individual's having more offspring, who themselves survive to produce offspring, is likely to spread through the population over time. This concept of adaptation, however, refers to traits or attributes that have a genetic basis—for example, color vision. One classic example of genetic adaptation among human beings is the development of the sickle-cell trait. Individuals whose hemoglobin cells produce sickle-cell anemia also have high resistance to malaria. It is believed that the prevalence of malaria in West Africa selected for sickle-cell anemia, as those who possessed the trait in heterozygous form were able to produce more offspring than those who succumbed more readily to malaria. Sickle-cell anemia still persists among black Americans and West Africans, even though its original adaptive advantage no longer remains. It is, however, decreasing in frequency as malaria itself is being rapidly eradicated in most areas.

For adaptation, or "problem solving," to occur through natural selection, the trait or response must have a genetic basis—as in the sickle-cell example. As we know, however, there are other ways in which an organism may adapt. Adaptation may be physiological and involve no genetic change, as when we shiver from cold or change our metabolic rates in situations of stress. Although there is, of course, a genetic basis for such physiological responses, which establishes the capacity and the potential of the individual to react, the actual occurrence takes place rapidly and without any shift in the genetic makeup of the population. Most physiological responses are involuntary; our bodies (like all organisms) are conditioned or programmed by "instinct" to react appropriately. Even then the role of natural selection is clear: These physiological capabilities arise and are continually shaped by individuals with different characteristics producing offspring at different rates. For example, Indians living at high altitudes in the Andes develop increased lung capacity as they grow to adulthood, to meet the demands of the rarefied atmosphere. This capacity is genetically determined, but the actual growth pattern is a response to environmental stimuli.

Far more complex, from the perspective of adaptation, is problem solving through learning. Learned behavior is found among all species of animals. The ability to learn is the ability to profit from experience and to direct one's behavior accordingly. Among human beings this ability is elaborated to the point at which we can speak of "culture" as our distinguishing characteristic. From an evolutionary perspective culture is adaptive and constitutes the distinguishing mark of our species.

Although the acquisition of culture sets people apart in the animal kingdom, we should not let the achievements of humankind blind us to the fact that it is our means of coping with problems. How, then, does culture fit in with the more obviously adaptive physiological or genetically determined traits? To answer this question, we have to step back and take a broad view of evolution, seeking what it is that determines the success or failure of individuals and species.

One recent attempt to do just that was made by Lawrence Slobodkin, a biologist. He described evolution metaphorically, as a game of "existential poker" in which the object is not to go home rich but simply to stay at the table. To leave the table, in this game, is to become extinct. Just as in poker, what really counts is the ability to minimize risk whenever possible and to maintain one's capacity to face the challenges posed by the other players. Slobodkin's model tells us that evolutionary success depends more on the maintenance of homeostasis than on opportunistic—and risky—innovation. To succeed, we should change just enough to stay the same; we should try to retain our options and avoid untried commitments. At first, this suggestion seems difficult to reconcile with what we know about human history, which is impressive both for rapid cultural development and for local diversity. But, as Slobodkin might put it, culture—at least in its genesis—is an evolutionary bastion of conservatism.

The reason lies in certain limitations that are inherent in the adaptation process. No organism, including ourselves, can ever catch up with the demands on it from the environment, for circumstances continually change in ways that are not fully predictable. Furthermore, any response to a challenge involves a cost measurable both in time necessary to become effective and in energy expended. The latter becomes critical, for it directly affects the future capacity of the organism to handle subsequent problems that will inevitably arise. Finally, any response or adaptation is constrained by the history of the organism, which must deal with its environment by means of whatever traits are available to it at that particular time. Given these limitations, anthropologist Gregory Bateson suggests that evolutionary success depends on the maintenance of "adaptive flexibility," a notion that accords with the biological model presented here. The idea is to be cost effective in solving environmental problems, thus keeping some reserve against future contingencies.

Faced with the limitations we have mentioned, how can we solve environmental problems in the cheapest possible way, and how can we retain maximum "adaptive flexibility"? Slobodkin and others suggest that the answer lies in the orchestration of a variety of ways of responding. Viewed from this perspective, learned behavior, even human culture, is part of a hierarchy of responses, ordered by the costs entailed;

the responses thus range from superficial behavioral shifts through permanent genetic changes in the population as a result of natural selection. Changes in behavior, especially learned social behavior, are considered "low cost" because of their rapid effectiveness and because they leave room for subsequent alteration or even reversal of a particular course of action. New responses that are closely determined by genetic changes, on the other hand, are slow to become effective and involve a costly commitment, as in the example of sickle-cell anemia, which is a genetic response to the prevalence of malaria. Accordingly, behavior —and the development of a capacity for learning—represents a first line of defense for both animals and human beings. But we have come to rely so heavily on learned behavior that genetic changes arising from our environment seem inconsequential. They are not inconsequential, however; rather the rate of change is so slow as to be scarcely discernible without elaborate research procedures. Actually behavior is more than a passive buffer against the necessity for more drastic measures of problem solving. It is a primary mechanism facilitating the biological success of the individual.

Even behavioral or cultural traits involve different costs to the individual and to the group. A brief human example makes this point clear. A farm family faced with a shortage of well water may at first attempt to dig a new well or to deepen an existing one. If the problem persists, the family will intensify efforts to secure reliable water, perhaps bringing it from distant sources. Family members may also alter their use of water and shift to a method of agriculture that requires less water. Finally, if the shortage becomes a drought, they may have to abandon their lands altogether, as so many did in the "Dust Bowl disaster" during the Depression in the American Southwest. The people in this example seem to be ordering their responses according to the "costs" of different strategies, and in general people seem to cope in ways designed to achieve flexibility. People are by no means wildly innovative in facing new problems, and around the world we see remarkable similarities in the ways in which people under comparable circumstances handle fundamental problems.

Let us turn our attention to some of the problems that occasion cultural or other solutions, for we have organized the following selections around them. The most important single point regarding adaptation at all levels is that people respond to very specific problems. The environment of an individual or group is not an array of "average conditions." For the American city dweller *patterns* of urban decay and *rates* of crime and unemployment are largely immaterial. What is important, and what constitutes an "environmental problem," is securing adequate shelter, paying the rent, coming home safely, and keeping a job. People cannot live on "average incomes" or count on "average health," nor do they have "average life expectancies." From the individual's vantage point, real problems are those that are immediate, specific, and personal.

The papers presented here all focus on people (or, in one instance, baboons) coping with specific problems. We have attempted to incorporate illustrations of both the sources of diverse problems and the complexity of human responses. We start, in Part One, with examples of how anthropologists experience their distinctive approach to research —fieldwork. It is by living with different peoples that anthropologists learn about their problems and how they cope with them. We will discuss this point later at somewhat greater length. In Part Two, "Responding to Environmental Pressures," we have grouped studies of human food procurement and land use. In many respects these articles directly build on our introductory comments about adaptation and behavioral responses to environmental challenges. After all, the problems are the familiar ones we read about in the daily papers, and all have some urgency. We also include an example of an ecological study, which may instruct us in practical decision making and planning.

At times it is difficult to think of advanced technology or modern economic systems as "problems" calling for solutions. Any element of technology is itself an answer to some demand or problem—and we Americans celebrate our abilities in this area almost to the extent of national fetishism. But, as the studies in Part Three show, there are costs involved. Technological innovation is a behavioral strategy, and the people involved must cope with the real costs of their actions, including often unanticipated penalties of pollution, social disruption, and environmental degradation.

Other sources of environmental problems are essentially social. People organize themselves in groups, establish social arrangements regulating access to resources by members of the group or society, establish conventions about whom to marry or how to view the opposite sex. Such arrangements almost inevitably involve varying degrees of inequality. Disturbing as it may be, the truly egalitarian society has yet to be discovered. One penalty of group life, or of human social organization, is thus that individuals derive different benefits from the social and economic transactions in which they participate. In some societies, particularly those we call "civilized," these inequalities cause entire segments of the society to live near-separate existences, in which their poverty maybe a source of profit for others. We have thus called Part Four "Sources and Consequences of Inequality."

Closely related to this subject are the sources of overt conflict within and among groups. The studies of conflict and warfare in Part Five reflect this part of the process of human response. Although Part Five, like the others, has a clear topical focus, the selections should encourage the student to go beyond the categories established here and to recognize obvious continuities in human behavior. Sometimes these continuities are emphasized in the chapter headings and introductory remarks for the articles. But the most important ones will be supplied by the reader as he or she relates them to personal experience. For example, papers dealing with the Memphis garbage strike and the Melanesian cargo cults appear in different parts of the book, and in each people are described as coping with different problems unique to them. Yet both studies encourage all of us to reconsider aspects of our own lives. A strike, a fight on the street, or a new storefront church is not a discrete event. Rather each represents continuing processes with special histories, perhaps best understood as people's efforts to solve problems presented by their participation in society.

The ways in which people deal with problems arising from environmental hazards, costs of technology, social inequality, and conflicts of interest are quite diverse from time to time and place to place. In Part Six, however, we attempt to underline some of the similarities among human responses by grouping together several instances in which people have responded to a variety of problems by the common means of turning to the "supernatural." At all levels of technological sophistication people invoke gods or spirits to provide comfort, explanation, and rationality, if not more material means of resolving pressures upon them. For human beings the symbolic ordering of the universe is as much a part of our system of adaptation as the technological, sociological, and biological devices that we have already mentioned. The role of concepts of the supernatural in human responses is noted in a number of papers in earlier sections as well. These selections help to make the point that, although the structure of human adaptation as a process is similar to that of other species, its content—involving beliefs and symbolic representations—is unique in the biological world.

Up to this point, the concepts we have been discussing are shared among the various scientific disciplines that study living things: biologists, ecologists, ethologists, and other natural historians concerned with the evolutionary process. But it is clear that anthropologists, who study human beings, have special problems and distinctive perspectives in their research, as a consequence of the peculiarities of the human animal, on one hand, and the paradox of being their own subjects of study, on the other. For this reason, we have placed particular emphasis upon the *experience* of anthropological research in this collection of articles.

Our emphasis upon the subjective experience of fieldwork should not obscure the fact that contemporary anthropological research is conducted within the framework of the scientific method. That is, our efforts in the field are generally directed toward the *testing of hypotheses.* Hypotheses are statements of relationships among variables (as, when $x$ grows, $y$ also grows), which are derived from a general explanatory theory (leading us to expect such a relationship). "Testing hypotheses" means checking by observation whether or not the expected relationship really exists. If it does, we have some confirmation of the validity of the theory; if not, we look for aspects of the theory or of the process of testing that need reassessment. All scientific activity involves this process of continual testing as part of a general effort to gain a more accurate model of the natural order.

The questions we ask, the data we choose to record, and the system of recording we use all derive from our theoretical interests and orientations. For example, an anthropologist interested in demographic theory may hypothesize that the number of people living together in a peasant household is positively related to demands placed on the household for labor to plant and harvest crops; that is, the higher the demand for agricultural labor, the larger the household. In order to test this hypothesis, the researcher in the field may collect information about the number of people who live in each household in one or more local communities, the age and sex composition of the household, the type of work done by each member, and so on. A demographic study generally requires relatively limited amounts of information from a large sample. By contrast, an investigation into the sources and control of conflict may require an extensive historical account of a small number of particular situations, with detailed biographic data on all participants and complex records of their daily activities. This contrast illustrates the ways in which a scientific *description,* which may strike the reader as simply a "record of fact," is actually governed by the researcher's theoretical concerns.

Like many other natural historians, anthropologists rarely engage in experimental research. Instead, they arrive at generalizations and tests of scientific hypotheses through observation of life as it occurs in natural settings. One reason for general avoidance of experiments on human beings' social behavior is obvious: Such experimentation would be unethical. We simply cannot "play" with the conditions of life of our fellow men and women. A second reason, also obvious, is that, as naturalists, we seek to comprehend human behavior in all its complexity, rather than to oversimplify through reliance on "laboratory" conditions. Anthropologists, therefore, frequently find themselves spending extended periods of their lives living among alien peoples in natural settings (doing "fieldwork"). Under such conditions, it becomes nearly impossible to separate "work" (research) from "life" (eating, sleeping, raising a family). The fieldworker tends to become deeply involved with the subjects of his or her research. Although fieldwork is intended to help the anthropologist become more objective about human beings by reducing "ethnocentrism," the fieldwork experience in itself is a subjective one. This reality has some disadvantages for the fieldworker, because it may result in personal problems, including emotional stress, but there are advantages as well—special insights resulting from intimate knowledge that can be obtained only through "participant observation."

Subjective participant observation, combined with objective cross-cultural comparison, lends a special perspective to anthropology. The collection of papers included in this volume is intended to convey not only the manner in which anthropological research partakes of the natural sciences by its dependence upon biological, ecological, and ethological theories but also its peculiarities and special insights as a profession that often requires the total absorption of the researcher in the research experience. We hope that our readers will learn from this collection about the problems other peoples face and the ways in which they cope, on one hand, and about the ways in which anthropologists have tried to contribute new understanding of our fellow human beings.

# Part I
## Being an Anthropologist

For nearly a century now, social anthropologists have committed themselves to a special way of learning about others. This commitment involves taking up residence *within* the community to be studied and encouraging one's new neighbors to teach one how to live, talk, and behave as a "native" does. We call this approach "participant observation." Through participant observation, the anthropologist hopes to gain a detailed understanding, from an outsider's point of view, of the working of another society and the ways in which its members see, feel, and respond to the world they live in. Although this approach may be rather difficult—for there are innumerable obstacles to absorbing an entire alien culture in the brief period of time available to the researcher, usually nine to eighteen months—it offers some advantages. The outsider, if he or she is well trained, may bring to a situation an objectivity that a member of the society under study can never have. Furthermore, the anthropologist who has learned about a new society from its members returns home with a new perspective on his or her own society. This perspective is an important intellectual tool for maintaining some level of objectivity when examining a variety of societies cross-culturally for purposes of generalization, as well as when seeking to understand specific situations. Although anthropological research involves a great deal more than fieldwork, it is fieldwork that distinguishes anthropologists from other scientists who study human beings.

While objectivity is essential to fieldwork, no one can do it in the complete absence of preconceptions. As Napoleon Chagnon's excerpt illustrates, our preconceptions govern our anticipations about what we shall find and how we shall work in the field as well. Some of our preconceptions disappear as we confront reality; others contribute to success in our research. Fieldworkers have specific jobs to do; they must carry out research that they have designed while still at home. They do not simply observe; they observe particular things and collect particular kinds of information, which they hope will be useful in answering the questions that they and their colleagues think are important for solving scientific and practical problems. These preconceptions, derived from the academic training of the anthropologists, direct and filter their observations in the field.

Still other preconceptions, having to do with ethics, justice, and morality, may affect the fieldwork experience also. The selection from Jean Briggs' book presents interpretations of events within a moral framework in conflict with that of the people she was studying. Such situations are relatively common in anthropological fieldwork, though authors rarely write about them. But the anthropologist's dilemma has long been recognized: At what point should cultural relativism stop? Whose interpretation of right and wrong should prevail? Can the anthropologist simply observe wife beating or murder if such behavior is acceptable to the people he or she is studying? Conversely, can the anthropologist support incarceration in prisons or taxation if they are morally unacceptable to the group he or she is living with, despite their propriety in his or her own culture and adoption by national governments with whose permission he or she is carrying out field research?

Finally, fieldwork involves imposition. We impose on the hospitality of the communities we study (sometimes they express resentment; sometimes they seem to welcome the diversion), and frequently their members impose on us in return, prying into our private affairs as we pry into theirs, taking our time and begging our limited resources as we do to them. Perhaps neglected in the usual portrayals of this sort of cultural imposition is the imposition by fieldworkers on the time, patience, and comfort of their own families. We have included Elizabeth Fernea's piece in order to bring out the demands made upon the families of anthropologists in the field, in this instance a wife (we have yet to hear the point of view of children). Having one's family in the field, most anthropologists agree, can be extremely helpful, both in establishing oneself as a mature and stable individual in a community in which all adults have families and in the day-to-day tasks of collecting information. Yet fieldwork can be a hardship for families when one of the spouses has a different career and children are of school age. There is no standard way to deal with such problems, which are not necessarily unique to anthropology.

# 1 | DOING FIELDWORK AMONG THE YĄNOMAMÖ

## Napoleon A. Chagnon

*As Chagnon shows in this excerpt from his monograph on the Yąnomamö Indians of the Amazon basin, young anthropologists may enter their first field situations with rather romantic notions of what fieldwork is going to be like. Whether that work is done in the remote tropical rainforest, as in this instance, or in a complex urban society, romantic notions will be quickly dispelled as the fieldworker discovers the hardships of being isolated from familiar surroundings. Fieldwork may involve physical hardships and mental frustration; this paper illustrates these factors in the extreme. Although Chagnon tells of the classic circumstances confronting the lone anthropologist in the field, few of us today are working in such situations. It is not so much the physical circumstances of fieldwork that we share as the intellectual and emotional problems of learning, from the beginning, about other people's ways of life by living among them.*

The Yąnomamö[1] Indians live in southern Venezuela and the adjacent portions of northern Brazil. . . . Some 125 widely scattered villages have populations ranging from 40 to 250 inhabitants, with 75 to 80 people the most usual number. In total numbers their population probably approaches 10,000 people, but this is merely a guess. Many of the villages have not yet been contacted by outsiders, and nobody knows for sure exactly how many uncontacted villages there are, or how many people live in them. By comparison to African or Melanesian tribes, the Yąnomamö population is small. Still, they are one of the largest unacculturated tribes left in all of South America.

But they have a significance apart from tribal size and cultural purity: the Yąnomamö are still actively conducting warfare. It is in the nature of man to fight, according to one of their myths, because the blood of "Moon" spilled on this layer of the cosmos, causing men to become fierce. I describe the Yąnomamö as "the fierce people" because that is the most accurate single phrase that describes them. That is how they conceive themselves to be, and that is how they would like others to think of them.

I spent nineteen months with the Yąnomamö,[2] during which time I acquired some proficiency in their language and, up to a point, submerged myself in their culture and way of life. The thing that impressed me most was the importance of aggression in their culture. I had the opportunity to witness a good many incidents that expressed individual vindictiveness on the one hand and collective bellicosity on the other. These ranged in seriousness from the ordinary incidents of wife beating and chest pounding to dueling and organized raiding by parties that set out with the intention of ambushing and killing men from enemy villages. . . . One of the villages . . . was raided approximately twenty-five times while I conducted the fieldwork, six times by the group I lived among.

The fact that the Yąnomamö live in a state of chronic warfare is reflected in their mythology, values, settlement pattern, political behavior, and marriage practices. Accordingly, I have organized this case study in such a way that students can appreciate the effects of warfare on Yąnomamö culture in general and on their social organization and politics in particular. . . .

I collected the data under somewhat trying circumstances, some of which I will describe in order to give the student a rough idea of what is generally meant when anthropologists speak of "culture shock" and "fieldwork." It should be borne in mind, however, that each field situation is in many respects unique, so that the problems I encountered do not necessarily exhaust the range of possible problems other anthropologists have confronted in other areas. There are a few problems, however, that seem to be nearly universal among anthropological fieldworkers, particularly those having to do with eating, bathing, sleeping, lack of privacy and loneliness, or discovering that primitive man is not always as noble as you originally thought.

This is not to state that primitive man everywhere is unpleasant. By way of contrast, I have also done limited fieldwork among the Yąnomamö's northern neighbors, the Carib-speaking Makiritare Indians. This group was very pleasant and charming, all of them anxious to help me and honor bound to show any visitor the numerous courtesies of their system of etiquette. In short, they approached the image of primitive man that I had conjured up, and it was sheer pleasure to work with them. The recent work by Colin Turnbull (1966) brings out dramatically the contrast in personal characteristics of two African peoples he has studied.

Hence, what I say about some of my experiences is probably equally true of the experiences of many other fieldworkers. I write about my own experiences because there is a conspicuous lack of fieldwork descriptions available to potential fieldworkers. I think I could have profited by reading about the private misfortunes of my own teachers; at least I might have been able to avoid some of the more stupid errors I made. In this regard there are a number of recent contributions by fieldworkers describing some of the discomforts and misfortunes they themselves sustained.[3] Students planning to conduct fieldwork are urged to consult them.

My first day in the field illustrated to me what my teachers meant when they spoke of "culture shock." I had traveled in a small, aluminum rowboat propelled by a large outboard motor for two and a half days.

This took me from the territorial capital, a small town on the Orinoco River, deep into Yąnomamö country. On the morning of the third day we reached a small mission settlement, the field "headquarters" of a group of Americans who were working in two Yąnomamö villages. The missionaries had come out of these villages to hold their annual conference on the progress of their mission work, and were conducting their meetings when I arrived. We picked up a passenger at the mission station, James P. Barker, the first non-Yąnomamö to make a sustained, permanent contact with the tribe (in 1950). He had just returned from a year's furlough in the United States, where I had earlier visited him before leaving for Venezuela. He agreed to accompany me to the village I had selected for my base of operations to introduce me to the Indians. This village was also his own home base, but he had not been there for over a year and did not plan to join me for another three months. Mr. Barker had been living with this particular group about five years.

We arrived at the village, Bisaasi-teri, about 2:00 PM and docked the boat along the muddy bank at the terminus of the path used by the Indians to fetch their drinking water. It was hot and muggy, and my clothing was soaked with perspiration. It clung uncomfortably to my body, as it did thereafter for the remainder of the work. The small, biting gnats were out in astronomical numbers, for it was the beginning of the dry season. My face and hands were swollen from the venom of their numerous stings. In just a few moments I was to meet my first Yąnomamö, my first primitive man. What would it be like? I had visions of entering the village and seeing 125 social facts running about calling each other kinship terms and sharing food, each waiting and anxious to have me collect his genealogy. I would wear them out in turn. Would they like me? This was important to me; I wanted them to be so fond of me that they would adopt me into their kinship system and way of life, because I had heard that successful anthropologists always get adopted by their people. I had learned during my seven years of anthropological training at the University of Michigan that kinship was equivalent to society in primitive tribes and that it was a moral way of life, "moral" being something "good" and "desirable." I was determined to work my way into their moral system of kinship and become a member of their society.

My heart began to pound as we approached the village and heard the buzz of activity within the circular compound. Mr. Barker commented that he was anxious to see if any changes had taken place while he was away and wondered how many of them had died during his absence. I felt into my back pocket to make sure that my notebook was still there and felt personally more secure when I touched it. Otherwise, I would not have known what to do with my hands.

The entrance to the village was covered over with brush and dry palm leaves. We pushed them aside to expose the low opening to the village. The excitement of meeting my first Indians was almost unbearable as I duck-waddled through the low passage into the village clearing.

I looked up and gasped when I saw a dozen burly, naked, filthy, hideous men staring at us down the shafts of their drawn arrows! Immense wads of green tobacco were stuck between their lower teeth and lips making them look even more hideous, and strands of dark-green slime dripped or hung from their noses. We arrived at the village while the men were blowing a hallucinogenic drug up their noses. One of the side effects of the drug is a runny nose. The mucus is always saturated with the green powder and the Indians usually let it run freely from their nostrils. My next discovery was that there were a dozen or so vicious, underfed dogs snapping at my legs, circling me as if I were going to be their next meal. I just stood there holding my notebook, helpless and pathetic. Then the stench of the decaying vegetation and filth struck me and I almost got sick. I was horrified. What sort of a welcome was this for the person who came here to live with you and learn your way of life, to become friends with you? They put their weapons down when they recognized Barker and returned to their chanting, keeping a nervous eye on the village entrances.

We had arrived just after a serious fight. Seven women had been abducted the day before by a neighboring group, and the local men and their guests had just that morning recovered five of them in a brutal club fight that nearly ended in a shooting war. The abductors, angry because they lost five of the seven captives, vowed to raid the Bisaasiteri. When we arrived and entered the village unexpectedly, the Indians feared that we were the raiders. On several occasions during the next two hours the men in the village jumped to their feet, armed themselves, and waited nervously for the noise outside the village to be identified. My enthusiasm for collecting ethnographic curiosities diminished in proportion to the number of times such an alarm was raised. In fact, I was relieved when Mr. Barker suggested that we sleep across the river for the evening. It would be safer over there.

As we walked down the path to the boat, I pondered the wisdom of having decided to spend a year and a half with this tribe before I had even seen what they were like. I am not ashamed to admit, either, that had there been a diplomatic way out, I would have ended my fieldwork then and there. I did not look forward to the next day when I would be left alone with the Indians; I did not speak a word of their language, and they were decidedly different from what I had imagined them to be. The whole situation was depressing, and I wondered why I ever decided to switch from civil engineering to anthropology in the first place. I had not eaten all day, I was soaking wet from perspiration, the gnats were biting me, and I was covered with red pigment, the result of a dozen or so complete examinations I had been given by as many burly Indians. These examinations capped an otherwise grim day. The Indians would blow their noses into their hands, flick as much of the mucus off that would separate in a snap of the wrist, wipe the residue into their hair, and then carefully examine my face, arms, legs, hair, and the contents of my pockets. I asked Mr. Barker how to say "Your hands are dirty"; my comments were met by the Indians in the following way:

They would "clean" their hands by spitting a quantity of slimy tobacco juice into them, rub them together and then proceed with the examination.

Mr. Barker and I crossed the river and slung our hammocks. When he pulled the hammock out of a rubber bag, a heavy, disagreeable odor of mildewed cotton came with it. "Even the missionaries are filthy," I thought to myself. Within two weeks, everything I owned smelled the same way, and I lived with that odor for the remainder of the fieldwork. My own habits of personal cleanliness reached such levels that I didn't even mind being examined by the Indians, as I was not much cleaner than they were after I had adjusted to the circumstances.

So much for my discovery that primitive man is not the picture of nobility and sanitation I had conceived him to be. I soon discovered that it was an enormously time-consuming task to maintain my own body in the manner to which it had grown accustomed in the relatively antiseptic environment of the northern United States. Either I could be relatively well fed and relatively comfortable in a fresh change of clothes and do very little fieldwork, or, I could do considerably more fieldwork and be less well fed and less comfortable.

It is appalling how complicated it can be to make oatmeal in the jungle. First, I had to make two trips to the river to haul the water. Next, I had to prime my kerosene stove with alcohol and get it burning, a tricky procedure when you are trying to mix powdered milk and fill a coffee pot at the same time: the alcohol prime always burned out before I could turn the kerosene on, and I would have to start all over. Or, I would turn the kerosene on, hoping that the element was still hot enough to vaporize the fuel and start a small fire in my palm-thatched hut as the liquid kerosene squirted all over the table and walls and ignited. It was safer to start over with the alcohol. Then I had to boil the oatmeal and pick the bugs out of it. All my supplies, of course, were carefully stored in Indian-proof, rat-proof, moisture-proof, and insect-proof containers, not one of which ever served its purpose adequately. Just taking things out of the multiplicity of containers and repacking them afterward was a minor project in itself. By the time I had hauled the water to cook with, unpacked my food, prepared the oatmeal, milk, and coffee, heated water for dishes, washed and dried the dishes, repacked the food in the containers, stored the containers in locked trunks, and cleaned up my mess, the ceremony of preparing breakfast had brought me almost up to lunch time!

Eating three meals a day was out of the question. I solved the problem by eating a single meal that could be prepared in a single container, or, at most, in two containers, washed my dishes only when there were no clean ones left, using cold river water, and wore each change of clothing at least a week to cut down on my laundry problem, a courageous undertaking in the tropics. I was also less concerned about sharing my provisions with the rats, insects, Indians, and the elements, thereby eliminating the need for my complicated storage process. I was able to last most of the day on *café con leche,* heavily sugared espresso coffee diluted about five to one with hot milk. I would prepare this in the evening and store it in a thermos. Frequently, my single meal was no more complicated than a can of sardines and a package of crackers. But at least two or three times a week I would do something sophisticated, like make oatmeal or boil rice and add a can of tuna fish or tomato paste to it. I even saved time by devising a water system that obviated the trips to the river. I had a few sheets of zinc roofing brought in and made a rain-water trap; I caught the water on the zinc surface, funneled it into an empty gasoline drum, and then ran a plastic hose from the drum to my hut. When the drum was exhausted in the dry season, I hired the Indians to fill it with water from the river.

I ate much less when I traveled with the Indians to visit other villages. Most of the time my travel diet consisted of roasted or boiled green plantains ( . . . ) that I obtained from the Indians, but I always carried a few cans of sardines with me in case I got lost or stayed away longer than I had planned. I found peanut butter and crackers a very nourishing food, and a simple one to prepare on trips. It was nutritious and portable, and only one tool was required to prepare the meal, a hunting knife that could be cleaned by wiping the blade on a leaf. More importantly, it was one of the few foods the Indians would let me eat in relative peace. It looked too much like animal feces to them to excite their appetites.

I once referred to the peanut butter as the dung of cattle. They found this quite repugnant. They did not know what "cattle" were, but were generally aware that I ate several canned products of such an animal. I perpetrated this myth, if for no other reason than to have some peace of mind while I ate. Fieldworkers develop strange defense mechanisms, and this was one of my own forms of adaptation. On another occasion I was eating a can of frankfurters and growing very weary of the demands of one of my guests for a share in my meal. When he asked me what I was eating, I replied: "Beef." He then asked, "What part of the animal are you eating?" to which I replied, "Guess!" He stopped asking for a share.

Meals were a problem in another way. Food sharing is important to the Yąnomamö in the context of displaying friendship. "I am hungry," is almost a form of greeting with them. I could not possibly have brought enough food with me to feed the entire village, yet they seemed not to understand this. All they could see was that I did not share my food with them at each and every meal. Nor could I enter into their system of reciprocities with respect to food; every time one of them gave me something "freely," he would dog me for months to pay him back, not with food, but with steel tools. Thus, if I accepted a plantain from someone in a different village while I was on a visit, he would most likely visit me in the future and demand a machete as payment for the time that he "fed" me. I usually reacted to these kinds of demands by giving a banana, the customary reciprocity in their culture—food for food—but this would be a disappointment for the individual who had visions of that single plantain growing into a machete over time.

Despite the fact that most of them knew I would not share my food with them at their request, some of them always showed up at my hut during mealtime. I gradually became accustomed to this and learned to ignore their persistent demands while I ate. Some of them would get angry because I failed to give in, but most of them accepted it as just a peculiarity of the subhuman foreigner. When I did give in, my hut quickly filled with Indians, each demanding a sample of the food that I had given one of them. If I did not give all a share, I was that much more despicable in their eyes.

A few of them went out of their way to make my meals unpleasant, to spite me for not sharing; for example, one man arrived and watched me eat a cracker with honey on it. He immediately recognized the honey, a particularly esteemed Yąnomamö food. He knew that I would not share my tiny bottle and that it would be futile to ask. Instead, he glared at me and queried icily, "Shaki!⁴ What kind of animal semen are you eating on that cracker?" His question had the desired effect, and my meal ended.

Finally, there was the problem of being lonely and separated from your own kind, especially your family. I tried to overcome this by seeking personal friendships among the Indians. This only complicated the matter because all my friends simply used my confidence to gain privileged access to my cache of steel tools and trade goods, and looted me. I would be bitterly disappointed that my "friend" thought no more of me than to finesse our relationship exclusively with the intention of getting at my locked up possessions, and my depression would hit new lows every time I discovered this. The loss of the possession bothered me much less than the shock that I was, as far as most of them were concerned, nothing more than a source of desirable items; no holds were barred in relieving me of these, since I was considered something subhuman, a non-Yąnomamö.

The thing that bothered me most was the incessant, passioned, and aggressive demands the Indians made. It would become so unbearable that I would have to lock myself in my mud hut every once in a while just to escape from it: Privacy is one of Western culture's greatest achievements. But I did not want privacy for its own sake; rather, I simply had to get away from the begging. Day and night for the entire time I lived with the Yąnomamö I was plagued by such demands as: "Give me a knife, I am poor!"; "If you don't take me with you on your next trip to Widokaiya-teri I'll chop a hole in your canoe!"; "Don't point your camera at me or I'll hit you!"; "Share your food with me!"; "Take me across the river in your canoe and be quick about it!"; "Give me a cooking pot!"; "Loan me your flashlight so I can go hunting tonight!"; "Give me medicine . . . I itch all over!"; "Take us on a week-long hunting trip with your shotgun!"; and "Give me an axe or I'll break into your hut when you are away visiting and steal one!" And so I was bombarded by such demands day after day, months on end, until I could not bear to see an Indian.

It was not as difficult to become calloused to the incessant begging as it was to ignore the sense of urgency, the impassioned tone of voice, or the intimidation and aggression with which the demands were made. It was likewise difficult to adjust to the fact that the Yąnomamö refused to accept "no" for an answer until or unless it seethed with passion and intimidation—which it did after six months. Giving in to a demand always established a new threshold; the next demand would be for a bigger item or favor, and the anger of the Indians even greater if the demand was not met. I soon learned that I had to become very much like the Yąnomamö to be able to get along with them on their terms: sly, aggressive, and intimidating.

Had I failed to adjust in this fashion I would have lost six months of supplies to them in a single day or would have spent most of my time ferrying them around in my canoe or hunting for them. As it was, I did spend a considerable amount of time doing these things and did succumb to their outrageous demands for axes and machetes, at least at first. More importantly, had I failed to demonstrate that I could not be pushed around beyond a certain point, I would have been the subject of far more ridicule, theft, and practical jokes than was the actual case. In short, I had to acquire a certain proficiency in their kind of interpersonal politics and to learn how to imply subtly that certain potentially undesirable consequences might follow if they did such and such to me. They do this to each other in order to establish precisely the point at which they cannot goad an individual any further without precipitating retaliation. As soon as I caught on to this and realized that much of their aggression was stimulated by their desire to discover my flash point, I got along much better with them and regained some lost ground. It was sort of like a political game that everyone played, but one in which each individual sooner or later had to display some sign that his bluffs and implied threats could be backed up. I suspect that the frequency of wife beating is a component of this syndrome, since men can display their ferocity and show others that they are capable of violence. Beating a wife with a club is considered to be an acceptable way of displaying ferocity and one that does not expose the male to much danger. The important thing is that the man has displayed his potential for violence and the implication is that other men better treat him with respect and caution.

After six months, the level of demand was tolerable in the village I used for my headquarters. The Indians and I adjusted to each other and knew what to expect with regard to demands on their part for goods, favors, and services. Had I confined my fieldwork to just that village alone, the field experience would have been far more enjoyable. But, as I was interested in the demographic pattern and social organization of a much larger area, I made regular trips to some dozen different villages in order to collect genealogies or to recheck those I already had. Hence, the intensity of begging and intimidation was fairly constant for the duration of the fieldwork. I had to establish my position in some sort of pecking order of ferocity at each and every village.

For the most part, my own "fierceness" took the form of shouting back at the Yąnomamö as loudly and as passionately as they shouted at me, especially at first, when I did not know much of their language. As I became more proficient in their language and learned more about their political tactics, I became more sophisticated in the art of bluffing. For example, I paid one young man a machete to cut palm trees and make boards from the wood. I used these to fashion a platform in the bottom of my dugout canoe to keep my possessions dry when I traveled by river. That afternoon I was doing informant work in the village; the long-awaited mission supply boat arrived, and most of the Indians ran out of the village to beg goods from the crew. I continued to work in the village for another hour or so and went down to the river to say "hello" to the men on the supply boat. I was angry when I discovered that the Indians had chopped up all my palm boards and used them to paddle their own canoes[5] across the river. I knew that if I overlooked this incident I would have invited them to take even greater liberties with my goods in the future. I crossed the river, docked amidst their dugouts, and shouted for the Indians to come out and see me. A few of the culprits appeared, mischievous grins on their faces. I gave a spirited lecture about how hard I had worked to put those boards in my canoe, how I had paid a machete for the wood, and how angry I was that they destroyed my work in their haste to cross the river. I then pulled out my hunting knife and, while their grins disappeared, cut each of their canoes loose, set it into the current, and let them float away. I left without further ado and without looking back.

They managed to borrow another canoe and, after some effort, recovered their dugouts. The headman of the village later told me with an approving chuckle that I had done the correct thing. Everyone in the village, except, of course, the culprits, supported and defended my action. This raised my status.

Whenever I took such action and defended my rights, I got along much better with the Yąnomamö. A good deal of their behavior toward me was directed with the forethought of establishing the point at which I would react defensively. Many of them later reminisced about the early days of my work when I was "timid" and a little afraid of them, and they could bully me into giving goods away.

Theft was the most persistent situation that required me to take some sort of defensive action. I simply could not keep everything I owned locked in trunks, and the Indians came into my hut and left at will. I developed a very effective means for recovering almost all the stolen items. I would simply ask a child who took the item and then take that person's hammock when he was not around, giving a spirited lecture to the others as I marched away in a faked rage with the thief's hammock. Nobody ever attempted to stop me from doing this, and almost all of them told me that my technique for recovering my possessions was admirable. By nightfall the thief would either appear with the stolen object or send it along with someone else to make an exchange. The others would heckle him for getting caught and being forced to return the item.

With respect to collecting the data I sought, there was a very frustrating problem. Primitive social organization is kinship organization, and to understand the Yąnomamö way of life I had to collect extensive genealogies. I could not have deliberately picked a more difficult group to work with in this regard: They have very stringent name taboos. They attempt to name people in such a way that when the person dies and they can no longer use his name, the loss of the word in the language is not inconvenient. Hence, they name people for specific and minute parts of things, such as "toenail of some rodent," thereby being able to retain the words "toenail" and "(specific) rodent," but not being able to refer directly to the toenail of that rodent. The taboo is maintained even for the living: One mark of prestige is the courtesy others show you by not using your name. The sanctions behind the taboo seem to be an unusual combination of fear and respect.

I tried to use kinship terms to collect genealogies at first, but the kinship terms were so ambiguous that I ultimately had to resort to names. They were quick to grasp that I was bound to learn everybody's name and reacted, without my knowing it, by inventing false names for everybody in the village. After having spent several months collecting names and learning them, this came as a disappointment to me: I could not cross-check the genealogies with other informants from distant villages.

They enjoyed watching me learn these names. I assumed, wrongly, that I would get the truth to each question and that I would get the best information by working in public. This set the stage for converting a serious project into a farce. Each informant tried to outdo his peers by inventing a name even more ridiculous than what I had been given earlier, or by asserting that the individual about whom I inquired was married to his mother or daughter, and the like. I would have the informant whisper the name of the individual in my ear, noting that he was the father of such and such a child. Everybody would then insist that I repeat the name aloud, roaring in hysterics as I clumsily pronounced the name. I assumed that the laughter was in response to the violation of the name taboo or to my pronunciation. This was a reasonable interpretation, since the individual whose name I said aloud invariably became angry. After I learned what some of the names meant, I began to understand what the laughter was all about. A few of the more colorful examples are: "hairy vagina," "long penis," "feces of the harpy eagle," and "dirty rectum." No wonder the victims were angry.

I was forced to do my genealogy work in private because of the horseplay and nonsense. Once I did so, my informants began to agree with each other and I managed to learn a few new names, real names. I could then test any new informant by collecting a genealogy from him that I knew to be accurate. I was able to weed out the more mischievous informants this way. Little by little I extended the genealogies and learned the real names. Still, I was unable to get the names of the dead and extend the genealogies back in time, and even my best informants continued to deceive me about their own close relatives. Most of them gave me the name of a living man as the father of some individual in order to avoid mentioning that the actual father was dead.

The quality of a genealogy depends in part on the number of generations it embraces, and the name taboo prevented me from getting any substantial information about deceased ancestors. Without this information, I could not detect marriage patterns through time. I had to rely on older informants for this information, but these were the most reluctant of all. As I became more proficient in the language and more skilled at detecting lies, my informants became better at lying. One of them in particular was so cunning and persuasive that I was shocked to discover that he had been inventing his information. He specialized in making a ceremony out of telling me false names. He would look around to make sure nobody was listening outside my hut, enjoin me to never mention the name again, act very nervous and spooky, and then grab me by the head to whisper the name very softly into my ear. I was always elated after an informant session with him, because I had several generations of dead ancestors for the living people. The others refused to give me this information. To show my gratitude, I paid him quadruple the rate I had given the others. When word got around that I had increased the pay, volunteers began pouring in to give me genealogies.

I discovered that the old man was lying quite by accident. A club fight broke out in the village one day, the result of a dispute over the possession of a woman. She had been promised to Rerebawä, a particularly aggressive young man who had married into the village. Rerebawä had already been given her older sister and was enraged when the younger girl began having an affair with another man in the village, making no attempt to conceal it from him. He challenged the young man to a club fight, but was so abusive in his challenge that the opponent's father took offense and entered the village circle with his son, wielding a long club. Rerebawä swaggered out to the duel and hurled insults at both of them, trying to goad them into striking him on the head with their clubs. This would have given him the opportunity to strike them on the head. His opponents refused to hit him, and the fight ended. Rerebawä had won a moral victory because his opponents were afraid to hit him. Thereafter, he swaggered around and insulted the two men behind their backs. He was genuinely angry with them, to the point of calling the older man by the name of his dead father. I quickly seized on this as an opportunity to collect an accurate genealogy and pumped him about his adversary's ancestors. Rerebawä had been particularly nasty to me up to this point, but we became staunch allies: We were both outsiders in the local village. I then asked about other dead ancestors and got immediate replies. He was angry with the whole group and not afraid to tell me the names of the dead. When I compared his version of the genealogies to that of the old man, it was obvious that one of them was lying. I challenged his information, and he explained that everybody knew that the old man was deceiving me and bragging about it in the village. The names the old man had given me were the dead ancestors of the members of a village so far away that he thought I would never have occasion to inquire about them. As it turned out, Rerebawä knew most of the people in that village and recognized the names.

I then went over the complete genealogical records with Rerebawä, genealogies I had presumed to be in final form. I had to revise them all because of the numerous lies and falsifications they contained. Thus, after five months of almost constant work on the genealogies of just one group, I had to begin almost from scratch!

Discouraging as it was to start over, it was still the first real turning point in my fieldwork. Thereafter, I began taking advantage of local arguments and animosities in selecting my informants, and used more extensively individuals who had married into the group. I began traveling to other villages to check the genealogies, picking villages that were on strained terms with the people about whom I wanted information. I would then return to my base camp and check with local informants the accuracy of the new information. If the informants became angry when I mentioned the new names I acquired from the unfriendly group, I was almost certain that the information was accurate. For this kind of checking I had to use informants whose genealogies I knew rather well: they had to be distantly enough related to the dead person that they would not go into a rage when I mentioned the name, but not so remotely related that they would be uncertain of the accuracy of the information. Thus, I had to make a list of names that I dared not use in the presence of each and every informant. Despite the precautions, I occasionally hit a name that put the informant into a rage, such as that of a dead brother or sister that other informants had not reported. This always terminated the day's work with that informant, for he would be too touchy to continue any further, and I would be reluctant to take a chance on accidentally discovering another dead kinsman so soon after the first.

These were always unpleasant experiences, and occasionally dangerous ones, depending on the temperament of the informant. On one occasion I was planning to visit a village that had been raided about a week earlier. A woman whose name I had on my list had been killed by the raiders. I planned to check each individual on the list one by one to estimate ages, and I wanted to remove her name so that I would not say it aloud in the village. I knew that I would be in considerable difficulty if I said this name aloud so soon after her death. I called on my original informant and asked him to tell me the name of the woman who had been killed. He refused, explaining that she was a close relative of his. I then asked him if he would become angry if I read off all the names on the list. This way he did not have to say her name and could merely nod when I mentioned the right one. He was a fairly good friend of mine, and I thought I could predict his reaction. He assured me that this would be a good way of doing it. We were alone in my hut so that nobody could overhear us. I read the names softly, continuing to the next when he gave a negative reply. When I finally spoke the name of the dead woman he flew out of his chair, raised his arm to strike me, and shouted: "You son-of-a-bitch! If you ever say that name again, I'll kill you!" He was shaking with rage, but left my hut quietly. I shudder to think what might have happened if I had said the name unknowingly in the woman's village. I had other, similar experiences in different villages, but luckily the dead person had been dead for some time and was not closely related to the individual into whose ear I whispered the name. I was merely cautioned to desist from saying any more names, lest I get people angry with me.

I had been working on the genealogies for nearly a year when another individual came to my aid. It was Kąobawä, the headman of Upper Bisaasi-teri, the group in which I spent most of my time. He visited me one day after the others had left the hut and volunteered to help me on the genealogies. He was poor, he explained, and needed a machete. He would work only on the condition that I did not ask him about his own parents and other very close kinsmen who were dead. He also added that he would not lie to me as the others had done in the past. This was perhaps the most important single event in my fieldwork, for out of this meeting evolved a very warm friendship and a very profitable informant-fieldworker relationship.

Kąobawä's familiarity with his group's history and his candidness were remarkable. His knowledge of details was almost encyclopedic. More than that, he was enthusiastic and encouraged me to learn details that I might otherwise have ignored. If there were things he did not know intimately, he would advise me to wait until he could check things out with someone in the village. This he would do clandestinely, giving me a report the next day. As I was constrained by my part of the bargain to avoid discussing his close dead kinsmen, I had to rely on Rerebawä for this information. I got Rerebawä's genealogy from Kąobawä.

Once again I went over the genealogies with Kąobawä to recheck them, a considerable task by this time: they included about two thousand names, representing several generations of individuals from four different villages. Rerebawä's information was very accurate, and Kąobawä's contribution enabled me to trace the genealogies further back in time. Thus, after nearly a year of constant work on genealogies, Yąnomamö demography and social organization began to fall into a pattern. Only then could I see how kin groups formed and exchanged women with each other over time, and only then did the fissioning of larger villages into smaller ones show a distinct pattern. At this point I was able to begin formulating more intelligent questions because there was now some sort of pattern to work with. Without the help of Rerebawä and Kąobawä I could not have made very much sense of the plethora of details I had collected from dozens of other informants. . . .

## NOTES

1. The word Yąnomamö is nasalized through its entire length, indicated by the diacritical mark [ą]. When this mark appears on a word, the entire word is nasalized. The terminal vowel [-ö] represents a sound that does not occur in the English language. It corresponds to the phone [†] of linguistic orthography. In normal conversation, Yąnomamö is pronounced like "Yah-no-mama," except that it is nasalized. Finally, the words having the [-ä] vowel are pronounced at that vowel with the "uh" sound of "duck." Thus, the name Kąobawä would be pronounced "cow-ba-wuh," again nasalized.
2. I spent a total of twenty-three months in South America of which nineteen were spent among the Yąnomamö on three separate field trips. The first trip, November 1964 through February 1966, was to Venezuela. During this time I spent thirteen months in direct contact with the Yąnomamö, using my periodic trips back to Caracas to visit my family and to collate the genealogical data I had collected up to that point. On my second trip, January through March 1967, I spent two months among Brazilian Yąnomamö and one more month with the Venezuelan Yąnomamö. Finally, I returned to Venezuela for three more months among the Yąnomamö, January through April 1968.
3. Maybury-Lewis, 1967: "Introduction," and 1965; Turnbull, 1966; L. Bohannan, 1964. Perhaps the most intimate account of the tribulations of a fieldworker is found in the posthumous diary of Bronislaw Malinowski (1967). Since the diary was not written for publication, it contains many intimate, very personal details about the writers' anxieties and hardships.
4. "Shaki," or, rather, "Shakiwä," is the name they gave me because they could not pronounce "Chagnon." They like to name people for some distinctive feature when possible. *Shaki* is the name of a species of noisome bee; they accumulate in large numbers around ripening bananas and make pests of themselves by eating into the fruit, showering the people below with the debris. They probably adopted this name for me because I was also a nuisance, continuously prying into their business, taking pictures of them, and, in general, being where they did not want me.
5. The canoes were obtained from missionaries, who, in turn, got them from a different tribe.

## REFERENCES

BOHANNAN, LAURA, 1964, *Return to Laughter.* New York: Doubleday & Co., Inc.

MALINOWSKI, BRONISLAW, 1967, *A Diary in the Strict Sense of the Term.* New York: Harcourt Brace Jovanovich, Inc.

MAYBURY-LEWIS, DAVID, 1965, *The Savage and the Innocent.* London: Evans Bros.

———, 1967, *Akwe-Shavante Society.* Oxford: Clarendon Press.

TURNBULL, COLIN M., 1966, "Report from Africa: A People Apart," *Natural History,* 75:8–14.

# 2 | KAPLUNA DAUGHTER: DOING FIELDWORK AMONG THE UTKU ESKIMOS

## Jean Briggs

*Anthropological fieldwork generally involves participant observation in the sense that the researcher lives among the people being studied and often joins them in their activities. But participation is always restricted—the anthropologist does not in fact become a member of the group. Furthermore, in order to observe, the researcher must avoid interfering with normal social processes. But refraining is often difficult, particularly when the anthropologist observes what appears to be social injustice and even more particularly when the community in which he or she lives is the target of injustice. In this instance we see what happens when an anthropologist speaks out against injustice. Much to Jean Briggs' dismay, "her people," the Eskimo group with whom she lived, resented her behavior; later she was punished for the way she had expressed herself by social ostracism. What she gained from this harsh experience was a deeper appreciation of the rules, attitudes, and values of people in the community.*

There remained more of an undercurrent of tension in my relationship with Inuttiaq and Allaq than I perceived at the time. I had come to accept the everyday vicissitudes of the relationship as matter-of-course; consciously, I felt the rewards far greater than the strains. The same was not true, I think, of Inuttiaq and Allaq; but I saw their feelings only at the end of April, when our iglu melted and Inuttiaq ordered a move into tents. Then he decided (as usual, without telling me) that I should return to my own tent, rather than joining the rest of the family in theirs. And during the five months in which I lived in my tent before moving back into Inuttiaq's qaqmaq in the following October, Allaq almost never visited me, as she had done in the first days after my arrival.

To be sure, during the last two months of that period almost no one else visited me, either. Short of murder, the ultimate sanction against the display of aggression in Utku society is, as I have said, ostracism. Niqi, Nilak's overly volatile wife, lived her life in its vacuum, and for a period of three months during my second summer and autumn at Back River, I experienced it, too. It was precipitated, in my case, by a misunderstanding that occurred in August, at the start of my second year. I am sure, however, that the tensions of the preceding winter added their residue of hostility, as well, to create a situation in which the kapluna [white] member of the community ceased to be treated as an educable child and was instead treated as an incorrigible offender who had, unfortunately, to be endured but who could not be incorporated into the social life of the group. The misunderstanding came about as follows.

At the time I went to live with the Utku, Chantrey Inlet was becoming increasingly known among sports fishermen in the provinces of Canada and in the United States. Every year in July and August small charter airlines in Ontario and Manitoba, which cater to sportsmen, flew men in, for a price incredible to me, to spend two or three or five days fishing for arctic char and salmon trout at the Rapids. Until a year or so before my arrival only a few had come each summer, perhaps five or six, but then they had begun to come in numbers. Fifteen or twenty, the Utku calculated, had come in 1963, and in 1964, when I was there, forty came, not all at once but in groups ranging in size from two or three to approximately fifteen. One or more of these groups was with us constantly from July 26 until August 23. They camped across the river from us, out of sight behind a point of land, and their outboard motors sputtered up and down the river from dawn to dark.

Some of these fishermen and their guide, a Canadian named Ray, kept to themselves on their side of the river. They traded generously with the Eskimos when the latter went to offer bone toys in exchange for tea, tobacco, and fishhooks, but otherwise they largely ignored the native inhabitants of the Inlet. The Utku—it was Nilak, Pala, Inuttiaq, and, later, Ipuituq, who were camped by the rapids that summer—liked Ray. He was a mild-mannered man, who had been bringing fishing parties to the Inlet for several years and who treated the Eskimos with dignity.

Individuals in other groups were less innocuous. Hard drinking, cigar smoking, and gruff-voiced, lacking in gentleness and sensitivity, they were the antithesis of everything Eskimo. They stared at the Eskimos; visited the Eskimo camp and photographed people without asking permission; peered into the tents; and when the Eskimos tried to trade for the coveted tea, tobacco, and fishhooks, one or two of these kaplunas offered instead strings of pink beads and other useless items, which the Eskimos were too timorous and too polite to refuse. The Eskimo women were particularly afraid *(kappia, iqhi)* of one of the plane pilots who, they said, had "wanted a woman" the previous year and had made his wishes known distinctly.

The Utku did not fail to notice differences among the fishermen and to judge some of them kinder *(quya)* than others, but whatever dislike they felt showed neither in avoidance nor, of course, in aggressive acts. The Eskimos looked forward with excitement to the coming of the kaplunas in July. As soon as the ice left the river, they began to listen for planes and, as they sat together on the gravel in front of the tents, they filed away at bits of caribou antler, shaping them into miniature replicas of fishhooks, pipes, knives, and other objects to trade to the kaplunas. Their talk was of tea and tobacco and of other things—food and clothing—which they had received from the fishermen in the past in very generous amounts, and which they hoped to receive again. When a plane was heard they hurried with one accord to the other side of the river in order to be present when the kaplunas landed, to help with the unloading of the plane, and to watch the strangers. Regardless of the quality of the men who had arrived, regardless of how the Utku felt about them, they treated all alike with the same obliging acquiescence with which they had treated me on my arrival. Their courtesy did not fail even when the kaplunas took advantage of their mildness to treat them in ways that I considered most humiliating. One champion wrestler picked up Mannik and held him horizontally, by shoulder and thigh, over his head: for a television ad, he explained to me. Mannik, who knew nothing of what was happening until he found himself in the air, giggled. On another occasion a loud-voiced man staggered off the plane, steeped in champagne, and wove his way over to Pala, whom he had singled out as the Eskimo "chief." Hugging Pala warmly, he inquired what his name was and invited him in incoherent English to be his friend. Pala, to my astonishment, understood the man to ask his name and replied "Peeterosi" (Peter, his Christian name). "Ha ha, Peeterosi!" roared the drunken kapluna. "Ha ha, Peeterosi! Le's be frens, I like Eskimos, nice Eskimos," and he stroked Pala's head, while Pala laughed mildly and resisted not at all. The other Utku watched, expressionless, in the background.

When we returned to our camp, later, I discovered that the Utku did have a way of retaliating against the kaplunas' condescending behavior; they made fun of it. They taught Saarak to imitate the drunken fisherman, and for months she ran from person to person, on request, stroking their heads and laughing with kapluna boisterousness in her piping voice: "Ha ha ha, Peeterosi, ha ha ha!" But even when I saw this mockery, my feelings were not relieved. I was ashamed of being a kapluna among such kaplunas, and I was humiliated on behalf of the Eskimos who watched, smiled, nodded, and submitted.

Yet I did not identify entirely with the Eskimos, and this fact made the situation even more painful. In spite of myself, I was drawn to the men camped across the river. Except for an exasperatingly brief conversation with a passing police officer in May, I had seen no member of my own culture and heard no English since the previous November. Neither had I tasted any kapluna food other than the few items: bannock, tea, rice, raisins, and chocolate, that I stocked in meagre quantities. Most trying of all, perhaps, I had had no mail since March, except for a few pitiful items, mostly bills and advertisements for camping equipment, which the police officer had brought in May. I deplored the insensitive ways of the men, and yet I was starved for the sights and sounds of my own world that they represented and for the familiar food that symbolized that world and that they had brought in enormous quantities.

But more detrimental to my peace of mind than the sudden sharp awareness of my deprivations was the fact that, since I was the only bilingual present, the members of each camp expected me to mediate with the other on their behalf. I often tangled the two languages hopelessly in my distress, unable to muster a coherent sentence in either one. It was not too hard to help the Utku in their attempts to trade with the kaplunas, since I almost always felt the Eskimos' requests reasonable. Difficulty arose only if a fisherman countered with beads a request for tea. Then I was tempted to demur on behalf of the unresisting Eskimo. Far more awkward were the requests that the kaplunas made of me. I was supposed to explain to Mannik why he had been so summarily hoisted skyward; to ask Nilak for his braided boot laces, though I knew no wool was to be had for replacements; and to negotiate with Allaq and with Niqi for the manufacture of fur mittens, though I knew that hides suitable for mittens were scarce and that our own winter mitten material would be used. The Eskimos would never refuse.

Most painful of all the transactions that I was expected to mediate were negotiations for the loan of the two Eskimo canoes. Once, each Utku family had owned a kapluna-style canoe of wood and painted canvas. The Canadian government had provided them after the famine of 1958, in order to encourage the Utku to depend more heavily on their rich fish resources than they had formerly done. One by one the canoes had been damaged and now either lay beached for lack of repair material or had been burned for firewood. Inuttiaq's and Pala's were the only two usable canoes remaining to our camp. During the spring, the canoes were used to transport the household goods up and down the river in the long series of moves, and during the summer and early autumn the men anchored them in midriver at the foot of the rapids and fished from them more efficiently than they could have fished from the shore. The canoes were used also to set and check the nets in the open river before freeze-up, and to ferry people back and forth across the river on various errands: to fetch birch twigs, which grew more plentifully on the far side of the river, to bring in needed possessions from caches, and to visit other families camped nearer the mouth of the river. The canoes had innumerable uses; without them Utku life would have been greatly constricted. Just how constricted I discovered when the kaplunas asked to borrow the boats.

All the groups, both the pleasanter ones and the less pleasant ones, wanted the use of these canoes. The kaplunas had two aluminum boats of their own, but these were not large enough to enable all of the men to go fishing at once. The ins and outs of the negotiations that I was forced to conduct are too complicated to record here, but the result was that from July 26, when the first plane arrived, until August 15, when the last large party of fishermen left, we seldom had the use of both of our canoes and sometimes we had the use of neither. The kaplunas suggested that to compensate us for the loan of the canoes, which prevented us from fishing as we would have done, they would bring us the fish that *they* caught during the day; Ray also offered to feed us a meal of kapluna food every evening. Of course, it was impossible to know what Inuttiaq and Pala thought of this plan when it was proposed, but they agreed to it with alacrity. I myself thought it sounded like a reasonable solution to the conflict of interests, one that would involve minimal discomfort for the Utku. In fact, however, the effects of the arrangement were more inconvenient than I had foreseen.

It was worst for the Utku, of course, when the kaplunas used both of our canoes. Then we were stranded on our shore and in many little ways were made dependent on the kaplunas. The days were spent not in fishing but in craftwork, as the men made toy after toy to trade to the kaplunas. Once Mannik went out to cast a throwline from the boulders along the edge of the rapids, but the hook, caught by the still swollen midsummer current, snagged under a stone and could not be retrieved until the kaplunas came to fetch us for our evening meal. Then they lent Mannik his canoe so he could paddle out to disentangle the hook. Once Inuttiaq shot a gull that was swimming near the camp. An occasional bird made welcome variety in our diet, but we could not fetch this one; we had to wait until it drifted to shore of its own accord. We ran out of sugar one morning, but the supply was cached on an island, so we had to drink bitter tea that day until, again, the kaplunas came to fetch us in the evening; then they took us out to the island in one of their outboards. We were deprived of our daily patau because we no longer had fresh fish to boil. The fish that the kaplunas brought us faithfully every evening were, inexplicably, fed to the dogs, and we ourselves ate the fish we had been drying for autumn and winter use. Not the least of the constrictions was our inability to visit the kaplunas freely. On the evenings when Ray was in the Inlet, if the wind had not whipped up the river too much, he came for us after the kaplunas had finished their supper and ferried us across to their camp for a meal, and after we had eaten, he ferried us home again. But often there was no visiting at all.

I do not know how strongly the Utku felt about the absence of their canoes and their dependence on the foreign visitors. Perhaps none of the alterations in the daily patterns troubled them as much as they did me. Characteristically, the Utku kept well under control whatever negative feelings they may have had. Gratitude was the feeling they expressed openly. Every week they thanked God in their prayers for the help the kaplunas were giving them with food, clothing, and equipment, and, indeed, the kaplunas were incredibly generous with their supplies; the leader of one party even brought boxes of discarded wool clothing to distribute among the Eskimos. I chafed against our enforced dependence on the kaplunas, against the loss of our patau, and perhaps most of all against the restrictions imposed on our visits to the kapluna camp, starved as I was for the sound of English and the taste of American food. From my point of view, it was most painful when we had one canoe. When we had none at all, no one went to visit except when the kaplunas fetched us, but when we had one, the men went, frequently and at length, leaving the women and children at home. When they returned, after hours of visiting, their pockets were filled with candy and gum for the children, and they regaled us with detailed accounts of all the good things they had eaten in the kapluna camp: canned pears, and steak, and potatoes, and oranges. Oranges! I would have sold my soul for an orange. Inwardly frantic with frustration and envy, I tried to conceal my feelings and to reason with myself: I was being treated the way the Eskimo women were treated; but the feelings remained and may have caused me to read more covert resentment into the Utkus' own behavior than was actually there.

Nevertheless, a change was clearly evident in the atmosphere of the Utku camp during the period of the kaplunas' sojourn, a change that indicated to me that feelings other than gratitude toward the kaplunas lay under the surface. Though I have no way of knowing whether the Utkus' feelings coincided in detail with mine, there was evidence that the loan of the canoes was to them, as it was to me, a source of strain.

The Utku were as fascinated with the kaplunas as I was. As they sat about on the gravel beach, filing bits of antler and soapstone into pipe-stems and knives for trade, they watched the kaplunas trolling up and down the river in their borrowed canoes and laughed at the odd cant of the boats, weighted down by the outboard motors that the kaplunas had attached. "It would be nice to have a kika (an outboard)," Inuttiaq joked; "paddling is no fun *(hujuujaq)."* The others laughed. Talk was all of the strangers, their personal and collective peculiarities: this one has a big nose; that one is frightening *(kappia, iqhi),* he doesn't smile, just stares; they are all disgustingly furry (that is, hairy); they drink liquor, and that is frightening *(kappia, iqhi),* too; they never eat fish, just catch them and throw them back or give them away. Most of all, talk centered on the bounties that the kaplunas would probably leave for the Eskimos when they departed, as they had done last year. And when the kaplunas disappeared at noon and in the evening into the cove where they were camped and their motors were silenced, the Utkus' thoughts followed them. "I wonder what they are eating?" someone would muse with a little laugh.

Given such absorption in the fishermen and their activities, it would have been strange had the Utku not felt regret at being unable to visit them at will. The year before, when the Utku were camped on the other side of the Rapids, when no water separated them from the kapluna campsite, they had spent many hours standing in a silent cluster on the slope just above the kapluna camp, watching the comings and goings below them, and accepting the food and tobacco they were offered.

There were several signs that something was, indeed, amiss in the Utku camp. For one thing, people were afflicted with a most unusual lethargy. They yawned, complaining of sleepiness in midday, something I had never seen at any other season. Inuttiaq and Allaq once fell sound asleep at noon. I remembered that lethargy one autumn day after the kaplunas had gone, when Amaaqtuq was describing to me how one could recognize that a person was upset *(huqu).* "He will sleep long hours during the summertime when people usually stay up late," she said, "and he'll sit idle instead of working."

Another puzzling phenomenon was the waste of the salmon trout that the kaplunas gave us. The fish were larger and fatter and more numerous than those we caught ourselves. In every obvious way they were desirable, and yet the Utku, who had accepted with such alacrity when the kaplunas offered us their catch, let the fish lie until they rotted on the beach where the kaplunas threw them; then they gave them to the dogs. Before the arrival of the kaplunas, the women had spent hours every day filleting the catches of their men and hanging them to dry in the sun. The dogs had been fed only the bones and heads. The kaplunas, good conservationists all, remarked on the cavalier way in which the Utku treated their gifts of fish, whereupon, wanting to justify to the kaplunas the apparently reprehensible behavior of the Eskimos, I tried to inquire into the latters' reasons for neglecting the fish. I was not satisfied with the replies I received. "The women feel too lazy to cut them up," said Inuttiaq. "Not at all," replied Allaq, "the fish are unpleasantly soft from having lain too long in the sun." The truth was, however, that even when the fishermen brought us fish caught only moments before, as they sometimes did after I had informed them of the Eskimos' dislike of sun-softened fish, the Utku still let most of them lie.

To be sure, neither the Utkus' lethargy nor their neglect of the kaplunas' fish was clearly attributable to the absence of the canoes. It was, characteristically, Inuttiaq who gave me the clearest evidence that the thoughts of the Utku did dwell on their canoes. One morning, two days after the kaplunas had borrowed both canoes, he asked me: "Are the kaplunas leaving tomorrow?" When I replied that those who had his canoe would be gone in two more days, he said with feeling: "That makes one grateful *(hatuq)."* The following day, he inquired again whether the kaplunas who had his boat would be leaving the next day, and when I assured him that they would, he went so far as to tell the guide of that party, through me, that "tomorrow" he would want his boat to fish in.

Curiously, though other Utku men, too, occasionally remarked as they sat stranded on the beach: "One feels like going fishing," or "One feels like eating fresh fish," nevertheless when the departing kaplunas returned the two canoes, nobody went fishing. The remaining kaplunas, covetously eyeing the beached canoes, commented on this inconsistency, too, and again I felt it incumbent on me to explain the Eskimos to the kaplunas. But when I tried, cautiously, to sound the Utkus' reasons for not fishing, telling them, truthfully, that the kaplunas had inquired, Pala replied: "When the kaplunas leave, we'll go fishing again"; and indeed, the day the last plane disappeared, the men sat and fished from their canoes all day in midriver. Not only that, they also set the nets for the first time since spring. What they did use the canoes for, as soon as they became available, was to cross the river to visit the kapluna camp, frequently and at length.

The strength of Inuttiaq's desire to retain his canoe, for whatever reason, appeared a few days after the first group had returned it. We were expecting another group of fishermen to arrive as soon as the clouds lifted. Knowing this, and knowing that Inuttiaq had been restless without his canoe, I tried to assure him that the kaplunas would not take it amiss if he refused to lend it again. If he wished, I said, I would tell them; and I warned him that if they used the boat when they were drunk, they might break it. Inuttiaq responded strongly. "I don't want to lend my canoe," he said. "I want to fish in it. If those kaplunas ask to borrow my canoe tell them they can't. The kapluna leader gave us those canoes because he cares for *(naklik)* us. It's Eskimos he cares for, not kaplunas, because we live under more difficult conditions *(ayuq)*, and he said that if any harm came to those canoes, the people who damaged them would be stabbed with something metal—I forget exactly what—something metal, yes? It will hurt." He made a stabbing gesture in the air and turned to Allaq for confirmation, which she silently gave. Little did I suspect how much trouble my literal interpretation of Inuttiaq's instruction that day was to cause me.

The fishermen arrived in due course, and shortly thereafter they came for a canoe. Trouble began almost at once, but I was not aware of it. The Utku did not lend their best canoe, Inuttiaq's; they lent Pala's, which was slightly leaky; but even so, I was annoyed at their compliance. I wished they had refused to lend either and, in my irritation, when the kapluna guide asked me for assurance that the Eskimos would really use the fish he offered as rental payment for the canoe, I replied that the Eskimos had not used the kapluna fish before when they were given, and probably would not do so now. Pala's fourteen-year-old son, Ukpik, freshly arrived in camp after a winter at school in Inuvik, listened, expressionless, to my remarks.

The rest of the day passed uneventfully. As usual when they had the use of a canoe, the men spent a large part of their time at the kapluna camp, but they returned with less booty than sometimes; this trip leader did not believe in "spoiling the natives." Next morning early, I woke to hear the sound of an outboard approaching, and kapluna voices down at the shore. Anxious not to lose an opportunity to use my native tongue, I dressed and joined the men, Eskimo and white, who clustered at the edge of the beach. Inuttiaq and Pala approached me as I went toward the group. "The kaplunas are going to borrow the other canoe," they told me. "They say they will return it when they are through with it."

The kapluna trip leader corroborated what Pala had said. "That first canoe is no good," he said; "it has a hole in it, so we have to borrow this other one." There was, indeed, a sizeable rent in the canvas, which had certainly not been there when we loaned it and which made the canoe unusable. The two men who had come with the guide were already attaching the outboard to Inuttiaq's canoe, as Inuttiaq and the other Utku men watched.

I exploded. Unsmilingly and in a cold voice I told the kapluna leader a variety of things that I thought he should know: that if he borrowed the second canoe we would be without a fishing boat, that if this boat also was damaged we would be in a very difficult position, since a previous guide had forgotten to bring on his return trip the repair materials that Inuttiaq had traded for, and that we would be unable to buy materials ourselves until the strait froze in November. I also pointed out the island where our supplies of tea, sugar, and kerosene were cached and mentioned our inability to reach it except by canoe. Then, armed with my memory of Inuttiaq's earlier instructions, I told the guide that the owner of that second canoe did not wish to lend it.

The guide was not unreasonable; he agreed at once that if the owner did not wish to lend his canoe, that was his option: "It's his canoe, after all." Slightly soothed, I turned to Inuttiaq, who stood nearby, expressionless like the other Utku. "Do you want me to tell him you don't want to lend your canoe?" I asked in Eskimo. "He will not borrow it if you say no."

Inuttiaq's expression dismayed me, but I did not know how to read it; I knew only that it registered strong feeling, as did his voice, which was unusually loud: "Let him have his will!"

I hoped my voice was calm when I replied to Inuttiaq: "As you like," but I was filled with fury at kapluna and Inuttiaq alike, as well as at myself for having undertaken the futile role of mediator, and my tone was icy when I said to the guide: "He says you can have it." Turning abruptly, I strode back to my tent, went to bed, and wept in silence. . . .

# 3 | HOUSEKEEPING IN EL NAHRA
## Elizabeth Fernea

*Because ethnographic fieldwork takes a long time and usually involves residing and participating in communities far from home, anthropologists engaged in research are generally accompanied by their families. The spouse of the field-worker often becomes as deeply involved in participant observation as the anthropologist does. This excerpt from Elizabeth Fernea's book about her life in the field with her anthropologist husband describes some of the practical problems of setting up house in a new environment—and some of the emotional adjustments that must be made by an anthropologist's wife as she discovers that she is to be subjected to as much scrutiny by her neighbors as is her husband. The book from which this report is excerpted goes beyond simply describing the author's circumstances in the village. It is a detailed and lucid account of Arab women, one that establishes Elizabeth Fernea as a first-rate ethnographer in her own right.*

In a few weeks our life in El Nahra settled into a working routine. After breakfast, Bob and I would listen to the BBC news and drill on Arabic, adding to each other's vocabulary new phrases and words we had heard for the first time the day before. By nine-thirty he had gone off for his morning interviewing and I began the household chores. My afternoons, like his, were given over to regular visits, he with the men, I with the women of the tribal settlement. The evenings we spent together, reviewing the events of the day, writing in our journals, reading or playing chess.

Most of the problems posed by everyday living in the village had been solved fairly easily. Our stove, refrigerator, new cupboard and the aluminum work table and folding chairs filled the bare kitchen. The dirt floors were covered with new reed mats, and we had screens made for the windows. Bob and Mohammed dug a garbage pit for tin cans and we burned refuse in the cylindrical oven. After many days of delicate negotiations, Bob finally found a man who was willing, once a month, to clean out our mud-brick toilet. We arranged to have our heavy laundry done in Diwaniya, as no one in El Nahra wanted to do a Christian's laundry, even at a price; the rest of the clothes I did by hand. We even became accustomed to taking baths out of two pails of water, one for washing, one for rinsing.

The preparation of food, however, was a major occupation. Shopping had to be done each day, for we were out of reach, literally as well as financially, of the luxuries of canned and frozen foods. Bob bought jam, dried yeast and coffee in Diwaniya, and otherwise we ate what was available locally: the vegetables and fruits currently in season, rice, eggs, yogurt, and, since we were rich by village standards, meat every day.

Mohammed did the marketing, and with his help I soon learned what every merchant had to offer, although in all the months in El Nahra I never visited them in person. Only women of very low status ever appeared in the public bazaar; rather than go personally, a woman sent her children, her servants, even her husband to buy groceries, pick up mail, or carry urgent messages to friends.

The village butcher slaughtered a goat or a sheep daily, and if Mohammed got to the market early, we had lamb kidneys for lunch, or liver, or the tenderloin which lies along the backbone. But if he was late we got a kilo chunk of unidentifiable meat, which might take one or four hours to cook, depending on the age of the animal. With Mohammed's help, I learned to strip off the tough membranes, and then he would either grind the meat or cut it into minute pieces suitable for stews of various kinds, which we ate with rice.

Onions and garlic to give flavor to the stringy meat were cheap and plentiful, and Mohammed brought me a fine supply of spices, cinnamon bark, whole nutmegs, turmeric root, peppercorns, saffron, dried celery leaves and mint. Whenever I needed spices for cooking, he would pound them fine with an old brass mortar and pestle which belonged to his mother.

Homemade tomato paste was the other ingredient essential to local cuisine. In the summer, when tomatoes glutted the market, every good housewife bought a supply, spread the tomatoes on flat tin trays and carried them up to the roof of her house. There, in the summer sun, the raw tomatoes dried and thickened, and salt was added every other day for about two weeks. The resulting tomato paste was then ready to be packed into earthenware jars to be kept throughout the winter. This paste had a delicious and distinctive flavor—the women asserted it was the combination of salt and summer sun.

We used locally made *ghee,* or clarified butter, for cooking, and after experimenting with a few tins of tasteless imported margarine (specially treated to maintain its texture in tropical climates!) we turned to local butter for all uses. One or two women in the tribal settlement specialized in making butter and selling it to the market to be clarified into ghee. If we ordered in advance and paid slightly more than the market price, we could usually get part of the supply. Many months after I arrived, I was visiting the butter-and-egg woman one day and asked the purpose of a shapeless leathery mass which lay near us on the ground. The woman demonstrated that it was her butter churn, a young lambskin which had been cleaned and dried in the sun, then greased for easy handling. The cream was poured in, both ends of the skin were securely tied, and then my neighbor simply shook the "churn" back and forth till the butter came. Occasionally the butter we bought was topped with a film of dirt, undoubtedly from the inside of that old and fragrant "churn." When this happened, Mohammed would simply scrape off the dirt and return it to the woman, explaining that we only paid for clean butter.

I made yogurt from water-buffalo milk, which was richer than the thin milk yielded by the settlement's undernourished cows. The *jamoosa,* or water buffalo, huge black slow-moving animals, were much better adapted to the local climate than were cows. They seldom contracted tuberculosis. Their milk was in demand and even the meat could be eaten, but, though the buffalo herders were prosperous by local standards, they did not enjoy a comparable social status. A cow was an animal conferring prestige, but a water buffalo was not. Still, several tribesmen owned buffalo, and from one of our neighbors Mohammed would buy a quart of milk each evening. Still foaming, the milk was put on to boil. It cooled during the night. In the morning we skimmed off the cream, a rich, thick butterlike substance *(gaymar)* which was delicious with jam on toast. To the rest I added a spoonful of yogurt starter, wrapped the pan in a towel to keep it at a constant temperature, and by late afternoon we had yogurt, for cooking, for eating, or for drinking if we diluted it with water.

We always got good rice, rice grown in Iraq, or the famous long-grain "amber" rice which supposedly came from Iran. When potatoes were available, we often buried them in our charcoal brazier and baked them. Other vegetables were seasonal; for weeks we might eat marrow squash, then spinach would come onto the market, followed by broad beans and okra. In the fall there were eggplant and carrots. The winter fruits, oranges and bananas, were excellent and in summer we ate watermelon and grapes.

For special occasions we could buy a chicken, which was, predictably,

very skinny and outrageously expensive, but had a good flavor if par-
boiled or marinated before roasting. On some nights we returned home
to find by our doorstep a brace of small partridges which had been shot
by one of Bob's friends. Plucked and cleaned and sautéed, they made
a fine change of diet.

The local bread, flat round cakes made of barley or wheat flour, salt
and water, was healthful and good when hot, but usually it was dry and
often tasteless. Finally I tried baking my own bread in our portable oven
and soon I was baking four fairly presentable loaves a week.

So we ate well, if monotonously, slept a reasonable amount and were
seldom sick. We were finding people generally pleasant and helpful,
and our painfully meager Arabic showed signs of improvement. Gradually we began to feel more or less at home in El Nahra, although new
problems kept arising, some more serious than others.

First there were the birds, which absolutely refused to leave. We
shooed them out of the house several times a day, and tried to keep the
windows and doors shut lest they swoop back in. Bob had screen doors
made with tight latches, and we crept in and out of the house, shutting
the doors quickly against the flocks of swallows that filled the yard,
perched on the roof or in the lemon trees, waiting for the door to be
opened the smallest crack.

One night I awakened, coughing, for a feather had fluttered down
into my face. What would come next? "This must stop," Bob said, and
in the morning he and Mohammed set out to "do something definite
about the birds," I was not sure just what. Mohammed returned with
a long bamboo pole, and every night thereafter before we retired, Bob
would probe in and around each of the beams, routing out the sly
swallows who had hidden there during the day, waiting for the peace
of the night to recommence their mating and nest building! After a
month of nightly probing, most of the swallows retired in defeat, but
the next spring they came again, small groups which camped in the
lemon tree, twittering sadly and obviously unable to understand what
had happened to their haven.

Bob was also in some perplexity about horses. Much of the visiting of
tribal clan settlements in the back country had to be done on horseback,
as there were no roads. Bob enjoyed this, for he had always liked to ride,
and he found it another area of common interest with the men of the
tribe. For these occasions the sheik insisted on lending Bob one of his
good Arab stallions. They were valuable and beautiful horses, worth at
least 500 pounds, and Bob lived in fear that, while he was riding the
borrowed animal, it might trip and break its leg, and then what would
we do? It was not only that we could not afford to replace the horse,
but that the sheik would probably not allow us to do so (after all, we
were his guests) and this would have been even worse.

One morning the gate opened and Bob and Mohammed led a horse
into our garden. He was small and light brown and slightly sway-
backed.

"I've bought him," Bob announced.

"Bought him?"

"Yes, what do you think of him?"

"Well—"

"I know he's not too beautiful, but he was only thirty pounds, and it seemed the best way to avoid borrowing the sheik's horses all the time."

I nodded. It did seem reasonable. But who would feed him and water him?

"I've already thought of that," said Bob. "I'm paying a man to feed and water him every day, and he can be tethered at the mudhif."

So it was. Bob was very pleased to have his own horse, and except for occasional visits to our garden to crop grass, the horse was completely cared for at the mudhif.

Meanwhile I was having my own troubles. These were serious, but they were hard to define, and I could not at first describe them even to Bob.

At this time we had been in El Nahra for two months. Bob had made many friends, not only among the tribe, but also in the town. He felt his study was going well, and he was enthusiastic and full of plans.

But I felt I was getting nowhere. I had conscientiously visited a number of houses in the settlement, some of them several times, had been welcomed and treated to tea and gossip in each. But not a single woman had come to call on me, and even in my own visiting, the women and I were still saying to each other approximately the same things we had said on the first occasions. My direct questions on subjects in which Bob was interested were parried by polite remarks. As my Arabic improved, I could often get the drift of conversations and understand occasional fragments. It seemed to me that many times the women were talking about me, and not in a particularly friendly manner. If I could have been certain they were talking about me, and understood exactly what was being said, then I could have dealt with it, replied to the comments and brought it out in the open. But the terrible thing was that I could not be certain. Were they talking about me or not? What errors in etiquette or custom had I committed? What in heaven's name were they *saying?* My uneasiness grew in this atmosphere of half-hearing and part-understanding.

I tried to tell myself that the women did not come to see me because they were busy with household chores and children, and that they seldom went out anywhere; this was all true. I realized that my novelty value was wearing off, and I was not developing any close relationships with the women which might have replaced it. Why? I did not know.

Finally I talked to Bob about it. He tried to help, pointing out that among the men, tradition prescribed how strangers were to be greeted and treated, but that this was not true of the women, who did not see a stranger from one year to the next, and were certainly not accustomed to dealing with them for long periods of time. Bob and I rarely visited together, so we had little opportunity to compare impressions of the same situation, which might have corrected my judgments and dispelled some of my doubts. He suggested that he speak to the men about having their wives visit me, but this I vetoed. I felt that if the women had to be forced by their husbands into coming to see me, they might better not come at all.

We discussed the situation very rationally, and I could even explain it to Bob, saying that of course the language barrier made all communication doubly difficult and was bound to exacerbate the situation in which I found myself. There was no doubt that the women did not answer direct questions. There was no doubt that they did not come to see me. But was there actual hostility? Unfriendliness? Coolness? I felt definitely that there was, but I had to admit that my isolation and loneliness might very well be magnifying this unfriendliness into a ridiculous and unrealistic bogey. But it was there, nonetheless, and I came to dread the daily visits, the tea drinking among the whispering, the smiles which now seemed artificial and insincere. And the giggling behind the abayahs. Twenty women, giggling, with their eyes fixed on me. Or were they?

Bob took me into Diwaniya, and we went to the movies. He stayed home in the evenings to read and play chess when he should have been in the mudhif, interviewing. He knew how miserable I was and he did his best, but in the end it was a problem I had to solve myself. We were very happy together in our little mud house. If only I could make some kind of breakthrough with the women, I thought. For one thing, I spent at least four hours a day with them. They were a major factor in my life, whether I liked it or not, and my only company, except for Bob and Mohammed. I felt very strongly that we must have some common humanity between us, although we were from such different worlds. But how to find it?

Things reached some sort of climax when Bob was invited on a long trip to visit one of the farthest-outlying clan settlements. The sheik's brother and his oldest son were going across the fields thirty miles on horseback, and would be gone at least two days and one night. I did not mind spending the time by myself, but the sheik decided it was not proper or safe that I stay alone at night, and decreed that Amina, Selma's servant, would sleep in the house with me. At that particular stage in my relations with the tribal women, a servant from the harem to watch my every movement as I brushed my teeth, washed my face and went to bed was the last thing on earth I wanted. But there was no help for it. The sheik said she was to come, and she came.

Poor Amina. I think she relished the night with me even less than I did, but there was no recourse for her either. She came at suppertime, and sat on the floor beside me, watching me as I ate. Then followed the hour when I usually read or wrote letters. Amina continued to watch me. A half hour of this intense, silent scrutiny was enough. I gave up, made tea and offered her some, and tried to talk. She was not very communicative, but she drank the tea. Mohammed came to set up a camp cot in the living room, beside the bed where I slept. Amina was to sleep on the cot and I was to wake her at five, so she could go and milk the cows. Mohammed bade us good night and departed. I wanted to undress and climb into bed but, feeling shy, went into the kitchen to change into my nightgown. Amina followed me. I came back to the living room; she did likewise. Apparently the sheik had warned her that things would go badly with her if she let me out of her sight for a single moment after darkness fell. I wondered whether she would accompany me to the toilet. She started to, but stopped halfway down the path to allow me some privacy. I came back, undressed as I had seen my grandmother do, putting the nightgown on over everything and gradually discarding clothes from beneath its protection, while Amina watched. I got into bed. Amina wrapped herself in her abayah and lay down on the cot, pulling up the blanket which I had offered her. Once more I got up to turn on the light and check the alarm, and at this point Amina spoke.

"Is your husband kind to you?" she asked. I said yes. She sighed, and burst into tears. I was appalled. I was trying to make up my mind whether to go over to her when she stopped dead in the middle of a sob, sat up cross-legged on the cot, dried her eyes on a corner of her tattered abayah, and launched into the story of her life.

How I wished then that my Arabic were letter-perfect! For the story poured out of her in a torrent of words, punctuated by occasional sobs. I caught perhaps a third of what she actually said, but she repeated so much that the outline was finally made fairly clear to me. As the tale emerged, I was tempted to break down and cry myself.

Amina was a slave, but she had not always been one. As a girl of fifteen, she had been married to a sixty-five-year-old man. Not even her father thought it was a good match, but there were twelve children in her family, and never enough barley bread and dried dates, the diet of the very poor, to go around. Her marriage brought her nothing but grief, for she nearly died delivering a stillborn son, and then her husband died, leaving her penniless. Her own family was destitute. Most of the members of her husband's family had died, and those who were alive did not want another mouth to feed. No one wanted her. What was she to do? At this point Sheik Hamid heard of her plight. He had then been married to Selma for three years; she had two sons and needed a servant. Hamid bought Amina from her father for twenty pounds, and gave her to Selma.

"And never have I had such a good life as since I came here," she averred. "Why, I can have as much bread as I want, every day, and rice, and sometimes meat. Selma even gives me cigarettes. And Haji—" here she raised her hands and her eyes to heaven and launched into a flowery eulogy of the generosity, the greatness, the goodness which were peculiar to Hamid's character.

"Do you ever see your family, Amina?" I asked, knowing that even through woe and poverty and separation, family ties are not soon severed in this society. The question was a mistake. Amina began to cry again, and between sobs she said she had not seen her family for seven years.

"But oh, Haji, he is a good man. There is no sheik in the Euphrates

Valley as good as Haji." She went on and on like this until she finally ran down. She was worn out and so was I. The recital had taken at least an hour. I suggested we might sleep, and she agreed. But when I turned out the light, the sound of muffled sniffling came to me through the darkness.

"What is the matter, Amina?"

"Nothing," she replied, but the sniffling continued.

"If your husband is really kind to you," she said inexplicably, "get a lot of gold jewelry from him while you are still young. You never know what will happen."

And before I could reply she was snoring loudly, fast asleep.

Bob came back at 6:30 the next evening. I had no time to recount the tale of Amina, for several members of the clan had returned with the men, and were eating in the mudhif. Bob was expected to make an appearance, and he changed his clothes and left. Not more than five minutes after he had gone there was a loud pounding at the gate. I thought he had forgotten something and ran to open it. Not Bob, but seven or eight black-veiled figures greeted me—the women! They had come at last. They marched up the path, giggling and whispering to each other like a bunch of schoolgirls on a field trip to the zoo. Not until they were all inside the house and had removed their face veils did I know who had come: Selma—yes, Selma, the social leader of my little settlement—and Sheddir, wife of Ali; Laila, one of the sheik's nieces; Fadhila, sister-in-law of Mohammed; two women I did not know; and Amina, my roommate of the night before. Aha, I thought, the business with Amina was not a waste of time, perhaps she has told them I am not such an ogre after all. I smiled at her in gratitude, but she was talking to Selma and did not respond.

No one paid any attention to me. They gazed around them, at our wardrobe with its full-length mirror, at the postcards and the calendar I had pinned up, at Bob's brick-and-board bookcase, at our narrow bed against the wall. I decided to let them look, and went to make tea, returning with seven glasses on a tray. Everyone refused. I offered it again. Again I was refused. Suddenly I was angry. This was a great insult, not to accept tea in a house where one was visiting, and they knew it and I knew it and they knew I knew it. I said, as sweetly as I could, "How is it that you receive me into your houses and insist that I drink your tea, but when you come to see me, you only want to look, and not accept my hospitality?"

There was a shocked silence.

Selma rose to the occasion. "The women are shy," she said. "They know your ways are different from ours, and think they should refuse the tea, since it is their first visit to your house."

She knew I knew she was making up every word she said, but I once more appreciated her tact and kindness in a difficult situation. "But," she said grandly, "I have been to secondary school in Diwaniya and have read about the West, I know your ways are much the same as ours, so I will drink some tea."

The crisis passed. Sheddir also accepted a glass, and Fadhila, but the others still refused. I passed around cigarettes. As I had thought, this was too great a temptation to resist, and everyone, even those whom I had never seen smoke, took a cigarette.

"What do you do all day here by yourself?" asked Fadhila.

"I cook, and clean the house."

"Why don't you do your washing in the canal as we do?" suggested Sheddir.

"Because I like to do it in my house," I said.

Then in a whispered conversation which followed, I distinctly heard Sheddir say that she often came to our garden to cut grass for their animals, and had never seen much laundry hanging on my line. She allowed as how I must be very lazy. I felt myself bristling, readying a tart reply to that one, but Selma intervened.

"You say you cook," she said. "What do you cook? I thought Western-ers ate all their meals from tin cans."

I told them what we had for lunch, and added that I had baked bread that morning.

"Bread like ours?" asked Sheddir.

"No," I said, "Western bread."

Selma explained to the group that this was a high loaf called "toast." Haji ate it all the time in Baghdad and had told her about it.

"Let us see some," they clamored.

I ran to the kitchen, proud that I was good for something, and re-turned with several slices of fresh bread, cut into quarters.

"You taste it, Sheddir," Selma instructed.

Everyone stopped talking and watched as Sheddir, very flustered indeed at being chosen the group guinea pig, picked up one of the squares of bread between thumb and forefinger and stuffed it in her mouth. She masticated a moment, then made a terrible face and spat it out on the floor. The ladies exploded and laughed till the tears ran down their cheeks. I was close to tears myself, and not humorous ones, but I realized that Selma was watching me.

"Sheddir is not accustomed to your bread—she finds it strange," she offered kindly, but she could not help shaking with laughter at this huge joke. At the height of the mirth, Sheddir thought of something else that was screamingly funny, and launched into a long tale which I did not understand, but which seemed to have something to do with me, for she kept watching me out of the corner of her eye as she talked.

"Do you know what she is saying?" Selma asked me. I shook my head. "Sheddir says you do not know how to cook rice, and because your rice is so bad, your husband comes to eat at the mudhif."

I admitted I did not know how to cook the rice in El Nahra because it was different from the rice in America.

Even Fadhila laughed at this. "Rice? Rice is the same everywhere," she asserted and people nodded. I was obviously slow-witted as well as lazy.

My face must have shown what I was feeling, for Selma changed the subject.

"Do you and Mr. Bob both sleep in that little bed?" she asked. I said yes.

"What fun they must have, I'm sure!" croaked Sheddir and the ladies were off again. I knew this was a good-hearted joke, but I had been tried too far that evening. Selma saw it too. She stood up and pulled her abayah around her, announcing that Haji Hamid would soon be back from the mudhif, and if he found her gone—she made an unmistakable gesture.

"Oh, no, Selma," protested Sheddir. "Haji would never beat you. You are too beautiful." Selma arched at this, but she did not deny it. The attention had been diverted from the strange American and the women's attitude changed. They rose and prepared to take their leave. I saw them to the gate, voicing the traditional farewells, and got a few halfhearted ones in reply. Then I shut the gate and burst into tears.

Six months before, I would not have believed that I could be so upset at being accused of laziness and incompetence by a group of illiterate tribal ladies. But there was no question but that it was a real and very terrible snub now. Not only the practical difficulties of continuing the visiting and maintaining good relations bothered me. It had now become important to me to be accepted by these people as a woman and as a human being. And tonight, when I had thought success was near, the evening had turned into a fiasco. I was indignant first, and told myself they were nothing but a group of curiosity seekers. Then I began to feel righteous. After all, they had insulted me by refusing my tea, spitting out my food, and telling me I was lazy and a bad cook. I felt hurt. They did not find me sympathetic or interesting or even human, but only amusing as a performing member of another species. I tried to feel tragic, superior, ironic, above it all—but failed utterly and wept again.

When Bob came home he told me to forget the whole incident, to remember that we were in El Nahra to do some specific work, not prove any romantic theories about humanity being the same everywhere. But this did not satisfy me. Bob said I should simply try to relax, and continue the visiting on a businesslike basis. I said I would try, but I was not convinced.

Next morning, after Bob had gone off to the mudhif, I was unreasonably depressed. Bob had suggested I should charge out and visit immediately one of the women who had been at our house the night before, apparently on the theory that if you get thrown from a horse, you must get back on it right away or you'll lose your grip forever. But I could not force myself out. I started lunch and then wandered into the garden, stopping to inspect a large hole in our mud wall where dogs sneaked in at night to raid the garbage pit. I bent down to look through the hole, and drew back in alarm as my gaze met three pairs of eyes, three black-framed faces looking in at me from the other side of the wall.

One of the women smiled. "Good morning," she said through the hole.

"Good morning," I replied.

"We hear you can't cook rice," she said.

I almost threw a rusty tin can at her, I was so annoyed.

But the third one said, "If you will open your gate, we will come in and show you how to cook rice, so your husband will be pleased with your food."

For the second time in twenty-four hours I was close to tears, but this was quite different. I opened the gate and let the ladies in (one was Laila, the sheik's niece; the other two I did not know). They marched purposefully up the path and into my kitchen, where they did indeed show me how to cook rice.

We picked over and washed the rice, covered it with cold water, then sat down on the floor to drink tea while it soaked. A large pot of salted water was put on the stove to boil, and the rice was cooked in the boiling water until the grains were separate and tasted right. When the rice was drained, clarified butter was put in the dry pot over the fire until it sizzled. Then the rice was poured back into the pot and stirred quickly until each grain was coated with the boiling butter. Then we covered the pot, turned down the heat, and let the buttered rice steam slowly. We drank another cup of tea, and I thanked the ladies profusely.

"We don't want your husband to beat you," said one. "After all, you are here alone without your mother."

"Come to see us soon," said Laila, as the gate closed behind her.

Lunch was quite a gay meal that day. Even Bob remarked on the rice, and when Mohammed came, he tasted it and pronounced it all right—the final seal of approval, I knew, for though Mohammed did not eat much, he was very particular about his food.

That afternoon I marched up the path to the sheik's house almost triumphantly. The rice-cooking lesson had reassured me, and I felt I could take on the whole harem. Mohammed had been sent to tell them I was coming, but apparently he had forgotten, for no one was at the door, and I crossed the courtyard to Selma's house without seeing a soul. At the door Amina met me.

"Oh," she said, obviously startled, *"ahlan wusahlan,"* and quickly led me into the sheik's bedroom, where the rugs were rolled up and the bed stripped. General housecleaning seemed to be under way. In yesterday's mood I would have gathered my abayah around me and departed, but not today. Amina hurried out to find someone, leaving me alone in the bedroom for the first time. The biggest chest was open, spilling out sheets and pillowcases, tablecloths, antimacassars and towels. Also I saw, to my amusement, that despite the splendor of the gilt bedstead and the satin spread, Sheik Hamid, like every other person in the village who could afford a bed at all, slept on bare boards covered with a cotton mattress. I was just screwing up courage to take a closer look at the contents of the open chest when Selma hurried in, in an old house dress.

*"Ahlan wusahlan!"* she said. She was flustered and preoccupied and

I apologized for arriving unannounced, explaining that I thought Mohammed had told her of my coming.

"Never mind," she said, "stay and have tea. But you must excuse me, because I have to make Haji's bed before he comes back from the mudhif."

I said I didn't mind at all, and she shouted for Amina, who came in and grinned at me as she helped Selma beat the mattress and lay it back carefully on the boards. By this time word of my arrival had spread and a few women and children straggled in. They joked with Selma as she puffed over the mattress, and nodded at me. Selma dug into the chest for sheets and pillowcases, heavy white cotton elaborately embroidered in bright colors. The bottom sheet was tucked in all around, but the top sheet had a wide border of embroidery which was draped down over the bedside. The pillowcases were skinned tightly over the long, narrow pillows, and tied in fancy bows at each end so the colored pillow covering (pink to match the bedspread) showed to good advantage. Mottoes were embroidered over the pillowcases—for good luck, said Selma, translating them for me. The most popular motto was "Sleep here and good health."

"Can you do embroidery like that?" asked Samira, the daughter of Kulthum, pointing to the complicated pattern which followed the border of the sheet.

"Not as beautiful as that, but I can embroider," I replied, remembering the few doll clothes I had painfully cross-stitched long ago under the watchful eye of my aunt.

"Why don't you embroider some nice pillowcases for your and Mr. Bob's bed?" continued Samira.

I was up to anything that day. "Oh, I'm already planning to," I lied airily. "Mr. Bob is bringing me some cloth and embroidery thread from Diwaniya."

"You can buy the cloth here," said Samira.

"Yes, I know," I answered, knowing absolutely nothing about it, "but the cotton is cheaper in Diwaniya and the selection is much better."

Another woman interrupted to say that cloth was cheaper in El Nahra, and there was no need to go all the way to Diwaniya for it.

"It may be cheaper," admitted Selma, turning from the bed, where she was applying a final pat to the satin spread, "but it is not as good quality as the cotton in Diwaniya. I know, because that was my home before I married, you remember."

That silenced them.

"What kind of pattern will you embroider?" asked Laila, the sheik's niece who had come to my house the evening of the bread episode.

"I haven't decided," I answered, quite truthfully this time. "I think I would like to do one like that"—and I pointed to the flowers and leaves and the good luck mottoes on Haji's clean pillowcase—"but I don't have any patterns."

"Oh," said Laila. "I have many, many patterns, because my sisters and I embroider all the time. Come to visit us when you get your cloth and you can choose one of ours."

I was suddenly unreasonably elated at the invitation. "I will," I promised. "I will get the cloth tomorrow, so I'll come day after tomorrow."

Selma had finished and locked the chest again. She sat down to rest, untying her *asha* and rearranging her hair under it. "Amina," she called, "bring us tea." Amina brought a tray of three glasses, one for me, one for Selma and one for the oldest woman in the room. I had been sitting on the floor the whole time, but no one had commented on it. Selma was too occupied with other things to think much about me and the proprieties of entertaining a guest. We all drank our tea together.

It was late and I felt that I should go, but we sat on. When I rose, Selma said, completely unexpectedly, "The sheik would like to meet you."

I looked blank.

"Would you like to see him here or at your house?"

The suddenness of it caught me off guard. I thought fast. I had been in purdah ever since I arrived and had neither spoken nor sat with any tribal men other than Mohammed, who didn't count as he was considered "my family" now. Yet Sheik Hamid was our host. What was the best thing to do?

"I must ask my husband," I said, and Selma nodded. It was apparently the answer they expected. . . .

# Part II
## Responding to Environmental Pressures

An important aspect of the study of any human population is the ways its members cope with problems in their immediate environments, problems as diverse as depletion of essential resources, multiplication of disease-causing parasites, or dramatic natural hazards like floods and earthquakes. As we shall see, although some of these problems are beyond human control, many actually result from human activities. Environments, then, are to be considered not as fixed but as changing, partly as a consequence of human behavior itself.

This insight is integral to the study of human ecology. Ecology is the science of relations among organisms of different species that interact with one another and with inorganic features of their environments. These relations are studied through systematic examination of the flows of energy, matter, and information among the component parts of the ecological community. In this way, we can isolate and measure the effects of one component in an "ecosystem" upon another. It becomes clear, then, how the behavior of one group of organisms—say human beings—affects the geographical distribution, abundance, or physical characteristics of other populations, like cattle, mosquitoes, or oak trees. It also becomes clear how change in one affects change in the others. For example, if a human population becomes larger, it may attempt to increase the size of its domestic cattle population. If there is limited grazing land, the cattle may overgraze it, thus preventing new grass from growing and permitting soil erosion. If soil erosion creates a desert that will not support either people or cattle at previous levels, both people and cattle will have to move, perhaps adopting a transhumant (seasonal-movement) pattern, rather than a sedentary one.

It has long been observed by anthropologists that many of the preindustrial peoples they study practice conservationist strategies. That is, many of their traditional practices seem to have resulted in balance between people and their resources, so that environmental relations have remained stable. Many different kinds of cultural practices have been recognized as functioning to preserve viable relations between human beings and their environments—from population control (birth spacing, infanticide, delayed marriage) to hunting and agriculture (randomizing directions in hunting expeditions, shifting crops so that land can lie fallow for long periods of time, and so forth).

Although research on the potential usefulness of such practices in promoting human survival has increased understanding about human-environmental relations, it has become clear in recent years that balanced and stable ecosystems are likely to be the exceptions, not the rule. The most salient observation is that contact between preindustrial and industrial-marketing systems consistently results in dramatic change in human-environmental relations in the former. As people begin to use local resources to meet nonlocal market demands, conservationist practices are replaced by others; as modern health practices are introduced, infant mortality declines, and the human population rises. These are only some of the obvious effects that integration into a larger, modern, industrial-marketing system has on human-environmental relationships everywhere.

But disruption of "natural" environments by human beings and the creation of unstable ecosystems may be far more typical of preindustrial societies than anthropologists once thought. Ecological research now enables us to see that peoples with relatively simple technologies have affected their environments in ways to which they themselves have had continually to adjust. Although environmental change and human adjustment may now be proceeding at a far more rapid pace than ever before, the phenomena themselves are by no means unprecedented anywhere that human beings exist. Furthermore, it must be understood that human beings are not unique in this respect: All organisms affect their environments simply by living in them. Sometimes the behavior of other organisms—be they ants or elephants—can be ecologically destructive, depleting essential resources. If the organisms are sufficiently destructive, of course, they may even cause their own extinction.

Human development of and dependence on technology as a special device for adjustment have meant that our scope for both destruction and survival may be far wider than that of other organisms, but we have certainly begun to worry that we may be approaching the limits of our own ability to adjust.

People deal with their environmental problems in a wide variety of ways, ranging from long-term biological accommodation to short-term emergency measures, as illustrated in the studies in Part Two. Not all responses, of course, are equally successful. Might we improve our chances by planning? A serious problem for planners is to try to understand the ingredients of a successful approach to dealing with human environments. C. S. Holling and M. A. Goldberg, in the last selection here, address themselves to this issue, with suggestions for the use of ecological principles in future planning.

# 4 | THE PREDATORY BABOONS OF KEKOPEY

## Robert S. O. Harding and Shirley C. Strum

*We open this section with a consideration of the means at our disposal for coping with problems arising from our relations with our environments. Some of our ways of coping are determined biologically, the products of long-term evolutionary adjustment. For example, when it is hot, we perspire, a response that helps to cool our bodies. When dust blows into our faces, we instinctively blink our eyes protectively.*

*But a very large proportion of human responses to environmental problems are far more flexible and diverse than those determined by biogenetic reflexes. We learn to take advantage of new opportunities and to abandon old patterns of life even without undergoing biological alteration. Our capacity to do so began to develop long before we emerged as the species we are today, for flexibility in behavioral adaptation is an ancient evolutionary device. The behavior of other animals is also not fixed or rigidly determined by instinct. This can be seen in the feeding behavior of baboons in the wild. Robert S. O. Harding and Shirley C. Strum examined a group of baboons, which were initially largely vegetarian in their eating habits but shifted to hunting and meat eating as new opportunities arose. Even such a fundamental pattern of behavior as food getting and diet, then, may change rapidly over a very short period of time, given a flexible organism and a change in the environment. This selection provides a valuable insight into some of the ways in which our early prehominid ancestors may have shifted their patterns of social behavior and feeding strategies in response to environmental change.*

The olive baboons moved slowly across the African plain that lay deep in the shadow of the cliffs on whose ledges the troop would sleep in safety for the night. Suddenly, an adult male stopped in the foot-high grass and pounced. The sharp bleat that followed betrayed the presence of a newborn Thomson's gazelle, still too weak to outrun its captor.

The baboon held the infant to the ground and tore at its soft belly with his teeth. When the antelope stopped moving, the baboon commenced eating, but perhaps intimidated by the presence of other male baboons, which had approached and were staring at the scene, he picked up the carcass in his jaws and ran twenty yards away. The others pursued. Within an hour the male had consumed most of the flesh, but as he walked away from the remains another male quickly seized the last bits of flesh and skin.

Incidents of this sort have become quite common among the baboon troops that range freely through Kekopey, a cattle ranch near the village of Gilgil, 70 miles northwest of Nairobi, in the Central Rift Valley of Kenya. Although Kekopey comprises 45,000 acres, the grass that grows sparsely in the arid climate supports only 4,500 cattle. Large portions of the ranch are covered with lava rubble, and other evidence of the volcanic activity that characterizes much of the rift valley is scattered throughout the area—steam hisses from cracks in the earth, and extinct ash cones and craters dot the landscape.

The central part of the ranch, however, consists of open grassland broken by patches of an aromatic camphorous shrub that the Masai people call *leleshwa.* Additional grassland has been created over the years by ranch workers who cleared away some of this scrub. Water troughs for cattle are scattered over much of this open land, and many kinds of animals take advantage of the ready supply.

Impala and Thomson's gazelle are the dominant antelope species in this part of the ranch. In 1970, when we first began our study, their exact numbers were not known, but a survey on 18,000 acres of open grassland and scrub on the ranch resulted in a count of 800 impala and 1,600 Thomson's gazelle. Baboons also inhabit this part of the ranch; our 1970 census, which covered some of this area, showed seven troops ranging in size from 35 to 135 animals and living in overlapping home ranges.

Predators had been greatly reduced but not completely eliminated. To permit the raising of domestic stock, the lion population had been systematically destroyed by shooting. And in recent years, ranch owners live-trapped some of the ranch's leopards for removal to national parks in Kenya. Some cheetah remained but we sighted them only infrequently.

The ecosystem at Kekopey has thus undergone considerable modification over the years. Baboons, however, have for the most part escaped the human harassment that is their lot elsewhere in Africa, where they are trapped for medical experimentation or killed because of their fondness for human food crops. Despite the obvious alterations in the ecosystem, we decided to proceed with our research in this natural laboratory.

Although baboons subsist mostly on grasses, seeds, roots, and other plant matter, they were known to occasionally capture and kill small animals. Sheepherders in southern Africa, for instance, have long complained of baboon troops raiding their herds and taking young lambs. And a number of scientists had described baboon predatory behavior, but in no case had they reported a troop killing more than twenty animals annually.

As a result we were not surprised to learn that the baboons at Kekopey killed and ate small animals, but we did not anticipate the extent to which they engaged in this behavior. During the first year's research, we saw members of the one troop we were studying kill and eat forty-seven small animals—principally baby gazelles and some hares. This was a meat-eating rate higher than any then reported for a nonhuman primate group.

Baboons spend the greater part of each day feeding and moving from one foraging site to another with other members of their troop. Movements are usually unhurried, with individuals stopping from time to time to feed on the grasses and other vegetation that cover the valley floors. Our observations disclosed that it was during such leisurely progressions that many of the killings of small prey took place. Since both hares and young antelopes attempt to conceal themselves from predators by crouching in long grass or behind bushes, some of the baboons located and killed these animals by chance in the course of normal troop movement.

Yet, as we became more accustomed to the baboons' usual movement patterns, we discovered that the troop was moving deliberately through herds of grazing Thomson's gazelle. And several times, adult males left the troop to detour through nearby gazelle herds, scanning the ground on all sides as they went. Males also explored the heavy scrub that small dik-diks frequent.

Of the fifty baboons in the troop in 1970, four were adult males and nineteen were adult females. At first, killing was predominantly a male activity. The adult females killed only three animals—infant hares. We never saw juvenile baboons even try to catch an animal. Of the three females who killed the hares, only one succeeded in keeping any part of her prey; the other two were chased and threatened by adult males until they dropped their catch. Capturing prey was not only largely a male activity, it was a solitary one as well. Although one male baboon once successfully took up the chase of a young gazelle driven near him by another male, the baboons did not seem to cooperate in running down prey nor did a male baboon voluntarily share his catch with another troop member.

In 1970 and 1971, two-thirds of all the animals killed were newborn antelope of various species, with Thomson's gazelle the most frequent. About one-quarter of the animals consumed were Cape hare, and the balance included a button quail and several other animals that we could not identify from the scraps the baboons left. We never saw troop members eating carrion, although they had several chances to do so, nor did they try to catch every animal of the appropriate size.

Their sleeping cliffs, for instance, abounded with rock hyrax, and although baboons eat these small furry creatures elsewhere in Africa, we never saw the study troop attempt to catch them. And although an adjacent troop often caught helmeted guinea fowl, the troop we were studying ignored flocks of these birds as they walked cackling through the baboons' midst.

By late 1972, the troop had grown to sixty baboons—the result of births and immigration of adult males from nearby troops—and the animals' meat-eating tendencies had increased. In 1,200 hours of observation between 1972 and 1974, we saw them capture 100 small animals, roughly twice as many as they killed during a similar number of hours in 1970–71.

Not only were the baboons consuming more meat; their behavior toward acquiring meat had changed as well. Adult females, which had shown little interest in meat eating during the first years of our study, began to capture prey in significant numbers—hares for the most part, but some infant antelopes as well. All females were now present at some of the kills but two, in particular, were present at more kills than several of the adult males, and always waited, patiently but persistently, at the site for the male to finish eating. While some watching males might give up and leave before the carcass was abandoned, these females remained, seemingly undaunted in their determination, and in the end, had their turn at the meat.

It did not take long before the females also became bolder; rather than drop an animal when a large adult male approached, a female might try to outrun or outmaneuver him and the attempt was often successful. During the period from 1972 to 1974, adult females caught 14 percent of all prey; we also noticed that immature baboons were becoming involved in meat eating. The offspring of the two females that seemed particularly interested in meat frequently had the opportunity to investigate prey, and predictably, they were the first immature baboons to eat meat. At first their presence in the vicinity of kills simply reflected their mothers' interest. But as they grew older and became more independent, their interest continued whether or not their mothers were present at a particular episode.

It was not only maternal bonds that helped meat-eating behavior to spread among the younger baboons; long-term male bonds with infants and juveniles also created opportunities for meat eating among the young baboons even when their mothers had no special interest in meat. Many young baboons thus began their meat-eating behavior as a result of their special, close relationship with a male.

Older juveniles often began eating meat by chance—stumbling across a meat-eating episode while chasing one another in play. Such incidents seemed to make little impression on the young baboons, unless one chanced to get a scrap or two of meat. Behavior changed markedly in such a case; the young baboon would begin to join the hangers-on at kills until, through patience and persistence, it too got some meat. Juveniles then began to seek out and capture prey on their own, to the point that in the period from 1972 to 1974, they caught 16 percent of the prey.

Over the years the tactics used by adult male baboons to obtain meat changed dramatically. They began to supplement fortuitous captures and occasional detours through grasslands rich in prey with more concerted and systematic efforts. Upon sighting a herd of gazelles as much as a quarter of a mile away, one or more males often left the troop and approached the herd. By January 1974, this was an almost daily event. At first each male acted independently, but adult males always remain constantly aware of each other's location and actions; as a result, when one male made a kill or seemed about to do so, the others often abandoned their own efforts and converged on the successful hunter.

In one such incident, three males noticed another male chasing a gazelle and ran toward him. To get to the scene of the chase, they had to ascend a small hill that concealed their approach from both predator and prey. Just as he was about to abandon the chase, the baboon in pursuit of the gazelle suddenly found the three other males blocking the prey's escape route. The closest male then took up the effort, and when he appeared to flag, another continued it. For a moment the gazelle appeared to be outrunning its pursuers, but it changed direction in response to a similar movement from the baboon chasing it, and in so doing, ran into the third of the newly arrived males. The gazelle almost escaped when the pursuing baboon momentarily hesitated, but a quick bite to the underbelly put an end to the chase.

From that point on, the male baboons gradually adopted this relay system as a regular stratagem, chasing their prey toward a nearby male instead of out on the open plain. Such joint ventures appeared to be more successful than those carried out by lone males.

Adult male baboons also began to scatter antelope herds more frequently in an apparent attempt to find young animals of suitable size. This tactic often revealed a young antelope breaking from cover in the grass to run after its mother. The baboons might then spend as much as two hours covering large amounts of ground in attempts to close in on the antelope mother and her infant. As this tactic became more successful, deliberate searching for other prey in different habitat—such as dik-dik in brushy areas—became less frequent.

The persistence of the male baboons' efforts was impressive. On several occasions the troop moved through one particular area for a number of consecutive days, and each time males unsuccessfully pursued the same young gazelle. Each venture lasted up to two hours and took the baboons as much as two miles from the rest of the troop, out of sight and, apparently, out of contact. Once, after hunting the same herd for three days, the males finally captured and consumed a young antelope.

In the beginning of 1973 the male baboons could not seem to discriminate between all-male herds and mixed or all-female herds of Thomson's gazelle. Since only those including females contained potential prey animals, the baboons at first wasted considerable time and energy in scattering male herds. Later, however, the baboons were able to assess the herds, ignoring all-male ones and pursuing only female group-ings within a mixed herd.

For their part, the Thomson's gazelle began to show vigilance toward baboons, especially those herds that had been hunted several times in a row. Once a baboon of any size appeared, the gazelles became alert and moved off, the adult females herding their infants away from the baboons. This vigilance, in turn, created new difficulties for the baboons and may have offset, at least partially, the advantage they had gained through their innovations in hunting behavior.

During the first year's observations, baboons did not share meat vol-untarily; indeed, the adult males who did most of the killing at that time were highly intolerant of other baboons in their vicinity. As predatory behavior spread through the troop over the years, however, we ob-served the animals eating simultaneously from the same piece of meat or pile of scraps and even moving aside to make room for other baboons. We saw none of the gestures that chimpanzees use in begging for meat nor did we see food items other than meat ever shared, even between a mother and her infant. Such meat-sharing relationships appear to coincide with already existing long-term bonds, such as those between mothers and infants or individual males and females.

Over the past five years, the troop appears to have developed more efficient and sophisticated methods of capturing and consuming prey. We shall never know how the predatory behavior began for the ba-boons were already eating meat when we began to study the troop, but we can make some educated guesses about why predation has devel-oped to such an extent. The most plausible has to do with the apparent antelope population explosion that resulted when the natural ecosys-tem of Kekopey was altered for raising cattle. Thomson's gazelle, predominantly grazing animals whose preferred habitat is open grass-land, have benefited the most from these changes.

While we can only speculate about the origins of the baboons' preda-tory behavior at Kekopey, we know a great deal about the social dynam-ics underlying its spread through the troop. The behavior clearly pro-ceeded along preexisting lines of social bonding—from mother to offspring, male to juvenile, and between male and female. We do not know whether the behavior was initiated by one or several individuals, but it seems to have become firmly established and is at this time independent of any one individual.

In a series of experiments involving the introduction of new foods to groups of macaques, Japanese anthropologists have documented the importance of individual behavior and social bonds in the diffusion of new behavior patterns involving different food items in a primate group. At Kekopey we witnessed a natural experiment in which, once again, individual behavior and social relationships played crucial roles in determining which animals acquired the new behavior.

There is no reason to think that we have seen the full development of the baboons' potential for predatory behavior, but of course there are limits to its expansion. Chief among these is probably the size of the prey animal, for nonhuman primates usually prey upon animals smaller than themselves; the anatomy typical of monkeys and apes allows for the easy capture and consumption of such prey. We would be greatly surprised if these baboons began to capture adult impala or even adult Thomson's gazelle.

Just as social factors facilitated the spread of predatory behavior within the troop, they may also set limits. Most troop members are physically capable of capturing prey and eating meat, but females and immature animals will probably not become involved in the hunting behavior that takes adult males far away from the troop for long periods. Adult males are relatively mobile, often transferring from troop to troop. Females and young baboons, however, would have to abandon old behavior patterns, which have important integrative functions within the troop, and acquire new ones if they were to take part in extended hunting forays. As evidence of this behavioral difference between adult males and other baboons, females and young approached only those kills that occurred near the troop. They usually ignored those that took place at a distance, unless the prey was carried close to the troop.

Anthropologists have traditionally believed that only humans among the primates kill and eat animals as a regular part of their diets. Some have even felt that the hunting, meat-eating adaptation has been so important in human evolution that we would be better advised to turn to social carnivores—such as lions—rather than nonhuman primates as models for early human populations. Documentation of hunting and meat eating by chimpanzees at the Gombe National Park in Tanzania and elsewhere in Africa, however, has forced a modification of this position. With predatory baboons now added to the equation, we can identify a primate potential for predation, one that our earliest hominid ancestors must have shared. The baboon and chimpanzee studies demonstrate how sophisticated and successful predation can be among primates without any of the unique attributes of the human hunting adaptation, such as the ability to manufacture tools.

There are many differences, of course, between the predatory behavior of human and nonhuman primates, for while the diet of the earliest hominids may have resembled that of today's baboons or chimpanzees, archeological evidence suggests that early man took part in organized hunting forays. The killing of large animals in large numbers is unique to humans among the primates, and it is tempting to speculate that the ability to manufacture tools and the development of sophisticated communication methods may have been the key to successful hunting of this nature.

As far as primates are concerned, however, there is no doubt that the capture, killing, or consumption of even a single large animal poses problems that are of a wholly different order from those encountered in the hunting of small animals. By comparing human and nonhuman primate hunting patterns, we can learn much both about the behaviors and behavioral potentials we share and those that are unique.

Predatory behavior in primates probably did not have a single origin but may have developed at many different places and at many different times, possibly even under widely varying environmental conditions. This notion is important in considering human evolution for it suggests that basic human adaptations may also have had multiple origins. Considering the speed with which the baboons elaborated their predatory behavior, it is also possible that after an initial adaptive shift to a new behavior in early human populations, further development of this behavior proceeded more rapidly than we think. The behavior of the baboons also shows that individual and social factors could well have had an important influence on the perpetuation of new behavioral adaptations.

The spread of predatory behavior among the Kekopey baboons prompts us to appreciate the complexity of adaptive shifts, both behavioral and anatomical, and adds to our growing realization that simple hypotheses tend to retard, rather than advance, an understanding of human evolution. The realization brings us back to the original insights of Darwin and Huxley, who theorized that all primates are linked along a single evolutionary continuum, one in which artificial barriers erected by humans to assure their own unique status have no rational grounds for existence.

# 5 | WHEN THE TURTLE COLLAPSES, THE WORLD ENDS
## Bernard Nietschmann

*Environmental crises are not always direct or dramatic. More often the problem is that some formerly abundant resource has become scarce or hard to obtain. Such scarcities can happen for a variety of reasons, from long-term climatic changes to unseasonably harsh winter storms. All too frequently, however, the crisis results from a simple imbalance between the demands made by human beings in their exploitation of a resource and the long-term ability of that resource to regenerate itself. For the Miskito Indians of Ecuador, the large green sea turtle once provided the mainstay of their diet. In the past it was harvested only for local needs, and as there was a strong emphasis on the sharing of turtle catches there was little incentive to kill more than needed for local consumption. Now conditions have changed, with the rise of an international market for the sea turtle. As we shall see, once the social context of consumption is set, it limits production. The Miskitos' situation illustrates what can happen when such controls are removed.*

*After delivering a lecture on the solar system, philosopher-psychologist William James was approached by an elderly lady who claimed she had a theory superior to the one described by him.*

*"We don't live on a ball rotating around the sun," she said. "We live on a crust of earth on the back of a giant turtle."*

*Not wishing to demolish this absurd argument with the massive scientific evidence at his command, James decided to dissuade his opponent gently.*

*"If your theory is correct, madam, what does this turtle stand on?"*

*"You're a very clever man, Mr. James, and that's a good question, but I can answer that. The first turtle stands on the back of a second, far larger, turtle."*

*"But what does this second turtle stand on?" James asked patiently.*

*The old lady crowed triumphantly, "It's no use, Mr. James—it's turtles all the way down."*

In the half-light of dawn, a sailing canoe approaches a shoal where nets have been set the day before. A Miskito turtleman stands in the bow and points to a distant splash that breaks the gray sheen of the Caribbean waters. Even from a hundred yards, he can tell that a green turtle has been caught in one of the nets. His two companions quickly bring the craft alongside the turtle, and as they pull it from the sea, its glistening shell reflects the first rays of the rising sun. As two men work to remove the heavy reptile from the net, the third keeps the canoe headed into the swells and beside the anchored net. After its fins have been pierced and lashed with bark fiber cord, the 250-pound turtle is placed on its back in the bottom of the canoe. The turtlemen are happy. Perhaps their luck will be good today and their other nets will also yield many turtles.

These green turtles, caught by Miskito Indian turtlemen off the eastern coast of Nicaragua, are destined for distant markets. Their butchered bodies will pass through many hands, local and foreign, eventually ending up in tins, bottles, and freezers far away. Their meat, leather, shell, oil, and calipee, a gelatinous substance that is the base for turtle soup, will be used to produce goods consumed in more affluent parts of the world.

The coastal Miskito Indians are very dependent on green turtles. Their culture has long been adapted to utilizing the once vast populations that inhabited the largest sea turtle feeding grounds in the Western Hemisphere. As the most important link between livelihood, social interaction, and environment, green turtles were the pivotal resource around which traditional Miskito Indian society revolved. These large reptiles also provided the major source of protein for Miskito subsistence. Now this priceless and limited resource has become a prized commodity that is being exploited almost entirely for economic reasons.

In the past, turtles fulfilled the nutritional needs as well as the social responsibilities of Miskito society. Today, however, the Miskito depend mainly on the sale of turtles to provide them with the money they need to purchase household goods and other necessities. But turtles are a declining resource; overdependence on them is leading the Miskito into an ecological blind alley. The cultural control mechanisms that once adapted the Miskito to their environment and faunal resources are now circumvented or inoperative, and they are caught up in a system of continued intensification of turtle fishing, which threatens to provide neither cash nor subsistence.

I have been studying this situation for several years, unraveling its historical context and piecing together its past and future effect on Miskito society, economy, and diet, and on the turtle population.

The coastal Miskito Indians are among the world's most adept small-craft seamen and turtlemen. Their traditional subsistence system provided dependable yields from the judicious scheduling of resource procurement activities. Agriculture, hunting, fishing, and gathering were organized in accordance with seasonal fluctuations in weather and resource availability and provided adequate amounts of food and materials without overexploiting any one species or site. Women cultivated the crops while men hunted and fished. Turtle fishing was the backbone of subsistence, providing meat throughout the year.

Miskito society and economy were interdependent. There was no economic activity without a social context and every social act had a reciprocal economic aspect. To the Miskito, meat, especially turtle meat, was the most esteemed and valuable resource, for it was not only a mainstay of subsistence, it was the item most commonly distributed to relatives and friends. Meat shared in this way satisfied mutual obligations and responsibilities and smoothed out daily and seasonal differences in the acquisition of animal protein. In this way, those too young, old, sick, or otherwise unable to secure meat received their share, and a certain balance in the village was achieved: minimal food requirements were met, meat surplus was disposed of to others, and social responsibilities were satisfied.

Today, the older Miskito recall that when meat was scarce in the village, a few turtlemen would put out to sea in their dugout canoes for a day's harpooning on the turtle feeding grounds. In the afternoon, the men would return, sailing before the northeast trade wind, bringing meat for all. Gathered on the beach, the villagers helped drag the canoes into thatched storage sheds. After the turtles were butchered and the meat distributed, everyone returned home to the cooking fires.

Historical circumstances and a series of boom-bust economic cycles disrupted the Miskito's society and environment. In the seventeenth and eighteenth centuries, intermittent trade with English and French buccaneers—based on the exchange of forest and marine resources for metal tools and utensils, rum, and firearms—prompted the Miskito to extend hunting, fishing, and gathering beyond subsistence needs to exploitative enterprises.

During the nineteenth and early twentieth centuries, foreign-owned companies operating in eastern Nicaragua exported rubber, lumber, and gold, and initiated commercial banana production. As alien economic and ecological influences were intensified, contract wage labor replaced seasonal, short-term economic relationships; company commissaries replaced limited trade goods; and large-scale exploitation of natural resources replaced sporadic, selective extraction. During economic boom periods the relationship between resources, subsistence, and environment was drastically altered for the Miskito. Resources became a commodity with a price tag, market exploitation a livelihood, and foreign wages and goods a necessity.

For more than 200 years, relations between the coastal Miskito and the English were based on sea turtles. It was from the Miskito that the English learned the art of turtling, which they then organized into intensive commercial exploitation of Caribbean turtle grounds and nesting beaches. Sea turtles were among the first resources involved in trade relations and foreign commerce in the Caribbean, Zoologist Archie Carr, an authority on sea turtles, has remarked that "more than any other dietary factor, the green turtle supported the opening up of the Caribbean." The once abundant turtle populations provided sustenance to ships' crews and to the new settlers and plantation laborers.

The Cayman Islands, settled by the English, became in the seventeenth and eighteenth centuries the center of commercial turtle fishing in the Caribbean. By the early nineteenth century, pressure on the Cayman turtle grounds and nesting beaches to supply meat to Caribbean and European markets became so great that the turtle population was decimated. The Cayman Islanders were forced to shift to other turtle areas off Cuba, the Gulf of Honduras, and the coast of eastern Nicaragua. They made annual expeditions, lasting four to seven weeks, to the Miskito turtle grounds to net green turtles, occasionally purchasing live ones, dried calipee, and the shells of hawksbill turtles *(Eretmochelys imbricata)* from the Miskito Indians. Reported catches of green turtles by the Cayman turtlers generally ranged between 2,000 and 3,000 a year up to the early 1960s, when the Nicaraguan government failed to renew the islanders' fishing privileges.

Intensive resource extraction by foreign companies led to seriously depleted and altered environments. By the 1940s, many of the economic booms had turned to busts. As the resources ran out and operating costs mounted, companies shut down production and moved to other areas in Central America. Thus, the economic mainstays that had helped provide the Miskito with jobs, currency, markets, and foreign goods were gone. The company supply ships and commissaries disappeared, money became scarce, and store-bought items expensive.

In the backwater of the passing golden boom period, the Miskito were left with an ethic of poverty, but they still had the subsistence skills that had maintained their culture for hundreds of years. Their land and water environment was still capable of providing reliable resources for local consumption. As it had been in the past, turtle fishing became a way of life, a provider of life itself. But traditional subsistence culture could no longer integrate Miskito society and environment in a state of equilibrium. Resources were now viewed as having a value and labor a price tag. All that was needed was a market.

Recently, two foreign turtle companies began operations along the east coast of Nicaragua. One was built in Puerto Cabezas in late 1968, and another was completed in Bluefields in 1969. Both companies were capable of processing and shipping large amounts of green turtle meat and by-products to markets in North America and Europe. Turtles were acquired by purchase from the Miskito. Each week company boats visited coastal Miskito communities and offshore island turtle camps to buy green turtles. The "company" was back, money was again available, and the Miskito were expert in securing the desired commodity. Another economic boom period was at hand. But the significant difference between this boom and previous ones was that the Miskito were now selling a subsistence resource.

As a result, the last large surviving green turtle population in the Caribbean was opened to intensive, almost year-round exploitation. Paradoxically, it would be the Miskito Indians, who once caught only what they needed for food, who would conduct the assault on the remaining turtle population.

Another contradictory element in the Miskito-turtle story is that only some 200 miles to the south at Tortuguero, Costa Rica, Archie Carr had devoted fifteen years to the study of sea turtles and to the conservation and protection of the Caribbean's last major sea turtle nesting beach. Carr estimates that more than half the green turtles that nest at Tortuguero are from Nicaraguan waters. The sad and exasperating paradox is that a conservation program insured the survival of an endangered species for commercial exploitation in nearby waters.

Green turtles, *Chelonia mydas,* are large, air-breathing, herbivorous marine reptiles. They congregate in large populations and graze on underwater beds of vegetation in relatively clear, shallow, tropical waters. A mature turtle can weigh 250 pounds or more and when caught, can live indefinitely in a saltwater enclosure or for a couple of weeks if kept in shade on land. Green turtles have at least six behavioral characteristics that are important in their exploitation: they occur in large numbers in localized areas; they are air breathing, so they have to surface; they are mass social nesters; they have an acute location-finding ability; when mature, they migrate seasonally on an overlapping two- or three-year cycle for mating and nesting; and they exhibit predictable local distributional patterns.

The extensive shallow shelf off eastern Nicaragua is dotted with numerous small coral islands, thousands of reefs, and vast underwater pastures of marine vegetation called "turtle banks." During the day, a large group of turtles may be found feeding at one of the many turtle banks, while adjacent marine pastures may have only a few turtles. They graze on the vegetation, rising periodically to the surface for air and to float for awhile before diving again. In the late afternoon, groups of turtles will leave the feeding areas and swim to shoals, some up to four or five miles away, to spend the night. By five the next morning, they gather to depart again for the banks. The turtles' precise, commuterlike behavior between sleeping and feeding areas is well known to the Miskito and helps insure good turtling.

Each coastal turtling village exploits an immense sea area, containing many turtle banks and shoals. For example, the Miskito of Tasbapauni utilize a marine area of approximately 600 square miles, with twenty major turtle banks and almost forty important shoals.

Having rather predictable patterns of movement and habitat preference, green turtles are commonly caught by the Miskito in three ways: on the turtle banks with harpoons; along the shoal-to-feeding area route with harpoons; and on the shoals using nets, which entangle the turtles when they surface for air.

The Miskito's traditional means of taking turtles was by harpoon—an eight- to ten-foot shaft fitted with a detachable short point tied to a strong line. The simple technology pitted two turtlemen in a small, sea-going canoe against the elusive turtles. Successful turtling with harpoons requires an extensive knowledge of turtle behavior and habits and tremendous skill and experience in handling a small canoe in what can be very rough seas. Turtlemen work in partnerships: a "strikerman" in the bow; the "captain" in the stern. Together, they make a single unit engaged in the delicate and almost silent pursuit of a wary prey, their movements coordinated by experience and rewarded by proficiency. Turtlemen have mental maps of all the banks and shoals in their area, each one named and located through a complex system of celestial navigation, distance reckoning, wind and current direction, and the individual surface-swell motion over each site. Traditionally, not all Miskito were sufficiently expert in seamanship and turtle lore to become respected "strikermen," capable of securing turtles even during hazardous sea conditions. Theirs was a very specialized calling. Harpooning restrained possible overexploitation since turtles were taken one at a time by two men directly involved in the chase, and there were only a limited number of really proficient "strikermen" in each village.

Those who still use harpoons must leave early to take advantage of the land breeze and to have enough time to reach the distant offshore turtle grounds by first light. Turtlemen who are going for the day, or for several days, will meet on the beach by 2:00 A.M. They drag the canoes on bamboo rollers from beachfront sheds to the water's edge. There, in the swash of spent breakers, food, water, paddles, lines, harpoons, and sails are loaded and secured. Using a long pole, the standing bowman propels the canoe through the foaming surf while the captain in the stern keeps the craft running straight with a six-foot mahogany paddle. Once past the inside break, the men count the dark rolling seas building outside until there is a momentary pause in the sets; then with paddles digging deep, they drive the narrow, twenty-foot canoe over the cresting swells, rising precipitously on each wave face and then plunging down the far side as the sea and sky seesaw into view. Once past the breakers, they rig the sail and, running with the land breeze, point the canoe toward a star in the eastern sky.

A course is set by star fix and by backsight on a prominent coconut palm on the mainland horizon. Course alterations are made to correct for the direction and intensity of winds and currents. After two or three hours of sailing the men reach a distant spot located between a turtle sleeping shoal and feeding bank. There they intercept and follow the turtles as they leave for specific banks.

On the banks the turtlemen paddle quietly, listening for the sound of a "blowing" turtle. When a turtle surfaces for air it emits a hissing sound audible for fifty yards or more on a calm day. Since a turtle will stay near the surface for only a minute or two before diving to feed, the men must approach quickly and silently, maneuvering the canoe directly in front of or behind the turtle. These are its blind spots. Once harpooned, a turtle explodes into a frenzy of action, pulling the canoe along at high speeds in its hopeless, underwater dash for escape until it tires and can be pulled alongside the canoe.

But turtle harpooning is a dying art. The dominant method of turtling today is the use of nets. Since their introduction, the widespread use of turtle nets has drastically altered turtling strategy and productivity. Originally brought to the Miskito by the Cayman Islanders, nets are now extensively distributed on credit by the turtle companies. This simple technological change, along with a market demand for turtles, has resulted in intensified pressure on green turtle populations.

Buoyed by wooden floats and anchored to the bottom by a single line, the fifty-foot-long by fourteen-foot-wide nets hang from the surface like underwater flags, shifting direction with the current. Nets are set in place during midday when the turtlemen can see the dark shoal areas. Two Miskito will set five to thirty nets from one canoe, often completely saturating a small shoal. In the late afternoon, green turtles return to their shoals to spend the night. There they will sleep beside or beneath a coral outcrop, periodically surfacing for air where a canopy of nets awaits them.

Catching turtles with nets requires little skill; anyone with a canoe can now be a turtleman. The Miskito set thousands of nets daily, providing continuous coverage in densely populated nocturnal habitats. Younger Miskito can become turtlemen almost overnight simply by following more experienced men to the shoal areas, thus circumventing the need for years of accumulated skill and knowledge that once were the domain of the "strikermen." All one has to do is learn where to set the nets, retire for the night, remove the entangled turtles the next morning, and reset the nets. The outcome is predictable: more turtlemen, using more effective methods, catch more turtles.

With an assured market for turtles, the Miskito devote more time to catching turtles, traveling farther and staying at sea longer. Increased dependence on turtles as a source of income and greater time inputs have meant disruption of subsistence agriculture and hunting and fishing. The Miskito no longer produce foodstuffs for themselves; they buy imported foods with money gained from the sale of turtles. Caught between contradictory priorities—their traditional subsistence system and the market economy—the Miskito are opting for cash.

The Miskito are now enveloped in a positive feedback system where change spawns change. Coastal villages rely on turtles for a livelihood. Decline of subsistence provisioning has led to the need to secure food from local shopkeepers on credit to feed the families in the villages and the men during their turtling expeditions. Initial high catches of turtles encouraged more Miskito to participate, and by 1972 the per person and per day catch began to decline noticeably.

In late 1972, several months after I had returned to Michigan, I received a letter from an old turtleman, who wrote: "Turtle is getting scarce, Mr. Barney. You said it would happen in five or ten years but it is happening now."

Burdened by an overdependence on an endangered species and with accumulating debts for food and nets, the Miskito are finding it increasingly difficult to break even, much less secure a profit. With few other economic alternatives, the inevitable step is to use more nets and stay out at sea longer.

The turtle companies encourage the Miskito to expand turtling activities by providing them with building materials so that they can construct houses on offshore cays, thereby eliminating the need to return to the mainland during rough weather. On their weekly runs up and down the coast, company boats bring food, turtle gear, and cash for turtles to fishing camps from the Miskito Cays to the Set Net Cays. Frequent visits keep the Miskito from becoming discouraged and returning to their villages with the turtles. On Saturdays, villagers look to sea, watching for returning canoes. A few men will bring turtle for their families; the majority will bring only money. Many return with neither.

Most Miskito prefer to be home on Sunday to visit with friends and for religious reasons. (There are Moravian, Anglican, and Catholic mission churches in many of the villages.) But more and more, turtlemen are staying out for two to four weeks. The church may promise salvation, but only the turtle companies can provide money.

Returning to their villages, turtlemen are confronted with a complex dilemma: how to satisfy both social and economic demands with a limited resource. Traditional Miskito social rules stipulate that turtle meat should be shared among kin, but the new economic system requires that turtles be sold for personal economic gain. Kin expect gifts of meat, and friends expect to be sold meat. Turtlemen are besieged with requests forcing them to decide between who will or will not receive meat. This is contrary to the traditional Miskito ethic, which is based on generosity and mutual concern for the well-being of others. The older Miskito ask why the turtlemen should have to allocate a food that was once abundant and available to all. Turtlemen sell and give to other turtlemen, thereby insuring reciprocal treatment for themselves, but there simply are not enough turtles to accommodate other economic and social requirements. In order to have enough turtles to sell, fewer are butchered in the villages. This means that less meat is being consumed than before the turtle companies began operations. The Miskito presently sell 70 to 90 percent of the turtles they catch; in the near future they will sell even more and eat less.

DISTRIBUTION OF TURTLE MEAT BY GIFT AND PURCHASE

| Percent of villagers* | Pounds received per person |
|---|---|
| 18 | 10–14+ |
| 28 | 6–9 |
| 32 | 2–5 |
| 22 | 0–1.9 |

During the one-month period from April 15 to May 15, 1971, 125 green turtles were caught by the turtlemen of Tasbapauni, Nicaragua. Of these, 91 were sold to turtle companies; the remaining 34 were butchered and the meat sold or given to villagers. In all, 3,900 pounds of turtle meat were distributed, but 54 percent of the villagers received 5 pounds or less, an insufficient amount for adult dietary protein requirements.

*Population of 998 converted to 711 adult male equivalents.

Social tension and friction are growing in the villages. Kinship relationships are being strained by what some villagers interpret as preferential and stingy meat distribution. Rather than endure the trauma caused by having to ration a limited item to fellow villagers, many turtlemen prefer to sell all their turtles to the company and return with money, which does not have to be shared. However, if a Miskito sells out to the company, he will probably be unable to acquire meat for himself in the village, regardless of kinship or purchasing power. I overheard an elderly turtleman muttering to himself as he butchered a turtle: "I no going to sell, neither give dem meat. Let dem eat de money."

The situation is bad and getting worse. Individuals too old or sick to provide for themselves often receive little meat or money from relatives. Families without turtlemen are families without money or access to meat. The trend is toward the individualization of nuclear families, operating for their own economic ends. Miskito villages are becoming neighborhoods rather than communities.

The Miskito diet has suffered in quality and quantity. Less protein and fewer diverse vegetables and fruits are consumed. Present dietary staples—rice, white flour, beans, sugar, and coffee—come from the store. In one Miskito village, 65 percent of all food eaten in a year was purchased.

Besides the nutritional significance of what is becoming a largely carbohydrate diet, dependence on purchased foods has also had major economic reverberations. Generated by national and international scarcities, inflationary fallout has hit the Miskito. Most of their purchased foods are imported, much coming from the United States. In the last five years prices for staples have increased 100 to 150 percent. This has had an overwhelming impact on the Miskito, who spend 50 to 75 percent of their income for food. Consequently, their entry into the market by selling a subsistence resource, diverting labor from agriculture, and intensifying exploitation of a vanishing species has resulted in their living off poorer-quality, higher-priced foods.

The Miskito now depend on outside systems to supply them with money and materials that are subject to world market fluctuations. They have lost their autonomy and their adaptive relationship with their environment. Life is no longer socially rewarding nor is their diet satisfying. The coastal Miskito have become a specialized and highly vulnerable sector of the global market economy.

Loss of the turtle market would be a serious economic blow to the Miskito, who have almost no other means of securing cash for what have now become necessities. Nevertheless, continued exploitation will surely reduce the turtle population to a critical level.

National and international legislation is urgently needed. At the very least, commercial turtle fishing must be curtailed for several years until the *Chelonia* population can rebound and exploitation quotas can be set. While turtle fishing for subsistence should be permitted, exportation of sea turtle products used in the gourmet, cosmetic, or jewelry trade should be banned.

Restrictive environmental legislation, however, is not a popular subject in Nicaragua, a country that has recently been torn by earthquakes, volcanic eruption, and hurricanes. A program for sea turtle conservation submitted to the Nicaraguan government for consideration ended up in a pile of rubble during the earthquake that devastated Managua in December, 1972, adding a sad footnote to the Miskito–sea turtle situation. With other problems to face, the government has not yet reviewed what is happening on the distant east coast, separated from the capital by more than 200 miles of rain forest—and years of neglect.

As it is now, the turtles are going down and along with them, the Miskito—seemingly, a small problem in terms of the scale of ongoing ecological and cultural change in the world. But each localized situation involves species and societies with long histories and, perhaps, short futures. They are weathervanes in the conflicting winds of economic and environmental priorities. As Bob Dylan sang: "You don't need a weatherman to tell which way the wind blows."

# 6 "DEVELOPMENT" AND THE PASTORAL PEOPLE OF KARAMOJA, NORTH-EASTERN UGANDA: An Example of the Treatment of Symptoms

## Randall Baker

*Many pastoral societies have developed over long periods of time patterns of animal management that minimize most risks of over-grazing. Often the nature of this achievement is not appreciated by outsiders, especially those trained in modern agricultural techniques. In this selection Randall Baker shows how, in an effort to promote animal production, well-intentioned administrators precipitated a number of environmental crises of great magnitude. For example, herd sizes were increased without thought for the stability of grass cover, and water tanks and wells were built without considering the potential effects of increased numbers of animals on very limited grazing. Traditional solutions to environmental problems are worthy of respect. If the developer or planner encourages changes in the methods of production, disease control, or whatever, it should be with full awareness of the complexity of the ecological context.*

*"The former disrespect for traditional systems . . . has given way to an increasing realisation of our own need for tutelage."—D. N. McMaster.*

At first sight most pastoralist societies appear very simple so that the popular picture is of a herder seated in the shade of a tree while his animals graze; of women poking at a desperately poor piece of ground to raise a few uncertain crops and of an almost total lack of the outward material show associated with more settled cultures.

This led many early observers and administrators to assume that the structure of the society and economy was as rudimentary as they appeared on the surface; that the pastoralists were generally "idle" in comparison with their settled neighbours; that they were lacking in imagination and initiative and that there was much that imported technology could do to "improve" the situation, winning the cooperation and gratitude of the people.

What was sadly misunderstood was the highly developed adjustment to the environment which the pastoralists had made to arrive at a system which offered them the minimum of risk in a very marginal physical environment and the very intimate knowledge of the physical resources which they had acquired in the process. Theirs was not a life of idleness, vandalism, aimless wandering and possibly, a few feeble attempts at cultivation; it represented an extremely delicately-adjusted ecological balance in which the threat of destruction was never very distant.

The administrators and "developers," therefore, instead of making a net addition to productivity (commercialization) and the pastoral resources of the district, as they hoped, often drastically upset the balance and once it was upset, the two parties concerned took diametrically opposed action to remedy the situation. The end result was hostility and the destruction of much of the resource base; which is all the more unfortunate for having arisen out of good intentions shrouded in misunderstanding.

What occurred during the period of external administration is analogous to treating the symptoms of a problem rather than the problem itself. In this case water development, disease control, destocking etc., all became ends in themselves without being considered within the framework of the pastoral system and society. As the "cure" progressed new "symptoms" emerged—often as a result of earlier "treatment" and were, in turn, given attention.

The real problem was the introduction of radical ecological, economic, and administrative change into a traditional system. All forms of "normal" responses were anticipated and when these were not forthcoming or unexpected ones occurred, cries of "irrationality," "perverseness," "reaction" or "conservatism" were raised. Yet each party acted, as it thought, in the direction of improvement but without any clear idea of the aims and methods of the other.

## LAND, PEOPLE AND ECONOMY

The district of Karamoja, with Karasuk, occupies 13,000 square miles of north-eastern Uganda having the form of a plain tilted towards the west. From the hills and mountains rising to 9,000 feet along the Kenya border, the land falls away westward into the great plateau of central and northern Uganda at 3,500–5,000 feet. Eastward the land falls dramatically along the line of the Rift to the Turkana plains in Kenya at 1,000 feet. The generally level horizons of Karamoja are broken by great volcanic remnants such as Mts. Moroto, Akisim, and Toror.

Over most of the district, rainfall totals are surprisingly high for a pastoral area, falling from over 40 inches along the western plains to below 20 inches in the driest parts of the east. Throughout the area the rainfall pattern is sharply seasonal with a dry season from October to March but it is the unreliability of the rainfall which is as critical to the way of life as the total fall. The greater part of the district falls into 30-inch reliability classes "poor" to "bad."[1]

The people of Karamoja are predominantly transhumant semi-pastoralists except for the tribes which inhabit the highland areas, some of whom have adopted cash cropping. In the southern half of the district are the Karamojong,[2] a grouping of three units: the Matheniko, the Bokora, and the Pian, all having close ties one with the other and with the people of the district's northern quarter—the Dodoth.[3] Separating these two groups are the Jie people[4] who have affinities with the Turkana of Kenya and with whom the Karamojong and Dodoth maintain frequently hostile relations. In the south-east are the Suk (Pokot) people of Upe county who have been migrating here from Kenya since the 1920s and who also have poor relations with the Karamojong.

The population of Karamoja is concentrated in a belt from north to south along the central backbone of the district and it is here that the homestead or *ere* is found where groups of full brothers and their families live. The homes may be regarded, for the purposes of this paper, as permanent, for if replaced, the replacement will be constructed in the same general area. It is here in this central belt that water is available for domestic needs throughout the year from open wells dug into the sandy river bottoms. Here also is the greatest security from hostile neighbours for the *cordon sanitaire* is a feature of pastoral societies in this area: even within the central belt there is a conspicuous break between the Karamojong and the Jie.

In this central belt live the women, elders, and children and it becomes the home of the young male herders during the wet season. Here also is the cultivation which plays a major role in feeding the permanently resident population of the household.[5] On the alluvial deposits along the inside of river bends, or on trash-bunded hill slopes the women plant sorghum, vegetables, and ground nuts with, in the more favoured areas, millet and maize.

It is not possible, in the conditions of rainfall reliability which prevail in Karamoja, to base family security on grains and this is the critical importance of livestock for, in a year of drought, they are the difference between starvation and survival. The evidence suggests that a drought of serious proportions occurs one year in four in the district.[6] However, because of the seasonality of rainfall and water availability it is not possible to keep the herds in the *ere* belt throughout the year and with the onset of the dry season the herders and their animals move outwards, possibly leaving their families with the nucleus of a milch herd and some small stock. Animals from the herd of one owner will often be run with those of other owners to reduce the risk of concentrated loss.

On arrival in the wetter plains the herders burn the tall stands of *Hyparrhenia* or *Themeda* grass to induce a "green flush," to kill off ticks and to control bush growth. During the early part of the dry season the animals are spread widely over the plains as watering points are relatively numerous but as the season hardens ever greater quantities of animals congregate around the few reliable waterholes and because of the number involved may drink only on alternate days. As the rains begin, the herders leave the temporary camps *(awi)* in the dry season areas and return to the *ere* zone.

For the last fifty years the pattern of life in Karamoja has been subject to increasing pressures: the herders have been wandering further and further in pursuit of rapidly diminishing pastures; raiding has increased dramatically leading to considerable death and destruction; large areas of what was once perennial grass have been turned into steppe or badlands and thousands of animals have died recently as a result of natural calamities. Even the tribes which have a tradition of cooperation have been raiding each other and in 1966 alone there were 740 deaths recorded as a result of raids.

As most of these problems have arisen from a failure to understand the nice but precarious balance between Man and the physical environment in Karamoja, this relationship will be examined first and then its undermining will be considered in the context of the various "development" programmes and projects.

## THE ECOLOGICAL BALANCE

The traditional pastoral system may be reduced, at its most basic, to two sets of opposing forces: those which attempt to increase selectively the number of animals and those which result in their destruction. Pastoralists are often accused of keeping large herds simply as a matter of pride and prestige (see penultimate paragraph) but the "quantitative" mentality has a very sound foundation. Most pastoral families can easily recall years of drought. Thus, their efforts are directed, in the main, towards minimizing this risk, which they do, primarily, by keeping the largest number of productive animals: "productive" in this case being a measure of the number of milkers, breeding oxen and breeding females.[7]

In addition there are considerable social pressures to maintain a large herd to increase the herder's standing in the community, for bride price, to establish relationships and as the exchange element of the local economy.

Checking the above are the twin elements of drought and disease. It has been estimated (see above) that one year in four is sufficiently dry seriously to retard crop growth or cause losses of crops and animals. Traditionally the people of Karamoja were unable to tap more than the most superficial alluvial aquifers and so had little storage capacity to protect them from the short-term vagaries of the climate. More dramatic in the past were the virulent epizootics which swept through the district causing heavy destruction. In addition, warfare and disease took a heavy toll of the human population.

So, while it might present a false sense of precision to speak of an equilibrium, there did exist a crude, albeit harsh, dynamic balance between these opposing forces which allowed either a sufficiently light stocking rate for the grazing resources to flourish or sufficient time after a disaster for them to regenerate. In extreme circumstances it was usually possible for a community to migrate and there are numerous examples of this for many parts of Africa. In such a marginal physical environment, however, the balance is of necessity very delicate with many of the vegetation complexes resulting from cultural practices so that adjustments to one element will have repercussions throughout the system in an extraordinarily short space of time.

## THE IMPACT OF DEVELOPMENT

Administration first came to Karamoja in 1915 when police patrols were started, but it was after the appointment of the first District Commissioner in 1921 that the misunderstandings began. Boundaries were to be drawn around the district and the "tribes" or "clans" whose areas would now become counties. When investigations were made to delineate these boundaries they were carried out in the wet season when the tribes and their herds were concentrated in the *ere* zone. This failure to appreciate the transhumant nature of the pastoral system or that the dry season grazing was as carefully delimited as the homestead area led to a serious misjudgement: an error accentuated by the false impression of "unused land" resulting from the decimation of the tribes by small-pox a few years before.[8] Two major areas of dry season grazing were considered to be "unoccupied" and were handed over to neighbouring tribes. In the south-western plains large areas of perennial grass which had been grazed by Bokora and Pian herds were given to the Iteso and in the south-east much of the county of Upe was given to the Suk (Pokot) of Kenya who promptly occupied it depriving the Pian and the Matheniko of valuable summer grasslands in times of hardship. As a consequence of this move, hostility has been marked in these border areas, worsening in recent years, while pressure was put on the central *ere* belt by the marked reduction in the total area of grazing.

The pressure on the central belt was further accentuated by the mistaken attitude of the administration towards cattle movement. Dyson-Hudson has shown how, in 1921, the authorities tried to limit movement in order to enforce compulsory labour regulations and to collect taxes so that herders were able to move only with the permission of the District Commissioner. Even this degree of flexibility was severely limited, for half the male population (i.e., that part of the community which normally takes the herds to the dry-season grazing) was required to stay behind to work on the roads. This regulation touched the very root of survival of the pastoral communities and met with a hostile response so that it is hardly surprising that much of the subsequent misunderstanding and non-cooperation dates from this poor start. Again Dyson-Hudson has shown how, among the Karamojong, the county boundaries which were eventually delimited were hopelessly inadequate within the context of the seasonal movement requirements: "It is not surprising that the three county system should have made little sense, territorially, to a society that recognises a permanent settlement zone distributed among ten territorial sections and an extensive outer margin of grazing land free to all."

At this point, with increased pressure on resources, the treatment of "symptoms" began with lamentable consequences. With the steady

destruction of perennials and the threat of soil loss through sheet flooding and gullying, attention was turned not to the fundamental cause of
the change, i.e., the disruption of a well-tried traditional system, but to
its control as a matter of soil-conservation policy (that is, it became an
end in itself rather than an index of a more basic problem). The authorities prohibited burning in an attempt at soil conservation with the
following results:

a. The nutritious value of the dry-season grazing was reduced dramatically; "the crude protein level was an average of 0.3% in March in
the western plains of Pian county and 6.0% at the onset of the
rains."[9] The same effect is produced by bringing on a "green flush"
with burning, reducing the fibrous matter and increasing the leaf/-
stem ratio.
b. By taking animals into tall, unburned grass the herders took them
into an ideal environment for ticks, especially *Rhipicephalus appen-
diculatus* which is the vector of East Coast Fever. In this way the
disease was taken back and established itself in the wetter areas of
Karamoja such as around Mt. Kadam.
c. The cessation of burning removed the main instrument of bush
control and the subsequent encroachment of bush led, in part, to the
invasion by tsetse which took place in the north of the district.

Ironically it was also part of the "soil erosion" fetish which prevailed
before the last war, that the goat was made the true villain in the
destruction of a vegetative cover and moves were made to reduce the
goat population. The goat, however, being a browser had a significant
role to play in controlling bush and, because of its browsing habit, it
represented a net addition to the biomass, rather than a competitor for
grazing resources.

As the destruction of the environment slowly advanced, two major
programmes were introduced which were to shatter the "balance,"
described earlier, almost completely; these programmes were water
development and disease control.

It was soon noted in official circles that considerable areas of the
western plain were never, or very rarely, grazed as either no water was
available or these areas represented a *cordon sanitaire* between hostile
tribes. The response was to consider it: "desirable to put in a large net
of water resources so that the greatest possible area is used during the
dry season"[10] . . . and that: "the main problem . . . in Karamoja is water,
not grazing . . . increased water supply will increase the amount of
grazing available."[11] As a consequence, in 1938 there began a programme of dam-building and, later, valley-tank construction which
continues at the present time covering the western and southern plains.

In the short term this programme had its desired effect; it did increase the area "used during the dry season" and allowed many cattle,
which might otherwise have died, to live through the summers. It did
not, however, explain how there was to be a parallel improvement in

grazing resources in the *ere* zone where the animals concentrated in ever greater numbers in the wet season. The result was dramatic as the perennials disappeared to be replaced by annuals, with the consequence that a smaller proportion of the total herd could now remain throughout the year in the central belt. More animals, therefore, had to venture further into the perennial plains thus accentuating the pressure. As the ground became more and more exposed during the dry season, the strong wind from Turkana soon shifted tons of topsoil westward into Teso and the first rains ripped open the land surface tearing gullies and, in Upe, removing the upper horizons right down to the regolith.

Again, eradication of the immediate "problem" had been seen as an end and not a means to an end, for the "solution" had ignored the relationship between the elements of the pastoral environment and the relationship between the prevailing aims of the society and these elements. The result of the water development programme was to spread the destruction of grazing resources into areas which had been conserved by the absence of water; to increase the pressure on resources in the *ere* zone far past breaking point and, eventually, to worsen the overall situation. There had been no parallel programme of rotational grazing, culling, destocking etc., despite assertions by government that programmes should be integrated.

At the same time as the water net was being established, the foundations of disease control were being laid. It must be admitted that the motives behind the introduction of this programme were rather different from those which lay behind water development, for the control of disease was seen in a national context as protecting the herds in more-developed parts of Uganda. It was also designed to eliminate the threat of another great panzootic such as the rinderpest plague of the 1880's. However, the programme was devastatingly successful and virtually removed the second major check on cattle numbers in the district. Although disease control was seen in this national context the point still emerges that it was considered *in vacuo.* Just as water development had no complementary grazing programme, so disease control had no rider to explain how all the extra surviving cattle were to be accommodated on the grazing available.

There was now virtually no mechanism to prevent the society's pressing its "insurance" concept forward at an alarming rate. In the absence of East Coast Fever and its attendant high calf mortality over most of Karamoja, the herds grew at approximately 5% per annum or twice the national average. It was not long before the district was showing further disturbing xerophytic trends (which one observer attributed to climatic change) and as more and more animals were moved west in the dry season so the annuals spread—about one mile per annum in the 1960s. Some of the annual areas were further degraded to semi-desert succulents and one writer speculated that the district was going through an abbreviated reconstruction of the formation of the Middle East deserts.[12]

In addition to factors affecting stock numbers, the control of warfare and the beginnings of preventive and curative medical treatment resulted in an increase in the human population growth rate which would in turn result in an increase in the demand for stock.

Still, however, the problem was not seen in the context of the total disruption of a stable traditional system. Comments such as "the people of Bokora, Pian, and Upe remain recalcitrant and uncooperative"[13] were possibly doing these people a serious injustice. They had, over centuries, developed a system which, within technological limits, offered them the best chance of survival. They knew what, under their system, they should do and they did it, but now it was leading to their own destruction. Understanding, on both sides, would have prevented this.

It was at this point, perhaps as a result of frustration, that some of the worst, and most familiar, generalizations came to the fore: the pastoralists were "only interested in keeping the maximum number of stock regardless of quality or type" (a glance at the herd structure would have shown this to be fallacious); "the excessive numbers of cattle are kept mainly for prestige" (Deshler wrote: "the 4 to 6 cattle per person . . . barely provide enough milk to supply the children [of the Dodoth] during the dry season"),[14] and, "raiding is akin to a national sport in Karamoja" (the relationship between periods of increased drought and increased raiding is indicative of why at least some of the major raids take place—see Dyson-Hudson [1966, p. 243] for a specific example). Sadly, many of the worst and most misleading generalizations have been taken up by the emerging élite in independent Uganda who commonly refer to the pastoralists as "primitive," "uncivilized," etc., or simply laugh at them. As there are few, if any, pastoralists among the élite this attitude is likely to prevail.

Dealing with problems of pastoralism on this *ad hoc* basis is analogous to dealing with energy; transmutation can be effected but never elimination. In the case of Karamoja the various programmes all served to shift the pressure on to the grazing resources.

The problem was now seen in terms of a surfeit of cattle numbers and attention was focused on this issue. There certainly was, as a result of the water development and disease control programmes, an excess of stock numbers in relation to seasonal grazing under unimproved range management. Once again the mistake was made of seeing the issue of cattle numbers as an end in itself and not as part of a growing maladjustment of a traditional system resulting from a struggle for security. This misunderstanding strikes at the basis of survival as perceived by the peoples of Karamoja for, as has been shown, the number of productive animals is the key to survival under traditional practices during drought.

The advancing destruction of the physical environment encouraged responses within the traditional framework which were destined to accentuate, rather than diminish, the problem. For, as the spread of annual grasses resulted in increased pressures during the dry season, eventually greater numbers of animals started to die from periodic starvation and the conventional response to this was, once more, to keep even larger herds and wander further in search of perennials.

The reaction of the authorities to the explosive growth of cattle numbers was to introduce a number of destocking measures. These operated at two levels but neither proved really successful in enforcing a check on the expansion of herds though they did succeed to some extent in reducing the number of older, non-breeding animals. Where cattle sales were attempted the problem arose from the fact that the buyers required a regular supply of beef steers related to the pattern of demand for quantity and quality while the sellers responded predominantly to the dictates of the weather.[15] In times of drought when large numbers of stock were offered, the marketing infrastructure proved inadequate to absorb these and so one means of periodic destocking was reduced in effectiveness. The other main problem arose from the very limited cash requirements of the people. The herders by offering older, sick, or barren animals were defeating the value of destocking as a limitation on growth and were simply adhering to their principle of retaining the maximum number of productive animals. Even where large numbers of animals were sold the reason was security, for it has been shown for the Dodoth that under these circumstances 60% of the money income was expended on food. The buyers, in expecting large, healthy males were being a little optimistic for, within the context of the traditional system it is evident that more than a very small number of breeding males would be a liability. Possibly, the mistake was that the people of Karamoja kept cattle for meat as well as milk, hides, urine, etc. A system such as that operated by the people of Karamoja could not afford to regard its stock in terms of terminal products.

The second means of reducing cattle numbers was by compulsory culling in connection with a meat processing plant at Namalu in Pian. This scheme was designed to net those animals too old or weak to be sold at the markets but which still competed with the younger stock for grazing. There was a resentment at being forced to give up animals without choice which the authorities attributed to the general malaise that "there are many improvements . . . the Karamojong will find them all incomprehensible" whereas, in reality, the herders chafed at being forced to accept 7 shs. per head[16] and considered the scheme as an attempt to deprive them of their cattle. The project failed eventually for a number of technical and economic reasons.

There was, by now, a rapidly developing *impasse* and a general hardening of attitudes but little attempt to understand the basis for the other party's actions. This led eventually to the acceptance by some officials of the belief that the herders were simply "conservative" (meaning reactionary) and resistant to change for reasons of sheer "perversity." In fact, although it is quite fair to assert that the pastoralists are conservative inasmuch as they try to protect a system which has protected them, the charge of being resistant to all change was false.

Where improvements demonstrably added to traditional measures of security they were taken up with extraordinary speed: the acceptance of the disease-control programme is a measure of this. Where there was an initial resistance it was often based on some very real fear[17] and when it is considered that any innovation involving cattle strikes at the very roots of tribal survival then the pastoralists appear more "progressive" than many of their settled counterparts.

As the position worsened during the great drought of the early 1950s when the annuals failed to appear, the question of law and order emerged as a major "symptom" for treatment: and that is how it was considered. With the failure of crops and grazing over large parts of the district the herders turned, in desperation, to raiding their neighbours. Their intrusions further and further into Teso on the west led to fighting and many casualties; the heavily fortified nature of Iteso settlements along this border is testimony to the intensity of the problem. In the south, by the mid-1960s, the Karamojong were raiding the settled communities of the Sebei plains and even into the cash crop belt of Bugisu on Mt. Elgon. Significantly they were seeking either food by raiding the fields or cattle by stealing herds.

The response of the authorities to the "law and order issue" was predictable: spears were impounded. This struck at the most superficial manifestation of a very serious problem. Later, units of the para-military Special Force were stationed in the district to follow up raids and ensure the payment of blood money: once again the pressure had been shifted not eliminated.

By the 1960s the crisis had reached overwhelming proportions whereby large areas of the district had been stripped almost bare in the dry season and, in the drought of 1961 100,000 head of cattle died[18] and another 35,000 were pushed through the cattle markets instead of the usual 10,000. The drought of 1965/6 was more severe but the number of cattle put through the markets (thus partially destocking) was low. This resulted from the free distribution of 240,000 lb of maize flour per week by the authorities as famine relief.

The recent history of Karamoja has been repeated in many other parts of Africa and, if a paper of this sort is to have any value beyond simply being an ideograph, it must try and illustrate the lessons to be learned from this experience and examine the implications these lessons have for planning in similar situations in the future.

Throughout this whole period examined above, workers in many fields were providing the answers to individual pieces of the jigsaw. Pasture regeneration, disease control, catchment protection and social factors were all the subject of excellent research and the prevailing attitude of research workers was summarized by one who stated: "the real frustration of working here is the fact that we know most of the answers to the technical problems, but how do we convince *them*?" Possibly the pastoral community would have expressed it: "we know what we want but how do we convince *them*?" Experience proved that the pastoralists are as adaptable as anyone and it is only the pressures resulting from their physical environment which must make them regard any change to the stock-keeping system with extreme caution. Where some development was clearly and immediately "beneficial" such as water development, then it was accepted without hesitation but where it was not so obviously "beneficial" then some form of demonstration was necessary. The secret of success in such cases was to make the demonstration in a context as familiar as possible to the pastoralist, otherwise it would be thought of as another "government scheme" born of incomprehensible technology and endless funds. The Moroto Farm School in Karamoja attempted just this, to create an environment as close as possible to that in which the people lived and to show them what they could do with their own capital and skills. There is an enormous amount of standing capital in the form of stock and a wealth of detailed knowledge waiting to be developed for the benefit of the district.

The key, then, is understanding on both sides. The quotation from a local field worker above is only half the story. It is not entirely a matter of "convincing *them*" however beneficial a programme or project is felt to be. If the frustrations are not eventually to lead to by-pass solutions such as State Ranches then an attempt must be made to understand the traditional system from all aspects and, if necessary, consider it as a working model or system. The social anthropologist, with his unique insight into and involvement with the traditional societies would seem uniquely well equipped to contribute to this process but, up to now, social anthropology has tended to concern itself with static rather than dynamic views of their subject communities. When this integrative analysis is achieved a more scientific approach towards prediction may be made which considers the essential interactions and the natural responses to change within a traditional context. In this way the total human and physical resources of the district may be developed rather than destroyed.

Unless this approach is accepted there is a strong argument for leaving the pastoralists well alone—though this is now quite impracticable everywhere as change has been initiated. In the case of Karamoja it is possible to end on an optimistic note, though in case it is thought that the lesson has been learned it is still possible to find statements such as the following: "Among many pastoralists . . . in many parts . . . of East Africa, cattle are kept merely as a symbol of power and prestige,"[19] and new 1,000,000 gallon valley tanks are even now being built in the western plains without a thought for the grazing resources.

To combat this type of approach a member of the Planning Dept. in Entebbe attempted to draw together all shades of opinion and expertise on Karamoja in order to develop a new policy towards the district. The lack of preconception boded well for future improvements and a serious attempt was made to consider development in terms of the traditional system though, now, it was necessary to consider also the limitations and constraints arising from the already well advanced destruction of resources. If the people of Karamoja are to survive as a pastoral group and if the resources of the district are not to be destroyed then there would seem little alternative to attempting a better understanding and working within the framework of this understanding. Otherwise the pastoralists will be eliminated altogether.

## NOTES

1. The "Poor to Bad" categories are measures of the prospect of receiving 30" of rainfall as defined in the *East African Royal Commission Report 1953/55*, p. 271.
2. Dyson-Hudson, N. (1966), gives an account of the three southern peoples.
3. Thomas, E. M. (1965), gives an account of life among the Dodoth people.
4. Gulliver, P. (1955), gives an account of the Jie people.
5. Gulliver (1954, pp. 67–8) states: "the Jie have an . . . economy wherein cereal foods are really no less important than animal foods, and this has been the case for generations. Scarcely a day passes when cereal foods are not eaten and they frequently form the only food (for the women, elders and children) until the dairy herds return in May."
6. Dyson-Hudson, N. (n.d.).
7. Hutchinson, H. G. (1965), gives an interesting account of the "insurance" concept.
8. This situation resembles the circumstances prevailing during the early days of white settlement in Kenya when large areas of land were thought to be unoccupied but were empty only because of the rinderpest and smallpox outbreaks at the end of the last century.
9. Bredon, R. M. and Thornton, D. D. (1965).
10. Letter from the District Commissioner, Moroto, Karamoja, January 1957.
11. Letter from the Provincial Commissioner, Northern Province, Gulu, January 1949.
12. Hursh, C. R. (1952, p. 30).
13. *Karamoja District Plan* (1958, p. 7).
14. Deshler, J., letter to the Secretariat, Entebbe, September 1953.
15. Baker, Randall, (1968, pp. 211–26), examines with statistics, one interpretation of the relationship between cattle sales and weather. See also (Baker, Randall) (1967).
16. At that time equivalent to $1.
17. It is interesting that when the Karamojong resisted disease-control measures on one occasion the reason was eventually found to be that they knew that the virulence of the vaccine did, among poorer stock, itself result in mortality.
18. Moroto: District Veterinary Officer (1961).
19. Abeywickrama, B. A. (1964, p. 54).

## REFERENCES

ABEYWICKRAMA, B. A., 1964, *The Ecology of Man in the Tropical Environment.* Nairobi.
BAKER, RANDALL, 1967, *Environmental Influences on Cattle Marketing in Karamoja.* Makerere.
——, 1968, *Problems of the Cattle Trade in Karamoja, Uganda. An Environmental Analysis.* Ostafrikanische Studien, Band 8. Nürnberg: Wirtschafts- und Sozialgeographischen Instituts der Friedrich-Alexander Universität.

BREDON, R. M., and THORNTON, D. D., 1965, *Grazing Proposals for South Pian.* Entebbe: Ministry of Agriculture (cyclo.).

DYSON-HUDSON, NOEL, n.d., *The Present Position of the Karimojong.* London: Colonial Office (cyclo.).

———, 1966, *Karimojong Politics.* Oxford.

EAST AFRICAN ROYAL COMMISSION, 1955, *Report: 1953/55.* London: HMSO, Cmd 9475.

ENTEBBE GOVERNMENT PRINTER, 1958, *Karamoja District Plan.*

GULLIVER, P. H., 1954, "Jie Agriculture," *Uganda Journal,* XVII.

———, 1955, *The Family Herds.* London: Routledge & Kegan Paul.

HURSH, C. R., 1952, *Forest Management in East Africa in Relation to Local Climate, Water and Soil Resources.* Nairobi: EAAFRO Report.

HUTCHINSON, H. G., 1965, *Development in Tanzania.* Dar-es-Salaam: Inst. of Publ. Admin.

MOROTO: DISTRICT VETERINARY OFFICER, 1961, *Annual Report* (cyclo.).

THOMAS, E. M., 1965, *Warrior Herdsmen.* New York.

# 7 | ECOLOGY AND PLANNING
## C. S. Holling and M. A. Goldberg

*So far we have seen examples of human beings responding to environmental problems that humans created. What can the ecologist tell us about ecological systems and environmental crisis in general? C. S. Holling, an ecologist, and M. A. Goldberg, an economist, have collaborated in addressing the question of how planners can make use of ecological principles. They argue that any approach should begin with a presumption of ignorance, rather than of knowledge, for our knowledge of environmental systems is extremely small.*

*In the following review of three case studies, the authors outline basic principles of ecological systems and make specific suggestions for planners. Their suggestions can be summed up in these words: "Adopt a boundary-oriented view of the world." This view entails an awareness of the potentially costly consequences of interventions in natural systems and an acceptance of the fact that, however flexible or resilient a particular system may appear, this resilience is limited.*

To offer an ecological view of urban systems to a planning audience is risky. But, the possibilities for collaboration appear to outweigh the risks. Ecologists and planners have much to learn from each other.

Since ecology emerged from its descriptive phase in the 1920's, its emphasis has been on understanding the operation of complex ecological processes and ecological systems. There has been little effort to develop effective *applications* of ecological principles. Within the last few years, however, there has been a major shift toward an interest in application; but ecologists' first efforts in this direction have been blundering and naive. The central role of planners, on the other hand, has been application and policy formulation and implementation. Ecologists can benefit enormously from an infusion of the pragmatic realism that is, of necessity, forced upon the planning profession. Perhaps, at the same time, planners may gain some insights about urban systems from ecological theory.

As a basis for dialogue between planners and ecologists, we propose a conceptual framework based on ecological concepts of ecosystem structure and stability. This framework suggests an approach for planning based on a presumption of ignorance rather than on a presumption of knowledge. Since the area of our knowledge of man/environment interaction is minutely small in comparison with our ignorance, this conceptual framework may have some merit for the planning process.

## THE NATURE AND BEHAVIOR OF ECOLOGICAL SYSTEMS

Rather than presenting an exhaustive treatment of ecological concepts and terms, we hope to apply the philosophy of the ecological approach to solve problems of a kind that recur in all complex systems.[1] The key insight of this approach is that ecological systems are not in a state of delicate balance. Long before man appeared on the scene, natural systems were subjected to traumas and shocks imposed by climatic changes and other geophysical processes. The ecological systems that have survived have been those that are able to absorb and adapt to these traumas. As a result, these systems have considerable internal resilience, but we know that this resilience is not infinite. A forest can be turned into a desert, as in the Middle East, or a lake into the aquatic analog of a desert. The key feature of the resilience of ecological systems is that incremental changes are absorbed. It is only when a series of incremental changes accumulate or a massive shock is imposed, that the resilience of the system is exceeded, generating dramatic and unexpected signals of change.

This has considerable consequence for planning, since, inherent in the philosophy of planning and intervention, is the presumption that an incremental change will quickly generate a signal of whether the intervention is correct or not.[2] If the signal indicates the intervention produces higher costs than benefits, then a new policy and a new incremental change can be developed. But because of the resilience of ecological systems, incremental changes do not generate immediate signals of their effect. As a result, planners can set in motion a sequence of incremental steps and face the reality of the inadequacy of the underlying policy only when the interventions accumulate to shatter the bounds of resilience within the system. By that time it can be too late. In order to demonstrate these features of ecosystems we will discuss two specific case histories, each based on man's intervention. The consequences of the interventions reveal some of the key properties of ecosystems.

## Malarial Control in Borneo

Since the Second World War, the World Health Organization (WHO) has developed a remarkably successful malarial eradication program throughout the world. We wish to emphasize that, in this example of intervention, there is no question that there has been a dramatic improvement in the quality of life of people in affected regions. But, we wish to explore a specific case in which the World Health Organization sprayed village huts in Borneo with DDT in order to kill the mosquito that carries the plasmodium of malaria. This case has been documented by Harrison (1965).

The inland Dayak people of Borneo live in large single homes or long houses with up to 500 or more under one roof. This concentration of population allowed WHO to develop a thorough and orderly spraying of every long house, hut, and human habitation with DDT. The effect on health standards was dramatic with a remarkable improvement in the energy and vitality of the people—particularly those remote tribes who had not previously had access to medical aid. Nevertheless, there were interesting consequences that illuminate some of the properties of ecological systems.

There is a small community of organisms that occupy the thatched huts of these villages—cats, cockroaches, and small lizards. The cockroaches picked up the DDT and were subsequently eaten by the lizards. In consuming the cockroaches, the lizards concentrated the DDT to a somewhat higher level than was present in the cockroaches. The cats ate the lizards and, by eating them, concentrated the level of DDT still further—to the point that it became lethal. The cats died. When the cats disappeared from the villages, woodland rats invaded, and it suddenly became apparent that the cats had been performing a hidden function—controlling rat populations. Now, with the rat came a new complex of organisms—fleas, lice, and parasites, and this community presented a new public health hazard of sylvatic plague. The problem became serious enough that finally the RAF was called to parachute living cats into these isolated villages in order to control the rats.

The story isn't finished at this point, however, since the DDT also killed the parasites and predators of a small caterpillar that normally causes minor damage to thatch roofs (Cheng 1963). The caterpillar populations, now uncontrolled, increased dramatically, causing the roofs of the huts to collapse.

We cite this example not because it has great substance, but simply because it shows the variety of interactive pathways that link parts of an ecological system, pathways that are sufficiently intricate and complicated so that manipulating one fragment causes a reverberation throughout the system. In addition, this case provides a simple example of a food chain in which energy and material moves from cockroaches to lizards to cats. Typically, in these food chains the number of organisms at a higher level in the chain are less abundant than those lower in the chain. This is the inevitable result of the loss of energy in moving from one trophic or nutritional, level to another, and the consequence is a biological amplification that concentrates certain material at higher and higher levels as one moves up the chain. A contaminant like DDT, for example, can be present in the environment in very low, innocuous levels but can reach serious concentrations after two or three steps in the food chain. Actually, this example is highly simplified; usually in such situations there is a food *web* rather than a single linear food chain. Several species operate at more than one trophic level. Moreover, there are competitive interactions that further complicate and link species within an ecosystem. Even in this example, however, it is clear that the whole is not a simple sum of the parts and that there are a large number of components in a system acting and interacting in a variety of complex ways.

## A Cotton Ecosystem in Peru

Unlike the preceding example, the case of cotton agriculture in many parts of the world has had a more serious outcome. Pest control practices in cotton have, until recently, been both ecological and economic disasters. A particularly well-documented case has been prepared by Smith and Van den Bosch (1967).

There are a series of valleys on the coast of Peru formed by streams running from the high Andes to the Pacific Ocean. Many of these valleys are under intensive agriculture and, because of the low rainfall, are irrigated. The result is that each valley is essentially a self-contained ecosystem isolated from others by barren ridges. In one of these valleys, the Canete, during the 1920's, the crop shifted from sugar cane to cotton. Over the years a group of seven native insects became significant cotton pests, including plant sucking insects, the Boll Weevil, the tobacco leaf worm, and some moths. The pest problem, however, was essentially modest, and the farmers of the region lived with the resulting economic damage. In 1949, chlorinated hydrocarbons like DDT, Benzene hexachloride, and toxaphene became widely available, and the opportunity to dramatically decrease pest damage and increase crop yields arose. The characteristics of these insecticides seemed admirably suited to achieve the goal of pest reduction or elimination in this case:

1. The insecticides are lethal to a large number of insects and are so mobile that they quickly and easily concentrate within insects.
2. They are highly toxic to invertebrates and less so to mammalian forms.
3. They have a long life in the environment so that, in theory, one application can have an effect over some time. It has been shown, for example, that DDT and its biologically active breakdown products have an environmental half life of over a decade.
4. They can be easily and inexpensively applied from aircraft.

**5.** The contained nature of the valley ecosystem made it possible to spray the entire area with the insecticide.

We emphasize these details because the general features of this policy seem to be shared by many of man's actions. First, the objective is *narrowly defined*—in this case elimination of seven insect pests. Second, the plan developed is the simplest and least expensive means to achieve the narrow objective. But the consequences of this approach generated a series of unexpected and disastrous consequences explicitly because of the narrow definition of the objectives and the intervention.

The initial response to the insecticide treatment was a dramatic decline in pests and a one and one-half times increase in cotton production. This lasted, however, for only two or three years, when it was noticed that new pests were appearing that had never been a problem during the history of cotton production. Six new species of insects became as serious a problem as the original seven. The reason for the appearance of these new pests was the elimination of parasites and predators that were selectively killed because of the biological amplification of the insecticides through the food web. Within six years the original seven insect pests began to develop resistance to the insecticide, and crop damage increased. In order to control this new resurgence the concentration of the insecticide had to be increased, and the spraying interval reduced from two weeks to every three days. As these responses began to fail, the chlorinated hydrocarbons were replaced by organophosphate insecticides which deteriorated more rapidly in the environment. But even with this change the cotton yield plummeted to well below yields experienced before the synthetic insecticide period.

The average yield in 1956 was the lowest in more than a decade, and the costs of control were the highest. The agricultural economy was close to bankruptcy, and this forced the development of a very sophisticated ecological control program that combined changed agricultural practices with the introduction and fostering of beneficial insects. Chemical control was minimized. These new practices allowed the reestablishment of the complexity of the food web with the result that the number of species of pests was again reduced to a manageable level. Cotton yields increased to the highest level experienced in the history of cotton production in the valley.

As in the Borneo example, this case demonstrates the complexity and the structure of one ecological system that gives the system the resilience to absorb unexpected changes. Application of the insecticide enormously reduced the complexity and diversity of the ecosystem with a dramatic loss in resilience. But there is a difference between the two examples. In the first example, the area of intervention was local, and although there was destabilization within the local region, the consequences never became serious enough to defeat the original purpose of the intervention. In the Peruvian example, on the other hand, the intervention was more global since the whole valley ecosystem was literally blanketed with insecticide. As a result, the short-term success of the narrow intervention led in the longer term to the complete opposite of the original goal.

## Nature of Ecological Systems

These two examples illuminate four essential properties of ecological systems. By encompassing many components with complex feedback interactions between them, they exhibit a *systems* property. By responding not just to present events but to past ones as well, they show an *historical* quality. By responding to events at more than one point in space, they show a *spatial* interlocking property, and through the appearance of lags, thresholds, and limits they present distinctive *nonlinear* structural properties. First, ecosystems are characterized not only by their parts but also by the interaction among these parts. It is because of the complexity of the interactions that it is so dangerous to take a fragmented view, to look at an isolated piece of the system. By concentrating on one fragment and trying to optimize the performance of that fragment, we find that the rest of the system responds in unsuspected ways.

Second, ecological systems have not been assembled out of preexisting parts like a machine: they have evolved in time and are defined in part by their history. This point does not emerge clearly from the examples quoted; nevertheless, the resilience described in the examples is very much the consequence of past history.

When a large area is stripped of vegetation, an historical process begins that leads to the evolution of a stable ecosystem through a series of successional stages. Early in this succession, pioneer species occupy the space, and the diversity and complexity are low. The species that can operate under these circumstances are highly resistant to extreme conditions of drought and temperature and are highly productive. Competition is low, and a large proportion of the incident solar energy is converted to the production of bio-mass (the standing stock of organic material). As this accumulates, the conditions of the area begin to improve and to permit the appearance of groups of plants and animals that otherwise could not survive. The result is a gradual increase in the variety of species and in the complexity of interaction, and this increase in complexity is accompanied by an increase in the resilience of the system and a decrease in productivity. Under stable conditions this successional history can continue until a stable climax ecosystem evolves.

Man's objective in agricultural management is to halt this history at an early successional stage when the productivity is high. The price of doing this is a continual effort to prevent the system from moving to its more stable and less productive stage: hence herbicides and cultural practices eliminate or reduce those organisms that compete with man for food. But by emphasizing high productivity as a narrow objective, man develops the simplest and most direct policy, and the result leads to decreased complexity—large monocultures, heavy use of chemical herbicides, insecticides, and fertilizers. For the short term, the narrow objective of increased productivity is achieved, but the price paid is a dramatic decline in the resilience of the system. Third, complex ecosystems have very significant spatial interactions. Just as they have been formed by events over time so they are affected by events over space. Ecosystems are not homogeneous structures but present a spatial mosaic of biological and physical characteristics. The differences noted above between the Borneo and Peruvian examples are explained, in part, by the difference in the spatial scale of the intervention. In the Borneo example, the intervention was local and, in fact, increased the spatial heterogeneity. In the Peruvian example, the intervention was global and dramatically decreased the spatial heterogeneity. The consequence was that the resilience in the cotton ecosystem vanished. Finally, there are a variety of structural properties of the processes that interrelate the components of an ecosystem. We do not wish to dwell on these details other than to say they present singular problems in mathematical analysis for they relate to the existence of thresholds, lags, limits, and discontinuities.

## Behavior of Ecosystems

The distinctive behavior of systems flows from these four properties. Together they produce both resilience and stability. Even simple systems have properties of stability. Consider the example discussed by Hardin (1963). Every warmblooded animal regulates its temperature. In man the temperature is close to 98.6°F. If through sickness or through dramatic change in external temperature, the body temperature begins to rise or fall, then negative feedback processes bring the temperature back to the equilibrium level. But we note this regulation occurs only within limits. If the body temperature is forced too high— above 106°F., the excessive heat input defeats the regulation. The higher temperature increases metabolism which produces more heat, which produces higher temperature, and so on. The result is death. The same happens if temperature drops below a critical boundary. We see, therefore, even in this simple system, that stability relates not just to the equilibrium point but to the domain of temperatures over which true temperature regulation can occur. It is this domain of stability that is the measure of resilience.

In a more complex system, there are many quantities and qualities that change. Each species in an ecosystem and each qualitatively different individual within a species are distinct dimensions that can change over time. If we monitor the change in the quantity or quality of one of these dimensions, we can envisage results. . . . Within the range of stable equilibrium, if we cause a change in the quantity being measured, it will return to equilibrium over time. But there is a limit to which we can perturb these quantities, and that limit is defined as a boundary of stability.

The domain of stability is contained within the upper and lower boundaries. In simple physiological and engineering control feedback systems, regulation is strong enough and conditions are stable enough that most of our attention can be fixed on or near the equilibrium. This is not true of ecological systems (Holling and Ewing 1969). Ecological systems exist in a highly variable physical environment so that the equilibrium point itself is continually shifting and changing over time. At any one moment, each dimension of the system is attempting to track the equilibrium point but rarely, if ever, is it achieved. Therefore, each species is drifting and shifting both in its quantity and quality. Because of this variability imposed upon ecological systems, the ones that have survived, the ones that have not exceeded the boundaries of stability, are those that have evolved tactics to keep the domain of stability, or resilience, broad enough to absorb the consequences of change. The regulation forces within the domain of stability tend to be weak until the system approaches the boundary. They are not efficient systems in an optimizing sense because the price paid for efficiency is a decreased resilience and a high probability of extinction.

This view of stability is, of course, highly simplified. There may not be just one stable equilibrium at any instantaneous point in time; there may be several. Moreover, the stable condition might not be a single value but a sequence of values that return to a common starting value. This stable condition is termed a *stable limit cycle.* . . . Finally, the sequence of stable values need never return to some common starting point. The earlier description of an ecological succession really represents such a condition—a *stable trajectory.* . . .

But, however the equilibrium conditions change, they are all bounded, and what we must ask in judging any policy is not only how effectively an equilibrium is achieved, but also how the resilience, or the domain of stability, is changed. The two insecticide examples illustrate the point. The policies used in these cases were characterized by three conditions:

1. The problem is first isolated from the whole; that is, pests are damaging cotton.
2. The objective is defined narrowly; that is, kill the insect pest.
3. The simplest and most direct intervention is selected; that is, broadscale application of a highly toxic long-lived insecticide.

Each of these conditions assumes unlimited resilience in the system. By adopting these policies, the problem and the solution are made simple enough to be highly successful in the short term. So long as there is sufficient resilience to absorb the consequences of our ignorance, then the success can persist for a very long time. It is successful in the sense that the agriculturist can return his system almost instantly to an equilibrium point of one crop and no competing pests. The price paid, however, is the contraction of the boundaries of stability, and an equilibrium-centered point of view can be disastrous from a boundary oriented view.

It is this boundary oriented view of stability emerging from ecology that can serve as a conceptual framework for man's intervention into ecological systems. Such a framework changes the emphasis from maximizing the probability of success to minimizing the chance of disaster. It shifts the concentration from the forces that lead to convergence on equilibrium, to the forces that lead to divergence from a boundary. It shifts our interest from increased efficiency to the need for resilience. Most important, it focuses attention on causes, not symptoms. There is now, for example, growing concern for pollution, but the causes are not just the *explosion* of population and consumption, but also the *implosion* of the boundaries of stability.

## THE NATURE AND BEHAVIOR OF URBAN SYSTEMS

Arguments related exclusively to the nature and behavior of ecological systems obviously cannot be uncritically transferred to urban systems. Analogies are dangerous instruments, and in this case the transfer should be made only when the structure and behavior of urban systems appear to be similar to the structure and behavior of ecological systems.

Ecology is the study of the interactions between organisms and the physical environment. Planning concerns itself with the interaction between man and the environment of which he is a part. But does this analogy go deeper than a simple verbal parallelism? There are specific examples that point to similarities between certain ecological and social processes.[3] But the real substance of an analogy between ecological and urban systems lies not in the similarities between parts or processes, but in fundamental similarities in the structure of entire systems. We earlier described four key properties of ecological systems which concern system interaction and feedback, historical succession, spatial linkage, and non-linear structure. The same properties seem to be important for urban systems.

In the first place, both urban and ecological systems are true systems functioning as a result of interaction between parts. Just as a narrow intervention in an ecological system causes unexpected reverberations, so will it in an urban system. A freeway is constructed as an efficient artery to move people, but the unanticipated social consequences stimulate urban sprawl and inner city decay. A ghetto is demolished in order to revitalize the urban core, and disrupted social interactions trigger violence. A tax subsidy is given to attract industry, leading to environmental pollution deteriorating the quality of life. Such narrow interventions demonstrate that the whole is not a simple sum of the parts.

Second, the city region, like an ecological system, has a history. The modern cities of North America are, to a major extent, the product of history since the industrial revolution. The technology of the industrial revolution removed the constraints imposed by limitations in the environment, permitting development to take place as if there were no environmental limitations. If, for transient moments of time, the signals of these limitations became apparent through the appearance of plague or famine, the problems were generally resolved by looking elsewhere for the solution. So long as there was an "elsewhere"—an undeveloped continent, an undeveloped West—then this approach provided the quickest solution. The only constraints were placed by economic needs, hence the great emphasis on economic growth. The result, therefore, is an urban system with many of the characteristics of an early stage in an ecological succession. The system is changing rapidly in time and is not closed. Without any apparent limitation, water and air are considered as free goods to receive, at no cost, the wastes of the system. Only now is it becoming generally recognized that there are environmental constraints, that water and air are not free goods, and that wastes cannot simply be transported "elsewhere." In a sense, the urban system, like an ecological one, has a memory which constrains it to respond to current events only as it has been conditioned by past events. In a rapidly changing present the responses can become dangerously inappropriate.

Third, the urban system has significant spatial characteristics and interactions. Just as the city has been formed by events over time, so it is affected by events over space. The city is not a homogeneous structure but a spatial mosaic of social, economic, and ecological variables that are connected by a variety of physical and social dispersal processes. Each individual human has a variety of needs—for shelter, recreation, and work. These activities are typically spatially separate, and any qualitative or quantitative change of a function at one point in space inevitably affects other functions at other points of space.

Finally, the same non-linear, discontinuous structural properties noted in ecological systems apply to urban systems. Thresholds and limits exist with regard to city size. We know that a city of 500,000 residents has more than five times the variety of activities a city of 100,000 has. We also know that below certain threshold levels, certain activities do not occur. Thus, suburban areas and smaller cities just do not have great art museums, operas, symphonies, and restaurants. These activities appear to occur above certain population, or density, thresholds. Finally, such notions as agglomeration and per capita servicing costs are all non-linear relationships with respect to city size.

Both the structure of the parts of an urban system and the whole system itself appear to have close similarities to ecological systems. Since we have argued that in ecological systems these distinctive structural features account for their behaviour, it follows that urban systems must behave in similar ways. There must be a set of urban equilibrium conditions. But more important, these equilibrium states must exist within a domain of stability that defines the resilience of the urban system.[4] And, as in ecological systems, the consequences of intervention in a city can be viewed very differently depending on whether we take an equilibrium centered or boundary oriented view. If this is true, then we should be able to demonstrate, through samples of interventions, the same kinds of effects we showed with the insecticide examples.

## Urban Programs with Unanticipated Consequences

For this purpose, we have selected examples of reasonably narrow interventions. A number of unexpected consequences emerge, and from them we can infer that the internal dynamics of urban systems are similar to ecological ones, and continued narrow interventions can lead to effects analagous to those which occur in natural systems. Our examples are chosen to demonstrate that simplification of urban systems, through such simple but large-scale interventions as urban freeway programs, urban renewal, and rent control, leads to large-scale unexpected consequences and a high likelihood of failure even with respect to the narrow objective of the intervention. This is the lesson from natural systems, and this, we think, is the experience to date in urban systems.

Three examples should suffice. The first two—rent control and residential urban renewal—represent simple and direct approaches to housing lower income people. Our third example is freeway construction which represents a similarly simple and direct approach to the "urban transportation problem." Each of these solutions has been carried out on a broad scale; each represents a considerable simplification of the real world; and each has had either little effect or negative effects vis-a-vis the original objective.

*Rent control* is a reasonable starting point. As in the insecticide examples there are three explicit policy conditions. First, the problem is isolated from the whole; in this case it is defined as inadequate low-cost housing. Second, the objective is narrowly defined: to limit the price increase in rental housing during periods of rapid economic growth. Third, the simplest and most direct policy is proposed: to apply government control of prices. Finally, the implicit assumption is that there is sufficient resilience in the system to absorb unexpected consequences.

Strong economic arguments have been presented against this narrow approach to rent control by Turvey (1957), Needleman (1965), and Lindbeck (1967), and empirical evidence supports the thesis that rent control in the long run can diminish the supply of housing and therefore extend or guarantee a shortage (Fisher 1966, Gelting 1967, and Muth 1968).[5] Available evidence thus indicates a negative effect.

*Residential urban renewal* yields another instance where the desired result is reversed. Slum clearance programs have been aimed at revitalizing the hearts of urban regions. In their broadest context, they include a multiplicity of land uses. For present purposes we are interested only in slum clearance programs aimed at providing better housing for low-income families and individuals.

It is fairly clear at present that these programs have not had the intended effect of providing more low-income housing. Hartman (1964) presents strong evidence that the programs have failed. Gans (1968) and Anderson (1964) have documented the shortcomings and have demonstrated that the reverse effect has often been achieved. They claim that the program has resulted in a decline of housing for low-income people and that the price of the remaining housing has in fact increased in the face of dubious increases in quality. In light of this evidence, Fried's (1963) criticisms of the social impact of relocation appear especially damning. It appears, therefore, that slum clearance has failed to provide more housing to low-income people, has failed to significantly upgrade the quality of their housing, has imposed a high psychic cost on slum residents, and perhaps has even had the reverse effect of removing low-income housing stock from existence.

Our final example concerns *freeways* and is meant to illustrate a variety of unexpected consequences, not only those that have effects opposite to the desired ones, but also those that produce significant "side effects" outside the narrow bounds of the original intervention. Our scenario runs as follows. Current dependence on the automobile has led to urban sprawl and congestion. This, in turn, has induced us to treat these symptoms with large-scale urban freeway programs. These have induced further sprawl and changed land use patterns which, in turn, have generated the need for more travel and therefore more traffic. The positive feedback of freeways to create traffic is illustrated in almost every major urban freeway system. Peak capacities are reached well ahead of design. The need for a more integrated and comprehensive transportation and land use planning program has been called for every year during the 1960's. Levinson and Wynn (1962) and Wendt and Goldberg (1969) summarize the arguments for such an integrated approach. Without it, freeway programs are bound to have an effect opposite to that desired (that is, creation of traffic congestion rather than alleviation of congestion).

Freeways have also brought with them a wide variety of environmental side effects. Freeways have changed the morphology of cities, stimulating sprawl that typically utilizes agricultural land. Each city can argue, with reason, that increased efficiency of agriculture and the development of marginal agricultural lands can partially fill the gap. But the price paid for this increased efficiency is the consequence of yet another "quick technological fix"—the increased dependency on chemicals to control insect pests and weeds and on chemicals to fertilize the land. Initially, the natural environment can absorb and cleanse these additives, but this resilience is limited and, when exceeded, results in the signals of pollution that are now so evident.

Interestingly enough, freeway planners have claimed that freeways should reduce air pollution by increasing average vehicle speed and facilitating the more complete burning of gasoline. Bellomo and Edgerley (1971) provide interesting evidence that this is not necessarily the case. They note that there are three major automobile pollutants: carbon monoxide, hydrocarbons, and oxides of nitrogen. Both carbon monoxide and hydrocarbon emissions are reduced as a result of increased speed and more complete burning. Oxides of nitrogen, however, are produced in proportion to fuel consumption which increases with vehicle speed. Thus, the Los Angeles freeway system, by increasing vehicle speeds, does reduce both carbon monoxide and hydrocarbon emissions. Unfortunately, it also increases the production of oxides of nitrogen, and it is these oxides that give Los Angeles its notorious photochemical smog. Here again we have the reverse of the desired state of affairs.

These examples illustrate the dangers inherent in focusing too narrowly on a component or symptom of a system problem. They have been chosen to relate the ideas developed for biological systems to urban systems to demonstrate that there are functional analogies that can be drawn from one to the other. Having illustrated these relationships, we can move on to some system oriented solutions of the kind that are evolving in the biological sciences and that (again hopefully) can successfully be transplanted to urban systems.

## Ecological Principles and Urban Plans

A variety of suggestions that have been made for urban systems are analogous to ecological control schemes in nature. They revolve around smaller-scale interventions and decentralized efforts rather than large-scale monolithic approaches.

There is a common theme running throughout the criticisms of the approaches to urban housing and transportation problems as well as through the suggestions for change. The criticisms concern the narrowness of the original approach and the failure to achieve stated goals while causing a variety of side effects. The suggestions for change are analogous to ecological control schemes and basically state that the system can cure itself if given a chance. The chance is provided if our interventions give credence to the basic complexity and resilience of our urban systems. Such basic respect for the system eliminates a host of policies like those that have been previously sketched out. The idea is to let the system do it, while our interventions are aimed at juggling internal system parameters without simplifying the interactions of parameters and components.

In this vein, Gans (1969), Anderson (1964), Fried (1963), and Cogen and Feidelson (1967) argue for increased flexibility and more decentralized approaches to the urban housing problem. Instead of large-scale clearance and public housing programs or rent control, they advocate smaller scale projects of rehabilitation, rent and income subsidies, tax credits and subsidies for property owners, and so on. These solutions allow individuals to make decisions as they see fit, while government decisionmakers provide them with information in the form of subsidies and credit as to the kinds of decisions society is willing to pay for. This decentralized approach will likely be more efficient in the long run and certainly more humane and enduring, since individuals will be making decisions about their future and will necessarily feel more a part of that future.

Completely analogous suggestions have been made for transportation planning. Again the central concept is to let individuals choose for themselves their transportation, the locations of their housing relative to their jobs, and the convenience they desire for their travel. Transportation and urban planners again merely provide information that will guide people toward socially desirable ends.

Pricing is the most widely mentioned means of achieving this end. Meyer, Kain, and Wohl (1966) describe pricing schemes both for congestion and peak hour use of roads and for parking. By changing the prices the individual traveller faces, he will more nearly bear the social costs that he creates in the form of congestion, pollution, and dispersed land use patterns. It is then up to him whether or not he chooses to pay these new prices or switch his travel mode, house location, job location, or time of travel to a pattern that is more consistent with broader social goals of reasonable urban form, uncongested roads, and reasonably clean air. At the same time a variety of modes of travel and housing locations must be provided so that meaningful choices exist. Provision of such alternatives is entirely consistent with our thesis since it does not diminish the basic complexity of the urban system (it may well add to it) and does not diminish the system's resilience (again we may score gains where previously the system was stretched to capacity of the preexisting mode be it freeway, subway, or ferry).

## CONCLUSION

Given an intuitive understanding of our complex urban system, we would hope that practicing planners and other private and public decisionmakers would draw several conclusions for themselves about the nature of their actions in the system. First, and most important, is that their actions be limited in scope and diverse in nature. Actions of this sort do preserve the complexity and resilience of the urban system and will limit the scale and potential harm of the inevitable unexpected consequences. Second, we feel that complexity is a worthwhile goal in its own right and should be preserved and encouraged. Finally, and really encompassing the above, we would hope decisionmakers and their advisors will adopt a more boundary oriented view of the world. We should be much more wary of success than failure. Again, rather than asking project directors to substantiate the ultimate success of their projects, they should be asked to ensure that unexpected and disastrous consequences be minimized. This is turning things around 180 degrees, but we feel this is the only way to proceed. Success has given us freeways, urban renewal, and public housing projects. We must reduce the size of our institutions to ensure their flexibility and respect for the system of which they are a small interacting part.

## NOTES

1. The reader specifically interested in an introduction to ecology can refer to Odum (1963) and Whittaker (1970).
2. The notion of incremental (or "marginal" in the economist's jargon) changes is part and parcel of cost-benefit analysis. Now marginal investments, which can change the structure of prices and the allocation of resources, are difficult to deal with under present cost-benefit approaches. Thus, resilience is usually assumed by ignoring changes in prices induced by large-scale projects. See Prest and Turvey (1965) for a discussion of the assumptions concerning marginal and non-marginal projects.
3. In one example (Holling, 1969), a simulation model of recreational land use was developed. It was clear from this study that many of the qualities and processes in land acquisition were similar to those found in the ecological process of predation. Moreover, the similarity between land acquisition and predation extended to the structure of the interrelations among the components of each. They differed only in the specific form of the functions describing the action of each component. Therefore, even at the level of processes there is at least a structural identity that can be usefully explored so long as it is recognized that there are functional differences.
4. See, Jacobs (1961, Chapter 13), for some interesting descriptions of the destruction of formerly diverse and stable urban systems.
5. The most complete study of the subject to date, by the RAND Corporation in New York, is not yet available, but preliminary evidence supports this statement.

## REFERENCES

ANDERSON, MARTIN, 1964, *The Federal Bulldozer.* Cambridge, Mass.: MIT Press.

BELLOMO, S. J., and E. EDGERLEY, 1971, "Ways to Reduce Air Pollution Through Planning Design and Operations." Presented at the 50th Annual Meeting, Highway Research Board. Washington, D.C.: January 1971.

CHENG, F. Y., 1963, "Deterioration of Thatch Roofs by Moth Larvae after House Spraying in the Course of a Malarial Eradication Programme in North Borneo," *Bulletin World Health Organization,* 28:136–7.

COGEN, J., and KATHRYN FEIDELSON, 1967, "Rental Assistance for Large Families: An Interim Report," in J. Bellush and M. Hausknecht (eds.), *Urban Renewal: People, Politics & Planning.* New York: Doubleday Anchor, especially Section VI, "New Directions," pp. 508–42.

FISHER, E. M., 1966, "Twenty Years of Rent Control in New York City," in *Essays in Urban Land Economics.* Los Angeles: University of California Real Estate Research Program, pp. 31–67.

FRIED, MARC, 1963, "Grieving for a Lost Home," in L. J. Duhl (ed.), *The Urban Condition.* New York: Basic Books, pp. 151–71.

GANS, HERBERT J., 1968, *People and Plans.* New York: Basic Books, especially Chapter 18, "The Failure of Urban Renewal: A Critique and Some Proposals," pp. 260–77.

GELTING, J. H., 1967, "On the Economic Effects of Rent Control in Denmark," in A. A. Nevitt (ed.), *The Economic Problems of Housing.* London: Macmillan, pp. 85–91.

HARDIN, GARRETT, 1963, "The Cybernetics of Competition: A Biologist's View of Society," *Perspectives in Biology & Medicine,* 7:58–84.

HARRISON, TOM, 1965, "Operation Cat Drop," *Animals,* 5:512–13.

HARTMAN, CHESTER, 1964, "The Housing of Relocated Families," *Journal of the American Institute of Planners,* 30 (November): 266–86.

HOLLING, C. S., 1969, "Stability in Ecological and Social Systems," *Brookhaven Symposia in Biology,* 22:128–41.

HOLLING, C. S., and S. EWING, 1969, "Blind Man's Bluff: Exploring the Response Space Generated by Realistic Ecological Simulation Models," in *Proceedings of the International Symposium of Statistical Ecology.* New Haven: Yale University Press.

JACOBS, JANE, 1961, *The Death and Life of Great American Cities.* New York: Random House.

LEVINSON, H. S., and F. H. WYNN, 1962, "Some Aspects of Future Transportation in Urban Areas," *Highway Research Board Bulletin,* 326:1–31.

LINDBECK, ASSAR, 1967, "Rent Control as an Instrument of Housing Policy," in A. A. Nevitt (ed.), *The Economic Problems of Housing.* London: Macmillan, pp. 53–72.

MEYER, J., J. KAIN, and M. WOHL, 1966, *The Urban Transportation Problem.* Cambridge, Mass.: Harvard University Press, especially Chapter 13, pp. 334–59.

MUTH, R. F., 1968, "Urban Land and Residential Housing Markets," in H. S. Perloff and L. Wingo (eds.), *Issues in Urban Economics.* Baltimore: Johns Hopkins Press, pp. 285–333.

NEEDLEMAN, LIONEL, 1965, *The Economics of Housing.* London: Staples Press.

ODUM, EUGENE P., 1963, *Ecology.* New York: Holt, Rinehart and Winston.

PREST, A. R., and R. TURVEY. 1965. "Cost-Benefit Analysis: A Survey," *Economic Journal,* 75.

SMITH, RAY F., and ROBERT VAN DEN BOSCH, 1967, "Integrated Control," in W. W. Kilgare and R. L. Doutt (eds.), *Pest Control.* New York: Academic Press.

TURREY, RALPH, 1957, *The Economics of Real Property.* London: George Allen & Unwin.

WENDT, P. F., and M. A. GOLDBERG, 1969, "The Use of Land Development Simulation Models on Transportation Planning," *Highway Research Record,* 285:82–91.

WHITTAKER, R. H., 1970, *Communities and Ecosystems.* New York: Macmillan Co.

# Part III
## Responding to Technological and Economic Change

Anthropologists who work in the field can rarely afford to be sentimental about traditional ways of survival. They are confronted on a daily basis with the fact that the peoples they study have been influenced by the world beyond their villages, their regions, their countries. Although the anthropologist-observer may be critical of the particular items adopted by a local group and of the ways that innovations are introduced into a society, it is clear that there is no way to prevent change from taking place.

The studies presented in Part Three document a variety of different kinds of technological and economic change in a wide range of social contexts. But general patterns emerge from comparison. In each instance the ramifications of adopting a new technological item or new resource were far wider than the immediate use of the item or resource itself. The impact of the innovation and its subsequent use were shaped very much by existing traditions of social organization. And usually a major consequence of change was increased dependence upon extralocal events and institutions. In fact, the world's societies are not only changing, but rates of change are also accelerating. Anthropologists have usually examined local economic and technological change in the course of "case studies" of particular communities. In Part Three William E. Mitchell's description of the impact of new weapons on life in rural New Guinea provides an example of this approach. In such societies people are rapidly drawn into dependence upon foreign sources of technology. This dependence is likely to increase with time as the people become more closely integrated into economies dominated by distant cities and markets. Even the Eskimos, described in chapter two, now hunt with motor boats, use rifles, and rely extensively upon food, gasoline, and supplies purchased at trading posts. Local self-sufficiency, if it ever existed, is now a thing of the past.

Many of the problems facing members of a community originate in their relations with other populations and in their dependence upon exchange for vital items. Such problems particularly affect farmers today. Studies of irrigation agriculture in Oaxaca, Mexico, and sisal production in Brazil focus on the effects of marketing on local communities and households. As rural communities are drawn into commitment to urban markets, they sacrifice much of their independence. In the Brazilian instance, it led to some families' giving up farming to become agricultural workers on estates owned by others. Often we see economic and technological change benefiting some individuals more than others. Sometimes such differences result in social and economic differentiation where little had existed before, a point explored in more detail in a later part of this book.

Although the examples we have mentioned so far come from either hunting-and-gathering or agricultural societies, the effects of economic change are obviously not limited to rural settings. Today almost as many people live in towns or cities as in the countryside. The world's cities have changed profoundly since the Industrial Revolution, achieving a size and organizational complexity unimaginable without elaborate organization for the supply of energy, food, and communications. The industrial city has imposed many changes on urban dwellers. One obvious development related to technology is that industrialized cities everywhere tend to resemble one another. Households belonging to the same economic class in different societies are increasingly similar in dress, daily routine, and general style of life. There is little difference between a worker in a French automobile factory and his Turkish counterpart. The organization of family ties and households is also shaped strongly by recent economic changes. But, perhaps more than in other areas of social life, we see new responses in families, who build on previous ways of doing things.

In approaching economic and technological change, perhaps the best question to ask is How have individual people benefited, and what costs have they paid? There can be no doubt that recent technological breakthroughs in health and transportation have brought great benefits to many. The life expectancy of members of industrial societies has increased, whether it is measured in longevity or in sharply lowered risk of infant mortality. Our lives may be enriched because we can travel and read about relatively distant places and experience the products of different lands and civilizations. There are, however, costs. For example, increased integration in a global economy means that even local problems can have potentially devastating far-reaching effects. We need only remember World War II and subsequent bloody conflagrations to recognize some of them. Another cost of economic integration is that inevitably some regions and some individuals benefit at the expense of others. Finally, there is a widespread and probably increasing disparity between general levels of productivity and actual individual benefits from production. From the individual's point of view this problem is far more important than abstract measures of increasing industrial and agricultural efficiency. Unfortunately, by this criterion, even in the most technologically advanced societies there are many who endure great personal deprivation.

Two final points are pertinent here. First, many anthropologists agree that it might be possible to alleviate some of the difficulties experienced by peoples of the world as the result of technological and economic change through improvements in planning and design of innovations. A number of anthropologists have actually been employed in this capacity, both in the United States and in developing countries; this work falls into what we call "applied anthropology." Second, many anthropologists (and other scientists) believe that we can learn a great deal from societies that, though technologically simpler than our own, are more stable, egalitarian, and personally rewarding. Not that they believe that we should "revert" to an earlier age or that simpler societies are without problems. Rather, they recognize our own imperfections and express hope that we can use to our advantage what we have learned. These latter points are well illustrated in the study of the Amish farmers, who live simply in the midst of a highly industrialized society.

# 8 | A NEW WEAPON STIRS UP OLD GHOSTS
## William E. Mitchell

*The impact of shotguns on the Wape people of New Guinea is partly related to the manner in which this new item of technology was introduced. Particularly important in this instance was the association between shotguns, on one hand, and the rules, ethics, and power of white colonists, on the other. An appreciation of these factors, along with traditional concepts and beliefs, has resulted in the emergence of a new cult centered on the use of shotguns in Wape society. The incorporation of this new tool has been accompanied, not by the breakdown of traditional values, but by their reinforcement and the simultaneous adoption of new values.*

When, in 1947, the Franciscan friars went to live among the nearly 10,000 Wape people of New Guinea, the principal native weapons were bone daggers and the bow and arrow. Even then, game was scarce in the heavily populated mountains where the Wape live, and the killing of a wild pig or a cassowary, New Guinea's major game animals, was an important village event. The Wape live in the western part of the Sepik River Basin. Their small villages lie along the narrow ridges of the Torricelli Mountains, above the sago palm swamps where women process palm pith, the Wape staff of life.

Today the Wape hunter's principal weapon is still the bow and arrow and game is even scarcer. This is partially the result of a new addition to the hunter's armory—the prosaic shotgun—which has had a profound moral impact on Wape village life.

The first guns were brought into this area in the late 1940s and early 1950s by missionaries, traders, and Australian government officials. Although natives were not permitted to own guns, they could use them if employed by a white man to shoot game for his table. This was a very prestigious job.

In 1960, government regulations were changed to permit natives to purchase single-shot shotguns. At first only a few Wape men, living in villages close to the government station and helpful to government officials, were granted gun permits. Eventually more permits were issued, but today, in hopes of preserving the remaining game, one permit is issued for every 100 people.

Within ten years of the granting of the first gun permits, a belief and behavioral system had evolved around the shotgun. It was based on traditional Wape hunting lore but had distinctive elaborations stemming from native perceptions of the teachings of government officials and missionaries. For descriptive purposes I call this system of formalized beliefs and ritual the "Wape shotgun cult." It is one of several Wape ceremonial cults, but the only one originating after contact with Europeans. Although the specific practices of the shotgun cult vary from village to village, the underlying beliefs are the same.

In creating the shotgun cult the Wape faced the challenge of adapting an introduced implement to their culture. Unlike steel axes and knives, which replaced stone adzes and bamboo knives, the shotgun has never replaced the bow and arrow. The shotgun is a scarce and expensive machine. This, together with the European sanctions imposed upon its introduction, places it in a unique position, both symbolically and behaviorally, among the Wape.

The cult is a conservative institution. It breaks no new cognitive ground by challenging established Wape concepts. Instead it merges traditional hunting concepts with European moral teachings to create a coherent system. The cult upholds traditional beliefs, accepts European authority, and most important, provides an explanation for unsuccessful hunting.

In 1970, my family and I arrived in Lumi, a small mountain settlement, which is the government's subdistrict headquarters in the middle

of Wapeland. For the next year and a half, we lived in the village of
Taute, near Lumi. There my wife and I studied Wape culture.

Taute, which has a population of 220, is reached by narrow foot trails,
root strewn and muddy, passing through the dense, damp forest. The
low houses—made of sago palm stems and roofed with sago thatch—are
scattered about in the sandy plaza and among the coconut palms and
breadfruit trees along the ridge. Towering poinsettias, red and pink
hibiscus, and multicolored shrubs contrast with the encircling forest's
greens and browns. A few small latrines perch on the steep slopes,
concessions to Western concepts of hygiene. In the morning, flocks of
screeching cockatoos glide below the ridge through the rising mists.
When the breadfruit trees are bearing, giant fruit bats flop across the
sky at dusk.

Since the mid-1950s the Franciscan friars have maintained, off and
on, a religious school in Taute. There, Wape boys are instructed by a
native catechist in Catholicism, simple arithmetic, and Melanesian Pidgin. A priest from Lumi visits the village several times a year, and the
villagers, Catholic and heathen alike, are proud of their affiliation with
the Franciscans and staunchly loyal to them. But their Catholicism is
nominal and superficial—a scant and brittle frosting that does not mask
their own religious beliefs, which dominate everyday life.

The ethos of Wape society is oriented around sacred curing rituals.
Whereas some Sepik cultures aggressively center their ceremonial life
around headhunting and the raising of sturdy and brave children, the
Wape defensively center theirs in the ritual appeasement of malevolent
ghosts and forest demons, who they believe cause sickness. Most men
belong to one of the demon-curing cults where, once initiated as priests,
they are responsible for producing the often elaborate curing ceremonies for exorcising the demon from the afflicted.

The little money that exists among the Wape is earned primarily by
the men, who work as two-year contract laborers on the coastal and
island copra plantations. Because of the lack of money to buy canned
meats, the scarcity of game, and the paucity of fish in the mountain
streams, the protein intake of the Wape is exceedingly low. The most
common meal is sago dumplings and boiled leaves. Malnutrition is
common among youngsters, and physical development is generally re-
tarded. According to studies by Dr. Lyn Wark, a medical missionary
who has worked widely among the Wape, the average birth weight of
the Wape baby is the lowest recorded in the world. Correspondingly,
secondary sex characteristics are delayed. For example, the mean age
for the onset of menses is over eighteen years.

Before contact with Westerners, Wape men were naked and the
women wore short string skirts. Today most men wear shorts and the
women wear skirts purchased from Lumi's four small stores. To appear
in a semblance of European dress, however meager or worn, is a matter
of pride and modesty to both sexes. "Savages" do not wear clothes, but
white men and those who have been enlightened by white men do. In
this sense, the Wape's Western-style dress represents an identification

with the politically and materially powerful white man. The identification is with power; it is an ego-enhancing maneuver that permits the Wape to live with dignity, even though they are subservient to Western rule and influence. The tendency of the Wape to identify with, and incorporate, the alien when it serves to preserve their culture will help us to understand how they have woven diverse cultural strands into the creation of the shotgun cult.

From the first day I arrived in Taute, the men repeatedly made two urgent requests of me. One was to open a store in the village, saving them the difficult walk into Lumi; the other was to buy a shotgun to help them kill game. This was the least, they seemed to indicate, a fair-minded and, in Wape terms, obviously rich neighbor should do. One of the hardest things the anthropologist in the field must learn is to say "no" to deserving people. To be stingy is almost to be un-American, but we had come halfway around the world to learn about the Wape way of life, not to introduce stores and shotguns that would alter the established trading and hunting patterns.

After several months the people of the major Taute hamlets, Kafiere, where we lived, and Mifu, a ten-minute walk away, each decided to buy a group-owned shotgun. The investment was a sizable forty-two Australian dollars: forty dollars for the gun and two dollars for the gun permit. Each hamlet made a volunteer collection from its members and I, as a fellow villager, contributed to both guns. A week later the villagers purchased the guns from one of the Lumi stores, and I began to learn about the shotgun's ritual and moral importance to the Wape. The villagers were already familiar with the significance of the shotgun for they had purchased one several years before. The cult ended, however, when the gun broke.

The shotgun, like Melanesian Pidgin, is associated by the Wape with Europeans and modernity. Not surprisingly, Pidgin is favored for shotgun parlance. The licensed gunman is not only called *sutboi* ("shoot-boy") but also *laman* ("law man"), the latter a term that connotes his official tie to European law and government as perceived by the villagers.

When a candidate for a gun permit appears before the government official in Lumi, he is examined orally on the use of firearms, then given an unloaded shotgun and tested on his handling knowledge. Under the direct and questioning gaze of the examining official, candidates sometimes become flustered. One inadvertently aimed the gun first toward the wife of the assistant district commissioner and then toward a group of observers. His examination ended ignominiously on the spot.

If the candidate passes the test and the examining official approves of his character, he is then lectured on the use of the gun: only the candidate can fire it, he must willingly shoot game for his fellow villagers, and the gun must be used exclusively for hunting. He is strongly warned that if any of these rules are broken or if there is trouble in the village, he will lose the gun and the permit and will be imprisoned.

The candidate's friends and the inevitable audience are present for the lecture. Here, as in many spheres of native life, the official's power is absolute, and the Wape know this from long experience. Guns have been confiscated or destroyed without reimbursement, and gunmen have been jailed.

The official's charge to the candidate is willingly accepted. Henceforth, he will never leave the village without carrying his gun. He is now a *laman,* and he has the gun and permit, printed entirely in English, to prove it.

The government official's strong sanctions against village quarrels are motivated by his fear that the gun might be used in a dispute among villagers. The sanctions are further upheld by the missionaries' and catechists' sermons against quarreling and wrongdoing as they attempt to teach the Christian doctrine of brotherly love. The message the villagers receive is this: To keep the white man's gun, they must follow the white man's rules. This the Wape do, not in servile submission, but with some pride because the presence of the gun and the public focus on morality mark the village as progressive and modern. The licensed gunman, therefore, is not only the guardian of the gun but of village morality as well.

Rain or shine, he is expected to go into the forest without compensation to hunt for his fellow villagers, who give him cartridges with some personal identifying mark upon them. After a gunman makes a kill, the owner of the cartridge receives the game and distributes it according to his economic obligations to others. But the gunman, like the bow and arrow hunter, is forbidden to eat from the kill; to do so would jeopardize further successful hunting.

In the hamlet of Kafiere, the clan that had contributed the most money toward the gun and on whose lands the most game was to be found appointed Auwe as gunman. But Auwe's wife, Naiasu, was initially against his selection. Her previous husband, Semer, now dead several years, had been Kafiere's first *sutboi* and she argued that the heavy hunting responsibilities of a *sutboi* took too much time, forcing him to neglect his own gardening and hunting obligations.

When Auwe first requested a gun permit he was turned away. The villagers believed that the ghost of Naiasu's dead husband, Semer, had followed Auwe to Lumi and influenced the examining official against him. Semer's ghost was acting to fulfill Naiasu's wish that her young son, now Auwe's stepson, would have a stepfather who was always available. This was the first of many stories I was to hear about the relationship between ghosts and the gun. When Auwe returned to Lumi for a second try, he passed the examination and was given the official permit.

The hamlet now had its own gun and hunting could begin in earnest. The first step was an annunciation feast called, in Pidgin, a *kapti* ("cup of tea"). Its purpose was to inform the villagers' dead ancestors about the new gun. This was important because ancestral ghosts roam the forest land of their lineage, protecting it from intruders and driving game to their hunting descendants. The hunter's most important hunting aide is his dead male relatives, to whom he prays for game upon entering his hunting lands. The dead remain active in the affairs of the living by protecting them from harm, providing them with meat, and punishing those who have wronged them.

The small sacrificial feast was held in front of Auwe's house. Placing the upright gun on a makeshift table in the midst of the food, Auwe rubbed it with sacred ginger. One of Auwe's elderly clansmen, standing and facing his land, called out to his ancestors by name and told them about the new gun. He implored them to send wild pigs and cassowaries to Auwe.

Several men spoke of the new morality that was to accompany hunting with a gun. The villagers should not argue or quarrel among themselves; problems must be settled quietly and without bitterness; malicious gossip and stealing were forbidden. If these rules were not obeyed, Auwe would not find game.

In traditional Wape culture there is no feast analogous to the *kapti*. Indeed, there are no general community-wide feasts. The *kapti* is apparently modeled on a European social gathering.

For the remainder of my stay in Taute, I followed closely the fortunes of the Taute guns and of guns in nearby villages as well. All seemed to be faced with the same two problems: game was rarely seen; and when seen, was rarely killed. Considering that a cartridge belongs to a villager, not the gunman, how was this economic loss handled? This presented a most intriguing and novel problem for there were no analogs to this type of predicament within the traditional culture. By Wape standards, the pecuniary implications of such a loss, although but a few Australian shillings, could not graciously be ignored by the loser. At the very least the loss had to be explained even if the money for the cartridges could not be retrieved.

Now I understood the concern about the ancestral ghosts. If the hunter shot and missed, the owner of the fired shells was being punished by being denied meat. Either he or a close family member had quarreled or wronged another person whose ghost-relative was securing revenge by causing the hunter to miss. This, then, was the functional meaning of the proscription against quarreling. By avoiding disputes, the villagers were trying to prevent the intervention of ancestral ghosts in human affairs. In a peaceful village without quarrels, the gunman could hunt undisturbed by vengeful ghosts chasing away game or misrouting costly shells.

Although a number of factors in European culture have influenced the shotgun cult, the cult's basic premise of a positive correlation between quarreling and bad hunting is derived directly from traditional Wape culture. In bow and arrow hunting, an individual who feels he was not given his fair share of a hunter's kill may punish the hunter by gossiping about him or quarreling openly with him. The aggrieved person's ancestral ghosts revenge the slight by chasing the game away from the offending hunter or misdirecting his arrows. But this is a private affair between the hunter and the angered person; their quarrel has no influence upon the hunting of others. And it is rare for an issue other than distribution of game to cause a ghost to hinder a bowman's success. The hunter's prowess is restored only when the angered person performs a brief supplication rite over the hunter.

This, then, is the conceptual basis for the tie between quarreling and bad hunting. Originally relevant only to bow and arrow hunting, it was then broadened to accommodate the government's pronouncements about the shotgun and keeping the village peace. And it applies perfectly to the special circumstances of shotgun hunting. Because the shotgun is community owned and many villagers buy cartridges for it, the villagers are identified with both the gun and the gunman. As a proxy hunter for the villagers, the gunman is potentially subject to the ghostly sanctions resulting from their collective wrongs. Thus gun hunting, unlike bow and arrow hunting, is a community affair and the community-wide taboo against quarrels and personal transgressions is the only effective way to prevent spiteful ghosts from wrecking the hunt.

No village, however, even if populated by people as disciplined and well behaved as the Wape, can constantly live in the state of pious peace considered necessary for continuous good gun hunting. When the hunting is poor, the gunman must discover the quarrels and wrongs within the village. After having identified the individuals whose ancestral ghosts are sabotaging the hunting, the gunman must also see to it that they implore the ghosts to stop. Embarrassed by the public disclosure, they will quickly comply.

The common method for detecting points of friction within the village is to bring the villagers together for a special meeting. The gunman will then document in detail his misfortunes and call on the villagers to find out what is ruining the hunting. If confessions of wrongdoing are not forthcoming, questioning accusations result. The meeting, beginning in Pidgin, moves into Wape as the discussion becomes more complex and voluble. It may last up to three hours; but even if there is no resolution, it always ends amiably—at least on the surface. For it is important to create no new antagonisms.

The other technique for locating the source of the hunting problem is to call in a professional clairvoyant. As the villagers must pay for his services, he is usually consulted only after a series of unsuccessful meetings. Clairvoyants have replaced the shamans, who were outlawed by the government and the mission because they practiced sorcery and ritual murders. The Wape do not consider a clairvoyant a sorcerer; he is a man with second sight who is experienced in discovering and treating the hidden causes of intractable problems. As such, shotguns are among his best patients.

Mewau, a clairvoyant from a neighboring village, held a "shotgun clinic" in Taute to examine the Mifu and Kafiere guns. For about an hour he examined the two guns and questioned the villagers. Then he declared the reasons for their misfortune.

Kapul, a dead Mifu shaman, was preventing the Mifu gun from killing game because a close relative of the gunman had allegedly stolen valuables from Kapul's daughter. Because of the family ties between the gunman and the thief, Kapul's ghost was punishing the gunman.

The Kafiere gun, Mewau declared, was not able to find game because a widow in the village felt that her dead husband's clan had not previously distributed game to her in a fair way. By interfering with the Kafiere gun, her husband's ghost was punishing his clan for the neglect of his family.

Once the source of trouble is named, there are several possible types of remedial ritual depending upon the seriousness of the situation. For example, the circumstances surrounding the naming of the husband's ghost were considered serious, and a *kapti* was held to placate him. Another, simpler ritual involves the preparation of taro soup, which the gunman consumes. But the simplest, commonest remedial rite is the supplication ritual without sacrificial food offerings, a ritual in which I became involved.

Mifu's gunman had shot a pig with one of his own cartridges but did not give me the small portion due me as a part owner of the gun. Partly as a test to see if my ancestors counted for anything in Taute and partly because I did not want to let this calculated slight go unchallenged, I, in typical Wape fashion, said nothing to the gunman but gossiped discreetly about his selfishness. The gunman continued to hunt but had no further success. When his bad luck persisted, a meeting was called to find out the reason. The gunman asked me if I was angry because I had not been given my portion of the pig. When I acknowledged my anger, he handed the shotgun to me and I dutifully spoke out to my ancestors to stop turning the game away from the gun.

But the gunman still had no success in the hunt, and the villagers decided there were other wrongs as well. The search for the offending ghosts continued. Eventually the villagers became so discouraged with the Mifu gun that they stopped giving cartridges to the gunman. The consensus was that a major undetected wrong existed in the hamlet, and until it was uncovered and the guilty ghost called off, hunting with the gun was senseless and extravagant. Thus the propriety of a remedial rite is established if there is success on the next hunt. The system is completely empirical; if no game is seen or if seen, is not killed, then the search for the wrong must continue.

Wape people are generally even tempered, and their villages, in contrast to many in New Guinea, strike the newcomer as almost serene. But the social impact of the guns at this time was pervasive, and life in Taute literally revolved around the guns and their hunting fortunes. Whereas the villagers previously had kept to their own affairs, they now became embroiled in meeting after meeting, seeking out transgressions, quarrels, and wrongdoing. As the gunman continued to have bad luck, his efforts to discover the cause became more zealous. A certain amount of polarization resulted: the gunman accused the villagers, the men accused the women, and the adults accused the young people of hiding their wrongs. And a few who had lost many cartridges wondered if the *sutboi* was keeping the game for himself. But no one ever suggested that he was an inexperienced shotgun hunter. The gunman was generally considered to be blameless; in fact, the more game he missed, the more self-righteous he became and the more miscreant the villagers.

Six months of poor hunting had gone by; the villagers felt that the only recourse left to them was to bring a bush demon named *mani* into the village from the jungle for a festival. The *mani*'s small stone heart is kept enshrined in a rustic altar in a corner of Kafiere's ceremonial house and after a kill the animal's blood is smeared upon it. The *mani* will reward the village with further kills only if he is fed with blood. *Mani* is the only spirit, other than ghosts, who can cause both good and bad hunting depending upon the way he is treated. Soon after the shotgun arrived in Taute, the gunman and some other men left their homes to sleep in the men's ceremonial house to keep *mani*'s stone heart warm. They thought *mani*, in appreciation, would send game to the gunman.

When little game was killed, the villagers decided on the hunting festival. In a special house outside of the village, men constructed the great conical mask that depicts *mani*. For several weeks they worked to cover the mask's frame with the spathes of sago palm fronds painted with designs traditional to *mani*. Finally, a priest of the *mani* cult, wearing a 20-foot-high mask festooned with feathers and leaves, pranced into the village to the thunderous beat of wooden drums.

For the next week and a half men from other villages who wished us well came and joined in the all-night singing of the *mani* song cycle. In the morning, if the weather was clear, *mani* led the bow and arrow hunters and the gunman to the edge of the village and sent them on their way to hunting success. But in spite of the careful attentions the villagers directed toward *mani*, he rewarded them with only one wild pig. The villagers became openly discouraged, then annoyed. Finally the hunters, disgusted and weary from numerous long futile hunts, and other men, their shoulders sore and bloody from constantly carrying the heavy mask around the plaza, decided that *mani* was simply taking advantage of them; all of their hard work was for nothing. Disgusted, they decided to send *mani* back to his home in the forest.

One late afternoon the *mani* appeared in the plaza but he did not prance. He walked slowly around the plaza, stopping at each house to throw ashes over himself with his single bark cloth arm. The villagers said he was in mourning because he had to leave by dusk and would miss the company of men. Silently the people watched the once gay and graceful *mani* lumber out of the village. The men and boys followed him into the forest. Then the gunman split open the mask, to insure the spirit's exit and eventual return to his forest home, and hurled it over the edge of the cliff into the bush below.

A few months after the *mani* hunting festival, the shotgun cult as I had known it in Taute ceased to function. All but one of the able young men of the hamlet of Kafiere went off to work on a coastal plantation for two years. With no young men, the ceremonial activities of the hunting and curing cults were suspended and the fault-finding meet-

ings halted until their return. The drama and excitement of the previous months had vanished with the men.

# 9 | HYDRAULIC DEVELOPMENT AND POLITICAL RESPONSE IN THE VALLEY OF OAXACA, MEXICO

## Susan H. Lees

*As with the Wape people of New Guinea and their new weapons, farmers in
the valley of Oaxaca, Mexico, are experiencing social, economic, and political
changes at an unprecedented rate. Although it is impossible to ascribe a single
cause to these changes, Susan H. Lees tries to show how they are related to
one another and especially the role of one technological feature, irrigation.
Particularly worth noting is that the use of new technology here too involves
increasing dependence upon outside authorities and economic systems.*

*In the Oaxaca Valley the persistence of traditional social relations within
agricultural communities depended upon relative isolation and relative independence from higher levels of government. These traditional relations involved a high degree of participation in community affairs by community members.*

*In order to increase agricultural production, however, Oaxaca villages had to
adopt new and more elaborate technical control of water resources. The technology was too expensive and too complex to obtain without outside help,
usually from government agencies. Reliance upon external sources of technological assistance contributed to an erosion of relative local isolation and autonomy; social change generally followed.*

One of the first things we learn when we study peasant society as a
cultural type is that the structure and operation of local community
organization is to a great extent a function of a larger social unit. Local
community political, social, and economic organizations must respond
not only to the requirements of their peasant members, but also to
specific conditions set by national policy, markets, class structure and
so forth. Eric Wolf (1955:457) has suggested, for example, that the
closed corporate community—a peasant community type found widely
in the highlands of Mesoamerica—was a social adaptation to conditions
set by Spanish colonial policy. Francois Chevalier (1963), Charles Gibson (1964) and William Taylor (1972) have shown how specific historical
policies during the Spanish colonial period served to shape Mexican
political, social and economic responses at the local community level.

These studies and others indicate that a full understanding of "micro-politics"—the political processes at the local level—requires investigation into the manner in which local units are linked with regional and national units, and integrated into the larger social systems.

The focus of this paper is upon the transformation of traditional, closed, corporate community political organizations in the Valley of Oaxaca, Mexico, to modernized forms. This transformation involves a systemic change in the relationship between local community units and national-level units. We will examine some ways in which the changes come about in the Valley, and the impact of this kind of change upon local political organization. The area of change investigated here will be that associated with agriculture in general, and irrigation in particular, both of which are critical elements in the many transformations occurring in Oaxaca today. Ethnographic material presented in this paper was gathered in the field during the years 1967 through 1970.[1]

This analysis borrows some concepts from ecology. One is that of *homeostasis,* a negative feedback process in which a system (or a subsystem, in this case) maintains a consistent relationship among certain variables under changing conditions through corrective adjustments. Certain elements of traditional community organization will be viewed as homeostatic mechanisms, in that they function to stabilize relations between members of a community and between those members and their resources through measures which tend to prevent deviation beyond a limited range. A second concept is *linearization,* a positive feedback mechanism in which lower-order controls are permanently bypassed for higher-order controls, with the result that the relations between parts of the system become altered under changing conditions. In social systems, this mechanism contributes to the process of centralization, an increasing "degree of linkages between the various subsystems and the highest-order controls in the society," (see Flannery 1972:409). The process of centralization will be seen here as resulting from certain changes in resource use and technology of exploitation which have altered the relationship between the community and the national governments.

Flannery suggests that linearization occurs after lower-order controls "have failed to maintain relevant variables in range for some critical length of time" (Flannery 1972:413). The critical variable in question here is the availability of ground and sub-surface water for irrigation. When, for reasons which will be explained below, traditional institutional and technological devices no longer work together to maintain adequate supplies of water, communities must turn to higher levels of the political hierarchy to provide access to this essential resource. By replacing local-level controls with national-level ones, communities lose relative autonomy and thereby lose one of the essential conditions for their operation in the traditional manner. Consequently, the internal political structure of local communities becomes altered in response to change in their relations with national level organization.

It is assumed in this paper that political organization and economic organization are not only mutually interdependent, but so intimately connected that it is impossible to understand one without understanding the other. Furthermore, as in tribal societies, many of the traditional institutions discussed here are difficult to classify as either political or economic, but are best viewed as both. It seems particularly important to consider the role of political organization in the regulation of economic variables, and vice versa, in the context of the question asked here: why are certain political changes at the community level taking place at *this* point in time, and not another?

## TRADITIONAL COMMUNITY GOVERNMENT: A HOMEOSTATIC SYSTEM

The traditional form of local community government in the Valley of Oaxaca depended largely upon three interrelated factors: isolation and autonomy; members' participation in local government through rotation of offices; and, under-production and stability.

1. *Isolation and Autonomy:* That relative political isolation and autonomy constituted an essential feature of traditional local organization has been established in the literature on closed corporate communities for some time (Wolf 1955). The Spanish colonial policy of indirect rule set a precedent for local autonomy during the seventeenth and eighteenth centuries which was outstandingly effective in the Valley of Oaxaca (Taylor 1972). Key features of this policy were the bestowal of communal rights to communal land to municipio units, the establishment of local official structures for internal self-government, and corporate responsibility for adherence to state legislation on such matters as taxation and tribute in the form of corvée labor. Colonial precedents for local autonomy persisted to some extent after independence, and were enhanced by the outcome of the twentieth century Mexican Revolution. As a consequence of the Revolution, land reform restoring agricultural lands to the control of corporate communities and ejidos, and the virtual elimination of the regional aristocracy, *hacendados* and major mine owners, were two important factors enhancing local village autonomy. Cultural, linguistic, class, economic, and still other barriers also contributed to the persistence of a substantial gap between rural peasants and national government agencies.

A high degree of variation among contemporary communities as seen in the details of local administrative forms attests to a considerable period of local autonomy. For example, villages vary significantly today in the organizational forms and personnel associated with water control: in some cases, access to canal water is directed by the *presidente,* sometimes by elected *regidores* or *jueces,* sometimes by special committees, sometimes by appointed low-level officials (Lees 1973:37–38). A remarkably strong tendency toward local autonomy in the Valley of Oaxaca is also evidenced by the proliferation of small independent municipios of a size well below that legislated by national policy (Pérez Jiménez 1968:9–45). Finally, linguistic diversity, in the form of marked dialectical differences in the Zapotec language still widely spoken in the Valley, not only attests to but contributes to relative isolation of villages from one another, as well as from the Spanish-speaking central government.

2. *Participation in local government through rotation of offices:* If communities are to govern themselves, they must provide their own officials. The *cargo* system or civil-religious hierarchy, which organizes recruitment for officeholding among villagers, has, like local autonomy, been the subject of considerable research in this area (see Cancian 1965). Most, if not all, adult male community members have been obliged to expend time, energy and often considerable amounts of money in discharging a social obligation to serve the community in a series of ranked political and religious offices. Their prescribed careers of a public service require that they progress from low-level posts to higher level positions of authority in the community administrative structure. Rotation of offices among these members is to ensure that no one is either over-exploited by the community, or gains too much political power. Although prestige accrues to those who serve in the highest offices, this honor is not frequently sought after, but rather is seen as the reward for doing one's duty to the community.

Service in both political and religious offices requires substantial monetary outlays (Corbett 1973:22). It has been argued convincingly that ceremonial sponsorship involved in holding religious offices in particular serves as a wealth-levelling device, in that as financial surpluses become available to individuals they are siphoned off to ceremonial funds rather than being accumulated so as to exaggerate financial inequalities in the community (Wolf 1955:458). Those inequalities which do exist may be sustained by the cargo institution (Cancian 1965: 140; Webster 1968). But because a good proportion of families in each community are not capable of providing such an outlay by themselves, the system of rotation of offices could not work without a means of distributing expendable wealth in such a way that all had access to wealth when they needed it. This distribution is frequently achieved by a traditional institution of delayed reciprocity, called *guelaguetza* in many Oaxacan communities, which circulates loans and debts among community members so that all can participate in ceremonial sponsorship and political office. Just as all take turns at serving in public office, so do all take turns at receiving one another's help.

3. *Underproduction and Stability:* The political system just described seems to be accomplished in traditional communities by a consistently low level of agricultural production and the maintenance of a relatively stable output through time. Dr. Anne Kirkby, a cultural geographer who studied land and water use in the Valley over a period of several years, pointed out that even taking into account the potential of the most primitive technology, Oaxaca Valley farmers were underusing their resources (Kirkby 1973:147). That is to say that, given their technological level, farmers were producing less than they could. Dr. Kirkby argues that both under-production and long-run stability are

indirect consequences of the cargo system and institutions of delayed reciprocity. Heavy demands on a farmer's time, energy and finances imposed by the cargo system and its associated obligations on the one hand, and limited opportunities for other productive uses of resources on the other, combine to give little incentive for economic development on the part of individuals. Farmers aim not at maximization of production, but at what Kirkby (1973:149) calls "satisficing" that is, they work to produce what they think will be an adequate income from year to year, but in a year predicted to be very good (i.e. plenty of rain at the right times), they work and plant less, in order to have more time to devote to discharging political and social obligations which provide the main paths to success and prestige in the community. Guelaguetza, the delayed exchange system, provides some degree of insurance for individual farmers against bad years, hence stability and flexibility over the long run for all (Kirkby 1972:15).

Thus, traditional community, political, social and economic institutions which developed in response to a socio-political environment inducing isolation and autonomy, functioned to regulate relations between farms and their natural environmental resources, particularly land and water. This regulation was homeostatic in effect, maintaining levels of use and production within a restricted range over time. Farmers responded to year-to-year variations in the natural environment, specifically water availability, in terms of local perturbations and regulatory devices. When water was more plentiful, acreage was reduced, so that as a result, more water was restored to sub-surface reservoirs. In bad years, when water was scarce, individuals would supplement their incomes through small-scale loans from others, and thus not be forced to drop out of community participation nor to radically alter their means of resource exploitation. It should be noted here that while land often tends to be treated as private property, and reduction of acreage by an individual farmer would not benefit another, water is a shared resource, and reduction in its use means that more is available for others, both within the community and, if it is plentiful enough for two or more communities to share, for members of other communities. In the ways that have been discussed traditional political institutions at the village level have served to regulate the relationships of farmers to a critical resource—water—whether it becomes abundant or scarce in its year-to-year variation.

The functioning of the social and political traditions as regulatory devices depended, of course, upon their effectiveness as responses to both wider social environments and the local natural environment. In a number of ways, they served as a mediator between the two. If local environmental resources were to vary beyond tolerable limits—for example if water were to become too scarce to permit successful farming —then villagers would not be able to continue to govern their use of these resources through traditional local institutions, but would have to reduce their village autonomy to get outside help. Similarly, if external political intervention were to reduce the effectiveness of traditional institutions, farmers would alter the means by which they exploited environmental resources, thereby affecting the availability of the resources themselves.

## PRESSURES FOR CHANGE AND RESPONSE: LINEARIZATION

Pressures for change in traditional political institutions have arisen, in fact, in both environmental sectors. The sources of change have been political, ideological, economic and technological in character.

1. *Political change:* Federal governmental initiatives have influenced directly and indirectly, the foundations of traditional community organization, particularly in the past decade or so. The government's motive in doing so, clearly enunciated in a variety of policy statements, is to raise the productive capacity of agricultural enterprise in rural areas (Secretaria de Agricultura y Ganderia 1968–69). Since the primary variable affecting productivity in the Valley of Oaxaca, as in other regions of Mexico, is control over water resources, hydraulic development is one of its major foci. In the Valley of Oaxaca itself, this development takes the form of constructing numbers of small-scale facilities including dams, lifting devices, and wells.

The Secretaria de Recursos Hydraulicos (SRH) of the federal government delegates the tasks of small-scale hydraulic development such as that found in the Valley, to the Secretaria de Agricultura y Ganderia (SAG). The SAG not only gives aid in materials, funds and engineering advice, but has a policy of improving the use of new facilities by reorganizing traditional local control organizations. It prescribes the form and membership of the local administration of the facilities, which is responsible not to the local community at large (as would formerly have been the case) but to the SAG, an agency of the central government. Simply in terms of formal characteristics, this policy undermines local autonomy and directly integrates local organization with the federal apparatus. Then, of course, dependence upon the federal agency for economic and technical aid in the maintenance of the new facilities cements the purely formal tie in practice. Both take activities and authority which once fell to traditional institutional processes out of context, making them part of a non-local system.

When the federal government installs a new facility, such as a dam, on a watercourse which is shared by more than one community, it also alters a previous administrative form. Traditionally, upstream communities controlled access to water sources originating in or passing through their territory, generally receiving payment from downstream farmers—a valuable source of income. But when the central government intervenes, upstream communities lose control—which now falls to the SRH—and hence lose both control and income. Once again, in relation to water resources, local organization gives way to a larger organization, and non-local imperatives. The most striking examples of this process are cases in the northern and central sectors of the Valley, where major streams which were once governed by upstream communities and which were used to irrigate extensive farmlands of the piedmont and upper alluvium, are now diverted in large part by the state government, so that the waters go to fulfill urban and industrial needs at the expense of irrigated agriculture (Lees 1973:43).

2. *Ideological Change:* One need not look far for sources of change in the outlook of Oaxacan farmers. The spread of national primary education, improved mass communication and transportation, growth of markets and urban and industrial development, have influenced world view and the opportunity for achieving changed goals in the rural population. Material gains begin to provide alternatives to ritual or ceremonial achievements as paths to prestige. Like the state governmental agencies, the rural population hopes to increase agricultural productivity through hydraulic development, as a means of improving their material welfare.

Because the outside world provides the means to material improvements through market opportunities, technological innovations and access to governmental aid, villagers have changed their attitudes toward recruitment to and participation in, community political office. In traditional communities, the prerequisite for full participation in public office was ceremonial sponsorship, an activity so costly that it was usually open only to older men who had spent a lifetime in saving and investing in this ritual institution. The prestige gained in this sponsorship was deemed adequate and necessary for service in high political office. But now, particularly in the face of increased ties with the state government, literacy rather than ceremonial prestige increasingly takes precedence as a prerequisite for office-holding. As a result, high office holders tend to be younger than before, since the older generation has a higher degree of illiteracy, and more and more communities are eliminating the ceremonial prerequisite altogether (Lees 1973:20). Releasing community members from this requirement for participation also releases funds which were previously absorbed by ceremonial expenditures, and makes them available for other types of investment.

A shift from ceremonial to materially-based prestige tends to channel such surpluses to investments in the productive process which result in intensified exploitation of resources. The goal of the "modernized" farmer is not to "satisfice" but to aim toward maximization of profits from agriculture (Kirkby 1973:149). This new orientation conflicts with traditional attitudes toward community service and supports the tendency to abandon the traditional institutions.

3. *Economic and technological change:* Traditional agriculture in the Valley is subsistence-oriented, though a certain proportion of the best arable land has always been devoted to small scale cash-crop production. In the northern piedmont area, an important irrigated cash-crop was once wheat. In the central and southern alluvial zones, flowers and garden vegetables were the most important irrigated market product. These crops involved two different types of hydraulic techniques: canal and pot irrigation. Canal irrigation was generally achieved simply by diverting small piedmont streams with stone and brush dams to adja-

cent piedmont and upper alluvial fields, using occasional small wood and stone aqueducts and earthen canals. Canal systems could be maintained in good working order through a day of communal labor each year on the part of the entire community (Lees 1973:29). Pot irrigation was a more private matter. It was restricted to the alluvial zone where the water rose to within three meters of the surface. After plowing every year, farmers excavated numbers of shallow wells in their fields, from which they drew buckets of water by hand to be poured over individual plants, one by one. The intensive labor requirements of pot irrigation restricted its use to less than 10% of the total cultivated land (Kirkby 1973:42), but as a means of providing cash, it had considerable economic importance.

The growth of an urban market for milk products has stimulated a new dairy industry, particularly in the northern area of the valley. This new industry has in turn provided a market for a new cash crop: alfalfa. Alfalfa is now being grown extensively throughout the Valley. Second only to corn, it is the major irrigated cash crop in the Valley.

Alfalfa requires very large quantities of water in order to be profitable, and since it is grown continuously for about seven years, it requires water during the winter dry season as well as during the summer wet season. Thus in the piedmont, it places very heavy demands upon stream resources using canal irrigation. It is unfeasible to try to irrigate alfalfa by pot-irrigation techniques, so that where it is planted in the alluvium, this method is replaced by pumps and furrows. That is, the sub-surface water table is tapped with greater intensity and efficiency by the use of diesel pumps. Labor is still quite intensive, since alfalfa is harvested in both regions every 20–30 days by hand.

Since alfalfa requires a great deal of water, unprecedented demands are being made upon the hydraulic resources themselves. Farmers must turn increasingly to new technological devices to help supply them with adequate quantities of water. In the upper piedmont zone, generally with the help of government agencies, villages install cement dams and reservoirs to tap stream resources more effectively, so that year-round supplies will be available. But this decreases water availability for lower piedmont and alluvial villages which formerly used the same resources. The latter have begun to sink deep wells to levels of 30–40 meters to tap sub-surface water supplies, again, with government aid. This process took place along the Rio de los Sabinos, for example (Lees 1973:43). While upstream San Juan del Estado tapped the stream in its new cement reservoir, downstream Santa Marta Elta and Magdalena Apasco shifted from the stream to reliance upon the subsurface water supplied by government-installed pumps. This intensive pumping, however, reduces the level of the water table downstream, making pot-irrigation unreliable and sometimes impossible in the alluvial zone. Therefore, here too, farmers turn increasingly to deeper wells and more powerful pumps in order to continue growing cash crops.

The fact that water is being used in greater quantities, year-round, means that this resource is no longer available to farmers using traditional techniques. Even farmers not wishing to grow alfalfa or other cash crops must turn to new technological devices in order to continue to irrigate. And this shift need not always be a community decision, as it is in the upper piedmont, for private wells are affected by the exploitation of upstream irrigators as well as public streams and wells. Thus a shift in cash-crops grown in certain areas of the valley has had the effect of increasing the cost of production by reducing the availability of the essential resource: water. As it becomes more expensive to get water, however, it also becomes more necessary to produce cash-crops to pay for technical devices to obtain water at all.

Thus, both upstream and downstream farmers find that in order to pay for their hydraulic facilities, they have to earn and keep earning capital. They now have not only the opportunity to do this, but the incentive of necessity; there is no possibility to return to the earlier conditions now that water resources once available by simple, traditional means are beyond reach. As a result, farmers become increasingly reluctant to spend time and funds discharging social and political responsibilities, now that they have both opportunities and incentives to divert them to capital-oriented enterprises. Thus, economic imperatives buttress ideological shifts in undermining traditional values associated with active participation in community affairs. Furthermore, this undermining of traditional values reduces the effectiveness of community institutions in maintaining ecological equilibrium in ways which were mentioned above, in that farmers intensify, rather than limit, their exploitation of resources.

Thus, farmers begin to over-use their water resources, and experience shortages which can only be corrected by increasing investments in technological innovations which tap water at more remote or deeper locations. This shift in economic orientation and technological usage unavoidably accompanies a shift in political orientation.

First, it is obvious that because communities, as well as individual farmers, cannot construct and maintain their new hydraulic facilities without outside help, they become increasingly dependent upon outside agencies just as they become increasingly dependent upon their new facilities. These outside agencies include, of course, the government itself, with its engineers, administrative bureaucrats, and so forth, but also agencies providing materials such as mechanical equipment, cement, petroleum, transportation and skilled labor.

Second, because hydraulic development here involves extra-local cooperation, it is likely that political orientation will become increasingly extra-local as well. Community members are likely to take more of an interest in national and state political parties, when they see that they have something at stake in that sector—a new dam, a new pump. Thus the effect of an economic change involving greater dependence on the part of local communities, while diminishing the control they have upon the use of their immediate resources, may also increase their participation in national affairs.

To say which of these changes had priority, either in time or in importance, would be difficult and probably misleading, in that they are interdependent. Suffice it to say that they occur contemporaneously, and that they affect one another in such a way as to increase one another's rate and impact. They are all part of the process by which a national system is now becoming more centralized through the establishment of strong linkages among its own parts which were once more or less buffered from one another by institutions maintaining relative local autonomy.

An important aspect of this change is an increasing responsiveness to regulation and controls at a higher level, more remote from local natural and social environment and more general in their operation. National market fluctuations and demands for particular products such as alfalfa, provide examples of new regulators of production. However, federal allocation of irrigation water according to its own political and economic priorities illustrates the growing influence of higher-level control.

## CONCLUSIONS

Subsequent to the Revolution of 1910, particularly during the 1930's, "progressive" factions in a number of Oaxacan villages attempted to abolish the costly ceremonial component of the cargo system, and in a number of cases they succeeded. However, in those cases reported or known to the author, such as in Santa Maria Guelace (Webster 1968), Matatlán (Kirkby 1973:148), and Absasolo, these villages returned to their ceremonial traditions within a few years of the effort at reform. While a certain proportion of the community members throughout the valley, particularly the younger men, continued to resent and oppose traditions which they viewed as impediments to economic advancement, custom prevailed. The conservative element of these communities consisted of older men who controlled (and still control) most of the land (Lees 1973:53–78). This element valued the social stability maintained by the ceremonial tradition more highly than potential economic gains to be attained by their abandonment.

But such an attitude was possible only so long as economic survival was possible under traditional conditions. Once environmental conditions began to change, the traditional framework could not operate and still allow farmers to "satisfice." Decreasing and insufficient water supplies would not allow farmers to continue to minimize time and energy spent on agricultural pursuits, nor to devote surpluses to ceremonial sponsorship. Thus, changing economic and environmental conditions made possible a breakdown in social traditions which could not be accomplished simply by attitude, reasoning, and reformatory decree.

While environmental changes such as a decrease in the availability of water through traditional means may provide or enhance a motive to reform social customs, such reforms have a feed-back effect upon the environmental conditions themselves. Villages which have abandoned the ceremonial expenditures of the mayordomia have also made substantial economic progress which in turn leads to intensified resource exploitation. This has been the case in a number of villages already, such as Zautla (Dennis 1968) and Soledad Elta (Iszaevich Fajerstein 1969). Social change can be seen then as both a cause and an effect of environmental change.

But neither type of change could be accounted for without consideration of the role played by the central government and other extra-local organizations. We must turn to the relationship between these and local communities if we wish to understand why these changes did not occur in the 1930's and why they do occur now.

## NOTE

1. This research was carried out in association with a project—the Prehistoric Cultural Ecology of the Valley of Oaxaca—directed by Professor Kent Flannery, and funded by grants from the National Institute of Mental Health and the National Science Foundation.

## REFERENCES

CANCIAN, FRANK, 1965, *Economies and prestige in a Maya Community*. Stanford: Stanford University Press.

CHEVALIER, FRANCOIS, 1963, *Land and Society in Colonial Mexico*. Berkeley: University of California Press.

CORBETT, JACK, 1973, "Aspects of recruitment to Civil Office in a Mexican Community," paper given at AAA meeting in New Orleans.

DENNIS, PHILLIP, 1968, "Wealth in Zautla," unpublished Dissertation, Stanford University.

FLANNERY, KENT V., 1972, "The Cultural Evolution of Civilizations," *Annual Review of Ecology and Systematics*, 3.

GIBSON, CHARLES, 1964, *The Aztecs Under Spanish Rule*. Stanford: Stanford University Press.

ISZAEVICH FAJERSTEIN, ABRAHAM, 1969, "Soledad Etla: Estudio de un Proceso de Modernización." Tesis Professional (M.A.), Escuela Nacional de Anthropología e Historia. Mexico, D.F.

KIRKBY, ANNE V. T., 1972, "Perception of Rainfall Variability and Agricultural and Social Adaptation to Hazard by Peasant Cultivators in the Valley of Oaxaca, Mexico," paper presented to Man and Environment Commission, 22nd International Geographic Congress, Calgary, Canada.

———, 1973, "The Use of Land and Water Resources in the Past and Present in the Valley of Oaxaca, Mexico," Memoirs of the Museum of Anthropology, #5. Ann Arbor: University of Michigan Press.

LEES, SUSAN H., 1973, "Sociopolitical Aspects of Canal Irrigation in the Valley of Oaxaca," Memoirs of the Museum of Anthropology, #6. Ann Arbor: University of Michigan Press.

PÉREZ JIMÉNEZ, GUSTAVO, 1968, *La Institución del Municipio Libre*. Mexico: Costa-Amie.

SECRETARIA DE AGRICULTURA Y GRANADERÍA, 1968–69, *Boletin Informativo de la Dirección General de Ingeniería Agrícola* #1, 2, 3. Mexico, D.F.

TAYLOR, WILLIAM B., 1972, *Landlord and Peasant in Colonial Oaxaca.* Stanford: Stanford University Press.

WEBSTER, STEVEN, 1968, "The Religious Cargo System and Socio-Economic Differentiation in Santa Maria Guelace," unpublished manuscript.

WOLF, ERIC, 1955, "Types of Latin American Peasantry," *American Anthropologist,* 57:3.

# 10 | THE GREAT SISAL SCHEME
## Daniel Gross

*In many, if not most, areas of the world experiencing technological development, negative impacts have occurred. In this paper about the introduction of a new cash crop, sisal, into northeastern Brazil, Daniel R. Gross tells a story all too common in the developing world. It begins with what it was hoped would bring an economic "boom": the adoption of a crop for sale on the world market and of the technology for processing it. Once the population of this region had become committed to this crop and the associated technology, however, prices for the crop fell dramatically. Gross tells of the consequences of commitment to sisal for the people of northeastern Brazil; the story exemplifies similar problems confronting peoples committed to producing cotton, rubber, sugar, and other cash crops.*

In northeastern Brazil, the lush green coastal vegetation almost hides the endemic human misery of the region. Unless you look closely, the busy streets of Salvador and Recife and the waving palm trees mask the desperation of city slums, the poverty of plantation workers. When you leave the well-traveled coastal highways and go—usually on a dusty, rutted road—toward the interior, the signs of suffering become more and more apparent.

The transition is quick and brutal. Within 50 miles the vegetation changes from palm, tropical fruit, and dark-green broad-leafed trees to scrawny brush only slightly greener than the dusty earth. Nearly every plant is armed with spines or thorns. The hills are jagged, with hard faces of rock exposed. This is the *sertão,* the interior of northeastern Brazil.

If the *sertão* were honest desert, it would probably contain only a few inhabitants and a fair share of human misery. But the *sertão* is deceitful and fickle. It will smile for several years in a row, with sufficient rains arriving for the growing seasons. Gardens and crops will flourish. Cattle fatten. Then, without warning, another growing season comes, but the rains don't. The drought may go on, year after dusty year. Crops fail. Cattle grow thin and die. Humans begin to do the same. In bad droughts, the people of the *sertão* migrate to other regions by the thousands.

The bandits, the mystics, the droughts and migrants, the dreams and schemes of the *sertão* hold a special place in Brazilian folklore, literature, and song. Even at its worst, the *sertão* has been a fertile ground for the human imagination.

For two years, I studied the impact of sisal crops—a recent dream and scheme—on the people of the *sertão*. Taking an ecological approach, I found that sisal, which some poetic dreamers call "green gold," has greatly changed northeastern Brazil. But the changes have not been what the economic planners anticipated. And misery has not left the *sertão*.

I lived in Vila Nova, a small village with a population of less than 500 about an hour's drive from the town of Victoria in Bahia State. Vila Nova is striking only for its drabness. Weeds grow in the middle of unpaved streets. Facing the plaza is an incomplete series of nondescript row houses. Some have faded pastel façades, others are mud brown because their owners never managed to plaster over the rough adobe walls. The village looks decadent, yet the oldest building is less than 20 years old and most were built after 1963.

Cattle raisers settled the *sertão* 400 years ago when the expanding sugar plantations of the coast demanded large supplies of beef and traction animals. A "civilization of leather" developed, with generations of colorful and intrepid cowboys *(vaqueiros)* clad entirely in rawhide to protect themselves against the thorny scrub vegetation. As the population of the *sertão* grew, many *sertanejos* settled down to subsistence farming. Gradually the entire region became a cul-de-sac, with many small and medium-sized estates occupied by descendants of the *vaqueiros* and others who had drifted into the region.

Life was never easy in this thorny land, for the work was hard and the environment cruel. Yet cooperation and mutual assistance provided assurance of survival even to the poorest. The chief crops were manioc, beans, and corn, and most of what was grown was consumed by the cultivator's family. Most families received some share of meat and milk, and consumed highly nutritious foods like beans and squash, in addition to starchy foods like manioc flour.

When droughts menaced the region all but the wealthiest ranchers migrated temporarily to the coast to work on the sugar plantations. When the rains came again to the *sertão,* they nearly always returned, for the work in the cane fields was brutal and labor relations had not changed greatly from the time when slaves worked the plantations.

Originally from Mexico, sisal was introduced to Brazil early in this century and reached the *sertão* in the 1930's. Farmers found sisal useful for hedgerows because its tough, pointed leaves effectively kept out cattle. The cellulose core of the long sisal leaf contains hard fibers, which can be twisted together into twine and rope. When World War

II cut off the supply of Manila hemp to the United States, buyers turned to Brazil for fiber. At first only hedgerow sisal was exploited, but the state of Bahia offered incentives for planting sisal as a cash crop. Since sisal plants require about four years to mature, Brazil did not begin to export the fiber in significant quantities until 1945. The demand persisted, and by 1951, Brazil was selling actively in the world market as prices rose.

In Vila Nova, a young entrepreneur who owned a mule team, David Castro, heard about the prices being paid for sisal fiber and planted the first acres of sisal in 1951. By 1968, in the county of Victoria where Vila Nova is located, so many people had caught "sisal fever" that half of the total land area was planted in the crop. Sisal is easily transplanted and cultivated, requires little care, and is highly resistant to drought. It has some drawbacks as a cultivated plant, however. At least one annual weeding is necessary or else the field may become choked with thorn bushes, weeds, and suckers (unwanted small sisal plants growing from the base of parent plants). A field abandoned for two years becomes unusable, practically unreclaimable. Despite these difficulties, many landowners planted sisal, especially in 1951 and 1962, years of high prices on the world market.

From the outset, sisal produced differential rewards for those who planted it. Owners of small plots (ten acres or less) planted proportionately more of their land in sisal than did large landowners. Many who owned just a few acres simply planted all their land in sisal in expectation of large profits. This deprived them of whatever subsistence they had managed to scratch out of the ground in the past. But work was easy to find because the need for labor in the sisal fields grew rapidly. When, after four years, the crops were ready to harvest, many small landholders discovered to their dismay that prices had dropped sharply, and that harvest teams did not want to work small crops. They had planted sisal with dreams of new clothes, new homes, even motor vehicles purchased with sisal profits, but found their fields choked with unusable sisal and became permanent field laborers harvesting sisal on large landholdings. In this way, sisal created its own labor force.

The separation of sisal fiber from the leaf is known as decortication. In Brazil, this process requires enormous amounts of manual labor. The decorticating machine is basically a spinning rasp powered by a gasoline or diesel motor. Sisal leaves are fed into it by hand, and the spinning rasp beats out the pulp or residue leaving only the fibers, which the worker pulls out of the whirling blades. Mounted on a trailer, the machine is well adapted to the scattered small-scale plantations of northeastern Brazil.

The decortication process requires constant labor for harvesting the year round. Sisal leaves, once cut, must be defibered quickly before the hot sun renders them useless. Each decorticating machine requires a crew of about seven working in close coordination. The first step is harvesting. Two cutters move from plant to plant, first lopping off the needle-sharp thorns from the leaves, then stooping to sever each leaf at the base. A transporter, working with each cutter, gathers the leaves and loads them on a burro. The leaves are taken to the machine and placed on a low stage for the defiberer to strip, one by one. A residue man removes the pulpy mass stripped from the leaves from under the motor, supplies the defiberer with leaves, and bundles and ties the freshly stripped fiber. Each bundle is weighed and counted in the day's production. Finally, the dryer spreads the wet, greenish fiber in the sun, where it dries and acquires its characteristic blond color.

For the planters and sisal buyers, this method of decortication operates profitably, but for the workers it exacts a terrible cost. The decorticating machine requires a man to stand in front of the whirling rasp for four or five hours at a shift, introducing first the foot and then the point of each leaf. The worker pulls against the powerful motor, which draws the leaf into the mouth of the machine. After half of each leaf is defibered, the defiberer grasps the raw fiber to insert the remaining half of the leaf. There is a constant danger that the fiber will entangle his hand and pull it into the machine. Several defiberers have lost arms this way. The strain and danger would seem to encourage slow and deliberate work; but in fact, defiberers decorticate about 25 leaves per minute. This is because the crew is paid according to the day's production of fiber. Although the defiberer is the highest-paid crew member, many of them must work both morning and afternoon shifts to make ends meet.

A residue man's work is also strenuous. According to measurements I made, this job requires that a man lift and carry about 2,700 pounds of material per hour. The residue man, moreover, does not work in shifts. He works as long as the machinery is running. The remaining jobs on the crew are less demanding and may be held by women or adolescents, but even these jobs are hard, requiring frequent lifting and stooping in the broiling semidesert sun.

With their own fields in sisal, to earn money the villagers had to work at harvesting sisal for large landowners. And because wages were low, more and more people had to work for families to survive. In 1968 two-thirds of all men and women employed in Vila Nova worked full time in the sisal decorticating process. Many of these were youths. Of 33 village boys between the ages of 10 and 14, 24 worked on sisal crews. Most people had completely abandoned subsistence agriculture.

Sisal brought other significant changes in the life of Vila Nova. Because most villagers no longer grew their food, it now had to be imported. Numerous shops, stocking beans, salt pork, and manioc flour, grew up in the village. A few villagers with capital or good contacts among wholesalers in the town of Victoria built small businesses based on this need. Other villagers secured credit from sisal buyers in Victoria to purchase sisal decorticating machinery.

The shopkeepers and sisal machine owners in the village formed a new economic class on whom the other villagers were economically dependent. The wealthier group enjoyed many advantages. Rather than going to work on the sisal machines, most of the children of these entrepreneurs went to school. All of the upper group married in a socially prescribed way: usually a church wedding with civil ceremonies as well. But among the workers, common-law marriages were frequent, reflecting their lack of resources for celebrating this important event.

CALORIE BUDGET OF A SISAL WORKER'S HOUSEHOLD

|  | Average daily caloric intake | Minimum daily caloric requirements | Percent of need met | Percent of standard weight of children |
|---|---|---|---|---|
| Household | 9,392 | 12,592 | 75% | |
| Worker | 3,642 | 3,642 | 100 | |
| Wife | 2,150 | 2,150 | 100 | |
| Son (age 8) | 1,112 | 2,100 | 53 | 62% |
| Daughter (6) | 900 | 1,700 | 53 | 70 |
| Son (5) | 900 | 1,700 | 53 | 85 |
| Son (3) | 688 | 1,300 | 53 | 90 |

The only villagers who became truly affluent were David Castro and his cousin. These men each owned extensive sisal plantations and several decorticating units. Most importantly, each became middlemen, collecting sisal in warehouses in the village and trucking the fiber into Victoria. David, moreover, owned the largest store in the village. Since the village was located on David's land, he sold house plots along the streets. He also acted as the representative of the dominant political party in Victoria, serving as a ward boss during elections and as an unofficial but effective police power. There was a difference between David and the large ranch owners of the past. While wealthy men were formerly on close terms with their dependents, helping them out during tough times, David's relations with the villagers were cold, businesslike, and exploitative. Most of the villagers disliked him, both for his alleged stinginess and because he never had time to talk to anyone.

During my stay in Vila Nova I gradually became aware of these changes in the social and economic structure. But I hoped to establish that the introduction of sisal had also resulted in a quantitative, ecological change in the village. At the suggestion of Dr. Barbara A. Underwood of the Institute of Human Nutrition at Columbia University, I undertook an intensive study to determine what influence sisal had on diet and other factors of a few representative households. When I looked at household budgets, I quickly discovered that those households that depended entirely on wages from sisal work spent nearly all their money on food. Families with few or no children or with several able-bodied workers seemed to be holding their own. But families with few workers or several dependents were less fortunate. To understand the condition of these families, I collected information not only on cash budgets but also on household *energy budgets.* Each household expends not only money, but also energy in the form of calories in performing work. "Income" in the latter case is the caloric value of the foods consumed by these households. By carefully measuring the amount and kind of food consumed, I was able to determine the total inflow and outflow of energy in individual households.

For example, Miguel Costa is a residue man who works steadily on a sisal unit belonging to a nearby planter. He lives in Vila Nova in a two-room adobe hut with his wife and four small children, ranging in age from three to eight. During the seven-day test period, Miguel worked at the sisal motor four and a half days, while his wife stayed home with the children. I was able to estimate Miguel's caloric expenditures during the test period. During the same period, I visited his home after every meal where his wife graciously permitted me to weigh the family's meager food supplies to determine food consumption. Each day the supply of beans diminished by less than one-half pound and the weight of the coarse manioc flour eaten with beans dropped by two or three pounds. Manioc flour is almost pure starch, high in calories but low in essential nutrients. At the beginning of the week about half a pound of fatty beef and pork were consumed each day, but this was exhausted by midweek. The remainder of the family's calories were consumed in the form of sugar, bread, and boiled sweet manioc, all high in calories but low in other nutrients.

Estimating the caloric requirements of the two adults from their activities and the children's by Food and Agriculture Organization minimum requirements, the household had a minimum need of 88,142 calories for the week. The household received only 65,744 calories, or 75 percent of need. Since the two adults did not lose weight while maintaining their regular levels of activity, they were apparently meeting their total calorie requirements. Miguel, for example, had been working steadily at his job for weeks before the test and continued to do so for weeks afterward. Had he not been maintaining himself calorically, he could not have sustained his performance at his demanding job. Despite his small stature (5 feet, 4 inches) Miguel required some 3,642 calories per day to keep going at the job. And Miguel's wife evidently also maintained herself calorically—pregnant at the time of my visit, she later gave birth to a normal child.

The caloric deficit in Miguel's household, then, was almost certainly being made up by systematically depriving the dependent children of sufficient calories. This was not intentional, nor were the parents aware of it. Nor could Miguel have done anything about it even if he had understood this process. If he were to work harder or longer to earn more money, he would incur greater caloric costs and would have to consume more. If he were to reduce his food intake to leave more food for his children, he would be obliged by his own physiology to work less, thereby earning less. If he were to provide his household with foods higher in caloric content (for example, more manioc), he would almost certainly push his children over the brink into a severe nutritional crisis that they might not survive for lack of protein and essential vitamins.

Thus, Miguel, a victim of ecological circumstances, is maintaining his family against terrible odds.

Miguel's children respond to this deprivation in a predictable manner. Nature has provided a mechanism to compensate for caloric deficiencies during critical growth periods: the rate of growth simply slows down. As a result, Miguel's children, and many other children of sisal workers, are much smaller than properly nourished children of the same age. The longer the deprivation goes on the more pronounced the tendency: thus Miguel's youngest boy, who is three, is 90 percent of standard weight for his age. The five-year-old boy is 85 percent; the six-year-old girl, 70 percent; and the oldest boy, at eight, is only 62 percent of standard weight. Caloric deprivation takes its toll in other ways than stunting. Caloric and other nutritional deficiencies are prime causes of such problems as reduced mental capacity and lower resistance to infection. In Vila Nova one-third of all children die by the age of 10.

When I surveyed the nutritional status of the people of Vila Nova, I found a distinct difference between the average body weights of the two economic groups formed since the introduction of sisal (shopkeepers and motor-owners on the one hand, and workers on the other). Since the introduction of sisal the upper economic group exhibited a marked improvement in nutritional status (as measured by body weight) while the lower group showed a decline in nutritional status. The statistics showed that while one group was better off than before, a majority of the population was actually worse off nutritionally.

This conclusion was unexpected in view of the widespread claim that sisal had brought lasting benefits to the people of the *sertão*, that sisal had narrowed the gap between the rich and the poor. Clearly, changes had come about. Towns like Victoria had grown far beyond their pre-sisal size.

But outside the towns, in the villages and rural farmsteads, the picture is different. Having abandoned subsistence agriculture, many workers moved to villages to find work on sisal units. In settlements such as Vila Nova wages and profits depend on the world price for sisal. When I arrived in 1967, the price was at the bottom of a trough that had paralyzed all growth and construction. Wages were so low that outmigration was showing signs of resuming as in the drought years. In spite of local symbols of wealth and "development," my observations revealed a continuation of endemic poverty throughout most of the countryside and even an intensification of the social and economic divisions that have always characterized the *sertão*.

Sisal is not the only example of an economic change that has brought unforeseen, deleterious consequences. The underdeveloped world is replete with examples of development schemes that brought progress only to a privileged few. The example of sisal in northeastern Brazil shows that an ecological approach is needed in all economic planning. Even more important, we must recognize that not all economic growth brings social and economic development in its true sense. As the sisal example shows, a system may be formed (often as part of a worldwide system) that only increases the store of human misery.

# 11 | ENERGY CONSERVATION IN AMISH AGRICULTURE

## Warren A. Johnson, Victor Stoltzfus, Peter Craumer

*This study builds on a point which was emphasized in Gross's study of sisal production in Brazil: agricultural productivity must be evaluated in terms of costs in human and other inputs as well as gains in yields. In this analysis of farming by the North American Amish and their neighbors, the authors compare energy inputs with outputs to discover whether limited use of energy leads necessarily to limited agriculture production.*

*The Amish, unlike their "English" neighbors, avoid reliance on industrial technology both in farming and in their general style of life, for ideological reasons. This study shows that they can maintain impressively high agricultural yields with far lower energy inputs than usually found in industrial agriculture. However, their achievements depend very much on a larger, favorable economic and environmental context. Thus, the implications of these achievements in the face of limited energy availability in the future are not clear-cut. The Amish system of farming, with its emphasis on human labor and frugality, is not necessarily a viable model for agriculture in the current energy crisis.*

*The Amish, perhaps more than any society studied, illustrate the effects of cultural values in determining the utilization of technology and natural resources. Their agricultural accomplishments challenge our own idelogically based rationales for the use of energy-costly technology—that it is somehow more "efficient." And yet, it is clear that there are other costs to be considered. The Amish value hard physical labor for its own sake, and prefer, for religious reasons, to forgo the conveniences of electricity in the home. But their values and preferences are not shared by their neighbors. This point must also be taken into consideration when we try to apply what we have learned from the Amish study to others whose values may well be different.*

The increasing agricultural yields of the last half-century have been achieved largely through the utilization of steadily increasing amounts of energy. Until the mid-1950's, total agricultural yields increased more rapidly than energy usage, but since then, the rate of increase in energy use has been faster than the increase in yields *(1)*. Not only does a farm use energy directly to power machinery and in the form of fertilizers, for example, but energy has indirectly led to greater agricultural production by eliminating the necessity for woods formerly used for household fuel and for pastures required by draught animals. Transportation and the processing of foods have also reduced food imbalances over space and time, enabling the products of all agricultural land to be fully and efficiently used.

If the current concern about future scarcity of energy is justified, will there inevitably be a decline in food production? Certainly such a pessimistic hypothesis could be made on the basis of the historical record. On the other hand, an optimistic hypothesis could be based on the current profligate use of inexpensive energy and the potential for maintaining high production by increasing the efficiency of energy use. Which of these hypotheses is correct could make all the difference to the poorly fed people in the world today and to their children.

To decide between these hypotheses on other than a theoretical or conjectural basis is difficult. Of the many examples of energy-efficient forms of agriculture in less-developed countries, most have low yields *(2, 3)*. The processes of population growth and economic development have been largely ones of increasing use of energy, first in terms of intensified human labor *(4)* and then in the use of fossil fuels *(5)*. In the developed countries, in which scientific knowledge and technology enable the development of productive and energy-efficient agriculture, economic factors have virtually forced the extensive use of energy to increase yields and reduce manpower in order for individual farmers to survive economically. Alternative forms of agriculture are still being developed *(6)*.

The Amish, however, are the exception because their religious beliefs have caused them to turn their backs on a number of energy-consuming techniques while still benefiting from modern scientific knowledge. Most Amish are not averse to having their soil and feed analyzed by specialists nor to purchasing scientifically bred stock, even though they plow with horses, ride in buggies, and live in homes without electricity. They provide an opportunity to shed some light on the question of whether high-yielding agriculture inevitably requires the heavy use of energy. This study was designed to determine (i) how much less energy the Amish use than their non-Amish neighbors and (ii) what penalty they pay in reduced yields because of their agricultural methods.

## THE AMISH

The Amish in America and Canada now number 70,000, most of whom live in communities in Pennsylvania, Ohio, Indiana, and Illinois. They are becoming increasingly visible to the general public as a result of tourism, journalism, and television. Although the study of their agricultural methods was initiated in the early 1940's *(7)*, little has been done since, even though published materials on other aspects of Amish ways have increased rapidly.

The Amish have their roots in the upheavals of the Protestant Reformation *(8)*. The reaction against the authority of the Catholic church was carried over into resistance by nonconformists to the authority of the new Protestant hierarchy. The Amish were a part of this Anabaptist left wing of the Protestant Reformation, which believed in individual interpretation of the Bible and adult baptism. In the 16th and 17th centuries, they were forced from Switzerland and Germany to other countries, including Russia, where their skills as farmers were needed. But in each country their nonconformist ways led to persecutions until they reached North America in the 18th century. The Amish, who in religious and agricultural matters were progressive for centuries, are now felt to be one of the best available sources of information on the farming life of 16th-century Germany *(9)*.

The religious functions of Amish agriculture are complex. Farming is not one among many neutral occupations but is strongly preferred as the optimum setting for the good life. This orientation stems most directly from their interpretation of Genesis 1:28, which directs humanity to replenish the earth and have dominance over animals and the land. They have a strong affinity for nature as God's work, as beautiful and orderly. Secondary choices are trades related to farming, such as carpentry, blacksmithing, and harness-making. Hard work is a moral value, which provides a context for the generally disciplined life. A simple technology is constantly adjusted to the right mix of sufficient labor intensity to provide jobs for the family and sufficient profitability to buy land, pay taxes, and support the shared obligations of the Amish community to cope with such problems as fire losses and medical bills. Education through the 8th grade is provided in their own schools. No government assistance is accepted, including social security or agricultural support programs, although they will consult agricultural advisers. They speak a dialect of German, and they refer to their non-Amish neighbors as "English."

The Amish belief in the literal interpretation of the Bible provides the basis for community integration. The biblical mention of horses but not of motorized vehicles has kept the scale of Amish communities small, the size being based on the power of the horse-drawn plow and the range of the buggy. In II Corinthians 6:14 it says, "Be ye not unequally yoked together with unbelievers," which the Amish interpret as forbidding their being tied directly to secular society by electrical lines or natural-gas pipelines. But in the modern era, many interpretations must of necessity be arbitrary when biblical wording does not apply directly to current questions. This fact, when combined with the independence of each Amish community, has led to much differentiation among them. Some Amish drive cars and are almost indistinguishable from the Mennonites, from whom the Amish split in 1697. But even among the Old Order Amish, the most numerous group, there are the very conservative who permit only stationary engines to drive belts for power (most Old Order Amish pull motorized balers behind their horses and may have a number of engines to power milking machines, refrigeration units, feed grinders, washing machines, and so forth). A market town in central Pennsylvania may have buggies of four different colors—white, yellow, grey, and black—indicating these different groups of Old Order Amish.

The market system of the larger society sets important constraints that the Amish must adjust to *(10)*. The price of land, the market for agricultural commodities, interest rates, and national economic factors all influence Amish operations. Since the Amish draw an ethical line between owning a machine and hiring custom agricultural work, they are beginning to use their neighbors' machinery, especially for specialized operations such as soybean harvest and the production of silage. The constraints of an ethically determined intermediate technology produce spatial differences in Amish agriculture as well. The Amish are not likely to spread into the Great Plains because that region is not conducive to the labor-intensive, unirrigated agriculture at which the Amish are so skilled *(11)*. The Amish not only must find the right area, but they must be able to purchase enough small farms to support their community and institutions without driving land prices too high. It is also desirable that a local market be available where they can sell the products of their gardens, barnyards, and farmhouses.

The Amish must adjust to the economic conditions as they find them, but in one major way they create their own economic pressures. The Amish family includes an average of seven children *(12)*, and the greatest task facing an Amish farmer is to see his sons established on farms. In their attitudes toward children, the Amish are like traditional agricultural societies worldwide.

## ENERGY ANALYSIS

With the increased realization that energy, which is essential to modern society, may become scarce, energy analysis has increasingly become a supplement to other methods of analyzing questions concerning resources and the environment. As with economic analysis, energy analysis permits different production processes to be compared, except that the costs are in terms of the energy degraded to obtain a desired product rather than of the dollars spent. Energy analysis is especially useful when imperfect markets or hidden subsidies distort prices and make economic analysis difficult, as is often the case with energy and agriculture. Energy analysis has provided a new understanding of policy questions as diverse as packaging *(13)*, housing *(14)*, and transportation *(15)*. One of its key advantages is that it is not culture bound, as economic analysis so often is. It has been used effectively, for instance, to show that the use of cows in India is a sensible practice in that cultural context. Cows provide milk (the major source of animal protein in the Indian diet), motive power for farm work and transport, and dung (which, in most cases, is the only fuel available). In addition, the cows are fed with materials that would otherwise be largely wasted *(16)*.

However, the process of carrying out an energy analysis is rarely as straightforward or concise as the laws of thermodynamics would suggest. Many studies of the same processes have led to different findings *(17)*, and international efforts have been initiated to standardize approaches and terminology *(18)*. Although standardization will be a great help, it will not resolve all the difficulties because of the necessity for tailoring each analysis to the objectives of the study.

In this study, the energy uses of Amish and "English" farmers were compared by calculating their energy ratios (sometimes called caloric gain), the amount of food energy produced per unit of energy spent to produce it *(2, 19)*. An energy ratio greater than 1.0 indicates that the process is a net producer of energy, and an energy ratio of less than 1.0, that it is a net consumer. The energy inputs to the agricultural process are traced back to the point at which additional energy costs make an acceptably small difference in the total energy costs. Outputs are calculated at the farm gate, on the basis that they are subsequently dependent on the allocation decisions of society rather than on the decisions of the farm operator.

In order to determine the penalty paid in lost production for energy conservation, the yields per acre (1 acre = 0.405 hectare) of each farm were determined. The total farm output, expressed in terms of 1000 kilocalories (Mcal) is divided by a corrected figure for farm acreage. The corrected acreage is obtained by adding to the total tillable land an additional acreage that would have been necessary to produce the supplemental feed that many farmers purchase. Acreages of woods and waste were not included, and rough pasture was discounted according to its equivalence to tillable land; the farmer suggested the terms of the trade, such as 3 acres of hillside pasture for 1 acre of tillable land.

The energy values of the major farm products are given in Table 1. For some, such as milk, eggs, and grains, the energy values are obvious. These are homogeneous commodities of relatively little variation in quality or nutritive value. With animals, however, there are large variations based on size, age, and quality of the animal. The product itself is complex: how should the analysis distinguish between prime meat cuts of low caloric value with high caloric fat and animal byproducts? The approach used here is that of Cook *(20)*, which assumes a standard percentage of the carcass to be separable lean meat, with bone and excess fat removed. The energy output per animal is, of course, more a function of these assumptions than a straightforward energy accounting, and as a result, the matter of whether a process is a net energy producer or consumer becomes less meaningful. However, these necessary assumptions do not impair the *comparisons* of energy ratios and yields between Amish and English farmers: indeed, any assumption of caloric values that is based on the weight of a fairly standard animal product would lead to the same relative responses to the questions posed by this study.

Table 2 gives the energy values used to convert major inputs into caloric values. For the most part, they are averages of selected data available in the literature, weighted to account for completeness of analysis and appropriateness for this study. Most energy figures that are available for agricultural inputs vary considerably. Not only do major differences stem from the completeness of the analysis, but also, fertilizers are produced by different processes, feeds come from different regions (some with irrigation and others without), and the use of different forms of energy and transportation all contribute to the differences in conversion figures. Agricultural equipment is particularly difficult to handle since there are normally many pieces on a farm, each of which has different rates of use, which makes the calculation of energy depreciation rates awkward.

Solar and human energy are not included in the analysis. Solar energy is considered a free good; if it were not used by agriculture it would go essentially unused. Human energy, even on the Amish farms, is still a tiny fraction of the total energy used, even though the work begins early, often 5 A.M., and ends with the after-dinner chores. There is also the question of whether labor would be more correctly viewed from the Amish perspective, as a benefit rather than as a cost.

## RESEARCH PROCEDURE

Three groups of Amish were studied—in central Pennsylvania, eastern Illinois, and southwestern Wisconsin—in order to obtain results from different environments. A smaller number of English farmers in the same areas were also interviewed. In Wisconsin, several recently completed studies (21, 22) provided comparative data, which necessitated a somewhat modified analysis and different conversion figures. Each farmer interviewed was asked a series of questions about the quantities of materials brought onto the farm and of the products sent out. Data were confirmed where possible by checking with distributors of fuel, feed, and fertilizer.

The number of horses used on each Amish farm was quite consistent. There were usually eight work horses or mules, even though farm size varied considerably. The number of "driving" horses varied more, between one and two in Pennsylvania to between two and four in Illinois. The Amish contend that a work horse will eat as much as a cow, which is an indication of one energy cost the Amish must overcome if their yields are to equal those of the English.

An input-output analysis such as this has the advantage of simplicity, since it is essentially concerned with what comes onto each farm and what leaves it; however, it sheds little light on the internal operations of each farm. The farmer is assumed to be using his land reasonably, given the constraints he operates under. The analysis assumes that the results will reflect the different constraints of labor and energy operated under by both the Amish and the English. However, there are variations among the farms. The Amish produce much of their own food and sell surplus vegetables, fruits, eggs, and baked goods at local markets. Theoretically, the food purchased and sold by each farm family should be included in the energy analysis, but such data are hard to obtain and were not a part of this study. Also, different farmers produce different crops and use different forms of crop rotation; the effects of these variables are unknown. It is not the highly controlled experiment that may be desired, but the results do reflect a substantial difference between Amish and English use of energy.

TABLE 1.   ENERGY VALUES OF MAJOR FOOD
PRODUCTS *(25)*.

| Item | Energy value (kcal) |
|------|---------------------|
| Milk | 650* |
| Eggs | 972† |
| Hogs | 3,040‡ |
| Cows | 2,440‡ |
| Chickens | 1,035‡ |
| Corn | 3,480§ |
| Wheat | 3,300§ |
| Soybeans | 1,340§ |

*Per kilogram, with 3.5 percent butter fat.
†Per dozen, large.
‡Per kilogram of live weight.
§Per kilogram.

## RESULTS

*Central Pennsylvania.* The study area is one of ridges and valleys just east of the Allegheny Front. The Amish have moved here only within the last 10 to 15 years, as land prices, tourism, and industry in Lancaster County have made it difficult for them to find farms for their growing numbers in that traditional center of Amish life. The Amish are now found in 40 of Pennsylvania's 67 counties. The valleys of central Pennsylvania provide good limestone soils, a degree of isolation, wooded hills, and good supplies of water. The sample consisted of 12 farms belonging to the Old Order Amish, five to the most conservative group of Amish (locally known as Nebraska Amish), and six English farms. All are primarily milk producers.

The overall energy ratio of the Old Order Amish indicates that there is virtually no net gain in energy in their dairy operations (Table 3), but in its final form of milk, the energy is directly useful to man. The English farmers' energy ratio of 0.553 means that they use 83 percent more energy to produce a unit of milk than the Amish. The yields per hectare for the two forms of agriculture are much the same, with the Amish yields 4 percent higher. In this case, there is no penalty in reduced production stemming from the reduced energy use of the Amish, which supports the optimistic hypothesis that high production can be maintained with reduced use of energy.

TABLE 2. ENERGY COSTS OF MAJOR INPUTS

| Item | Energy cost (Mcal) | Efficiency of production (%) | References |
|---|---|---|---|
| Fuels | | | |
| Gasoline | 9.30* | 89.6 | *2,26* |
| Diesel | 10.40* | 89.6 | |
| Liquefied petroleum gas | 6.45* | 95.0 | |
| Kerosene | 10.30* | 84.6 | |
| Naptha | 7.70* | 89.6 | |
| Electricity | 2.54† | 34.0 | |
| Fertilizer | | | |
| Nitrogen | 15.9‡ | | *2,3,27,28* |
| Phosphorus | 3.5‡ | | |
| Potassium | 1.4‡ | | |
| Pesticides | | | |
| Atrazine | 45.2‡ | | *2,28–30* |
| All others | 33.0‡ | | |
| Feed | | | |
| Corn | 1,300§ | | *28* |
| Soybean meal‖ | 1,100§ | | *2,3,30* |
| Hay | 400§ | | *3,20,28,30* |
| Transport | 0.345¶ | | *2,3,20* |
| Farm equipment | 160# | | *1–3* |

*Per liter.
†Per kilowatt hour.
‡Per kilogram.
§Per ton.
‖The total energy cost to produce a ton of soybeans, estimated to be 2200 Mcal, is divided equally between the soybean oil and meal.
*Per ton per kilometer.
#Per horsepower per year. For Amish farms, the number of motors and their horsepower were recorded. For non-Amish, who power most of their farm implements from tractors, the horsepower of the tractors was doubled to account for their other equipment.

For the Nebraska Amish, however, the historical relationship between energy use and yields appears. Their energy ratio is 49 percent higher than that of the Old Order Amish, but their yields are 47 percent lower. Since they use only one stationary engine, the Nebraska Amish must sell their milk as grade B milk, cooled only by spring water. In addition, they are less likely to take advantage of the services offered by agricultural extension agents and farm suppliers. Their farms are 27 percent smaller than those of the Old Order Amish, but they have many fewer cows, in part because they do not use milking machines. The Nebraska Amish generally reflect greater self-sufficiency. The farms appear noticeably poorer, and the farmers are more reluctant to be interviewed. The Nebraska Amish can perhaps best be thought of as failing to utilize the scientific developments as extensively as other Amish and are therefore similar to farms in less-developed countries.

Figure 1A provides a comparison of the major energy inputs per hectare for the three groups. The main energy savings of the Amish come in their use of fuel and equipment, as would be expected. The Old Order Amish use more purchased feed than the English; 100 acres (40.5

TABLE 3.   ENERGY RATIOS AND YIELDS PER FARM (CENTRAL PENNSYLVANIA). SUMMARY DATA ARE SHOWN IN BOLDFACE TYPE TO FACILITATE COMPARISON WITH DATA IN TABLES 4 AND 5

| Group | Energy ratio | Yield (Mcal/ha) | Output (Mcal) | Input (Mcal) | Size (ha) | Corrected size (ha) | Cows *(N)* |
|---|---|---|---|---|---|---|---|
| Old Order Amish | **1.009** | **3,151** | 134,527 | 113,367 | 32.6 | 42.7 | 31.0 |
| English | **0.553** | **3,071** | 245,715 | 444,453 | 73.4 | 80.0 | 47.3 |
| Nebraska Amish | **1.508** | **1,710** | 53,014 | 35,151 | 30.0 | 31.0 | 12.8 |

TABLE 4.   ENERGY RATIOS AND YIELDS PER FARM (EASTERN ILLINOIS). SUMMARY DATA ARE SHOWN IN BOLDFACE TYPE

| Group | Energy ratio | Yield (Mcal/ha) | Output (Mcal) | Input (Mcal) | Size (ha) | Corrected size (ha) |
|---|---|---|---|---|---|---|
| | | | *Data as collected* | | | |
| Amish | **0.974** | **3,165** | 173,134 | 177,821 | 38.9 | 54.7 |
| English | **2.003** | **11,444** | 2,466,156 | 1,230,769 | 200.6 | 215.5 |
| | | | *Assuming all grains fed to hogs* | | | |
| Amish | **0.886** | **2,879** | 157,494 | 177,821 | | |
| English | **0.707** | **4,644** | 1,000,820 | 1,415,384 | | |

TABLE 5.   ENERGY RATIOS AND YIELDS PER FARM (SOUTHWESTERN WISCONSIN). SUMMARY DATA ARE SHOWN IN BOLDFACE TYPE

| Group | Energy ratio | Yield (Mcal/ha) | Output (Mcal) | Input (Mcal) | Size (ha) | Corrected size (ha) | Cows *(N)* |
|---|---|---|---|---|---|---|---|
| Amish | **1.614** | **1,305** | 50,631 | 31,379 | 60.8 | 38.8 | 14.5 |
| English | | | | | | | |
| Small farms* | **0.274** | **1,668** | 99,399 | 362,990 | 71.6 | 59.6 | 24.5 |
| Large farms† | **0.395** | **2,079** | 204,800 | 518,890 | 107.6 | 98.5 | 40.9 |

*Number of cows, < 30.
†Number of cows, 30 to 49.

hectares) is about the limit of horse farming, and many farms have fewer tillable acres than that; if the Amish wish to have additional cows they must purchase additional feed.

An additional contrast between the Amish and the English is their household use of energy. The Amish use liquefied petroleum gas for cooking, refrigeration, and hot water; naptha for lighting (in Coleman lanterns); and wood for space heating. The English use energy in much the same way as most American families do. In our sample, the average Amish family used 15,330 Mcal per year, and the English families used 160,280 Mcal. The English, in fact, used 20 percent more energy in their homes than the Amish to produce 173,650 kilograms of milk, the average farm output. The conservation achievements of the Amish here are greater in their homes than in their farming.

*Eastern Illinois.* The Amish community in Douglas County, Illinois, was established in 1864 with the purchase of railroad land for $8.10 per acre. The land is excellent, with deep fertile soil, although its flatness creates some drainage difficulties. The uniformly good soil presents a problem to the Amish since it does not permit them to allocate any of it to woods and the 5 to 15 acres used as pasture on each farm are inefficiently used in comparison with the English farms. In the absence of woods, household heating is by fossil fuels, and in the absence of gravity-fed water systems, windmills are used to lift water to insulated water tanks.

As Amish farms dominate this part of Douglas County, it was not possible to pair Amish farms with adjacent English farms. The nearest English farms were substantially larger than the Amish farms; the five English farms surveyed averaged 495 acres (200 ha) compared with 96 acres (39 ha) for 11 Amish farms. The Amish use very little chemical pesticides and, because of the good soil in the area, they have traditionally not used chemical fertilizer, although some farmers are beginning to apply small amounts (some organic fertilizers are used). However, unlike another recent study of organic farming *(23),* we found that the Amish yields of corn, 115 bushels per acre (7200 kg/ha), are less than the English figures of 165 bushels per acre (10,400 kg/ha). The largest single energy input to an Amish farm is for supplementary feed (especially soybeans) which is grown in only limited quantities (Fig. 1B). Hogs are the major product in the area, although the English farmers export substantial amounts of grain as well.

The initial calculation of the energy ratios (Table 4) reflects the grains exported by English farmers, which pushes their energy ratios above 2.0. Since it would not be correct to compare outputs of animal products to grain, a calculation was made of the hogs that could be produced if the exported grain had been fed to hogs, using local feeding efficiencies of 4.25 kg of grain per kilogram of animal weight gain. A 15 percent energy surcharge was added for the estimated energy cost of this hypothetical feeding operation. On this basis, the energy ratio of the Amish was 25.3 percent higher than that of the English, but their yields were 38.1 percent lower. These results support the pessimistic hypothesis, that a decline in energy available to agriculture would cause a decline in food production.

There are several possible explanations for the differences in the results from Illinois and Pennsylvania. The use of chemical fertilizers would increase Amish yields significantly, but it would also lower their energy ratios toward the English figures, thus generally reducing the differences between the two farming operations. It is also possible that hog farming, being less labor-intensive than dairy farming, is less amenable to energy conservation through Amish methods. However, since crop production is the major energy consumer, it seems unlikely that this factor would be important.

The differences between the two sets of results probably stem from the differences between the two environments. The diversity of central Pennsylvania, with its long narrow valleys, steep wooded hills, and marginal pasture, can be used efficiently by the Amish, while the uniformly good soil of Illinois is ideal for modern agricultural technology. Each environment presents certain obstacles and opportunities, and although it is easy to visualize the obstacles to using large machines on the irregular topography of Pennsylvania, it is not so easy to identify the obstacles to the Amish in Illinois. Household uses of energy are not included in these figures. In fact, since the energy ratios and yields of the Amish are similar in Illinois and Pennsylvania, it is probably more correct to say only that the Amish cannot utilize the Illinois site as effectively as the English.

The differences between the results for Illinois and Pennsylvania suggest that if energy were to become scarce in the future, the changes in agriculture would vary depending on the site. In diverse environments, agricultural practices may move away from energy-intensive methods more rapidly than in areas that are now treated most intensively by modern methods. If labor is substituted for increasingly expensive energy, idle small farms may be returned to production to the extent that they permit the utilization of local energy sources such as woods and pastures. Sites that enable farmers to avoid the high cost of equipment and fuel will increasingly be advantageous.

*Southwestern Wisconsin.* Vernon County and the adjacent part of Monroe County is the site of the Cashton-Westby Amish settlement. Consisting of approximately 55 farms, the community has been expanding as Amish have moved in from other areas where land pressure and prices are higher. The Amish here are conservative, in many ways similar to the Nebraska Amish in their use of stationary engines and belt power and the limited use they make of available scientific assistance. The region is characterized by a rolling upland topography cut by flat-bottomed valleys, with rocky, wooded slopes making up much of the landscape between. The soils are deep forest soils overlying dolomite and sandstone, but the farms are large because of the amount of unproductive land on the hillsides. Dairy farming predominates, and nearly all cropland is planted with corn, hay, and oats.

Data were collected from ten farms in this settlement and were

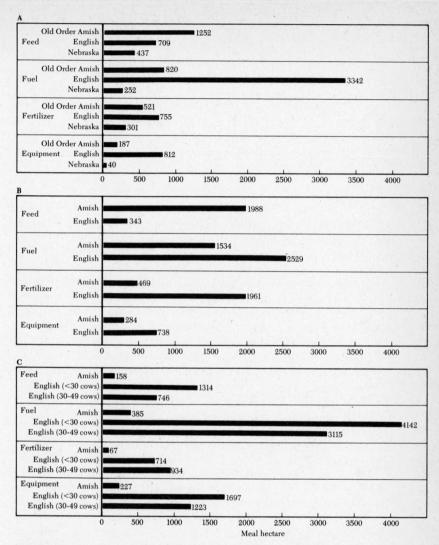

FIGURE 1. Major energy inputs per hectare for Amish and English farms in (A) central Pennsylvania, (B) eastern Illinois, and (C) southwestern Wisconsin.

compared with a statistical sample of 14 farms obtained from the 1975 Wisconsin Farm Business Summary *(21)* and with supplementary data from other sources *(22)*. While not providing a sample of farms in the same area, this sampling method did offer the opportunity to select English farms of the same approximate size and with the same number of cows; thus, differences in these variables should not affect the outcome. However, compared with English dairy farms in Pennsylvania, the small English farms (with an average of 24.5 cows) were relatively inefficient in their use of energy, and yields were less. Therefore, a sample of larger Wisconsin farms (30 to 49 cows) was also evaluated to see if the scale of operation affected the results.

The energy conservation of the Amish is striking (Table 5). The Amish yields are 22 percent less than those of the smaller English farms and 37 percent less than those of the larger ones, and yields on all types of farms are well below those in Pennsylvania. The Amish inputs for all major items—feed, fertilizer, fuel, and equipment—are low, whereas for the English farms they are high, especially for fuel (Fig. 1C). The data for English farms in all three study areas suggest that larger farms are more energy-efficient than the smaller ones.

## CONCLUSIONS

The data do not clearly support either the optimistic or the pessimistic hypothesis. The results from the more progressive Old Order Amish in Pennsylvania, who perhaps best approximate a traditional culture taking advantage of modern science and technology, do support the optimistic hypothesis, but the Amish in Illinois, who are progressive in most matters, do not. A number of other factors, such as the effects of different environments and the differences in farm size and operation, are also important. An input-output analysis such as this does not permit a detailed understanding of the specific reasons for the variations. To obtain the data necessary for such an analysis would require the collection of a vast amount of information from each farmer throughout the year and necessitate a degree of involvement in the farm operation that Amish farmers may not be willing to grant. Even with such data, the interrelationships might not become clear.

In one respect, however, the results are clear and do support the optimistic hypothesis, if slightly modified to pertain to energy conservation on farms in general rather than just in agricultural production. An Amish farmer told us that to buy a car he would have to milk five more cows. One may ask how many cows it would take to purchase a recreation vehicle or a color television or to pay an electric bill. If the Amish are conservationists, it is primarily in their consumption pattern. Their major contribution to energy conservation is in the limited demands they make on available resources to support their way of life. Their major purchases are limited to clothing, bread flour, sugar and a few other food items, and household equipment and furnishings. The Amish buggies and harnesses, which are made by Amish craftsmen, will last 20 to 30 years; a horse may live that long as well, although the average life span is approximately 20 years. Probably more than any other group in this country, the Amish could survive without the support of industrial society.

Amish conservation and its economic consequences also account for the prosperity and expansion of Amish agriculture, a striking factor in itself in this era of poverty-stricken small farms and large commercial agriculture. The frugality of their consumption patterns and their willingness to use a labor-intensive intermediate technology has meant that the Amish could bank most of the proceeds of their farming operations and accumulate the funds to obtain land for their sons as the need arises. Their simple technology has enabled the Amish to avoid the major causes of small farm poverty and bankruptcy, the difficulty of obtaining the capital to purchase modern agricultural machinery or the heavy debt payments required if it is obtained *(24)*.

If energy becomes scarce in the future, the effects will not be felt uniformly. Agriculture would almost certainly be able to procure supplies needed for energy-efficient purposes such as fertilizing crops and preserving food. Even though the results we have described are mixed, they do suggest the potential for reintroducing human labor without major losses in production as long as key supplies such as fertilizers are available. The requirements of human labor could even be a benefit if energy shortages reduced the jobs available in other sectors of the economy.

The Amish experience should make us more confident about the future if energy should become progressively scarcer. It is often said that the Amish provide a vignette of early America; is it also possible that they may provide an image of the future?

## NOTES

1. J. S. Steinhart, and C. E. Steinhart, *Science* 184, 307 (1974).
2. G. Leach, *Energy and Food Production* (International Institute for Environment and Development, Washington, D.C., 1975).
3. M. Slesser, *J. Sci. Food Agric.* 24, 1193 (1973).
4. E. Boserup, *The Conditions of Agricultural Growth* (Aldine, Chicago, 1965).
5. R. G. Wilkinson, *Poverty and Progress: An Ecological Perspective on Economic Development* (Praeger, New York, 1973).
6. R. Merrill, Ed., *Radical Agriculture* (Harper & Row, New York, 1976).
7. W. M. Kollmorgen, *Rural Life Stud. No. 4* (U.S. Department of Agriculture, Washington, D.C., 1942); *Am. J. Sociol.* 49, 233 (1943).
8. J. A. Hostetler, *Amish Society* (Johns Hopkins Press, Baltimore, 1963).
9. W. I. Schreiber, *Our Amish Neighbors* (Univ. of Chicago Press, Chicago, 1962), pp. 88–98.
10. V. Stoltzfus, *Rural Sociol.* 38, (1973).
11. E. W. Schwieder and D. A. Schwieder. *A Peculiar People: Iowa's Old Order Amish* (Iowa State Univ. Press, Ames, 1975).
12. H. E. Cross, *Nature (London)* 262, 19 (1976).
13. B. M. Hannon, *Environment* 14, 11 (1972).
14. A. Mackillop, *Ecologist* 2 (No. 12), 4 (1972).
15. E. Hirst and J. C. Moyers, *Science* 179, 1299 (1973).
16. S. Odend'hal, *Hum. Ecol.* 1, 3 (1972).
17. B. F. Chapman, *Energy Policy* 2, 91 (1974).
18. International Federation of Institutes for Advanced Study, *Energy Analysis Methodology, Workshop Rep. No. 6* (Nobel House, Stockholm).
19. G. H. Heichel, *Am. Sci.* 64, 64 (1976).

20. C. W. Cook, *J. Range Manage.* 29, 268 (1976); ———, A. H. Denham, E. T. Bartlett, R. D. Child, *ibid.*, p. 186.
21. *Wisconsin Farm Business Summary, 1975* (Univ. of Wisconsin Extension, Madison, 1976).
22. U.S. Department of Agriculture, *Agric. Inf. Bull. No. 230* (1968);———, *Selected U.S. Crop Budgets: Yields, Inputs and Variable Costs* (1971), vol. 2.
23. W. Lockeretz, R. Klepper, B. Commoner, M. Gertler, S. Fast, D. O'Leary, R. Blobaum, *Center for the Biology of Natural Systems Rep. No. CBNS-AE-4* (1975).
24. E. Higbee, *Farms and Farmers in an Urban Age* (Twentieth Century Fund, New York, 1963), p. 47.
25. A. L. Merrill and B. K. Watt, *Energy Value of Food, U.S. Department of Agriculture Handbook No. 74* (1963).
26. *Handbook of Tables for Applied Engineering Sciences* (Chemical Rubber Co., Cleveland, 1970), p. 304; V. Cervinka, W. J. Chancell, R. J. Coffelt, R. G. Curley, J. B. Dobie, B. D. Harrison, *Trans. Am. Soc. Agric. Eng.* 18, 246 (1975).
27. W. Lockeretz, R. Klepper, M. Gertler, S. Fast, D. O'Leary, *Center for the Biology of Natural Systems Rep. No. CBNS-AE-6* (1975).
28. D. Pimentel, L. E. Hurd, A. C. Bellotti, M. J. Forster, I. N. Oka, O. D. Sholes, R. J. Whitman, *Science* 182, 443 (1973).
29. M. B. Green and A. McCulloch, *J. Sci. Food Agric.* 27, (1976).
30. B. Commoner, *Center for the Biology of Natural Systems Rep. No. CNBS-AE-1* (1974).

# Part IV
## Sources and Consequences of Inequality

One of the most important motives for inquiry in the social sciences through the centuries has been the search for a basis of social justice. Social philosophers from ancient Greece to industrial England observed various forms of injustice, which they sought to remedy by designing what they considered more rational and appropriate governmental systems.

Anthropologists, no less than other social scientists, have been concerned with at least one aspect of social justice, that related to social equality and inequality. Observation of largely egalitarian horticultural and hunting-gathering societies has led us to reevaluate the structures of societies divided into social classes. There has been considerable research into and theorizing about the ways in which social stratification emerges from egalitarian beginnings. These studies are generally concerned with explaining the origins of inequalities in power and economic position among social classes; recently, however, some authors have sought to explain how this relates to inequalities among individuals, between the sexes, and among different age groups.

It may be that some social inequality is an inevitable fact of social life. Differences in age and sex, as well as in talent, temperament, and experience, provide a potential basis for social discrimination, hence inequality, in human and other animal societies. Charles Darwin pointed out that variability among members of the same species who compete for the same resources is the very foundation of natural selection; those who are best equipped to solve the problems they face produce more offspring than do those with fewer advantages.

Yet it is not this sort of inequality based on individual endowment that concerns most anthropologists. In most human societies inequality in access to resources and social status or power is founded not on attributes of individuals but on attributes of the larger groups of which they are members. Smaller, less complex societies, in which inequality is more individualized, are increasingly rare.

Such societies, generally considered "egalitarian," do not necessarily provide equal access to all resources for all members. Division of labor by age and sex is a human universal; so, probably, are inequalities of one sort or another based on these attributes. Among members of the same age and sex category, there may be other inequalities. We illustrate this point by means of one study, by C. W. M. Hart and Arnold R. Pilling, of an "egalitarian" society of Australian hunter-gatherers, in which there are inequalities in the outcome of competition among adult men for wives. Some men manage to control the marriages of many others, whereas less fortunate men may remain monogamous and may thus suffer from lack of adequate food, not to mention lack of social or political influence. Inequalities in access to potential marriage partners are by no means limited to hunting-gathering societies like the Tiwi. In a number of horticultural societies where polygyny is practiced and where women are the main cultivators, a man with several wives is wealthier and more powerful than others because of his ability to distribute the food and other goods that his wives produce.

Inequalities in material goods may be derived from other factors as well. The Kwakiutl, native Americans of the northwest coast, had a stratified society based on apparently unequal control of certain natural resources, like advantageous fishing sites. In order to validate high social positions, individuals in this society (as in many other societies of the world) were obliged to share their wealth, to show generosity. As Marcel Mauss showed in his classic essay, "The Gift," among the Kwakiutl the giver has social and psychological power over the receiver. Competition for prestige in this society took the form of rivalry in generosity. The principles of this rivalry are not hard to understand; we see them operating in our own society. Social rivals may compete in "one-upmanship," in gift giving at Christmas time, or in such entertainment as elaborate parties. Although our society has been characterized as "acquisitive," prestige is acquired by ostentatious displays of generosity—from the proud host or hostess to the famous philanthropist.

Although rewards to individuals in the form of prestige may explain the motivation of individuals to be generous or to give goods to others, the social *functions* of generosity may include economic circulation of wealth and "leveling," that is, diminution of the material basis for social differentiation. If individuals are motivated to reduce their material accumulations of wealth, then the material differences between the rich and the not-so-rich will be diminished. In societies that lack facilities for the preservation and storage of material goods and particularly in those that lack money, it is clear that hoarding of wealth is not only antisocial but also pointless. In such instances an individual's only motive for producing beyond his or her own needs will be the prestige to be gained through generosity. But, where wealth can be stored and converted into money for later use, accumulation may proceed at a rapid rate. Although the wealthy may continue to exhibit some generosity, the differences between themselves and the poor become exaggerated as wealth is accumulated over the generations.

In preindustrial societies private land holding provides the most important basis for social differentiation in terms of wealth and power. Those who own land have clear means of controlling those who do not but who need its products for survival. What is not so obvious is that those who own more land than they can cultivate depend upon others who work for them. This interdependence is illustrated in Scarlett Epstein's paper on rural caste relations in India. Although landowners are unequal beneficiaries in this interdependent relationship, provisions for the landless ensure the survival of both during "bad years."

Unequal control over land itself may become less critical in industrial and market-oriented societies, where control over capital, another form of property, and over distribution of goods and services becomes the most significant base for social and economic inequalities. In such systems, decisions can affect the lives of people remote from, sometimes entirely unknown to, the people who make them. Allen Ehrlich's study shows this happening to a group of East Indians in Jamaica.

Social inequality is not viewed everywhere, or in all contexts, as unjust. But, where it *is* perceived as unjust, bringing about change toward equality may be quite problematic. The most radical efforts at redressing social injustice can be observed in revolutions. To illustrate some of the problems a revolutionary society may have in achieving social equality, we have included an article by Norma Diamond that addresses the question of equality between the sexes in the People's Republic of China.

# 12 | THE PRESTIGE AND INFLUENCE SYSTEM

## C. W. M. Hart and Arnold R. Pilling

*This paper is taken from a joint study by two anthropologists of a hunting-gathering society, the Tiwi of Bathurst Island. Often we idealize the living practices of peoples who do not have state systems or participate in market economies. In particular, hunters and gatherers are sometimes held up as examples of "the original affluent society" because of their leisure time, apparent social equality, and absence of formal political institutions. What we often forget is that the roots of inequality go deeper than simply the institutional arrangement of class-stratified states.*

*The Tiwi, like all known human groups, thus find much to compete for, and, despite the lack of formal office, an individual can devote a lifetime to the pursuit of power and influence. An important means to this end is the acquisition of wives and the bestowal of daughters, sisters, and even mothers in marriage to other men. The career of Ki-in-kumi illustrates this point. He accumulated twenty-one wives and bestowed numerous others. It is not that women are a commodity in this society, but, rather, that they are viewed as a productive resource, the scarcity of which is ensured by the fact that older men acquire numerous wives, thus leaving younger men to take elderly widows as their first spouses. Even among hunter-gatherers who have few material possessions to compete for, social inequality is founded upon unequal access to scarce resources, in this instance women.*

The most influential man in Malau and the head of the biggest household was Ki-in-kumi. Since he had been born around 1863–64 and had been a "young operator" somewhat before 1900, the deals by which he got his career launched were difficult to reconstruct. The results of them, plus the fact that he lived long enough to draw full dividends from them, gave him by 1928–29 a wife-list of twenty-one. These had been accumulated as follows:

> When around 30 years old he remarried two elderly widows and a year or two later received his first bestowal. Thus by age 33 he had three wives. On that foundation he went ahead thus:

Thus his list of twenty-one wives was made up of six elderly widows and fifteen bestowed or rebestowed young wives.

| | Total |
|---|---|
| *At age 33* | |
| Had two widows and one bestowed wife | 3 |
| *Between age 33 and age 43* | |
|   Remarried two more widows and had three more | |
|   bestowed wives join him | +5   8 |
| *Between age 43 and age 53* | |
|   Three more bestowed wives came into residence | +3  11 |
| (During these twenty years at least five bestowed wives | |
| died in infancy or childhood) | +5  16 |
| *Between age 53 and age 65* | |
|   Two more bestowed wives joined him and he married | |
|   2 more widows (one the mother of Boya) | +4  20 |
| Now at age 66 there is still one more bestowed wife, aged | |
| about 9, in her father's household | +1  21 |

By 1928–29 five of his bestowed wives had died before puberty and one was still with her father. Three of his six widows were dead. Subtracting these nine women, we find that his current household contained twelve resident and active wives: the oldest about sixty, two in their fifties, four in their forties or thirties, three in their twenties, and the two youngest around seventeen or eighteen years of age. Almost all of them had borne children since joining his household, but the death rate had been high among Ki-in-kumi's children and from all of his wives he had only eight living children of whom six were girls. Five of these six daughters he had bestowed or rebestowed on Padimo . . . and the sixth on a middle-aged Rangwila. His oldest living daughter was the girl of 20 married to Padimo. His oldest living son was a boy of 18, despite the fact that Ki-in-kumi had been "a married man" for over thirty-five years. This was a situation which many Tiwi elders found themselves in at the close of long and successful lives. With numerous wives, numerous step-sons, large households to be managed, and large estates to be liquidated after their deaths, their oldest real sons (as distinct from step-sons) were still boys or youths and as such quite unsuitable as executive assistants while the old man lived or as heirs or executors after the old man died. Quite apart from kinship considerations, the Tiwi emphasis on age and seniority made it impossible for Ki-in-kumi to utilize in any capacity his 18-year-old son. A youth of that age was a nonentity, whoever his father.

Confronted by this situation, Ki-in-kumi in his advancing years had summoned Padimo, a sister's son in his early thirties, to come from Rangu and become his chief lieutenant. The youth of his own son had been a factor in his selection of Padimo. The presence in his camp of an older step-son, Boya, had been another factor. Boya, the step-son, was more than twenty years older than the son, and at least six years older than Padimo, the chosen instrument. Padimo, as we have seen, moved right in, fused his own small household with Ki-in-kumi's large one, and became Ki-in-kumi's Man Friday. Boya, the step-son, though married to a widow, refused to move out. Thus, among other things, we have to distinguish between Ki-in-kumi's household of twelve resident wives enumerated above, and Ki-in-kumi's establishment which contained Padimo, Boya, and the various people attached by marriage or kinship to them. Padimo had an old wife and two young wives (daughters of Ki-in-kumi). Boya had an old wife and a younger brother. There were a number of younger step-children of both sexes also resident with Ki-in-kumi. The full size and make-up of his establishment is given in Table 1.

TABLE 1.   KI-IN-KUMI'S ESTABLISHMENT

(Ages in brackets)

|  |  | Males | Females |
|---|---|---|---|
| Head (Ki-in-kumi | 66) | 1 | 0 |
| Oldest step-son (Boya | 42) | 1 | 0 |
| Sister's son (Padimo | 36) | 1 | 0 |
| Old wives (of all three adult men) |  | 0 | 5 |
| Young wives (including Padimo's 2) |  | 0 | 11 |
| Young males (sons and step-sons) |  | 8 | 0 |
| Young females (daughters and step-daughters) |  | 0 | 5 |
|  | Totals | 11 | 21 |

## THE ESTABLISHMENTS OF MALAU

There were, besides Ki-in-kumi, six other elders of the Malauila band. Two of these, the brothers Enquirio and Merapanui, were well over sixty and deserve, both by age and by success, to be labeled senior elders. The remaining four ranged in age from about 45 to nearly 60 and since none of them were particularly successful we call them the junior elders. In Table 2 we have listed the seven "establishments" in which lived all the members of the band. We mean by an establishment a food-production and food-consumption unit. Ki-in-kumi's establishment contained three married men—himself, Boya, and Padimo—and therefore contained three households. Economically it was one establishment, since the sixteen wives it contained worked as a team and the food they produced was consumed by the thirty-two total members of the establishment. For comparative purposes in Table 2 we list Ki-in-kumi's establishment as Unit I and give the personnel breakdown of the other six establishments that made up the total population of Malau.

Unit II is the joint enterprise maintained by the other two senior elders, the brothers Enquirio and Merapanui. To this we have added the pathetic and ostracized Teapot and his motherless son, since when they ate at all they ate as hangers-on of the Enquirio-Merapanui menage. Unit III is the establishment jointly maintained by the brothers White Man and Ku-nai-u-ua. Since the oldest wife of Ku-nai-u-ua was Summit's mother, that young man, together with the elderly ex-widow who was so far his only resident wife, lived in this establishment. Units IV and V present no difficulty; they are the small households of the other two junior elders Pingirimini and Tipiperna-gerai respectively. Unit VI is the joint enterprise of Gitjara and L. F. B., containing largely old ladies and young men. Unit VII is the remarkable menage that had gathered round the elderly widow whom young Banana had illegally "married." To this couple had attached themselves Tiberun (Banana's unmarried older brother), two younger brothers, and another male orphan who had apparently moved in for want of some better place to eat. The Banana menage thus had somewhat the appearance of a case of economic polyandry and somewhat the look of a fraternity house with an elderly housemother in residence. We include it as Unit VII since by so doing we are able to include in Table 2 all the hundred and nine people who made up the Malauila band in 1928–29 and allocate all of them to the economic units in which they functioned as food producers and food consumers.

TABLE 2.   THE FOOD PRODUCTION UNITS OF MALAU

| Unit | Married Males | Unmarried Males[a] | Old Wives[b] | Young Wives | Girls Under 14 | Total Persons |
|------|------|------|------|------|------|------|
| I    | 3  | 8  | 5  | 11 | 5  | 32  |
| II   | 3  | 9  | 1  | 7  | 11 | 31  |
| III  | 3  | 2  | 2  | 3  | 5  | 15  |
| IV   | 1  | 5  | 0  | 1  | 1  | 8   |
| V    | 1  | 2  | 0  | 1  | 2  | 6   |
| VI   | 2  | 5  | 3  | 0  | 1  | 11  |
| VII  | 1  | 4  | 1  | 0  | 0  | 6   |
| Total | 14 | 35 | 12 | 23 | 25 | 109 |

[a]Unmarried males include all males from male infants to men around 30, or more.
[b]The division between old wives and young wives is arbitrary. Several of the young wives were 40, others only 14 or 15.
?The question mark in Unit VII refers to the difficulty of deciding whether Banana should be classified as married.

The data in Table 2 merit close study. These seven establishments illustrate in capsule form several of the more significant emphases in Tiwi career patterns; indeed each might be said to illustrate some time point in the life careers of adult men and/or some degree of success or lack of success in becoming an influential man.

## THE POLITICS OF WIDOW REMARRIAGE

Ki-in-kumi's large establishment was the sort of set-up that every Tiwi sought to achieve but few accomplished. An establishment such as his meant wealth, power, prestige, and influence for its head, and, in Malau, Ki-in-kumi was the only man with such a household. With eleven males, many of them food producing; sixteen women, all of them food producing; and several of the girls under fourteen able to assist the older women, the amount of food this unit could collect in a day provided an ample food surplus for the establishment. A man whose household was a surplus food producer was a successful man. Moreover, since the large work force that produced the food surplus contained numerous young wives who (usually) could be relied upon also to produce numerous female babies, he was doubly blessed with both the requisites —surplus food and surplus daughters—necessary to increase his influence and make more people beholden to him or dependent on him. Of the thirty-five married women in Malau, sixteen, or over 45 percent, were in this one establishment.

By comparison, the other old men of Malau were less successful.[1] Through pooling their work forces, Enquirio and Merapanui had achieved an establishment (Unit II) almost as big as that of Ki-in-kumi, and probably its members ate almost as well as the members of his, but their effort was a shared effort and their influence and prestige had to be divided between them. They had been lucky with daughters but, divided between the two fathers, the eleven daughters in their establishment were less impressive than Ki-in-kumi's eight, and the total of seven young wives between them was quite overshadowed by Ki-in-kumi's nine. The two old brothers were successful men and headed a successful operation, but their prestige and success must be rated at least one whole degree below that of Ki-in-kumi.

Another pair of elderly brothers, White Man and Ku-nai-u-ua, had also joined forces (Unit III), but the results can be judged as only fair. They were at least the best off of their age group, the 45- to 55-year-olds, but the competition in that age group was weak, as can be seen by comparison of their establishment with Units IV and V, the households of Pingirimini and Tipiperna-gerai. Perhaps the best indication of the respective success in life of the seven oldest men is that given in the column of Table 2 headed "young wives." Of the twenty-three such women in the band, eighteen were in the establishments[2] of the three oldest men (Units I and II); the next five men in age shared the remaining five (Units III, IV, and V).

It might be thought that the small establishments of the unsuccessful junior elders like White Man, Ku-nai-u-ua, Pingirimini, and Tipiperna-gerai could be expected to increase sharply in size and these men to grow in relative prestige and influence when death removed the three old men at the heads of Units I and II and made their wives available for redistribution. The working of the Tiwi system made this possibility unlikely. Unsuccessful junior elders could not expect to step into the shoes of successful senior elders merely by outliving them; nor could one rise to power in the gerontocratic system merely by living past fifty-five. What was necessary was age *plus* ability, and the time to demonstrate the ability was in one's thirties. If it was not demonstrated and recognized by then, a man could not forge ahead in his middle forties and early fifties, for by then it was too late. This fact gave a certain cyclical quality to the transfer of influence in Tiwi. The influence of successful senior elders, to the extent that such an intangible thing was transferable at all, tended to skip a decade and bypass the men currently in the junior elder category in favor of the men in the current "young operator" category. Since Ki-in-kumi was already quite old, there was in 1929 a great deal of political maneuvering going on in Malau and elsewhere in anticipation of his death, and it was clear that the people most likely to profit by his death and the redistribution of his twelve resident wives (one-third of all resident wives in the band) were the men aged from thirty-two to forty-two such as Padimo, Boya, Summit, and Gitjara, all of whom were jockeying for position to take advantage of the death of any old man, especially such a wealthy elder as Ki-in-kumi. Some of the widows would undoubtedly remarry into other bands, but these younger Malauila, living with or near the old man's establishment, were already taking advantage of their strategic location to make some preliminary deals and marriage arrangements for the old man's widows even before his death. Neither Padimo, as Ki-in-kumi's son-in-law, nor Boya, as his nominal "son," could themselves marry any of the widows, but as resident members of his establishment and the only two men so situated, each was in an excellent spot to act as an honest broker in the disposal of Ki-in-kumi's large estate. Anybody interested in obtaining a widow or two at the death of Ki-in-kumi was well advised to have a few quiet words with either Padimo or Boya well ahead of time. Both of them had wives who lived and worked every day alongside Ki-in-kumi's womenfolk and thus they each had ideal communication systems to the women's side of the band. This was why they had held off setting up their own separate establishments though they were both married men. Neither were "heirs" of Ki-in-kumi in any strict Western use of that word, but it was obvious that it was their careers that would be promoted and their spheres of influence that would be enhanced by the death of Ki-in-kumi. The junior elders, all approaching or past the age of fifty with only small establishments and small spheres of influence, were being bypassed in the transfer of the old man's assets.

Every Tiwi anxious to obtain a Ki-in-kumi widow recognized the strategic positions of Padimo and Boya; the problem was to decide which broker to retain, since the positions of the two men in relation to Ki-in-kumi were so different. For the past four or five years Padimo had been the right-hand man and trusted lieutenant and undoubtedly it was he upon whom Ki-in-kumi was relying to carry out his own wishes about the distribution of his widows. . . . Old men found it difficult to control the remarriage of their widows with the same unchallenged authority with which they bestowed their daughters. Nevertheless they tried hard in many cases to do so. Ki-in-kumi was one who tried hard to make the decisions for his widows, by selecting Padimo as his trusted executor. If Padimo faithfully carried out the old man's wishes after he died, then the widows were not likely to come on the open market; they would be redistributed in accordance with the terms of Ki-in-kumi's will (in both senses of the word "will").

Though, of course, Padimo might prove to be a dishonest executor of the estate, there was a safeguard provided in that the new husbands whom Ki-in-kumi had selected for his wives were all aware of his wishes and hence if Padimo tried to depart from those wishes the cheated heirs would bring charges of double dealing and broken promises against him. But regardless of Padimo's honesty after the death, his position as Ki-in-kumi's trusted lieutenant clearly made him an unsuitable agent before the death for those numerous men who wanted some of Ki-in-kumi's future widows and who had not seen any indication that Ki-in-kumi had included them among his beneficiaries. The obvious young man for such men to use as their go-between and agent was Boya. Ki-in-kumi was hostile to him and had given him nothing willingly. Boya's presence in the old man's establishment was based on the nominal tie of Ki-in-kumi being the last husband of his mother to rename him before she died. Viewed thus, the two young men in Ki-in-kumi's household can be said to have become agents for two different networks of intrigue. Padimo was the manager and agent for all the men, including Ki-in-kumi himself, who wanted to perpetuate and continue the existing alliances and arrangements that Ki-in-kumi had built or helped to build during his long and successful career; Boya was the natural agent for all the men who, being outside that set of alliances, had nothing to gain from Ki-in-kumi's death unless his death dissolved the network of alliances and arrangements of which Ki-in-kumi had been the main architect. Padimo's responsibility was necessarily a sort of holding-together and preserving operation as the executor of an existing estate; Boya's clients were men hoping for fragmentation and subdivision not only of Ki-in-kumi's widows but also of the alliances and deals of which the widows were a part.

It is incidentally amusing, and also indicative of how the ever-present kinship ties affected all such deals and redeals, to note that if some of Boya's clients succeeded in grabbing off some of Ki-in-kumi's widows—despite the opposition, before his death, of Ki-in-kumi and the presumed opposition, after the death, of Padimo the executor—they were very liable thus to become automatically fathers-in-law of Padimo, since several of Ki-in-kumi's wives already had daughters who were bestowed on Padimo.

The question then of which agent was employed by the numerous men yearning to acquire one or more of Ki-in-kumi's widows was fairly well settled by the respective roles which the two young men occupied in the household. Men already well inside the Ki-in-kumi-centered alliances were relying on Padimo; men outside those alliances were rely-

ing on Boya to engineer a fluid situation and a more open market. In
choosing an agent in this as in any other "deal," there was also the
question of fee. Neither Padimo nor Boya would become involved or
make any soundings among the widows unless there was something in
it for them. Hence the client had to find out whether a promise of
general goodwill and friendship was all that Boya (or Padimo) would ask
in return for his services or whether the price would be much higher
—perhaps as high as the bestowal of the client's next baby daughter. It
was in such ways that widow-remarriage arrangements and infant bestowals were intertwined; a much-delayed bestowal to an apparently
unrelated individual would be the ultimate pay-off to the broker or
agent who had engineered a widow remarriage for the bestower years
before.

This role of agent in the disposal of a dead man's widows was a type
of operation best suited to men in the first stages of their own married
lives—that is, to men in their middle thirties or very early forties who
had perhaps married their first or second widows and who had as yet
no young wives of their own in residence. Having no young wives to
guard, they were able to get around easily on diplomatic missions and
they had their own listening posts inside the world of women in the
person of their own mothers (if still alive) and in the elderly widows
whom they themselves had married. The ambitious young brokers
were tipped off by their mothers and elderly wives as to how the young
wives wished to be distributed and what the competing young brokers
were trying to arrange. Thus when a wealthy old man like Ki-in-kumi
died, the redistribution of his wives through remarriage was a matter
that had been decided beforehand by an extraordinary complex tangle
of semisecret arrangements and deals and promises, but the people
most influential in arranging the redistribution were the young brokers
who usually got few, if any, of the young widows for themselves but who
collected their rewards in reputation, influence, alliances, and future
bestowals from the men for whom they had acted as agents.

Thus the death of Ki-in-kumi or of any other old man with many
wives tended to disperse the wives all over the tribe, with only one or
two, or at most three, going to any one new husband. A large estate was
almost always fragmented by the death of the old man who had built
it up, and any one of his contemporaries was able to take over only a
very small fraction of it at best. The levirate and sororate principles,
though present, worked very feebly. The men who benefited most—not
immediately, but eventually—were the young operators.[3] In such a
manner Padimo and Boya were sure to be the long-term beneficiaries
of Ki-in-kumi's death though neither of them could remarry any of his
widows. The real heirs of the wealthy old men of sixty and over were
the young men who happened to be between thirty-two and forty-two
when those old men got near to death. The men between forty-five and
fifty-five whose brokerage business ten years earlier had not been very
skillfully handled, or who happened to be at the brokering age when
no big households were being liquidated, found themselves in the posi-

tion that Pingirimini and Tipiperna-gerai occupied in 1928–29. We know they had not been successful dealers in their thirties because we found them around the age of fifty with only one resident wife each and relatively few bestowals in prospect. Their earlier dealings in widows had not laid the right foundations for successful careers as elders. Even before he was forty, Padimo had five or six bestowed wives either in residence or in prospect, and Boya, not much over forty, had several already promised. The death of Ki-in-kumi in the near future would bring both of them more reputation and ultimately more bestowals in return for their skill (if they showed it) in the disposition of the estate. The inferiority of Pingirimini and Tipiperna-gerai to these younger men in the marriage and influence struggle was already apparent and would be even more accentuated by Ki-in-kumi's death.

## THE POLITICS OF BESTOWAL

The above discussion of how younger men were indirectly benefited by the deaths or impending deaths of wealthy older men does not pretend to give an exhaustive list of all the considerations that went into the reallocation of a dead man's widows. We built our analysis around those factors which were paramount in the case of Ki-in-kumi's household. Other cases were different to the extent that there were real adult sons involved in them rather than a nominal "son" like Boya, or because in them the old man had not chosen a clear-cut executor as Ki-in-kumi had chosen Padimo, or because an old man had surviving brothers close to him in age and alliance who would emphasize the levirate principle and seek to have it followed in the relocation of their dead brother's widows. The few points we are seeking to emphasize among the many that might be emphasized in any exhaustive treatment of Tiwi widow remarriage are: 1) that widow remarriage was a very flexible area in which the ultimate disposition of the widows was decided by the manipulations and wishes of a wide range of individuals including both relatives and nonrelatives. The dead man himself; the fathers of the wives, if still alive; the brothers of the widows, if adults; the widows themselves, if strong minded; the executors of the dead man, if clearly nominated; and the numerous dealers and brokers on behalf of remote clients or even on their own account—all tried to make their own wishes prevail. The result was that no two cases were ever alike, but on balance 2) it was younger men rather than older men who were most likely to enhance their reputations and increase their assets in the long run as the results of these widow redeals, even though in the short run it was the older men who remarried most of the widows, especially the younger widows.

We have briefly discussed what we have labeled the politics of widow remarriage before discussing the politics of infant bestowal, although logically it might appear that infant bestowal should be taken up first. We have followed this order because, in Tiwi life, infant bestowal was reserved for fathers, and a Tiwi was at least a middle-aged man before he became a father at all. Before he could have a daughter to bestow, he had to be the father of one; and before he could become a father, he had to have a baby girl bestowed upon him and wait for her to grow up to child-bearing age. The much-married Ki-in-kumi did not have his first actual daughter (as distinct from wives' daughters begotten by previous husbands) until he was forty-five, and Enquirio was closer to fifty than to forty when his first real daughter was born. We are inclined to call such daughters free or unencumbered daughters since the step-daughters brought into a man's household by widows, even young widows, were already bestowed by act of the widows' previous husbands and the new husband's control over their marriage was therefore encumbered by the dispositions made by his predecessors.

Thus most men did not have and could not expect to have any free or unencumbered daughters to bestow until they were well into their forties. By that time a man was a prisoner of his past. When at last he had free daughters he was no longer a free man but a junior elder with a mass of obligations both to older men and to younger men, which he had contracted in the previous twenty or thirty years. Even his initiation, which had started when he was only about fifteen, left him under obligation to the older men who had initiated him. Any bestowals he had received had almost necessarily come to him from older men. In his thirties, it is true, he had operated in the widow remarriage area and put some older men under obligation to him by acting as their agent. But in his agency activities he had also contracted debts, usually in fee-splitting or log-rolling agreements with other agents of about his own age. Thus all his past activities, from his initiation at fifteen until the arrival of his first free daughter at (let us say) age forty-five, were on balance a story of obligations contracted and debts of gratitude assumed in his career of upward mobility. The more successful he had been up to now, the stronger the pressure on him to begin paying off those who had helped him, since it was assumed that his very success was a clear indication of how much obligation he must have to other men, especially older men and contemporaries.

If this line of reasoning had been the only relevant one, a Tiwi of age forty-five just presented with his first free daughter would have had problem enough deciding which of his many obligations to liquidate first by his bestowal decision for that daughter. Unfortunately he was at the age when he had to consider the future as well as the past. Some of his old obligations were to men who were very old and unlikely to live much longer. Others were to men of his own age with whom he had been partners ten years before, but by now it was clear that some of these would never amount to much and paying them off would reap no dividends for the future. Failure to meet the obligation might incur their enmity, but in view of their lack of success, perhaps their hostility was a lesser evil. In 1929, Gitjara, who had needed L. F. B. to get his own career launched, was ready to drop him as a partner now that Gitjara had attracted favorable notice in the form of two bestowals. The junior elders, though obligated to older men like Ki-in-kumi, were not bestowing their scanty free daughters on the older men but upon each other while waiting for the power alignment in Malau to change with Ki-in-kumi's death. Perhaps the clearest case of the pull between the obligations of the past and the planning for the future in the bestowal of free daughters was provided by Merapanui. He was a man who owed or thought he owed very little to his elders. None of them had ever bestowed a girl on him, and he reached fifty with nothing but an ancient widow. The fortunate death of an elder brother had suddenly provided him with bestowable daughters rather later in life than the average. By 1929 he had been able to bestow no less than four, and every one of them went to men much younger than himself and in other bands. Merapanui, being relatively free of old debts, was investing his daughters in young men with a future, but unlike Ki-in-kumi who had invested most of his daughters in one younger man, Padimo, old Merapanui believed in diversifying his investments.

Thus the politics of bestowal marriage were just as complicated as the politics of widow remarriage but, since a man was ten or more years older when he became involved in the former than when he became involved in the latter, a rather different set of motivations prevailed. At thirty-five as a mobile operator in the widow field, a man was trying to launch a career, and if he had no obvious assets—no living sisters or mother or important mother's brothers—he was often trying to launch it on a shoestring. By forty-five the same man was well along in his career and was a junior elder—the head of a household with at least one young wife in residence and a man beginning to have bestowable daughters of his very own. He now saw tribal politics and reputation building in different perspective from the way they had looked to him ten years earlier. Then he had put his services and his wits and his diplomatic skills at the disposal of older men in order to gain favorable notice from the elders. But now that he was an elder himself, albeit still low in the pecking order of elders, he was no longer their satellite but rather one of them and therefore in competition with them. Now he no longer wanted to build up his client's business; he wanted to build up his own household and his own influence. With the arrival of his first free daughters he was no longer content to work for and accept the leadership of older clients; he was in business as an elder for himself. His free daughters were therefore bestowed not as acknowledgments of his obligations to older men but as inducements to younger men to accept him as their patron. With his first free daughters a man was in position to become emancipated from the dominance of the elders because with the arrival of those daughters he could start bidding against them for the allegiance of men younger than himself.

One of the neatest examples of the switch in life career was provided in 1928 by the case of Tomitari. All Tiwi life careers and marriage arrangements were so tangled that one was delighted to find a relatively open and shut case. Some of the principals involved were relatives of Padimo, who was originally a Rangwila before Ki-in-kumi, his patron, lured him to Malau. Padimo and three sisters were the children of a Rangwila man and woman whom for simplicity's sake we will call Padimo's real father and real mother. The father bestowed the three girls on another Rangwila named Inglis who was about the same age as himself. (If we tried to answer *why* he did, the case would no longer be simple.) Padimo's father died while the four children were still young, and their mother remarried a relatively young man named Tomitari. This occurred in about 1914 and the situation then was as follows:

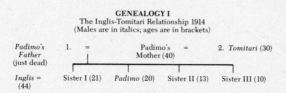

**GENEALOGY I**
The Inglis-Tomitari Relationship 1914
(Males are in italics; ages are in brackets)

Fifteen years or so later, all parties were still alive; the two youngest sisters had joined Inglis as wives and all three sisters had borne children to him, including girls. Thus the situation in 1928–29 was:

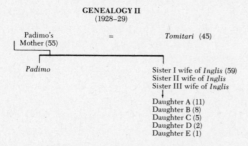

**GENEALOGY II**
(1928–29)

The three sisters of Padimo had borne five daughters to Inglis and as they were successively born Inglis had bestowed the first three on Tomitari. He did not bestow the fourth or fifth nor any of his daughters by other wives.

The master clue to the whole matter was the marriage in 1914 of Padimo's widowed mother to Tomitari, then little more than thirty. His function had been to act as trustee or stand-in for Inglis' interest, not in the widow but in her daughters who had been bestowed on Inglis by their dead father. The young Tomitari as step-father of the girls had to ensure their safe delivery to Inglis' household. (One was there already but the other two were not.) Tomitari accomplished his mission, acquiring the widow, of course, as a wife in the process; the girls arrived safely in Inglis' household and Inglis paid off handsomely by bestowing their daughters on his honest agent who had held off the competitors.

But by 1923 or thereabouts Inglis had stopped paying off. Tomitari by then had received three bestowals from Inglis. (Actually he had received about six, but three died in infancy). Moreover, he was no longer a young man but was entering the junior elder class and, having received wives from other sources than Inglis, was getting to the point where he would soon have free daughters of his own. He had no intention of performing any more services for Inglis who was now nearly sixty. Hence Inglis had not bestowed any daughters on Tomitari since 1923; those of his daughters who had been born since that year were bestowed on men other than Tomitari and men who were younger and less successful than he.

As we see it, the deals involving widows, particularly the pay-offs to young agents for acting to promote the interests of older men, had distorted what might be called the pure theory of Tiwi bestowal. According to the pure theory, mothers' brothers bestowed their daughters on selected sisters' sons, and the older man who gave a young man a wife and became his wife's father, was performing a kindness toward a favorite nephew for which the nephew should be grateful. But the Inglis-Tomitari operation shows how the theory had become distorted in practice. In order that Inglis might have some young daughters whom he would be free to bestow on his favored young nephew, Tomitari, in 1914 he had had to arrange the young man's marriage with an elderly widow to ensure safe delivery to him (Inglis) of some young wives who would bear him those daughters. Everything went smoothly and no slip-up occurred, yet by the time Inglis was in a position to give a wife to his favored young nephew, he found that the latter was no longer a dependent young man but a successful junior elder competing with him in his own field of identifying and using talent among the younger men. Tomitari's first daughter, born in 1927—not to any daughter of Inglis but to an older wife—was bestowed by its father on the distant but very promising Gitjara, a man of thirty-two. Gitjara was thus selected by Tomitari as a promising satellite at about the same age as Tomitari in 1914 had been selected by Inglis. Moreover, Tomitari by this time, far from being the grateful nephew of old Inglis (as the theory stipulated), was looking forward with anticipation to the old man's death, since when that occurred, among the widows of Inglis would be the three sisters of Padimo of whom he was still the nominal father. It was by acting as their step-father when they were children that he had got his own career started. They were indeed the foundation stone of his own career and, having profited so much from them as children, he was keenly interested in their redisposition whenever Inglis' death should put them on the market again. Thus he was simultaneously the husband of some of Inglis' daughters and nominal father of some of Inglis' wives. In the first status, he was expected by the theory to be a grateful son-in-law of Inglis; in the second status, the facts of Tiwi life required him to see Inglis' death as providing him with an opportunity to derive some new benefits for himself from his position as nominal father of the three wives of Inglis whose delivery to Inglis' household he had himself engineered.

Thus the politics of bestowal cannot be separated from the politics of widow remarriage. Every case of one had endless repercussions in the other. Sisters' sons who were promised young wives by their mothers' brothers were always too old to be grateful by the time the bestowal occurred or by the even later time when the bestowed child was old enough to come into residence. Mothers' brothers, in turn, were unable to endow their nephews any earlier because they as younger men had been caught in the same trap. The only way out was by deals in which older men and younger men collaborated. Ideally such collaborative efforts should always have been between mothers' brothers and sisters' sons, but amid such fierce competition and endless log rolling this was not possible, and in many cases the mother's-brother–sister's-son relationship was a *result* of collaboration between older man and younger man rather than a cause. The bond arose from the deal rather than from their original kinship, particularly when the two men involved were very close in age.

The collaborative deals between older men and younger men were essentially designed to compensate for the older man's inability to bestow a young wife upon the younger man at a reasonable age. As was stated before, not until he was about forty-five would the older man have a free or unencumbered daughter. By then his younger collaborator and satellite had attracted the attention of older and wealthier men with many unencumbered daughters. After performing all his services to Inglis, young Tomitari had not had to depend on him for his first bestowal. A wealthier man than Inglis had reached over Inglis' head, so to speak, and bought Tomitari's allegiance by the bestowal of a young wife who provided Tomitari with a free daughter several years earlier than any child the daughters of Inglis could provide. With this first unencumbered daughter, Tomitari promptly bid for the allegiance of Gitjara. Put in terms of allegiances, Tomitari had from 1914 until about 1923 been the henchman of Inglis. During those years he passed from about age thirty to age forty, and his main patron was Inglis, who passed from about forty-four and on the fringes of the elder group to about fifty-four and accepted among the elder group. Then—and this was typical of the shift of allegiance that occurred in most life careers—a senior elder more wealthy in wives and daughters than Inglis bid for Tomitari's allegiance, and Tomitari became his henchman. Five years later, in 1928, Tomitari was a coming junior elder in Rangu and a man of influence in his own right. His oldest bestowed wife had already borne him a daughter whom he used to make Gitjara *his* henchman. The three wives (daughters A, B, and C) of Inglis were nearing the stage when they would join his household and he had other bestowals from other quarters. His relation to Inglis was no longer that of henchman but of rival, since they were now both successful elders in the same band and competitors in the struggle to make younger men dependent on them. Far from bestowing any more daughters on Tomitari, Inglis was bestowing his daughters (now plentiful) on men of Gitjara's generation (though not on Gitjara). Having more free daughters than Tomitari, he had more men of that generation to patronize, but since Inglis was sixty and Tomitari only forty-five, time was obviously on the side of the latter.

Thus the crux of the Tiwi system of influence-satelliteship-marriage arrangement-wealth centered around what happened to a man in his thirties. This is what we meant when we said earlier that old men with many daughters bestowed them on young men who looked to them like "comers." Old men with many free daughters were usually men well over fifty. "Comers" were men in their thirties. In so choosing the "comers," the old and wealthy men reached right over the junior elders and the forty-year-old group down to the ranks of the young operators. In this way we may say that the real power group, the successful old gerontocrats, chose their own successors. They chose young men twenty or more years younger than themselves (as Ki-in-kumi chose Padimo) because men at such an age were not rivals or competitors. A man so chosen in his thirties could be already powerful and fairly wealthy by his middle forties (like Tomitari in 1928) and very wealthy in his fifties. Such men went up fast because of their selection by the group in power. Those not so chosen had to go up the hard way by accumulating what position and influence they could by manipulations of the few available females not controlled by the wealthy old men. The "haves" left a small minority of women available to the "have-not" men to keep them quiet, but the great majority of females were concentrated in the hands of a few old men and these old men chose their own successors. Thus the Tiwi system actually deserves to be called a primitive oligarchy as much as it deserves to be called a gerontocracy. It was run by a few old men who ruled it not so much because they were old but because as young men they had been clever and then had lived long enough to reap the rewards of their cleverness. These rewards made up Tiwi wealth—many wives, much leisure, many daughters to bestow, many satellites and henchmen, and much power and influence over other people and tribal affairs.

### NOTES

1. It will be noticed that as we move into the older group of men we have to use their native names, since most of them had no "whiteman" names.
2. Two of these eighteen were of course actually married to Padimo, but still part of the establishment of their father, Ki-in-kumi, since Padimo's wives all lived with Ki-in-kumi's wives.
3. At least some of the so-called "stolen" or disputed wives were widows who had insisted on marrying the younger agent instead of the older client, which put the young broker in the embarrassing position of saying to his client, "I cannot make delivery of the widow I acquired on your account; she insists on marrying me instead." Such an incident did not do his agency business much good but tended rather to frighten off clients.

# 13 PRODUCTIVE EFFICIENCY AND CUSTOMARY SYSTEMS OF REWARDS IN RURAL SOUTH INDIA

## Scarlett Epstein

*India represents an extreme in the extent and formalization of its system of social stratification. Traditionally Indian society has been organized on the basis of hereditary castes, each of which has been identified with a distinctive profession, as well as customary rituals and other cultural practices. Within a traditional community, then, the various tasks of community life, from farming to education, from clothes washing to sanitation, are allocated among the participant castes, each in long-term relations with other castes, on a family-to-family basis. The castes themselves are ranked in social status, from the Untouchables at the lowest end of the social spectrum, to the educated, often land-owning Brahmins at the highest end of the social spectrum. Goods and services are provided year round by each family to the others with which it is in association; those who provide services to land-owning farmers receive fixed payments in agricultural goods every year.*

*Although the caste system has long been denounced as unjust and as an impediment to progress, it is important to try to understand how this system has been maintained over such a long time. Scarlett Epstein views the system of "fixed rewards" inherent in economic caste relations as an adaptation to the particular environmental and technological means of ensuring a good harvest. In good years landowners profit greatly by the system of fixed rewards, but in bad years poor, low-caste workers are ensured of incomes.*

*Epstein goes beyond considering merely past adaptive advantages of the caste system. She also attempts to explain why, in the context of this system, some technical innovations were acceptable and others not. When innovations threatened traditional labor relations, they were viewed as too risky, even though they offered the prospect of profits over the short run. This situation illustrates the importance of a clear understanding, by those who seek to introduce technical change, of traditional economic adjustments.*

## INTRODUCTION

Economics is concerned with the phenomena of production and distribution. Market and non-market economies alike have to meet the same problems: goods have to be produced and distributed among the population. It is on the former that economists have concentrated their attention. At the same time they have tended to neglect the interactions and conflicts between the market and other social institutions. However, in the study of societies which are changing over from non-market to market economies such factors cannot be so easily ignored. Since the majority of the world's population lives in societies where this transition is now occurring, the development of underdeveloped areas has become a central problem in world affairs, and a central concern of economists and others. Ways and means have to be devised to increase output so as to allow for a surplus to be sold, by which the economy is incorporated in the market system. Economic development involves here not only the use of new and more productive methods, it also depends on the presence of appropriate incentives which will induce the population to adopt the new techniques. In these circumstances, therefore, the recognition of the interplay of all social institutions becomes particularly important. This probably explains why economists have developed so few models to show the working of traditional non-market economies. They have concentrated their attention rather on the emerging and growing capitalist sector (Lewis, 1954, pp. 139–191, and 1958; pp. 1–32). Yet in order to establish the conditions for the emergence and growth of a capitalist sector in underdeveloped countries an understanding of the principles underlying the customary non-market economies is essential. Apart from its purely theoretical interest, this is necessary to explain why some development schemes are successful and others fail; why the indigenous population of underdeveloped areas is prepared to react positively to some new economic opportunities and not to others.

Here I seek to explore some of these issues by focusing on hereditary labour relationships as they operate in India. My analysis is concerned to examine the implications of this system for productive efficiency, for the principles that underlie it and the way in which these differ from forms of capitalist economic organization. I shall show the importance of average productivity in underdeveloped Indian villages as opposed to the emphasis placed on marginal productivity in industrial economies.

## THE JAJMANI SYSTEM

Economists sometimes assume that all farming economies are composed of self-sufficient owner-occupier households (e.g. Lewis, 1954, p. 148). However, there are many rural societies in which members perform specialized functions: Indian farming communities with their complex division of labour provide a good example. The character of economic relationships in Indian villages is largely determined by the high degree of specialization that exists and by the particular sets of beliefs and observances that underlie and perpetuate this division of labour. It is in fact the caste system that throws into relief the complex division of labour in Indian society. A major feature of the caste system is that labour relationships between the landowning castes and their dependent servicing castes are usually hereditary and rewards are paid annually in the form of fixed quantities of farming produce.

In the past, villages were largely self-sufficient; goods and services were mutually exchanged by the different specialist castes within small rural communities. Services and duties which the various castes performed for one another and the rewards associated with these were regulated by a socio-economic system known as the *jajmani* system. According to Sanscritic Indian usage, *"jajmani"* refers to a client who receives religious services and gives gifts in return for them. But, following Wiser, the term *jajmani* has come to be accepted for the system as a whole. He defined *jajmani* as follows: "These service relationships reveal that the priest, bard, accountant, goldsmith, florist, vegetable grower, etc. etc. are served by all the other castes. They are the *jajmans* of these other castes. In turn each of these castes has a form of service to perform for the others. Each in turn is master. Each in turn is servant. Each has his own clientele comprising members of different castes which is his *"jajmani"* or *"birt."* This system of interrelatedness in service within the Hindu community is called the Hindu *'jajmani* system'" (Wiser, 1958, p. xxi). Beidelman has criticized Wiser for describing a Hindu caste village as a system of idyllic mutuality, whereas in reality castes are linked in unequal relationships based upon power (1959, p. 6). This asymmetrical dimension of the *jajmani* system had its roots in land tenure, numerical predominance, political influence, and ritual differentiation in the caste hierarchy. From this point of view, Gould has described *jajmani* as "a matter of landowning, wealth and power controlling castes providing a structurally fixed share of their agricultural produce along with numerous "considerations," in exchange for craft and menial services rendered by the mainly landless impoverished, politically weak lower castes" (1958, p. 431). Similarly, Beidelman speaks of *jajmani* as "a feudalistic system of prescribed hereditary obligations of payment and of occupational and ceremonial duties between two or more specific families of different castes in the same locality" (1959, p. 6). In short, where Wiser talks of mutual rights and obligations, Beidelman and Gould emphasize the high degree of economic and political differentiation characteristic of India's customary system of labour relations. On the face of it, these views of the *jajmani* system are plainly inconsistent. I shall try to show later, however, that both are in a sense correct; the inconsistency arises from the fact that each stresses only one aspect of the total system.

All writers on the *jajmani* system stress the point that rewards and duties were strictly defined. The interdependence between the different caste occupations was based on hereditary ties. Rewards were in terms of agricultural produce, and quantities were fixed. As a result, methods of work were handed down from generation to generation and a certain rhythm of productive activities became a fixed aspect of the Indian villager's life.

## TYPES OF TRADITIONAL LABOUR RELATIONS

In order to understand the traditional economic relationships which have been described as falling within the *jajmani* system, their component parts and variations in different places and under different conditions must be made clear. The extreme form of *jajmani,* that is the prescribed hereditary relationship involving all castes in any one rural settlement, appears to have been largely limited to certain areas in North India. Yet the division of labour supported by the caste system, and expressed in the hereditary ties between different caste households, occurred to some extent in most Indian villages. Thus in Mysore in South India I found two types of hereditary link in the villages: one between Peasant[1] masters and their Untouchable labourers, the other between Peasants and certain functionary castes, such as Washerman, Barber, and Blacksmith, whose services were continually required. Village craftsmen, such as the Goldsmith and Potter, whose services were not in regular demand, had no hereditary relationship with Peasant caste households; they were not rewarded annually, but rather on the occasions when their services were required. In these Mysore villages landholding was vested in Peasants, who possessed what Srinivas has called "decisive dominance" (1959, pp. 1–16), that is they dominated numerically, economically, politically, and also largely ritually. (There were no Brahmins in this village.) Though most of the servicing caste households had some land of their own, their holdings were too small to suffice for their subsistence. Therefore the castes with little land contributed their labour and/or skills to the life of the community and in return received a fixed share of the total agricultural output produced. These economic relations were, however, only one aspect of the multiple relations which linked the different caste households in the Indian village. For instance, the hereditary relationship between a Peasant master and his Untouchable labourer operated not only in the economic but also in the political and ritual spheres. If an Untouchable was involved in a dispute with another, whether Untouchable or not, his Peasant master had to come to his support. Similarly, the Untouchable allied himself with his Peasant master in disputes. He was expected to be prepared to fight for the latter, even against Untouchables aligned with other Peasants in conflict with his own master. Perhaps even more important, the Untouchable had to perform a number of ritual services for his Peasant master, such as carrying a torch ahead of a funeral procession from his master's household. These different types of relations—political, economic, and ritual —reinforced each other and in turn helped to ensure the stability of Indian peasant economies. Furthermore, the Hindu concepts of Karma (destiny) and Dharma (innate endowment), as well as beliefs in ritual pollution, stressed the maintenance of the *status quo.* Caste indeed pervaded the total complex of Indian society. There are, therefore, many aspects to caste relations. For the purpose of the present argument, however, we need concern ourselves only with the way in which the different aspects of the hereditary ties affected the purely economic part of the relationship. The more general social and political advantages, which, as we have seen, are part of the system of customary labour relationships, acted as additional incentive to landowners to meet their economic liabilities in good and bad harvest years alike. The noneconomic aspects of labour relations are probably even more important from the workers' point of view. Not only are Untouchable labourers assured of a minimum subsistence level in bad harvests, but the hereditary relationship provides them with a benevolent master who is expected to look after them as a father provides for his children. In fact, the customary relationship between Peasant masters and Untouchable labourers is couched in kinship terms; a Peasant calls his Untouchable labourer his "Old Son" *(Hale maga).* Moreover, by leading the good life of an Untouchable, a labourer can hope to be reborn into a higher caste in his next existence.

The caste system incorporated two types of economic relationship. There were strictly hereditary ties between landowners and their servicing castes; these were highly prescribed. There were also the less prescribed but more personally contractual relationships between landowners and certain artisan castes, such as Basketmaker and Potter, whose services were not in regular demand. The establishment of links with outside markets brought new economic opportunities to Indian villages. The possibility of selling crops and labour offered incentives to enterprising men to improve their productive efficiency. We can investigate, therefore, whether these different types of socio-economic relationship produced different reactions to the new opportunities. I shall illustrate my discussion mainly with material from two villages: Wangala, with its strictly prescribed hereditary system of rewards; and Dalena, where the diversification of economic activities had already largely undermined the traditional relationships (Epstein, 1962).

## CUSTOMARY SYSTEMS OF REWARDS AND IMPROVED PRODUCTION TECHNIQUES

Following irrigation, Wangala lands required more and deeper ploughing. Farmers, therefore, had to replace their customary wooden ploughs with iron ones. Not only did these need more maintenance than wooden ploughs, but repairs also demanded greater skill. Wangala's Blacksmith, who had hereditary relations with Peasant farmers in the village, found that he had to learn how to repair the new iron ploughs. He also found that he was kept busier by his Peasant clients than he had been prior to irrigation. Yet his annual reward in kind remained the same. When he approached Peasant elders about an increase in the customary reward, they flatly refused it. They argued that it had been fixed by elders in the distant past and they saw no reason to increase the quantity of agricultural produce given annually to the Blacksmith, since it was still adequate to feed him.

The Blacksmith then carefully considered his position and came to the conclusion that it would be in his best interest to discontinue his hereditary relations with Peasant households altogether and work instead for cash. However, when he proposed this to Wangala's Peasant elders, who composed the village *panchayat,* they opposed his suggestion most strongly. They pointed out to him that relations which had lasted through generations could not be broken off at one stroke. It was, of course, in their own interest that the traditional arrangement should be maintained. They threatened that if the Blacksmith refused to perform his customary duties they would make his life in the village pretty much impossible. Since he had a small landholding in Wangala he was reluctant to move to another village. Nevertheless, being a very enterprising man, he was determined to be rid of his customary obligations, which he regarded as obstacles in his way to success. He wanted to be able to branch out into other activities, not directly connected with his craft, such as making doors and window-frames. He continued to argue with the Peasant elders until they finally offered a compromise. They suggested that if he could find some other Blacksmith prepared to carry on the traditional relations on customary terms, he himself would then be free to work as he liked. Wangala's Blacksmith managed to find a classificatory brother from another village who, as the youngest of a large family, was pleased to be able to take over the position which Wangala's Blacksmith had come to find so burdensome. Thereafter the new Blacksmith repaired wooden ploughs and other traditional tools belonging to the Peasants for which he received his annual reward of a fixed quantity of agricultural produce; the indigenous Blacksmith repaired their more recently acquired iron ploughs, for which he was paid in cash. Whereas Peasant farmers had at first not been prepared to grant even a small increase in the quantity of annual reward in kind the blacksmith received, they were now quite ready to pay extra cash for the services, which they had previously expected from him as part of their customary arrangements. Though this behaviour may appear strange, I shall show that the rationale and the principles on which it was based are quite clear.

Admittedly irrigation had increased the productivity of land. However, Peasants tended to regard the greater yield as part of the normal windfall profits which had been associated with the system of prescribed hereditary rewards. They rationalized their argument in terms of subsistence requirements and told the Blacksmith that the customary reward was still sufficient to feed him and his family. But the expansion of a cash sector induced the Blacksmith to hold out for higher rewards; this meant that he was no longer prepared to work for a minimum of subsistence. After the Blacksmith had managed to disentangle himself from his customary obligations and had provided a substitute for himself, Peasants were quite prepared to pay different amounts of cash for the various jobs he performed for them and which his substitute was not able to do. As soon as the hereditary ties between Wangala's indigenous Blacksmith and his Peasant clients had been broken as a result of the contact with the wider cash economy, Wangala Peasants acted as typical entrepreneurs in advanced economies. They were prepared to pay extra for the blacksmith's work because it could be associated with a considerable increase in total output.

In the case of Wangala's Blacksmith we are dealing with an extremely enterprising man: he designed a new and improved iron plough and started making it himself; he branched out into house-building and other activities for which the growing prosperity in the area produced a demand. However, before he could take advantage of the new economic opportunities he had to disentangle himself from his hereditary relationship with his Peasant clients. Peasant elders, village *panchayat* members, had used their political influence and power to force the indigenous Blacksmith to provide a substitute for himself to carry out his traditional duties. Thus the customary system of rights and duties continued to exist and exert pressures to ensure conformity. Customary ties are obligatory not only for workers but also and equally, for employers. "Workers were entitled to their rights from every villager, according to the rules of the village communities; and if the villagers declined to employ their services to which they were entitled, they must still pay the *bullcottee hucks* (reward in kind)" (Wiser, 1958, p. xxvi). What is also worth noting, incidentally, is how this system of relationships is modified to operate in India's large and rapidly growing cities. I became aware of this when I stayed with one of my English friends in Bombay. It appears that individual Washermen managed to establish a system of "customary" relationships with tenants in particular blocks of flats. The Washerman washes all the clothes for the resident families and in turn receives a fixed monthly reward from each of them. When my hosts' Washerman decided to return to his natal village for a few months a year, he arranged for one of his kin to carry on his duties during his absence. Though my hosts were satisfied with their "own" Washerman, they found the services of his substitute highly unsatisfactory; they therefore wanted to find a different Washerman. However, none of the many underemployed Washermen in Bombay was prepared to take on the job. They all regarded it as the prerogative of the "customary" Washerman, who in turn had the right and duty to provide a substitute in his stead, if he went absent. In fact my hosts were boycotted by Bombay's Washermen, because they had attempted to change their "customary" Washerman. The system of customary relationships in this way gives labour relations great stability and tends to eliminate competition, even in a highly competitive urban environment.

Similarly, Wangala's new Blacksmith continued to work according to long-established rules and was completely unaffected by the new economic opportunities in his environment. The existence of hereditary labour relations and fixed annual rewards, therefore, acted as a force to maintain the *status quo* and accordingly as an obstacle to economic growth and expansion. Wiser reports that "there is very little stimulus for better work. The Washerman has no desire to buy a flat iron to iron his *jajmani's* clothes. If he were to get one, he would simply increase his own labour and get very little, if any more, pay for it" (1958, p. 142).

Craftsmen who have no such prescribed and highly formalized relations with their clients can much more easily branch out into new activities than those who, like Wangala's Blacksmith, are subject to traditional labour relations. For example, in Dalena there were a number of immigrant craftsmen caste households, such as the Basketmaker, whose enterprise was not in any way hampered by traditional agreements. When the growing urban demand for more colourful and nicely shaped mats and baskets became effective, Dalena's Basketmaker changed his products and methods of production. (There was no Basketmaker in Wangala with which to compare him but a comparable craftsman there, a Jeweller, preferred to cultivate his own small plot of land instead of seeking the advantage of the new urban market.) Moreover, the Basketmaker's close links with the nearby urban centre made him realize there was a big demand for pork—which may be eaten by lower-caste Hindus. Accordingly, he started rearing pigs in Dalena itself and sold them with considerable profit at the nearest urban market. His enterprise proved so successful that he even sent word to his brother to join him. The latter came and they continued to expand their business. A comparison of the case of Wangala's indigenous Blacksmith with that of Dalena's Basketmaker clearly indicates the drawback of a prescribed system of rewards and obligations when it comes to economic expansion. This point can be further illustrated by the reaction of Wangala Peasants to the introduction of improved production techniques.

Wangala had had some tank-irrigated lands even before canal irrigation reached the village. Thus some of Wangala's peasants were already accustomed to growing paddy (rice) long before canal irrigation made the growing of wet crops a practical proposition. Traditionally, a *gumpu* group of ten or twelve women was employed as a team to transplant the paddy seedlings from the nursery to the paddy fields. Each *gumpu* had a leader, whose responsibility it was to see that her co-workers turned up on the day arranged between her and the Peasant: the leader also received a certain fixed amount of crops per acre of paddy her group transplanted. She gave equal shares of this agricultural produce to each member of her *gumpu* while she kept a slightly larger proportion for herself. Each Peasant always employed the *gumpu* of the wife of the Untouchable with whom he had hereditary relations. Accordingly, there was a traditional relationship between a Peasant farmer and his *gumpu*, involving fixed customary rewards. About 20 years after canal irrigation reached Wangala, the Agricultural Department tried to introduce the Japanese method of paddy cultivation to Wangala farmers. The officials stressed the considerable increase in yield which would result from the new method. Though farmers were quite prepared to believe this, only a few were ready to experiment with the new method, which involved a more laborious way of spacing plants properly. First of all, farmers were not prepared to pay the *gumpu* more for transplanting the new way, because there was pressure from the more conservative farmers against raising the fixed reward for the services of a group of women. Secondly, the few more enterprising men who were prepared to offer a higher reward to their *gumpu* found that the women had developed a certain rhythm of work and were reluctant to change it; besides no one was prepared to pay them for re-training. Similarly, when officials from the Agricultural Department tried to introduce a cheap and most efficient weeding hook, the use of which would have considerably reduced the cultivation labour required, Wangala farmers were not prepared to employ the new tool. At first sight their reaction appears difficult to understand, but it becomes more readily explicable when viewed in the context of hereditary relationships. These make them responsible for providing a minimum of subsistence for their Untouchable labourers. If they substituted tools for labour and therefore saved some agricultural produce in terms of rewards, they might then have to give in charity what they had initially saved. They would therefore have no net gain. Besides, they would be criticized for being mean and selfish.

In these instances we see the Peasants of Wangala rejecting new techniques which would have increased output. But their response cannot be attributed simply to conservatism—which in any case often indicates a recognition of diffuse benefits not seen on the surface. For in other spheres, which were not covered by the hereditary system of rewards, Wangala Peasant farmers displayed a considerable degree of enterprise. They were, for example, extremely progressive in their attitude towards sugar-cane cultivation, an entirely new venture to them. Since sugar-cane had not been one of the traditionally cultivated crops, there were no customary production techniques or traditional rewards associated with it. Thus farmers felt free to experiment with the new techniques and methods and adopted those that proved most productive and efficient. They paid their labourers in cash on a daily basis. The number of labourers any one farmer employed was largely determined by the interaction between the wage-rate and marginal productivity, as is the case in any capitalist system. Since the problem of the subsistence for the village population was taken care of by the system of hereditary labour relations, a Wangala farmer could operate in spheres outside the customary system like any "rational" employer in an industrial society; he attempted to maximize his returns by equating marginal returns with marginal costs. A Peasant's hereditary obligation to provide a minimum of subsistence for his dependent households provides an obstacle to improving productive efficiency and maximizing returns. Wherever this obligation is not in existence or has been abandoned, we can expect a more positive reaction to new economic opportunities. This becomes clear when we examine Dalena's economic activities.

Dalena lands had remained dry even after irrigation had reached the area. Dalena farmers therefore sought to participate in the growing prosperity of the region by diversifying their economic activities and by purchasing wet lands in neighbouring villages. This resulted in the breakdown of hereditary ties between Peasant farmers and their Untouchable labourers. In turn, this meant that farmers were left free to employ labourers with whom they had no customary arrangements. Nor were they bound by customary rewards in the form of a fixed quantity of agricultural produce. Unlike his Wangala counterpart, a Dalena Peasant farmer was thus able to select his labourers, who worked for him according to his instructions and under his supervision. His relationship with his labourers was mainly contractual; he paid them in cash on a daily basis. The better worker received a higher daily wage. Moreover, since his hereditary obligation to provide a minimum of subsistence for his dependent Untouchable households had already disappeared, he was keen to employ the new weeding hook, which Wangala farmers were reluctant to accept. This resulted in a considerable saving of labour and therefore in a sizeable gain. Paddy was a new crop to Dalena farmers. But, unlike Wangala landowners, Dalena Peasants were not tied to any customary techniques and arrangements for paddy cultivation, and they showed themselves eager to experiment with the Japanese method of paddy cultivation, which promised them greater returns. In fact, the adoption of the new method of paddy cultivation enabled Dalena farmers to get a considerably higher output per acre of paddy than Wangala farmers with their customary method. According to a stratified random sample, which I compiled in the same way in both villages in 1955 and 1956, the average output per acre of paddy cultivation by Dalena farmers was as much as Rs. 362 (1962, p. 218), while it amounted to only Rs. 281 in Wangala (1962, p. 47). Thus the average yield per acre of paddy was about 30 per cent higher for Dalena than for Wangala farmers. As a matter of fact, Dalena's village headman won the prize in 1953 for the best yield per acre of paddy in the whole district. Although Dalena farmers have less wet land and have to walk longer distances to their fields than Wangala Peasant farmers, yet the disappearance of the prescribed hereditary system of labour relations enabled them to adopt more efficient and productive methods of paddy cultivation and therefore ensured them a considerably higher yield.

## AVERAGE PRODUCT AND CUSTOMARY REWARDS

Having discussed the operation of customary systems of reward and shown that they provide serious obstacles to increasing productivity and economic growth in general I want now to attempt an analysis of the principles underlying these labour relations in stagnant village economies. Here I seek to suggest answers to such questions as: What determined the number of masters any one craftsman or agricultural labourer sought? What determined the number of customary labour relationships any one farmer was prepared to continue? And, again, what determined the amount of the fixed annual reward?

Since hereditary labour relationships still operate in Wangala, I shall utilize the numerical data I collected there as the basis for this discussion. Prior to irrigation, *ragi* (*Eleusine corocana,* a millet) used to be the major crop in Wangala; it also provided the staple diet for the villagers.

The population was composed of 128 Peasant, 28 Untouchable, 2 Washerman, and 1 Blacksmith households. The total area of dry land cultivated by Wangala villagers was about 540 acres. Output of *ragi* varied from year to year according to climatic conditions. Bad years were those when rainfall was insufficient or fell at the wrong time; famine years were those when most crops failed and a considerable proportion of the population had to go hungry and many even died. Informants told me that bad years used to occur with a frequency of about one in every five or six years; this is borne out by Mysore rainfall statistics. Accordingly, we find that the output per acre of *ragi* varied from a minimum of just over two *pallas* (one *palla* of *ragi* equals 208 lb) in bad seasons to a maximum of about eight or nine *pallas* in good ones. The average daily subsistence requirement of *ragi* per household is just under two *seers* (one *seer* is one-hundredth of one *palla,* or 2 lb); this makes the annual *ragi* requirements for each household about seven *pallas* and for the whole village composed of 159 households 1,113 *pallas.* In bad years Wangala's total *ragi* output of approximately 1,300 pallas was thus slightly more than sufficient to keep all the households fed, provided it was distributed equally among all of them. The average output per household in bad seasons was, therefore, an important factor in determining the size of any one settlement. I shall subsequently return to the importance of the average in stagnant economies. At this stage in the argument it is sufficient to note that in bad years the total product of the village had to be distributed equally among all households in order to keep the population alive. Yet the discrepancy in the landholding by Peasants and their dependent Untouchable labouring households was, and still is, considerable. The average land holding per Untouchable household was about 1½ acres, while that of Peasants was about 4 acres. This meant that in bad years Wangala Untouchable households managed to produce only approximately 3½ *pallas of ragi*, while each needed at least 7 *pallas* to survive. By contrast, the average Peasant household produced over 9 *pallas* of *ragi.* Average labour requirements per acre of *ragi* amount to about 35 labour days in bad years. The average Peasant household thus needed a minimum of about 120 labour days to cultivate its *ragi* fields. As cultivation of *ragi* is concentrated into a short period in the year—*ragi* is a two to four months crop—each Peasant farmer needed at least one or two helpers. It is extremely difficult for the Indian farmer to know the marginal product of his labour, i.e. the addition to total output produced by the last unit of labour employed: sometimes two men produce as much as three do, at other times there are differences in return. For the Peasant farmer it is much easier and more reliable to calculate the average product per labourer: this can readily be done by sharing the output equally among all cultivators. In bad years Wangala villagers, Peasants and their dependent households alike, all received an equal share of the total quantity of *ragi* produced. This meant that each Peasant had to give 50 *seers* of *ragi* to each of his two dependent Untouchable households. Fifty *seers* of *ragi* is in fact the quantity of fixed annual reward given by

Wangala Peasant masters to their Untouchable servants. Each Untouchable household had to have hereditary relationships with about eight or nine Peasant masters in order to make up the deficiency in bad years between his family's food requirements and his own output of *ragi.*

Clearly, in bad years Peasants had no more *ragi* supplies than their dependent Untouchables. However, masters were prepared to accept this egalitarian distribution always in the hope of better seasons: In years of bumper crops the average Peasant farmer could produce a surplus of about 25 *pallas* of *ragi* over and above his subsistence needs including the fixed rewards to his Untouchable labourers. This surplus enabled him to throw large feasts, arrange for elaborate weddings, invest in better bullocks or houses, etc. (cash saving was very rare). Good harvests, therefore, provided Peasants with the means with which to conduct their struggle for prestige. Economic differentiation was clearly taking place in good years, whereas in bad seasons the emphasis was on egalitarianism. In order to maximize his total product the Peasant farmer needed helpers; he needed them even more in good years than in bad. To make certain that his helpers were on the spot when required, he in turn was prepared to maintain hereditary relationships with them and give them fixed annual rewards. Other considerations besides the purely economic, such as ritual and political, reinforced the Peasant's preparedness to maintain his customary relationships.

Good years meant better yields also for Untouchables. However, since their landholdings were so much smaller than those of Peasants and their masters had prior claim on their work performance, their own output never reached the village maximum. Labour requirements per acre of *ragi* were higher in good than in bad years: bumper crops needed more weeding and more harvesting. Therefore, in good years Untouchables had even less time for their own fields than in bad seasons. The major part of their food requirements was always provided by their Peasant masters in the form of fixed quantities of annual rewards. Untouchables were prepared to accept the system of fixed rewards because it provided them with security even in bad years. Though no dependent Untouchable ever managed to have a surplus even approaching that of Peasant households in good seasons, the servicing castes did also benefit indirectly from good harvests: they watched the Peasants' lavish weddings and collected food at feasts. They could also get loans from their masters to help purchase cattle. Moreover, the hereditary relationships offered to the dependent Untouchables a number of advantages of more diverse economic and social nature: each Untouchable could count on his Peasant masters to help him in arranging and conducting weddings and in settling disputes and to give him some degree of social security in general.

In our Wangala example we have seen how the small landholdings of the Untouchables buttressed the system of fixed customary rewards. On the basis of this, we may postulate that the quantity of fixed annual rewards will vary according to the total village produce in bad years, the size of the labourers' landholdings, and the number of labour relations any one of them can maintain. This statement may be verified in different ways: first, by examining the fixed annual rewards of landless dependent households; second, by finding out whether there is any correlation between the quantity of fixed rewards and the size of the dependent household's acreage; and, third, by establishing whether or not there are differences in the quantity of fixed rewards in different villages in the same area.

We can satisfy the first point by examining the hereditary relationships in which Wangala's two Washerman households were involved. Prior to irrigation they were completely landless. Each had hereditary relationships with 64 Peasant masters. In turn each Peasant gave his Washerman 15 *seers* of *ragi* per year. This meant that the Washerman households' annual income in terms of *ragi* amounted to 9½ *pallas*, which in bad years was probably more than the *ragi* intake in Peasant households. However, since these Washerman households were completely dependent for their own requirements on their annual rewards, which did not vary at all according to bad or good seasons, Peasants as a group were prepared to let them have slightly more than the average *ragi* output of a bad year. By contrast, the Blacksmith, who owned one acre of dry land and had hereditary relationships with all 128 Peasant households, received only 5 *seers* of *ragi* annually from each of them. Since one Blacksmith could quite easily meet the work requirements of 128 Peasant households and since he owned some land himself, his annual reward from each of his masters was only one-third of that of the Washerman. This clearly indicates that annual rewards were fixed regardless of the service involved.

Furthermore, neighbouring villages in the Wangala area, where the landholding pattern as well as the caste composition of the population is different, also had different quantities of *ragi* making up the annual rewards given by Peasant masters to their dependent households.

The importance of the average product in underdeveloped economies has already been emphasized by Lewis, when he referred to it as setting an objective standard for wages in the capitalist sector; "men will not leave the family farm to seek employment if the wage is worth less than they would be able to consume if they remained at home" (1954, pp. 148–149). However, this is not entirely true, because other incentives besides wages may attract men to cities and often they do not understand how much subsistence costs in money terms. In any case, since Lewis's main concern at the time was to show how a newly emerging capitalist sector operates, rather than to analyse the subsistence sector, he did not pursue the point further.

In order to throw into relief the importance of the average product in Indian village economies I shall now describe the operation of a customary system of rewards by a composite picture of a traditional large settlement made up of one Peasant farmer, controlling 50 acres of dry land, and 14 dependent Untouchable households. The output of approximately 120 *pallas* of *ragi* in bad seasons was slightly more than sufficient to keep the small community alive—7 *pallas* of *ragi* being the annual subsistence minimum per household. The Peasant master, who always hoped for better harvests, wanted to retain his labour force and, therefore, in bad years distributed his total product equally: his own as well as each of his 14 dependent households received 8 *pallas* each.

If, owing to the improvement in climatic conditions, a number of good harvests were experienced in succession, more labour was required to cope with cultivation and, in particular, with harvesting so as to maximize the total product. Thus one or more servicing households may have been attracted to join the 14 Untouchables' households. However, it probably took quite some time before the news of the more favourable harvests spread to less fortunate areas. Furthermore, time had to elapse before putative kinship ties—since hereditary labour relations are couched in kinship terms—could be manipulated so as to arrange for a grafting on to the system of hereditary labour relationships, as in the case of the Blacksmith cited earlier. Conversely, if after an increase in the number of dependent households once more some bad harvests occurred which reduced the output again to 120 *pallas* per year, pressures will have begun to operate on the last accepted member of the group to migrate and lighten the burden of the Peasant's obligation to provide subsistence for his labourers. The time-lag between the variations in harvests and the appropriate adjustment in the size of the labour force helps to explain cases of zero or even negative marginal productivity, as well as incidents of strains and stress in the political and social system of Indian villages.

The share of the Peasant landholder, who himself participated in cultivating, was in bad seasons no larger than the annual reward he had to give to each of his dependent Untouchable households. By contrast, good harvests gave him a surplus of as much as 300 *pallas* of *ragi* over and above the rewards he had to pay to his labourers. He could utilize this surplus to throw large feasts and establish status and prestige for himself. Labourers, on the other hand, were prepared to accept the system of fixed annual rewards, because it assured them of their subsistence requirements, even in bad seasons. Thus, it was the expectation of good harvests which induced the Peasant master to accept in bad years a share equal to the annual rewards his labourers received, whereas the continued threat of bad harvests induced Untouchable labourers to accept a reward which did not vary according to labour performed or according to harvest. The system was, therefore, maintained by the chance occurrences of good and bad harvests. Its essence was chance of profit for the Peasant and assurance of security for the Untouchable. It broke down only in extremely bad harvests, when the total product was not sufficiently large to provide a minimum of subsistence for all the members of the society. Such years were famine periods, during which the customary system of rewards had to be completely suspended. But in normal times, when bad and good harvests occurred fairly regularly, the fixed rewards for customary services were based on the average product produced in bad seasons.

Indian villagers, rich and poor alike, used to be largely at the mercy of climatic conditions. In bad seasons "share and share alike" was their motto, whereas good harvests facilitated large feasting and economic differentiation with its concomitant struggle for prestige. This may help to explain the contradictory views of the *jajmani* system expressed by Wiser, on the one hand, and by Gould and Beidelman, on the other. Wiser may have examined the *jajmani* system as it operated in bad seasons with its emphasis on equal distribution of output, while Gould and Beidelman may have concentrated their attention on good harvests when extreme economic differentiation occurred and when masters appeared to exploit their dependent helpers as capitalists are supposed to exploit their workers. But the difference may also be due to different philosophical approaches. However, while the success of a capitalist enterprise is largely due to the foresight and organizing ability of its managers, traditional Indian landowners and landless alike relied completely on favourable climatic conditions to provide them with good harvests. No one, of Wiser, Gould, or Beidelman, seems to appreciate that Indian villagers, rich and poor alike, were all subject to the hazards of their environment, over which they had very little control. Mere survival was therefore of the utmost importance to the population of these underdeveloped economies. Indian villagers did not have the technological know-how nor did they have any incentives to initiate growth in these economies, which were geared to stability.

In traditional Indian village economies with hereditary systems of reward, landowners were chiefly concerned with the quantity of the average product in bad years—or to put it in time-perspective: they were interested in the long-term average product, rather than in the marginal addition to total output which any one worker might contribute. This emphasis on the average is noticeable not only in economic relations; it pervades many other aspects of the culture. Beliefs in sorcery and witchcraft sanction "average" behaviour. For instance, when a Wangala Peasant builds a new house with the surplus he produced in good years, he always hangs a broken pot on to the outside. This is done to protect the new house from evil and jealous spirits. The broken mudpot is supposed to give the impression that the house is not new but really old like all the other houses in the vicinity.

As soon as external forces break down the isolation of Indian villages and new economic opportunities are introduced, innovations and changes at the margin tend to become important. This is precisely what happened in Wangala after irrigation had facilitated cash cropping. As we have seen, Wangala Peasant farmers were not prepared to grant the Blacksmith even a small increase in his customary fixed reward of five *seers* per household. This had been based on the average product in bad years and was regarded as more than sufficient for subsistence. However, as soon as the Blacksmith managed to disentangle himself from his hereditary obligations, Peasants started to think of his work in terms of the contribution it made to the cultivation of their lands. The Blacksmith was obviously an innovator: he designed an improved plough and became a housing contractor. Peasants then began to appreciate their Blacksmith and his contribution to their output, i.e. wet crops, the cultivation of which necessitated iron ploughs in place of the customary wooden ones. Thus the transition from a non-market to a market economy involves a change from emphasis on average productivity to one on marginal productivity. However, before such change in emphasis can take place customary labour relations must be eliminated. Planners would be well advised to bear in mind that it may be easier to improve productive efficiency by introducing entirely new crops or products, rather than by attempting to change the traditional methods and techniques of production. For example, in Saurashtra "attempts were made to introduce improved methods of cultivation like the Russian method of *bajri* cultivation and the Japanese method of paddy cultivation. Only 34 acres were brought under the Russian method of *bajri* cultivation against the overall target of about 2,600 acres and for the Japanese method, the respective figures were 52 acres and 865 acres" (Government of India, 1954, p. 247). If the agricultural officials responsible for this programme had appreciated the principles underlying the traditional organization of labour, they would never have attempted to introduce improved methods for cultivating customary crops, but would have tried to introduce entirely new crops, which could then have been cultivated outside the system of traditional labour relations.

This change-over from emphasis on the average product to stress on the marginal product is not only a symbol of important changes in the economic organization of previously isolated economies, but is also marked by radical changes in the social and political systems. In non-market economies nonconformity is usually penalized. By contrast, economic growth necessitates innovation and needs men who are prepared to take risks. These new entrepreneurs who try to take advantage of the new economic opportunities then want to translate their wealth into social status. They want to replace the system of ascribed social status with one in which status can be achieved. This has been happening in Dalena (Epstein, 1962, pp. 276–293) and is evidenced in a great number of societies which are in the process of being integrated into the wider economy and polity. The strains and stresses associated with these changes provide a fascinating field for study and analysis.

## CONCLUSION

A prescribed hereditary system of rights and duties of the kind I have been describing is a mark of a stagnant rather than a developing economy. India's customary systems of rewards and obligations placed great emphasis on stability. In a country such as India, with low soil fertility and little and/or irregular rainfall, there are usually great fluctuations in harvests occurring side by side with small margins of agricultural profits. Accordingly, the security value offered by the stable system of prescribed rights and duties was of great importance. Landowners knew in advance the exact quantity of agricultural produce they had to give as reward for services rendered them throughout the year. A good harvest brought them windfall profits. However, making allowances for differences of individual skill—and some were very adept in getting the best yield out of a poor soil—the greater yield was due primarily not to any positive efforts of their own, but to more favourable climatic conditions. On the other hand, a good harvest also meant more work for labourers, as well as for certain functionaries, for which they received no extra rewards, though they did get greater fringe benefits. Yet a poor harvest still provided the dependent castes with a minimum of subsistence. Since Indian villagers, landowners and landless alike, were all subject to the hazards of their climate and environment, they were all prepared to participate in a system which offered all of them at least the minimum necessities of life, except in times of extreme crop failure and general famine. There were, therefore, no incentives to initiate growth in these stagnant economies. The relative isolation of traditional Indian villages and the absence of outside markets helped to perpetuate the system of hereditary relationships, which defined most obligations and rewards.

The equal distribution of the total output in bad seasons may help to explain migration whenever population increased to such an extent that the average product in bad years became insufficient to provide a minimum standard of subsistence for villagers. There may be also some correlation with infanticide and the frequency of abortion though this is much more difficult to measure. Moreover, the appreciation of fixed annual rewards, i.e. fixed labour costs, associated with variations in output may clarify the fact of economic differentiation in traditional non-market peasant economies as well as the forms such differentiation has taken.

If my analysis of traditional Indian peasant economies is valid—and I hope I have shown that it is—it may also be relevant to other pre-industrial societies. For instance, we may find that many societies with a low level of technological knowledge and consequent inability to control their environment tend to distribute produce in a standard pattern equally in bad as in good seasons. What good seasons do is to facilitate economic differentiation. This tentative suggestion gains support from a study of African farming practices. Allan, an agriculturalist, reckons that before the introduction of cash crops to Africa, men cultivated enough land to bring them in a small surplus in normal years —he calls this a normal surplus. However, in good seasons, when there were favourable climatic conditions, they had bumper harvests with a large surplus; in bad years they went on short commons. Allan worked this out in trying to explain the considerable annual variations in the crops that African tribes now sell on the open market. Before the creation of this external European market, the bumper seasons presumably produced large-scale feasting, while bad harvests involved mutual assistance in terms of the same relations (Allan, 1965, pp. 38–49). Though African landholding patterns and labour relations differ from those in India, there seems to be a general similarity. The emphasis on average productivity in bad seasons may also help to throw light on witchcraft beliefs and sorcery in many primitive societies. These are but a few of the many interesting problems raised by the preceding analysis of Indian village economies.

## NOTE

1. Caste names are written with capital initials: thus a Peasant is a member of the Peasant caste, whereas a peasant is a farmer.

## REFERENCES

ALLAN, W., 1965, *The African Husbandman.* London: Oliver & Boyd.

BEIDELMAN, T. O., 1959, *A Comparative Analysis of the Jajmani System.* New York: J. J. Augustin.

EPSTEIN, T. S., 1962, *Economic Development and Social Change in South India.* Manchester: Manchester University Press.

GOULD, H. A., 1958, "The Hindu Jajmani System," *Southwestern Journal of Anthropology,* 14:428–437.

GOVERNMENT OF INDIA, 1954, *Evaluation Report.* Delhi: Planning Commission.

LEWIS, W. A., 1954, "Economic Development with Unlimited Supplies of Labour," *The Manchester School of Economic and Social Studies,* 22:139–191.

———, 1958, "Unlimited Labour: Further Notes," *The Manchester School of Economic and Social Studies,* 26:1–32.

SRINIVAS, M. N., 1959, "The Dominant Caste in Rampura," *American Anthropologist,* 61:1–16.

WISER, W. H., 1958, *The Hindu Jajmani System.* Lucknow: Lucknow Publishing House.

# 14 | ECOLOGICAL PERCEPTION AND ECONOMIC ADAPTATION IN JAMAICA

## Allen S. Ehrlich

*The opening up of new lands often seems to offer the opportunity to immigrants to break out of a previous condition of dependence and economic subordination. In this selection, we see how a group of Indians attempted to do just that and met with partial success for a time. But their success was dependent upon their occupation of lands that others, more powerful than they, viewed as worthless. When this perception changed, the impoverishment of the Jamaican Indians soon followed.*

*East Indians came to Jamaica as indentured servants to work on the sugar- cane plantations. Many were able to buy land and established themselves as peasant farmers. From Ehrlich's analysis we learn how the Indians initially profited from the fact that plantation owners regarded marsh lands as unusable. The Indians settled there and achieved a high degree of self-sufficiency through rice cultivation.*

*This situation changed when plantation owners came to regard the wet lands as a resource. The subsequent impoverishment of the Indian population is typical of situations around the world. Formerly the Indian household could rely on its own fields and gardens for food, only slightly supplemented by wage labor. Now that wet lands have been drained and turned over to production of cane, even the owners of small fields find it hard to maintain their families adequately when they must purchase food, rather than grow it. Landless Indian families are even worse off, as there is less food available locally. There is a lesson here. Development strategies designed in terms of the national economy may exact a great cost locally. Ehrlich's study reveals an increasingly common phenomenon: the formation of a rural proletariat, consisting of workers who have nothing to sell but their own labor.*

For anthropologists interested in the study of cultural adaptation, the way in which groups define their environment and select out specific resources for exploitation is of crucial importance. Without exaggera- tion, it can be said that the history of Jamaica has been characterized by a series of adaptations which groups have made to the selective factor of large-scale monocrop production embodied in the sugar plan- tation. Until quite recently, resources were continuously perceived as being useful or marginal depending upon their incorporation into the plantation system of production, and this consideration strongly in- fluenced modes of adaptation in the island. Probably the most striking example of this pattern is seen in the well-documented rise of a Jamai- can peasantry after emancipation in 1838 (Sires 1940; Mintz 1958), wherein large numbers of former slaves were able to establish freehold peasant villages in hilly and mountainous regions of the island which were considered of no importance to the sugar plantations located in the plains. In essence, the peasant adaptation of the freed slaves was a direct consequence of the way in which sugar estate owners defined their environmental boundaries. The present essay argues that a similar set of conditions also controlled the adaptations of the rural East Indian[1] population. The paper will focus upon the adaptational responses which Indians have made to the sugar plantation system as they worked their way out of contracts of indentured labor and became first, a part-time peasantry, and then, a rural proletariat.

## HISTORICAL BACKGROUND OF EAST INDIANS IN JAMAICA

At the outset, it can be said that the Indian population living in rural Jamaica represents the interplay of larger historical and economic forces—a set of forces which linked a colonial people and sugar cane into a bitter alliance. After emancipation, a critical labor shortage developed within the Jamaican plantation economy as freed slaves, successful in their peasant adaptation, eschewed laboring for their former masters. With "massah day done" and few black hands to work in the canes, a new source of labor was sought by the planter class. The frantic search for a replacement of the African laborer eventually came to focus upon the Crown colony of India. Hence, during the period between 1845 and 1917, approximately 36,000 East Indians came to Jamaica under contract to work as indentured servants on sugar estates. Of that number, it is estimated that approximately half remained on the island and made Jamaica their permanent home.

The initial connection between the Indian and the sugar estate appears to have been a tie which was not easily broken. Movement off the estates was gradual, with departure primarily dependent upon the availability of land and the accumulation of capital to purchase land. As late as 1915, in a report to the government of India, it was noted: "One matter about which complaint was commonly made was *not* concerned with conditions on estates, but rather, the difficulty of acquiring land" (McNeill and Lal 1915:213).

Materials collected from Indian informants living in the western part of the island (the parish of Westmoreland), indicate that a significant number of indentured laborers continued residence on the estates for long periods after their contracts had expired. The situation in Jamaica seems to have been similar to that of the indentured cane worker in Guyana (Jayawardena 1963:27)—in both cases, living within the confines of the estate system provided the Indians with a certain amount of security. By remaining on the estate proper and continuing to supply their labor to it, they were assured of free shelter. In addition, small cultivation plots and grazing privileges at nominal fees were made available to such laborers. These conditions, coupled with a scarcity of land and capital, initially kept Indians in Jamaica on the sugar estates.[2]

At the turn of the century, however, movement away from habitation on the estates did begin to occur in the parish of Westmoreland. Some of the Indians were able to save part of their wages, invest their savings in land, and move onto their holdings; others, for a variety of reasons, left the estates to live on rented household sites. As Indian laborers moved away, they clustered in households strung along the boundaries of the larger sugar estates. However, while still dependent upon the sugar estates for wage employment, the Indians were proceeding to make a bifaceted adaptation.

## EAST INDIANS AS PART-TIME PEASANTS

The adaptation which Indians in Jamaica were able to effect is alluded to in geographical accounts as well as general historical surveys of the island. These sources continuously note that certain sections of the western part of the island have been rice growing areas. The appearance of rice production in these areas resulted from the convergence of two factors: (1) the existence of tracts of morass lands which were unsuitable for cane cultivation . . . and (2) the presence of Indian cane workers who saw in the marsh lands an opportunity to utilize the rice growing techniques which they had brought with them from India. The situation was essentially one of ecological perception. From the vantage of the estate owners, the coastal plain provided but one ecological niche suitable for economic exploitation. To the Indians, however, the environment presented two ecological niches—one suitable for rice cultivation as well as a second, for cane farming.[3] Indians living in Westmoreland eagerly took to the morass areas, renting small plots upon which to plant rice. The annual reports of the colonial government invariably record larger numbers of acres put into rice cultivation in Westmoreland than in other parts of the island (see Table 1).

TABLE 1.   ACREAGE OF RICE CULTIVATION BY EAST INDIANS IN FIVE
PARISHES, 1919–43

| Year | Westmore-land | Hanover | St. Elizabeth | St. Catherine | Clarendon |
|------|------|------|------|------|------|
| 1919 | 53 | 4 | 67 | 1 | 16 |
| 1921 | 200 | n.d.* | n.d. | n.d. | 2 |
| 1923 | 263 | n.d. | n.d. | 16 | n.d. |
| 1925 | 302 | 3 | n.d. | 10 | n.d. |
| 1927 | 350 | 15 | n.d. | 20 | n.d. |
| 1929 | 102 | 80 | n.d. | 23 | n.d. |
| 1931 | 130 | 15 | 5 | 20 | 25 |
| 1933 | 303 | 30 | 6 | 20 | 25 |
| 1935 | 645 | 30 | 9 | 4.5 | 25 |
| 1937 | 645 | 30 | 9 | 3 | 17 |
| 1939 | 700 | 20 | n.d. | 10 | 13 |
| 1941 | 978 | 20 | 10 | 13 | 13 |
| 1943 | 1200 | 53 | 50 | 180 | 15 |

*n.d. = no data

Source: *Annual Reports of the Immigration Department*

While East Indian existence revolved around the cultivation of two crops—sugar cane and rice—their participation in the growing of these crops, however, represented two very different economic stances. In the cultivation of sugar cane they sold their labor outright; in the growing of rice they were able to utilize their labor for themselves. The

Indians thus channeled their physical energies into two different ecological niches and the rewards from this dual expenditure of energy
provided a set of conditions in which the people felt they could live a
comfortable life. The secret of success was to be sure one had a good
foothold in both of these ventures.

The rice lands upon which the Indians planted their crops were
primarily available from two sources. One was from a private landowner who rented out approximately 500 acres; the other consisted of
estate lands totaling another 400 acres. The rentals reported for these
lands revealed a wide spread, ranging from $1.04 (U.S.) to secure one
acre from the estates, to $15.40 (U.S.) for the rental of one acre from
the individual landowner.[4] However, the point to be emphasized is that
regardless of the amount of rent requested, none of the rice lands went
begging for renters. In fact, one of the findings noted by the government's Department of Statistics in doing a census of rice growers in
1954 was that the "[enumeration] procedure proved particularly laborious in the parish of Westmoreland where the major portion of total
production is represented by large numbers of small growers" (1955:3).
Table 2 clearly shows how very widespread the dependence upon rice
cultivation became in Westmoreland, with 97% of the Indian rice growers planting their crops on small plots of five acres or less.

TABLE 2.   NUMBER OF RICE GROWERS BY PARISH AND ACREAGE, 1954

| Parishes | Total | 0–1 | 1–5 | 5–10 | 10–25 | 25–100 | 100 & Over |
|---|---|---|---|---|---|---|---|
| All Parishes | 5,379 | 2,923 | 2,197 | 115 | 56 | 77 | 11 |
| St. Catherine | 191 | 12 | 80 | 38 | 29 | 28 | 4 |
| Clarendon | 123 | 12 | 67 | 16 | 10 | 16 | 2 |
| St. Elizabeth | 904 | 284 | 581 | 23 | 4 | 8 | 4 |
| Westmoreland | 2,913 | 1,629 | 1,210 | 36 | 12 | 25 | 1 |
| Hanover | 712 | 525 | 184 | 2 | 1 | – | – |
| Other Parishes | (536) | (461) | (75) | – | – | – | – |

Source: Department of Statistics 1955:7

The cultivation of rice, then, became an integral part of the livelihood
of Indian villagers. It provided them with the major portion of their
food needs, freeing the wages they earned on the sugar estates from
being spent on large food expenditures. As one man remarked, "Plant
an acre of rice and a man's family can live off it for a year." In addition
to money saved from sugar wages, some of the rice crop was often sold
and thereby provided a second means of capital accumulation. Families
in the village of Canelot reported that they would keep one-half to
three-quarters of the harvested rice for food and sell off the remainder
of the crop. Villagers were also quick to point out that the husks from
the milled rice, locally referred as as "cana" or "trash," made excellent

feed for pigs. Hence, the cultivation of rice provided the Indians with: (1) food for consumption, (2) a means of capitalization, and (3) the opportunity for inexpensive pig-rearing. A woman villager stood as a personal testament of the three-fold function of rice cultivation when she pointed to her house and remarked:

> Rice bought the house we live in. We planted rice and its yield was good. We sold some of the rice and with that money bought some pigs and a heifer. When the animals grew big, we sold them, and bought this house. If you have the land to plant rice, life is good—very nice. Rice is a nice thing.[5]

All of the Indian families who, by local standards were well-to-do, had achieved their success through rice cultivation. There was uniform agreement that without the opportunity to grow rice they would not have held their higher economic position in the village.

In molding a way of life for the Indians in Canelot, the combination of rice and cane cultivation can be viewed as having an adaptive advantage in another sense. One can argue that the two-crop adaptation permitted the Indians to maximize the use of their labor for productive purposes (see Figure 1). Rice could be sown in April, and transplanted in June and July when the cane crop was coming to an end. The harvesting of rice was near competition approximately at the time when the cane season was just getting underway toward the end of November and beginning of December. The amount of overlap between the two crops was quite small. Rice and cane competed minimally for manpower and, from the Indian's viewpoint, the two crops were complementary—one could plant his rice plot and earn sugar wages as well, without a strong conflict of interest.[6]

FIGURE 1. SEASONAL EXPENDITURE OF LABOR INTO RICE AND CANE

In addition to the benefits accrued from the rice itself, there were other benefits which came to the Indians. The presence of large tracts of swampy areas suitable for rice exploitation actually meant the availability of food resources other than the rice crop which was purposively cultivated. Men in the village reported that they frequently were able to kill ducks in the swampy rice-growing areas. Gray and whistling ducks were hunted, as were baldpates and teals. But of far greater importance was the abundant fish life of the morass, especially crayfish. The point to be underscored is that not only were the fish available, but they were free. Villagers did not have to go out to the road and wait to purchase fish from peddlers who brought them from the sea or from nearby rivers. They merely went to the marsh lands and set a few fishpots. Hence, the swampy areas in Westmoreland literally provided the Indians with a variety of foods for their subsistence needs.[7]

## THE EXPANSION OF CANE AND THE CREATION OF A RURAL PROLETARIAT

Today, the bulk of morass lands which the Indians rented no longer exists. The withdrawal of these lands in 1959 resulted from a perceptual change of the nature of the international sugar market on the part of the West Indies Sugar Company, the largest owner of estate lands in Westmoreland; this, in turn, led to a shift in the company's perception of the marginality of the morass lands. Convinced that agreement to an international sugar quota was imminent, the sugar company felt it should expand its cane acreage. The decision was based upon the assumption that the larger the amount of estate land the company had in sugar cane at the time of the agreement, the larger would be its quota.[8] Given this new selective pressure for increased cane cultivation, the former marginal swampy estate lands came to be viewed as a rich untapped resource in the race for as large a cane quota as possible.

In order to convert the swampy tracts into lands suitable for cane cultivation, the West Indies Sugar Company proceeded to drain the morass. Since the estate lands were adjacent to the other rice lands, and the drainage pipes had to pass through both properties, the sugar company sought permission to run the pipes through the morass area of the private landowner; in return, the company offered to drain off his lands as well. The request was granted and subsequently both of the marsh areas were drained. Thus an ecosystem was destroyed and the networks of biotic relationships which supported the abundant fish and bird life were shattered. The wet swampy lands which were so conducive to the growth of rice seedlings had rotted cane roots—in their place a new environment for promoting the growth of sugar cane was created. Cane was literally made to spread at the expense of rice through the manipulation of modern technology. Concomitantly, the Indians in the village say they have now come to know the meaning of poverty. Most families argue that their well-being has been one steady decline since the draining of the rice lands. Today, an air of depression and hopelessness characterizes village life. Reference to the "hard times" of the present versus the "softer times" of the past is continuously expressed in conversation.

With the ecological shift of land use, the most obvious change has been the proletarianizing effect it has had upon the Indians. From their previous twofold adaptation of peasant and wage earning activities, they have now become a full-blown rural proletariat lacking any means of production other than their own labor. Their complete dependence upon the sugar industry for existence has bred a cash-orientation to life which previously was nonexistent. In the former times of rice cultivation, money was scarce because of the poor wages paid. However, more significantly, the availability of rice lands played down the importance of wages—security came from rice cultivation rather than from the accumulation of earnings. This point was emphasized repeatedly in discussions of the "old days," prior to 1938, when the morass lands were owned by the James Charley estates.

In "Charley-days" you didn't get much money—work a full day for 9 pence and if it rained for even two, three minutes, they took back 3 pence. But things did not cost much either. You could buy a pound of mutton for 6 pence. And we had a rice piece—got 35 bags of rice from it. That was plenty to sustain us and we could sell some too. If you got sick and were not able to work, you didn't have to worry. You always had some rice to eat. Not like now when we have nothing. And every Indian family had at least one cow. You could put him on Charley's land for 1 shilling a month —12 shillings a year. That wasn't bad. So every Indian family had plenty of milk. The children grew up healthy. You could go into any yard and get a quart of milk free. People were glad to share. If you had hard times you could get enough rice "on trust" from someone for three months. People always had plenty of rice in their "battrys" [storage houses]. Those were nice times.

Today, sharing and borrowing "on trust" are conspicuously absent among the villagers of Canelot. With work in the cane fields available only six months of the year, the wages earned must be carefully guarded and doled out sparingly within the family if earnings are to last the entire year.[9] Fragmentation, rather than cooperation, appears to characterize the attitudes and behavior of the Indian villagers—each man for himself with the major value placed upon cold hard cash.[10] As an elderly informant commented in summing up the prevailing sentiment of the village, "It is money which makes things turn." One might note that because money is now a very scarce commodity in the village, "things do not turn" very much in Canelot. Celebrations and religious rituals which previously had brought together large numbers of villagers are now confined to smaller, more select groupings of people. From the viewpoint of population distribution, it might be said that the people of Canelot form a village; however, in terms of social interaction, a sense of solidarity linking the various households into a community no longer exists. Proletarianization and poverty have atomized the Indians of Canelot.

In looking at the situation of the Indians of Canelot, it has been stated in government circles that it behooves Jamaica to import rice from Guyana rather than to encourage its cultivation locally because Guyanese rice can be grown so much more cheaply. This factual statement can easily be shown to be true. Yet it does not follow, as some government officials have said, that the Indians are better off buying Guyanese rice because of its lower cost of production. This is a meaningless line of argument at the village level of economics. On the contrary, it can be argued that almost any price the Indians in Canelot have to pay for rice is far more costly than if they grew it themselves.

Labor can only be thought of as having value if there are available alternatives to which it might be put, and economic alternatives are the very things that do not exist in the village or in the general area. It is not a situation in which individuals can sit and rationally calculate how to manipulate their labor so as to gain the greatest profit. Without rice lands, the dead season now marks an end to the Indians' labor as a capital-earning asset. Like so many other people in the Third World, their labor and time are meaningless variables in the economist's macroscopic analyses of cost production. That rice from Guyana can be marketed more cheaply than island-grown rice is of little matter to the Indian villagers. What matters is that they must now pay cash for every store-bought bag of rice. When families had rice lands, their rice came from their own labor which cost them nothing. With the rice lands withdrawn, that same potentially productive labor lies idle. And so, today the Indians in Canelot sit out half of their lives waiting for croptime. In the words of a middle-aged caneworker, "Half of the year, you just ping-pong. You sit and talk a little, play some dominoes, drink, find a little day work, and just jump around from one thing to another—just ping-pong."

In conclusion, one final but profound effect which the ecological shift in the environment has had upon the villagers might be noted. The draining of the morass lands has made the Indians into seekers of the past. From a temporal viewpoint, life in the village is now completely dominated by a backward-looking stance. The future holds no future. For the Indians in Canelot, the best future would be a return to the past —to "Charley-days," when everybody could rent a rice plot, parlay part of the yield into an animal or two, catch plenty of fish, and feel secure with a storage house full of rice.

It is said that Man tends to romanticize the past and see former events of his life in a mellower light than they really were. From the vantage of the field materials presented, it would appear one can argue that the Indians' view of the past is rooted in the realities of their past, rather than in its romanticization.

## NOTES

1. In the Caribbean literature, the term "East Indian" is used to distinguish persons of Indian descent from the aboriginal Amerindians. Throughout the paper, the terms "Indian" and "East Indian" have been used interchangeably, as there are no persons of Amerindian descent in Jamaica.
2. For a comparative discussion of Indian adaptation to the plantation system in the British Caribbean, see Ehrlich (1971:166–80).
3. The material on rural Jamaican Indians supports some of Wolf's comments on the patterns of adaptation of immigrant groups to larger host societies: ". . . migrants are often able to see opportunities, fields for manoeuver, in the host culture which the local inhabitants fail to perceive. This sharpened perception on the part of the migrant group is due partly to their possession of a distinct cultural lens

through which they view the outside world, partly to their need to strive for an improved balance of risks and chances in a situation in which they have cut their connections with an established way of life. They may thus find and create new niches in the local ecology, and then stake their claims to these niches . . ." (1959: 144).

4. The prices given are for rentals in 1958 and are based upon a conversion rate of £ 1 = $2.80 (U.S.) which was in effect during most of the fieldwork period.

5. All quotes from village informants have been transposed from the Jamaican patois into standardized English.

6. For an overview of the types of economic strategies taken by cane workers after the crop has been harvested, see Hicks' recent essay, "Making a Living During the Dead Seasons in Sugar-Producing Regions of the Caribbean" (1972:73–81).

7. Paul Friedrich, in his study of a Tarascan village in southwestern Mexico, has also commented upon the diversity of wild food resources available to the community because of its location near a marshy lake (1970:10–11).

8. To date, no such international agreement has been reached.

9. Few families dependent upon cane wages are actually able to make it through the year without some form of purchasing on credit. In neighboring towns, stores owned mainly by Chinese extend small amounts of credit to the people during the dead season.

10. The social situation in Canelot contrasts rather sharply with Mintz' work among cane workers in Puerto Rico where *compadrazgo* relations appear to have countered the type of fragmentary and isolating condition which has developed in Jamaica (see Mintz 1956:389–90; also Mintz and Wolf 1950:359–60).

# REFERENCES

EHRLICH, A. S., 1971, "History, Ecology and Demography in the British Caribbean: An Analysis of East Indian Ethnicity," *Southwestern Journal of Anthropology,* 27:166–80.

FRIEDRICH, P., 1970, *Agrarian Revolt in a Mexican Village.* Englewood Cliffs: Prentice-Hall.

HICKS, F., 1972, "Making a Living During the Dead Season in Sugar-Producing Regions of the Caribbean," *Human Organization,* 31:73–81.

JAMAICAN COLONIAL GOVERNMENT–DEPARTMENT OF IMMIGRATION, 1919–43, *Annual Report of the Immigration Department.* Kingston: Government Printing Office.

JAMAICAN COLONIAL GOVERNMENT–DEPARTMENT OF STATISTICS, 1955, *Rice Acreage in Jamaica.* Kingston: Mimeograph.

JAYAWARDENA, C., 1963, *Conflict and Solidarity in a Guianse Plantation.* London: The Athlone Press.

MACNEILL, J., AND C. LAL, 1915, *Report to the Government of India on the Conditions of Indian Immigrants in Four British Colonies and Surinam:* Part II—*Surinam, Jamaica, Fiji, and General Remarks.* London: His Majesty's Stationery Office.

MINTZ, S. W., 1956, "Cañamelar: the Subculture of a Rural Sugar Plantation Proletariat," in *The People of Puerto Rico.* Julian H. Steward, (ed.) Urbana: University of Illinois Press.

———, 1958, "Historical Sociology of the Jamaican Church-Founded Free Village System," *De West-Indische Gids,* 38:46–70.

MINTZ, S. W., AND E. R. WOLF, 1950, "An Analysis of Ritual Co-parenthood (Compadrazgo)," *Southwestern Journal of Anthropology,* 6:341–68.

SIRES, R. V., 1940, "Negro Labor in Jamaica in the Years Following Emancipation," *The Journal of Negro History,* 25:484–97.

WOLF, E. R., 1959, "Specific Aspects of Plantation Systems in the New World: Community Sub-cultures and Social Classes," in Vera Rubin (ed.), *Plantation Systems of the New World,* Social Science Monographs VII. Washington, D.C.: Pan American Union.

# 15 COLLECTIVIZATION, KINSHIP, AND THE STATUS OF WOMEN IN RURAL CHINA

## Norma Diamond

*Coming full circle to the universal inequalities found in human societies, we examine, in this last selection, one inequality that some societies have attempted to overcome: that between the sexes. Feminist movements in the United States and Europe, for example, have made efforts to eradicate political and economic inequalities by changing discriminatory laws and social practices; socialist and communist movements in such countries as Israel, Cuba, and the Soviet Union have contributed to similar efforts.*

*In this selection Norma Diamond considers the impact of contemporary China's efforts to eliminate sexual inequality. She addresses herself particularly to areas in which the goal of equality has not been reached; we thus see once again that a knowledge of cultural traditions is crucial to a grasp of the impact of change.*

The marked improvements in the status of women in China since Liberation have attracted the attention not only of scholars but also of those of us involved in the women's liberation movement. Some observers feel that the question of women's equality has been solved in China through the destruction of feudalism and capitalism, by the introduction of new legislation (particularly the 1950 Marriage Law), and by the entry of large numbers of women into the agricultural and industrial work force. Others, more skeptical, point to the undeniably lesser participation of women in positions of leadership and in political life, to the problem of lower pay rates for women, and the continuation of a sexual division of labor despite the presence of women in a wide variety of jobs. They take these as evidence that a socialist system still fails to come to grips with the basic question of male oppression and the special conditions of women.

Janet Salaff and Judith Merkle (1973), for example, argue that while the revolution freed women to the extent that it removed the legal restrictions that bound them to the family and prevented them from participating in production, it failed to take the final step of liberating women from their special form of oppression within "the most intimate private areas of life," or from the male-supremacist thinking imbedded in the traditions and historical experience of the society. The Chinese do not deny that there is a struggle against continuing male chauvinism in the home and the local community. Salaff and Merkle's position is that these male-chauvinist attitudes are perpetuated and buttressed by (1) the continuation of the nuclear family, (2) the cost considerations of socializing housework, and (3) the relative nonparticipation of women in the military either now or during earlier stages of the revolution; and they are pessimistic that China can or will end the oppression of women as a social group.

In her rebuttal, Nancy Milton (1973) points out that the demands of revolutionary Chinese women never included the total abolition of the family, but only of the feudal-patriarchal family and the restriction on free choice in marriage. The goal was a happier family life, not universal divorce. Speaking to the point of women gaining the means of coercion (armed force), she points to the inclusion of women in the PLA since 1958 and the military role of women in the mass media. And on the third point, she argues that it is a question of time and economic means in a society like China's, which is not yet an advanced industrial society. The question of housework is gradually being resolved as living standards rise and more funds become available for child-care facilities, services, and simplification of household tasks. In brief, she counsels patience, as opposed to the school of thought which says "once again we have been betrayed by promises."

Both analyses are wrong in part, in what they fail to include in their discussions. The problem is more than one of "bourgeois" versus "revolutionary" feminist demands, or of traditional versus modern industrializing societies.

In 1972 Soong Ch'ing-ling, head of the All-China Federation of Women and a vice-chairman of the People's Republic, wrote a key article discussing these issues (1973:201–209). She is less sanguine than Milton. Although she asserts that women's liberation, which begins with a democratic revolution, will be completed only within the socialist revolution, she states firmly that it is not yet time for the women's movement in China to close up shop or for the women's associations to disband. Among the peasantry, still 85 percent of the population, the "feudal-patriarchal ideology" continues despite the presence of women in many kinds of work, in the schools, and in the military. There are still real problems to be grappled with: unequal pay, unequal access to education, the pressure to produce sons, and the burden of household chores hindering women from full participation in public life.

More recent statements also stress the problem of the persistence of older thinking. Fu Wen (1974:16–18) and Hsu Kwang (1974:12–15) point to the existence of backward elements representing the landlord and capitalist classes, those who look down on women, bar their way to full participation in society, and try to turn back the clock. These and other recent commentators on the woman question see the campaign to criticize Lin Piao and Confucius as a mass movement that will sweep away the old ideas about women and propel China's women to win complete liberation.

To some extent the problem may be ideology, as the Chinese say it is. But it is my feeling that this analysis also fails to ask certain questions, specifically what is there in the current organization of society, particularly rural society, that allows for the continuation of the feudal-patriarchal ideology, or that creates it in new guise? Must we assume that male oppression of women is so deeply rooted in the human species that even revolution and major restructurings of society are insufficient to abolish it?

What I shall do in this paper is try to deal with how the rural sector has been reorganized since 1949, how this has affected women, and to what extent traditional structures *were* abolished (since everyone seems to assume blithely that they have been). Everywhere in China the process of socialist transformation of the countryside followed the same sequence: equalization of landholdings during land reform, the formation of mutual-aid teams which gradually became the basis for cooperatives, the organization of these into collectives, and the coordination of these under the commune system after 1958. However, units smaller than the commune have considerable autonomy. The production brigade, usually based on the natural village, is the unit for collective ownership of land, livestock, machinery, and small workshops. The smaller production team, which often coincides with hamlet or neighborhood, is the basic accounting unit in many communes. These residential units hold land-use rights and own some machines, tools, and livestock. Below that, there is also some property ownership at the household level, including the private plots that represent 5 percent of the total agricultural land.

Before Liberation landholding took two basic forms: household ownership and lineage ownership (with perhaps a third variant of corporate business ownership in the late Ch'ing and Republican periods). Both local and absentee landlordism could result either from small household ownership of surplus lands or from lineage ownership. In either case, the title to land and control over it passed along male lines of descent. Since surname exogamy was mandatory, women usually were married to men outside of their natal community. Villages and hamlets were often composed of large clusters of male kinsmen whose wives came from outside and whose sisters left the community at marriage. A different pattern was found in those areas where recurrent political upheavals, natural disasters, and/or the pressures of landlordism led to frequent population movement. There villages tended to be more heterogeneous in terms of surname, and women stood a better chance of remaining in their home communities after marriage. This was particularly true in the north and northwest.

Within the traditional system, women were essentially propertyless, save for the dowry goods they received at marriage. They did not inherit land or receive it as part of their dowry, and in poor families they often did not even receive a dowry. At all social levels women were the means through which to produce sons and continue the family (male) line. At all but the top social level, they also represented an input of labor to the household economy. Sometimes this was crucial, particularly in the southern rice area, and where tea, silk, cotton, or production of cloth constituted a major part of household income. In addition, women were responsible for domestic chores and child care. Their labor was under the direct control of male household heads or an older woman (mother-in-law, eldest sister-in-law) acting as a surrogate for male authority. Where women earned agricultural wages, these were paid directly to the household head. Women's powerlessness in the economic sphere was reflected in the customary inheritance rulings that gave widows only temporary control over household-owned land. They held it in trust for their minor sons, and as sometimes happened, the land reverted in use and ownership to the deceased husband's brothers or lineage cousins.

Along with lack of economic power went lack of social power. Women had little or no role to play in lineage organizations. They were lost to their lineage of birth when they married and were never fully incorporated into their husband's lineage until death, when they were commemorated as ancestors.

The land-reform program destroyed the landlords as a class, cut the power of the rich peasants, and undercut the base of lineage power and wealth by breaking up and redistributing lineage estates. These corporate forms of land ownership disappeared as land reverted to household ownership, although technically it was distributed to individuals. In many places, even though women received title to land, their status was not markedly changed. Their lands continued to be worked and administered by fathers, husbands, or sons. Isabel and David Crook, for example, comment that in the area of Hopei where they were, the individual land deeds were in the keeping of the male family head, who also controlled household finances. Women's consent was needed for selling the land, but it was difficult for women to exercise the right of withholding their consent (1966:242). Secondly, women often lacked the agricultural expertise needed to take over control of their newly received land. In some regions, women were not involved in agricultural labor at all, or they worked only at certain tasks during peak seasons (weeding, transplanting, harvesting). In a speech in 1947, Teng Ying-chao foresaw the problems that women would have during land reform (1949:40–46). She urged that there be training of women in all facets of production, including side occupations and handicrafts, but most importantly in all aspects of agricultural production as determined by the particular conditions of the area. This organized training for women does not seem to have been universal policy. Had it been, it would have made more realistic the exhortations to women to engage in production in order to win economic equality. As it was, many women remained untrained and unable to participate in agriculture. Their threat to withdraw their landholdings in the course of a divorce was a somewhat empty one: they might have been left economically helpless. The holdings of unmarried daughters were also treated as household property. The writings of the period are unclear about what would be done with a daughter's share when she married. Since marriages continued to be village-exogamous, the best she might do would be to "lease" her share to her father or brothers. However, we are talking about a short period of time. By 1952, with the formation of mutual-aid teams and lower-level cooperatives, a new situation emerged. What were essentially male groups pooled their household lands and labor resources into a larger work unit than the household.

Thirdly, during the land-reform period women were encouraged to participate and to throw off all remaining oppression. "Speaking bitterness" through the forum of the women's associations was at first difficult, but as it gained momentum and the criticisms targeted in on male oppression within the family, the women were persuaded to desist. Poor peasant men were in the forefront of the struggle for land reform. Attacks directed at them were thought by some to be a way of aiding the class enemy. Most of the early activists in the women's associations were women from poor peasant households: the husbands, fathers, or fathers-in-law of whom they complained were at the same time the activists in the revolutionary struggle, and as such, "erring comrades to be reasoned with" rather than the main oppressors (Crook, 1966:241). There may have been some truth in this, but it took the edge off criticisms of male-chauvinist thinking at that time.

With the development of collectives in the mid-1950s, a new situation emerged. Little property was retained by the household, and economic powers were vested in a larger group based for the most part on neighborhood and/or former social ties. This development created the conditions for a reconstitution of the localized lineage in ways neither planned nor anticipated. The lineage, minus its gentry/landlord/rich peasant leadership and stripped of religious functions, too often formed the basis of the new cooperative units. Together, a group of male kinsmen held usage rights over land, ponds, forests, orchards, livestock, and equipment. A woman usually became a member of her husband's team when she joined his residence at marriage. Many of the current small-production teams are still referred to by family name, except in multi-surname hamlets or in the case of specialized production teams that recruit across neighborhood boundaries.

With the work unit based on neighborhood, there is often no way to avoid the overlap with kinship ties. Nor is it necessarily undesirable. Ties of kinship, like ties of friendship, feed into cooperative efficiency and help meet the goal of greater productivity, assuming that kin loyalties do not override class awareness. That teams and brigades often have a kinship base is not a new observation. John Lewis, in his study of leadership, makes reference to this (1963:236–38). He presents a chart analysis of a production team in Hupei in which the team leader, the assistant leader in charge of field management, and the section leader guiding subsidiary occupations are all members of the Yang family of the same generation level, while two other men of the Yang family of another generation are in charge of livelihood and techniques. He further comments:

> In still another production team in Kiangsu which received national recognition in 1960, moreover, the team leader is Liu So-chin. His first elder brother is a secretary of the party branch, his second elder brother is a group work leader, his fourth younger brother is an "advanced worker" and his two sisters are Young Communist League members. For a team of 105 households, it is highly revealing that this single family has attained such a pervasive leadership position. The "proletarian" relationships among family members must be assumed to be of an order different from the strictly neutral relationships dictated by Communist ethics. Although a great deal of research is still required to demonstrate the prevalence of family-dominated leadership at the production levels, it is probable that at this level Confucian concepts of "relational leadership" have found considerable tacit support. (Ibid.:238)

The same frequency of "relational leadership" is evident also in Jan Myrdal's study (1965) where the sons, daughters, nephews, and other kin of Li Yueh-hua, the old Party secretary, hold positions of responsibility from the team level up to the commune. At the time of Myrdal's writing, a son and a daughter served with him on the management committee of the brigade. Another son was a team bookkeeper. Two nephews served as leader and member of the management committee of a second team within the brigade. Two others were in cadre posts at the commune level. The daughter and two of the nephews were Party members. The Li households came to the village as migrants in the 1930s, but most of the current residents are also migrants who came fleeing the famines of the late 1920s, the war, and the KMT White terror. In this situation, the Lis formed a significantly large solidarity block. They comprised seven or eight of the village's fifty households, including its most complex extended ones, easily outnumbering any other surname group in the brigade. But they by no means held a clear majority: cadre positions were filled by a range of surnames, while some Li family members held no positions of responsibility at all. However, in communities with more time-depth and stable population, a single surname group can dominate decision-making simply because they clearly outnumber any other contenders.

Nanwang village, cited as a model in the early days of cooperativization, is a case in point (Li Kai and Ching Shen, 1957:115–27). It is clearly a lineage village, and the three founders of the first cooperatives were Wang Yu-kun, Wang Hsiao-chi, and Wang Hsiao-pang—all poor peasants. They were joined by three upper-middle-peasant Wang households, which led to struggle between those who were from poor peasant households and those who were better off. On one occasion "some of the members wanted to elect Li Wu, a Party member [as chairman], but he [Wang Wen-shuang, an upper-middle peasant] made them elect Wang Tan-tan, who was politically backward and no good as a leader" (ibid.:120). The situation was eventually resolved successfully, with 85 percent of the village households being drawn into the cooperative under poor peasant leadership, but the struggle to put national and collective interests in first place and to be aware of class struggle still goes on in what is now Nanwang Village Production Brigade, according to recent reports (*Hung-chi,* March 1974).

The dangers resulting from the lack of attention to class struggle are not only the move backward to the individualistic "capitalist road," but a return to an even older order. The Kwangtang press in the early 1960s printed critiques of several production brigades in the region which were apportioning collective funds to repair the ancestral halls, paint new ancestral tablets, and rebuild local temples (Ting Chung, 1962).

Western scholars and Chinese commentators alike have made little connection between the patrilineal structure and lineage control of collective work units, and the difficulties of realizing the goal of full equality for women in the rural areas. The household in many rural teams and brigades remains embedded in a network of male kinsmen that has been strengthened by collectivization. To avoid this development, it would have been necessary to force massive transfers of the population, with all the attendant economic chaos and psychological suffering—clearly unfeasible and undesirable. The equalization of women's status has thus been held back by the necessities of the situation.

One of the results of the current structure is that team and brigade affiliations are seen as passing from father to sons. Women still are either in-marrying strangers who have to prove themselves or temporary residents who will soon be departing to get married. There is little incentive for the work unit to recommend girls over boys for higher education or specialized training, or to prepare them for increasing degrees of responsibility and leadership. Of course, there *are* some women in positions of leadership and responsibility. In the rural areas women are cited as making up anywhere from 10 percent to 37 percent of the cadres. But this figure includes those assigned to "women's work" —creche and nursery attendants, and the leaders of all-female small work groups within the team or brigade. When it comes to holding wider powers, including leadership over men, the number of women is small.

Moreover, the women who become leading cadres in the rural areas seem often to have led atypical lives. This assertion can be documented somewhat by the existent literature and by the small amounts of interviewing I was able to do over a two-month period in 1973 during a visit to China. In Myrdal's study, referred to earlier, the leading woman cadre was not only the daughter of the Party secretary and kinswoman to several other male cadres, but in addition she resided after marriage in her father's house while her husband worked in nearby Yenan city. In short, an atypical marriage allowed her to stay in the village of her birth and to advance politically. The Crooks' earlier study (1959:43) similarly points out that the first woman activist in the community had "the advantage over most married women of Ten-Mile Inn of being a native of the village." Contrary to local custom, she married a man from a nearby hamlet. Her daughter followed the same pattern, thus giving her a wide range of ties.

Matrilocal marriage obviously works in women's favor. But there are other atypical patterns as well that produced cadres and activists. The first labor heroine in Ten-Mile Inn was an adopted daughter-in-law, brought in as a small child to be a future wife and treated as a household slave. When the Peasant Women's Association formed, she was the first to take her domestic grievances to them, and when they resolved her case successfully, she became one of the most active members. After years of humiliation, she set out to earn respect for herself by becoming a pacesetter in spinning and weaving (ibid.:73). The first head of the Peasant Women's Association was herself an adopted daughter-in-law in a family that had sunk into poverty. She worked in the fields at heavy labor, though this was not usual for women. Her husband died when she was thirty-six, and she had her first taste of independence. She became an active supporter of the anti-Japanese village government, an opera fan, and the only female member of the village music club. She even took up smoking in public. When the Peasant Women's Association formed, she "found herself pushed to the fore by the rather shy and timid members of the new organization because she was one of the few poor women who never feared to speak her mind" (ibid.:106).

The outstanding woman cadre of a village two miles from where the Crooks did their original study was separated even earlier in life from male authority. Her father died before she was born. She and her mother were thrown on their own resources, living as fuel gatherers and doing coolie labor. She was married at fifteen, but soon abandoned. At seventeen, she was completely on her own. Contacted as a representative of the poorest peasants by a Communist cadre, she sheltered her for two years, aided the anti-Japanese guerrilla forces, and at twenty-four became a Party member herself. The following year (1944) she became a labor heroine and was elected as head of her village's women's association. When her husband finally returned to the community, well after Liberation, she was already firmly established as a cadre, heading the first mutual-aid group in the village and later the first lower-level Agricultural Producers' Cooperative (Crook, 1966:16–19).

Moreover, as the Crooks indicate, the initial members of the Peasant Women's Association were recruited from among the poorest in the village. They were those who had suffered the most from both class oppression and male oppression. Some had been forced into prostitution. Others had been abandoned without any means of livelihood and either forced to find their own way or to take temporary husbands. Some were runaways from cruel husbands or unbearable household circumstances. Generally, they were seen as "disreputable" women by the middle peasants, including middle-peasant women who had led more conventional lives.

And there were still others whose lives took them beyond "Confucian morality" and male authority. C. K. Yang cites the case of the woman representative who in the old society was a "female sorcerer." She was a poor peasant woman who made a living through shamanistic séances in the old days. After Liberation she developed into an articulate and politically sophisticated cadre. Her earlier skills in human relations and her verbal abilities, Yang suggests, were invaluable assets. So was her class background, and even more so, her marginal position—since, "unlike economically more fortunate women, she had apparently not had a man to speak for her and thus had overcome *before* the revolution one of the traditional patterns of 'proper' behavior that restrained women from direct action" (1959:132). In short, she was not tied into the kinship system through marriage ties, but in order to survive had been forced to create a position of influence for herself—in this case, one where backing by supernatural authority would override male authority.

My own limited interviewing elicited a high percentage of similar life experiences. In Shashihyu Brigade, Tsunghwa County, the leading woman cadre and head of the women's association was a former adopted daughter-in-law who remained in the community after marriage. The leader of the crack women's work group of "Iron Wives" was village-born, and had married within the village to another cadre. In Hsuhang Commune, near Shanghai, the leading woman cadre at the commune level was locally born and had moved back to her native village with her husband after many years of working in city industry. A second of the women's leaders was a former adopted daughter-in-law who at the time of Liberation demanded the right to free choice in marriage, in this case a young man living in the hamlet where she had been raised. Adopted daughters-in-law as cadres and activists in the over-forty age group also turned up at Ch'i-li-ying in Honan and elsewhere, as did women who had essentially made matrilocal marriages.

It is still unusual for women to stay in their home communities after marriage unless they are married to someone in the People's Liberation Army or a worker in the nearby city or county town. However, in the current birth-control campaigns, families are being urged to have no more than three children and to think about bringing in a son-in-law if all three should turn out to be girls. Joining your wife's residence no longer carries the stigma it did in the past, when it was an unfilial act that only the poorest men would agree to. Resettlement of educated youths in the countryside also widens the marriage pool and makes it possible for young women to remain in their home communities.

The adoption of child brides stopped at Liberation, as well it should, but in some areas it has had negative effects on the recruitment of women cadres in the younger generation of women. In some teams in Hsuhang, almost 70 percent of the women over forty had been adopted as small children, and in overall terms women's participation in political life was high (25 percent of the commune Party Committee and 30 percent of the commune Revolutionary Committee were women; and women led not only all of the all-women work teams, but some mixed work teams and one brigade). Yet there was concern about the absence of upcoming new cadres among the younger women. The teams, many of which were dominated by one surname group, were less willing to educate and train their own daughters. Brides were selected from outside the team, and often from outside the commune. Like departing daughters, the new brides lacked training and experience. They were also under pressure to produce sons during the early years of marriage. They were not in the work force full time for several years (although in this commune women were 55 percent of the agricultural work force and 40 percent of the industrial work force). Even when their children all reached school age, these women were ineligible for responsible posts because of their broken work records, their lesser participation in political work, their lack of experience, and their lack of special skills. When I visited, the women cadres were grappling with the problem of how to recruit new leadership from out of this younger group.

There remains the need to look at the problem in terms of ideology and the retention of traditional ways of thinking about women. The long legacy of second-class status is not that easily obliterated. In many areas, women are excused or even barred from doing agricultural work during menses: the reason given is that it would be detrimental to their health, but the underlying reason is that in traditional thinking, menstruating women were polluting and would affect the crops. This kind of thinking is still being struggled against.

The evaluation of the work that women do also reflects older thinking. Housework, for example, continues to go unrewarded and is defined as "nonwork." There is no payment for food preparation, cooking, child care, laundry, or clothing production unless it is done outside of the home in a team or brigade workshop. Moreover, these tasks are seen as women's responsibilities, particularly in the countryside. A recent article in the *Kuang-ming Daily* reflects the ambivalence toward sharing of household tasks:

> . . . due to the influence of feudalism and capitalism, there are still persons who tend to look down upon and discriminate against women. This has been reflected in many of their activities. Some of them merely pay lip service to the role of women who must shoulder half of the worldly responsibilities, while refusing to take any action to bring that role into full play. Others assign women cadres as much housework as possible, as if women are cut out only for household chores which they consider to be outside their own responsibility. (Lu Yuan, 1973)

That last line can only refer to husbands or male household heads, since housework is hardly "assigned" by the team, brigade, factory, or office unit. The article continues, in a somewhat compromising vein:

> It is true that after marriage, a woman must spend much of her time and energy on household chores. Yet a revolutionary woman certainly does not allow such chores to cut into her social responsibilities. Men comrades should *offer to share a portion* [italics mine] of the household chores from the standpoint of equality, to enable the women comrades to participate properly in socialist revolution and socialist construction. (Ibid.)

In short, household chores remain the responsibility of the woman: a man can choose to "help her with her work," but if he does not, the woman must still manage to find time to engage in political activity and productive labor. This may be a big step forward from saying women's place is in the home or that men have no responsibility for the management of the household, but it's still a long way from egalitarianism. In many households, the young wife's source of help is an older woman whose age and state of health precludes her participation in productive labor outside the home. This transfer has changed the daughter-in-law/mother-in-law relationship considerably, but it has not changed the relationship between men and women or improved the status of women.

Just as household tasks continue to be sex-typed, productive labor may continue to be assigned by sex. Throughout the work force there are now women doing jobs that were once thought of as "men's work." Some are exceptional cases such as aviators and high-tension powerline operators who stand as symbols for the promise that "anything male comrades can do, female comrades can do." In the countryside, women continue to be excluded from some jobs. To some degree this is necessary for the protection of pregnant women, for the convenience of those who are breast-feeding, or for older women whose feet were bound. But women are pregnant or breast-feeding for a relatively short span of years, and sometimes the division of labor by sex seems to reflect earlier role definitions and attitudes toward women.

A case in point is the report of an investigating team of the county Revolutionary Committee in Ch'i-tung county, Kiangsu (*Hung-ch'i,* March 1973). The team investigated a fishing village where 85 percent of the agricultural work force was women. As in pre-Liberation times, few or none were engaged in fishing. Tasks like soil loosening, weeding, fruit picking, and cotton trimming were assigned to women. Other tasks were regarded as only suitable for men:

> Some women have high enthusiasm and demand farm jobs which are beyond their capacity, and they are urged to think of the long-range interests and work realistically within their capacity. (Ibid.)

The article goes on to approve the example of a hard-working woman who was permanently removed from agricultural work and assigned to be an attendant in the creche after having an operation, and to explain that pregnant, lactating, and menstruating women were all excluded from transplanting work. Men were excluded from other things: "domestic work should be shared by men and women, but some household chores, such as looking after children, sewing, etc., should generally be done by women."

In some places, women have been insistent that they have the same capacities as men, or at least some of them do. There are teams of "Iron Girls" or "Iron Wives" that do heavy and difficult work or all phases of agricultural work and often take on more than the normal quota to prove their point. It seems to be easier to prove that point in the northern areas where women did little agricultural work prior to Liberation. Their relatively recent entry into the work force, doing "men's work" has raised their consciousness and that of the men as well. But in areas where some agricultural jobs were traditionally done by women, agricultural labor is more sex-typed and not always given equal payment.

Productive agricultural labor is rewarded by work points, converted into cash paid to the individual. There is a guiding principle of equal pay for equal work, and certainly some women earn as much as some men. But often, women are less productive and efficient in the same job. They work a shorter labor day in order to meet domestic responsibilities, and lose several work days a month during menses, which further reduces their income. Women's work groups often do tasks which receive a lower work-point evaluation in terms of effort or skills required. These tend to be jobs done by women before Liberation.

At Holo Brigade, near Wuxi, yearly income for women falls between 280 *yuan* and 360 *yuan*. Men's income ranges between 480 and 520. The women's income range reflects shorter work days, fewer work days per month, and sex-assigned tasks. The highest earners in the brigade are those in male work groups raising pond fish and cultivating pearls. Both men and women work in grain-production teams, but women work only twenty-five days of the month and receive lower work points for what they do. In the brigade-run embroidery shop, the women workers' points and earnings are determined not by the market value of what the shop produces, but what their husbands' or fathers' team accords them—these women earn between 6½ and 9 points a day, but never a full 10.

Impressionistically, it would seem, then, that where women continue to do the same productive jobs they did before Liberation, the demand for equal pay is less easily won. The value of women's work was adjudged long ago. Another, and admittedly extreme, example of this occurs in the tea brigades near Hangchow. The major income of the community stems from women's labor. Tea accounts for 90 percent of brigade income, with women engaged in tea picking eight months of the year and also doing most of the processing. Men work in forestry and rice production, which accounts for most of the remaining 10 percent. Yet a man's work day is given 10 points, while a woman's is worth 8. Accounting is done at the brigade level, rather than at the level of the production team, as is still the rule elsewhere. Since work points are unequal, almost every man in the brigade receives a higher cash income than any woman. If accounting were done at the team level, the all-women tea teams would be earning anywhere from eight to nine times more than the men. With the accounting at the brigade level, income could still be equal if women received the same number of work points. Instead, males, as a group, receive the difference between the wages of the actual producers and the market value of the item produced. I was told that this system followed the Tachai model: in form, yes, by accounting at the brigade level and thus equalizing team incomes; but in spirit, no. And one wonders whether the system would be so enthusiastically followed if the men's work produced a markedly more valuable product. Certainly that was not the case in our earlier example of Holo Brigade.

Of course, this is not an economic rip-off, as in the days when the landlord pocketed the difference between the market price of tea and the meager wages of his women day workers. It all becomes household income now, shared with spouse, children, and aged parents. But it's a political rip-off: despite their importance in production and being 51 percent of the work force, women are only 27 percent of the cadres in the brigade and commune committees, and 40 percent of the leaders and specialists at the small team levels.

However, the various failures to achieve total equality do not cancel out the tremendous progress that has been made. Chinese women, prior to Liberation, were victims of the most terrible kinds of oppression. They had no economic independence or access to education or political leadership. Today they come close to being half the work force. Even though they participate politically in lesser numbers than the ideal, it is a tremendous leap forward from their total powerlessness in traditional society. They have come a long way since 1949, and we should look at the recent developments that may serve to realize the goal of sex equality more completely.

One such development is the encouragement to move up to the brigade level of accounting, coupled with equalization of work points for all tasks (as in Tachai). This assures women of a potentially equal income. In addition, the move to the brigade as the major social unit beyond the household could lead to more rationalized decision-making about education and training of women for leadership. In multi-surname villages, a young woman may have to leave her parental team at marriage, but she will not always be leaving the brigade. The growth of commune industry, and commune- or brigade-sponsored work groups similarly take decisions about women out of the hands of the localized lineage.

A second development is the relocation of educated youths in the countryside. Some of these are permanent assignments, bringing in potential marriage partners. The educated young women are unlikely to accept a traditional role, and will serve also to spur people into reconsidering their expectations for their own daughters. And if the educated young men marry into the community, their wives will have more status and leverage than if they were coming as strangers into a new place.

Thirdly, there are the stirrings in the newly revived women's associations which were disbanded during the Cultural Revolution. Starting in 1972, they were reorganized and quickly became involved in educational projects, family planning, encouragement of women into production, and concern for the special needs of women. Starting in the summer of 1973, women's congresses were held at the county, regional, and municipal levels, and by late summer were beginning to convene at the provincial level.[1] The provincial congresses, each of which met for five or six days, dealt with such issues as implementation of the principle of equal pay for equal work, labor protection for women, sharing of housework, planned parenthood, encouragement of late marriage, greater participation of women in production, increasing the number of women cadres and bringing women into more political activity and study, recruitment of more women into the Party and the Young Communist League, attention to the special problems of educated young women resettling in the countryside, and criticism and struggle against the forces of old ideas and habits reflecting male-chauvinist thinking. Press reports available here unfortunately did not detail the resolutions that came out of these meetings, but one from the Hainan Administrative Region is perhaps indicative:

"There must be women Party members in each brigade by the end of this year and in each production team by the end of June next year" (*Daily Report*, October 18, 1973).

Also encouraging is the fusion of the woman question with the campaign to criticize Lin Piao and Confucius. Direct linkages still seem to be limited to the writings of women cadres and women's collectives, but they have been very much in evidence in the press since the onset of the mass movement. Since at least early January 1974, Lin Piao has been targeted as a spokesman and symbol for male-chauvinist thinking. He has been charged with slandering women as being "backward in thought and ideas" (*Kuang-ming-jih-pao,* January 14, 1974), and with having said such things as "a woman cannot be expected to have a bright future" (Fu Wen, 1974), "a woman's future is determined by that of her husband," and "a woman must devote herself to her husband." He is accused of having urged a return to "loyalty, filial piety, chastity, and righteousness" (New China News Agency, March 8, 1974), in order to once again bind women with "reactionary, feudal ethics." He is also said to have stated that women "think only about how to get oil, salt, soy sauce, vinegar, and firewood" (NCNA, March 12, 1974). All of these attacks on mistaken ideas about women are, of course, part of a larger criticism of worship of the past and the desire to restore capitalism or even aspects of feudalism. The women's movement is strengthened by being a part of that wider criticism.

Also encouraging, but more muted in the anti-Confucian campaign, are the attacks on clan loyalties over class unity. Several articles have appeared discussing the experiences in the brigades in Chufu County, Shantung, which is the home of the K'ung lineage, the descendants of Confucius (NCNA, January 31, 1974; see also *Jen-Min-Jih-Pao,* March 1, 1974). Pointing to the problems of landlordism and exploitation in the old society that involved those of the same surname, and to the class struggle that continued after Liberation, the message of the articles is that "those of the same class are dear, not those of the same clan," and that historical experience proves the hypocrisy of the Confucian principles of "jen" and "I."

Class awareness versus clan loyalties appears in another context, one that praises women's political astuteness. In one such article the director of the commune women's association was singled out for commendation because when an unreformed landlord in her production brigade

> ... used clan relations to corrode a cadre, she aroused *the masses of women* to struggle against him. She mobilized an elderly woman who had worked as a servant for the landlord in the old society to pour out her grievances and expose his crimes. This helped raise the women's consciousness of class struggle. (NCNA, March 7, 1974; italics added)

And who is better suited to do this than the women, who are outsiders to the male solidarity group and have no special interest in protecting clan privilege?

Merged also into the anti-Confucius campaign is discussion of the underlay of traditional religious beliefs that defined women as polluting agents either in agriculture or in the fishing industry (NCNA, February 27, March 10, March 11, 1974). The old taboos are criticized as a part of the doctrine of "male superiority," linked to Confucian thought even if not discussed in the Confucian classics.

At the same time, there is still reluctance within the anti-Confucian campaign to separate the issue of oppression of women as women, from the question of class struggle. In many, though by no means all, of the articles, Confucian ideas are said to have oppressed the "working women" (*lao-dung-fu-nu*), rather than women in general.

> For over two thousand years until Liberation, the working women were subjected to oppression by the reactionary political authority, clan authority, religious authority, and the authority of the husband and downtrodden at the lowest stratum of society. . . . The establishment of the socialist system in China has eliminated the class cause of oppression and exploitation of working women and liberated the masses of women politically, economically, and culturally. (*Jen-Min-Jih-Pao*, March 8, 1974; see also NCNA, February 22, 1974)

Undeniably, working women suffered the most: their oppression as women was an added element to their oppression as peasants and workers, to their oppression as youth in a gerontocracy. But one could argue that all women shared some of the same oppression because of the value assigned to gender. The oppression stemming from clan authority, religious authority, and the authority of the husband touched the lives of all but an exceptional handful. There were few Empress Dowagers through the two thousand years of history.

There are still other developments which are of positive value in raising the status of women. Birth-control methods are being actively promoted and increasingly adopted, thus giving women control over their own bodies and providing alternatives to motherhood as women's only or major role. Child-care facilities are expanding. And finally, there is the sincere concern with the problem of training and promoting more women cadres. The December 1973 issue of *Hung-ch'i* contained an article specifically on the need to train and recruit more women cadres and bring them into the Party. The same month an article in the *Jen-Min-Jih-Pao* on training of new cadres in Linhsi County, Hopei, pointed out that since the Ninth Party Congress half of the cadres promoted to commune and county posts have been women, and that at the production-brigade and team levels, 37 percent of the cadres are women (*Jen-Min-Jih-Pao*, December 12, 1973). Similarly, we might assume that the campaign in Hsinfang County, Kwangtung, is not an isolated case: there, over the past two years, some 209 women went through special training classes preparing them for positions at the commune and county levels, while another 3,720 attended commune-sponsored classes to enable them to move into lower-level posts (*Jen-Min-Jih-Pao*, October 9, 1973). Some of the educated youth resettled in the area were drawn into the educational work with women, particularly literacy classes to bring them up to the level where they could become involved in ideological study.

There is also sharp protest in the press when local situations are markedly out of line with government policy. Recently there was a letter in the *Kuang-Ming Daily* strongly criticizing the school system in the Kwangsi-Chuang Autonomous Region (*Kuang-Ming Daily*, September 21, 1973). The writer complained that in his/her commune only 12 percent of the teachers were women, none of whom were allowed to hold any positions of responsibility. Within the country, where women were between 20 percent and 30 percent of the teachers, only one had been given a responsible post as deputy director of the Revolutionary Leadership Group in a brigade primary school. The letter concluded by strongly urging more female representation, and investigation of the situation by responsible persons.

Looking at the overall situation some twenty-five years since Liberation, there is still cause for optimism. Although the changes have not been as far-reaching as some might have hoped, they are considerable, and recent developments are encouraging. The anti-Confucius movement is very complex and deals with a number of issues. The scholarly polemics on the Spring and Autumn Period, on the nature of slave society and the rise of feudalism, and on the meaning of Confucian terms and phrases are but one part of it. To the anthropologist's eye, there is more importance to the meetings and discussions going on in the countryside and in urban neighborhoods and work places. The past is not being discussed for its own sake, but because of its relevance to contemporary life, in this case its negative effects on the current scene. In relating this discussion to their own lives and experiences, it is conceivable that people's consciousness will be raised and further changes will occur. Some of those changes will have to be structural ones. Consciousness alone does not resolve the problem of realizing full equality for women, just as years of exposure to the concept of class struggle have not always led to success in breaking down the insularity of kinship groups and expanding the size of the cooperating group. There are still backward communes, like the one I visited near Canton, where almost every team represented a single surname group, each clearly separated from the others in residence clusters and guarding its own resources, and hesitant to pool some of its wealth into brigade projects and enterprises. The revolution is not yet completed, but one can hope that it will continue to move along the right path, breaking down the last vestiges of privilege and inherited power and doing away with outmoded social structures and ideas whose origins go back to tribal society.

## NOTE

1. It is improbable that the Chinese press and radio did not give more detail about the resolutions and speeches at these congresses. Our various government-sponsored monitoring services did not find the subject very important. *Daily Report,* for example, confined its efforts to translating only the speeches given by the high-ranking invited male guest at each opening session. One such appeared under the incredible lead line composed by someone at *Daily Report:* "XXX Lauds Distaff Role." Fortunately, he had done no such thing! And although the *Jen-Min-Jih-Pao* literally devoted pages to articles by, for, and about women during the first two weeks of March, the *Survey of the China Mainland Press* seems to have regarded them as just so many blank pages. Anyway, according to the radio monitoring done by *Daily Report,* from mid-July to the beginning of the Tenth Party Congress in late August, women's congresses were held in Kwangtung, Fukien, Kansu, Heilungkiang, Tibet, the Kwangsi-Chuang Autonomous Region, Chekiang, Szechuan, Yunnan, Shensi, Liaoning, Kiangsu, Kiangsi and various regions of Sinkiang. All of these made some linkage between Liu Shao-chi and the persistence of old ideas about women. After the Tenth Party Congress, there were meetings in Shanghai and Peking, Honan, Hunan, Kweichow, Hainan, and Inner Mongolia. I was not able to find reports for the remaining provinces. These later meetings added criticism of Lin Piao and study of the Tenth Party Congress documents to the discussion agendas.

## REFERENCES

CROOK, ISABEL and DAVID, 1959, *Revolution in a Chinese Village: Ten-Mile Inn.* New York: Humanities.

———, 1966, *The First Years of Yangyi Commune.* New York: Humanities.

FU WEN, 1974, "Doctrine of Confucius and Menicius—The Shackle That Keeps Women in Bondage," *Peking Review,* 17, no. 10 (March 18): 16–18.

*Hung-ch'i,* March 1973, Investigating Team of the County Revolutionary Committee, Ch'i-tung County, Kiangsu, "Bring into Fuller Play the Role of Women as a Labor Force," trans. in *Survey of China Mainland Magazines 1973–1974,* pp. 51–54.

———, March 1974, Party Branch, Nan Wang Village Production Brigade, Anping County, Hopei, "Lienxi Luxian Doujeng: Shiji Pi Lin Pi Kung," pp. 45–57.

*Jen-Min-Jih-Pao,* October 9, 1973, "CCP Committee of Hsinfeng County, Kwangtung, Actively Help Women Cadres Improve Their Leadership," trans. in *Daily Report,* 1, no. 214 (November 6, 1973).

———, December 12, 1973, Reporting Unit, Linhsi Hsien Revolutionary Committee, "Training of New Cadres," trans. in *SCMP* (January 9, 1974).

————, March 8, 1974, editorial for International Women's Day, NCNA English release, Peking.

*Kuang-Ming Daily,* September 21, 1973, trans. in *Daily Report,* 1, no. 203 (October 19, 1973).

*Kuang-ming-jih-pao,* January 14, 1974, "Women Can Prop Up Half of Heaven," trans. in *SCMP* (February 4–8, 1974).

LEWIS, JOHN, 1963, *Leadership in Communist China.* Ithaca: Cornell Univ. Press.

LI KAI and CHING SHEN, 1957, "The Road for Five Hundred Million Peasants," in *Socialist Upsurge in China's Countryside,* Mao Tse-tung (ed.). Peking: Foreign Languages Press.

LU YUAN, 1973, "Hail to Them for Shouldering Half of the Worldly Responsibilities," *Kuang-ming Daily,* July 8, 1973, trans. in *Daily Report,* 1, no. 180 (August 3, 1973).

MILTON, NANCY, 1973, "A Response to 'Women and Revolution,' " in *Women in China,* Marilyn Young (ed.), Michigan Papers in Chinese Studies No. 15. Ann Arbor: University of Michigan, Center for Chinese Studies.

MYRDAL, JAN, 1965, *Report from a Chinese Village.* New York: Pantheon.

New China News Agency (NCNA), January 31, 1974, "Former Tenants of Confucius' Descendants Denounce Lin Piao," English release, Peking.

————, February 22, 1974, "Women Alternate Members of Party Central Committee Criticize Lin Piao, Confucius," English release, Peking.

————, February 27, 1974, "East China Peasant Women Criticize Lin Piao, Confucius," English release, Nanking.

————, March 7, 1974, "Central China Region Actively Trains Women Cadres," English release, Changsha.

————, March 8, 1974, "Tachai Women Criticize Lin Piao and Confucius," English release, Changsha.

————, March 10, 1974, Interview with all-woman fishing team in Chantung, English release, Tainan.

————, March 11, 1974, "Chinese Fisherwomen Criticize Lin Piao's Contempt for Women's Notions as Reactionary," English release, Shenyang.

————, March 12, 1974, "Woman Oil Tender Goes to College," English release, Peking.

SALAFF, JANET, and JUDITH MERKLE, 1973, "Women and Revolution: The Lessons of the Soviet Union and China," in *Women in China,* Marilyn Young (ed.), Michigan Papers in Chinese Studies no. 15. Ann Arbor: University of Michigan, Center for Chinese Studies.

SOONG CHING-LING, 1973, "Women's Liberation," in *Women in China,* Marilyn Young (ed.), Michigan Papers in Chinese Studies no. 15. Ann Arbor: University of Michigan, Center for Chinese Studies.

TENG YING-CHAO, 1949, "Tudi Gaige yu Funu Gongzuoti Xin Renwu," in *Funu Yundong Wenxian.* Hong Kong: Xinminju Publishers.

YANG, C. K., 1959, *The Chinese Family in the Community Revolution.* Cambridge: The Technology Press.

# Part V
# People in Conflict

Anthropologists have long been interested in the sources of conflict among members of societies and the ways in which conflicts are—or are not—resolved. In Part Five we examine a variety of contexts in which social conflict has been studied. We look at chronic warfare between tribal villages, at conflict and competition between young and old, at conflict over marital arrangements, at revolts by different ethnic groups in an urban setting, and at a strike by an occupational group in one city. Wars, feuds, strikes, and family quarrels are all forms of conflict. We cannot hope to generalize about them. Rather, we hope to show that the processes of response to real problems can be analyzed in the context of social competition, scarce resources, and organizational change; these processes may involve conflict among individuals and groups.

One way to begin such an analysis is to consider the obvious fact that people everywhere live in social groups. As a consequence there are inevitably conflicts of interest, some trivial, some of great intensity. Even within families or groups that meet daily face to face, the interests of all members are not the same. We know in our own society that what may serve a husband's career can be harmful to that of his wife. Children, too, have interests apart from those of their parents, and in fact brothers and sisters may compete for the attention of their parents. Such realities establish the potential for conflict even among people whose ties are close and mutually rewarding.

That this potential is frequently realized needs little documentation. Divorce ends a substantial percentage of all American marriages, and sibling rivalry is part of Western folklore, beginning with the fatal encounter of Cain and Abel. Families and households are continually adjusting to the changing interests of their members, much as larger groups adjust to the ever-changing requirements and objectives of their participants. In these studies we see not only conflict but also ways of resolving it or at least of minimizing its costs. Although conflict resolution may be fundamental to every society, we know too that people may resort to physical violence, murder, and warfare.

In order to understand this behavior, we must distinguish conflict from aggression, which is simply one rather extreme expression of conflict. "Aggression" usually refers to a physical approach to an opponent and the infliction of some sort of damage. It involves face-to-face encounter among members of the same species. No aggression is involved when a butcher slaughters a cow or when we eat hamburgers. Aggression also entails an altered emotional state associated with a determination or threat to inflict bodily harm on someone else. Although many animals display aggression in some form or other, human beings are notorious for inflicting damage. Not only is homicide known in every human society, but homicide on a large scale in the form of raiding and warfare is also a widespread pattern, one perhaps as ancient as our species itself. What makes us fight?

There have been attempts to relate human violence to an "instinct" for aggression, presumed to have been shaped by our 4-million-year prehistory as nomadic hunters. Although there may be an "instinctive" or "closely programmed" basis for some sorts of aggressive response to threat or attack, we are still a long way from explaining the complex ways in which human beings act against others. It does not account for the fact that human aggression varies greatly and in accordance with human situations. People will suffer greatly at the hands of others, only to respond violently to what may appear to be a trivial change in circumstances. What seems to happen is that, though we all share a capacity for aggressive behavior, whether or not we actually behave aggressively and to what degree depend on the problem and the alternatives open to us. Rather than behaving on blind instinct, people seem to gauge available options and costs of particular solutions, a point that we have stressed in the Introduction to this book. For example, some groups may find it necessary to fight to defend resources that are concentrated or represent an investment in time or labor. People engaged in agriculture are likely to fight to retain their exclusive use of their fields. Other groups may have little interest in maintaining exclusive rights to a territory—perhaps because resources are diffuse and fluctuate greatly during the year. Hunters and gatherers sometimes take a relaxed view toward other groups' use of territory. Fishermen in our country usually treat fish and fishing grounds as an open resource and make no attempt forcibly to restrict others. Lobstermen, however, will carefully defend their lobster pots and the territories in which they are placed. Reacting

aggressively or attempting to control the behavior of others can be costly—
and violence is frequently a last resort. It is therefore useful to view
full-fledged warfare or raiding as the final stage in a *series* of conflicts—one
that would be avoided if there were available less violent solutions to the
problems facing the group or groups. Although these problems may be
external, like disputes over territory, access to resources, and the like, there
are other problems that cause entire groups to fight one another. Often
they are internal to one of the groups or societies. For example, people
wage war to acquire resources needed to sustain existing standards of
living, to relieve domestic pressures on resources, or to perpetuate a
particular social order.

So far we have been referring to conflict involving individual face-to-face
confrontation. We have not considered some of the ways in which people
organize themselves for intergroup aggression or warfare. In some
technologically less complex societies, usually organized tribally, every
healthy adult male may be expected to stand ready to involve himself
personally in community defense or to participate in raids on other groups.
With the development of the early agrarian empires of Asia perhaps six to
seven thousand years ago and those of Latin America some two thousand
years ago, warfare and organized conflict took a new turn. Standing armies
and self-perpetuating classes of military specialists greatly expanded the
scope of organized aggression. At the same time intergroup aggression
took on a less personal cast. Instead of raiding parties, "chains of
command" now structure the actions of large numbers of specialists, most
of whom are unknown to one another. The motivations of individuals
mobilized for war may be quite varied: The conscript may fight in order to
avoid a worse fate as a deserter, the professional soldier may simply be
"doing a job," and the officer may be seeking distinction and future political
rewards. As a consequence, warfare has become a part of "normal
statecraft"—quite removed from physical or emotional manifestations of
aggression. This latter change is not entirely irrelevant. Basic training in
even the most technologically advanced armies still involves training in
hand-to-hand combat and attempts to instill a psychological readiness to kill.

The development of modern military establishments has extended the
impact of war on human societies beyond limits suggested by advances in
technology alone. As warfare has become depersonalized and the "enemy"
distant societies—established in places unknown to the average soldier—
fighting can escalate beyond the point at which any purpose will be served
by continuing the slaughter. Twenty million Soviet citizens died during
World War II—most of them after it was reasonably clear that Germany was
not going to prevail. The German government's decision to fight on and to
continue the sacrifice of German and Russian lives had little to do with a
concern for the well-being of the German citizenry. It seems clearly to have
resulted from the decision of élite members of a threatened regime to

maintain themselves. The establishment of a large-scale military apparatus makes disengagement difficult as long as those in command continue to benefit from continued hostilities. As Chagnon noted in Part One, the Yąnomamö may be among the last people on earth who have the luxury of being able to declare wars without international ramifications. We might add that they also have the capacity to cease fighting when the interests of the combatants dictate.

Although modern states engage in large-scale and often devastatingly bloody wars, they are often also the scenes of organized internal disturbances, which we usually call "civil unrest," "riots," and occasionally "rebellion" and "civil war." In many respects these forms of conflict parallel the processes leading to warfare among politically discrete societies. For example, the garbage collectors of Memphis, Tennessee, were recruited from among rural-dwelling poor blacks. After accepting low wages and degrading working conditions for many years, they at last began to organize themselves. This drive culminated in a long strike that drew national attention. Why did the garbage collectors finally organize to express their grievances? Although the sequence of events is spelled out by Thomas W. Collins, we can answer generally that they organized when the risk of confrontation with the local white power structure appeared less than the penalty of continued exploitation. They had hope. Around the world we see people accepting great oppression but willing to challenge the established order when it appears either that they have little to lose or that the risks are outweighed by the chances for improving their positions. Frequently those who perceive the greatest threat or see the chances for improving their own positions in society are not the most oppressed. Rather leaders of strikes, even of full-scale rebellions, are often people with some education, professional training, or other means who are being displaced by social changes or whose positions do not match their expectations.

In these few pages we have touched on complex issues of a very controversial sort. We hope that the following papers will indicate at least the breadth of the problem and some of its more general features.

# 16

## SHARING, TALKING AND GIVING: RELIEF OF SOCIAL TENSIONS AMONG !KUNG BUSHMEN

## Lorna Marshall

*In this report on the !Kung Bushmen, Lorna Marshall describes a "paradox unique to human societies": usually security, comfort, and the warmth of inter-personal relations must be achieved in the face of self-interest and competition. We learn the important distinction between talking and conversation, as well as the significance of sharing and gift giving. We see, too, that social tensions are considerable; even warfare is not unknown. But we can also see some of the social means that mitigate conflict and provide the richness of life that is also peculiarly human. This treatment of a hunting-gathering society helps to expand our understanding of how people manage to control conflict, just as it indicates some universal sources of disagreement.*

### BEHAVIOR AND BELIEF

This chapter describes customs practiced by the !Kung which help them to avoid situations that are likely to arouse ill will and hostility among individuals within bands and between bands. My observations were made among !Kung in the Nyae Nyae area in Namibia (South West Africa). Two customs which I consider to be especially important and which I describe in detail are meat-sharing and gift-giving. I discuss also the ways in which mannerliness, the custom of talking out grievances, the customs of borrowing and lending and of not stealing function to prevent tension from building up dangerously between members of a group and help to bring about peaceful relationships.

The common human needs for cooperation and companionship are particularly apparent among the !Kung. An individual never lives alone nor does a single nuclear family live alone. All live in bands composed of several families joined by consanguineous or affinal bonds. The ardu-ous hunting-gathering life would be insupportable for a single person or a single nuclear family without the cooperation and companionship of the larger group. Moreover, in this society, the ownership of the resources of plant foods and waterholes and the utilization of them are organized through the band structure, and individuals have rights to the resources through their band affiliation. Thus, the !Kung are dependent for their living on belonging to a band. They must belong; they can live no other way. They are also extremely dependent emotionally on the sense of belonging and on companionship. Separation and loneliness are unendurable to them. I believe their wanting to belong and be near is actually visible in the way families cluster together in an encampment and in the way they sit huddled together, often touching someone, shoulder against shoulder, ankle across ankle. Security and comfort for them lie in their belonging to their group, free from the threat of rejection and hostility.

Their security and comfort must be achieved side-by-side with self-interest and much jealous watchfulness. Altruism, kindness, sympathy, or genuine generosity were not qualities that I observed often in their behavior. However, these qualities were not entirely lacking, especially between parents and offspring, between siblings, and between spouses. One mother carried her sick adult daughter on her back for three days in searing summer heat for us to give her medicine. N/haka carried her lame son, Lame ≠Gau, for years. Gau clucked and fussed over his second wife, Hwan//ka, when she was sick. When !'Ku had a baby, her sister, /Ti!kai, gathered food for her for five days. On the other hand, people do not generally help each other. They laugh when the lame man, !Xəm, falls down and do not help him up. !'Ku's jealous eyes were like those of a viper when we gave more attention to her husband, ≠ Toma, than to her on one occasion because he was much more ill than she. And, in the extreme, there was a report from the 1958 Marshall expedition of an instance of apparently callous indifference in one band on the part of some young relatives to a dying, old, childless woman, an old aunt, when her sister with whom she lived had died.

Occasions when tempers have got out of control are remembered with awe. The deadly poisoned arrows are always at hand. Men have killed each other with them in quarrels—though rarely—and the !Kung fear fighting with a conscious and active fear. They speak about it often. Any expression of discord ("bad words") makes them uneasy. Their desire to avoid both hostility and rejection leads them to conform in high degree to the unspoken social laws. I think that most !Kung cannot bear the sense of rejection that even mild disapproval makes them feel. If they do deviate, they usually yield readily to expressed group opinion and reform their ways. They also conform strictly to certain specific useful customs that are instruments for avoiding discord. . . .

## TALKING AND "TALKS"

I mention talking as an aid to peaceful social relations because it is so very much a part of the daily experience of the !Kung and, I believe, usefully serves three particular functions. It keeps up good open communication among the members of the band; through its constantly flowing expression it is a salutary outlet for emotions; and it serves as the principal sanction in social discipline. Songs are also used for social discipline. The !Kung say that a song composed specifically about someone's behaviour and sung to express disapproval, perhaps from the deepest shadow of the werf at night, is a very effective means of bringing people who deviate back into the pattern of approved behaviour. Nevertheless, during our observations, songs were not used as much as talking. If people disapprove of an individual's behaviour, they may criticize him or her directly, usually putting a question, "Why do you do that?" or they may gossip a bit or make oblique hints. In the more intense instances "a talk" may ensue.

The !Kung are the most loquacious people I know. Conversation in a !Kung werf is a constant sound like the sound of a brook, and as low and lapping, except for shrieks of laughter. People cluster together in little groups during the day, talking, perhaps making artifacts at the same time. At night families talk late by their fires, or visit at other family fires with their children between their knees or in their arms if the wind is cold.

There always seems to be plenty to talk about. People tell about events with much detail and repetition and discuss the comings and goings of their relatives and friends and make plans. Their greatest preoccupation and the subject they talk about most often, I think, is food. The men's imaginations turn to hunting. They converse musingly, as though enjoying a sort of day-dream together, about past hunts, telling over and over where game was found and who killed it. They wonder where the game is at present and say what fat bucks they hope to kill. They also plan their next hunts with practicality. Women (who, incidentally, do not talk as much as men) gave me the impression of talking more about who gave or did not give them food and their anxieties about not having food. They spoke to me about women who were remembered for being especially quick and able gatherers, but did not have pleasurable satisfaction in remembering their hot, monotonous, arduous days of digging and picking and trudging home with their heavy loads.

Another frequent subject of conversation is gift-giving. Men and women speak of the persons to whom they have given or propose to give gifts. They express satisfaction or dissatisfaction with what they have received. If someone has delayed unexpectedly long in making a return gift the people discuss this. One man was excused by his friends because his wife, they said, had got things into her hands and made him poor, so that he now had nothing suitable to give. Sometimes, on the other hand, people were blamed for being ungenerous ("far-hearted") or not very capable in managing their lives, and no one defended them for these defects or asked others to have patience with them.

As far as we know, only two general subjects are taboo in conversation. Men and women must not speak openly together of sexual matters except as they make jokes in the joking relationship. The !Kung avoid speaking the names of the gods aloud and do not converse about the gods for fear of attracting their attention and perhaps their displeasure. They told us their myths, but only when we asked them to. It is evidently not the habit of these Bushmen to recount the myths as they sit by their fires. They do not invent stories. They said they had no interest in hearing things that are not true and wonder why anybody has.

While a person speaks the listeners are in vibrant response, repeating the phrases and interposing a contrapuntal "eh." "Yesterday," "eh," "at Deboragu," "eh," "I saw old !Gaishay." "You saw Old !Gaishay," "eh, eh." "He said he had seen the great python under the bank." "EH!," "The PYTHON!" "He wants us," "eh, eh, eh," "to help him catch it." The "ehs" overlap and coincide with the phrase and the people so often all talk at once that one wonders how anyone knows what the speaker has said.

Bursts of laughter accompany the conversations. Sometimes the !Kung laugh mildly with what I would call a sense of humour about people and events, often they shriek and howl as though laughter were an outlet for tension. They laugh at mishaps that happen to other people, like the lions eating up someone else's meat, and shriek over particularly telling and insulting sexual sallies in the joking relationship. Individual singing of lyrical songs, accompanied by the *//guashi,* or snatches of the medicine music, the playing of rhythmical games, the ceremonial dances themselves occupy the evenings, as well, but mostly the evening hours are spent in talk.

"A talk," as the !Kung call it, differs from a conversation or an arranged, purposeful discussion. It flares spontaneously, I believe from stress, when something is going on in which people are seriously concerned and in disagreement. I think that no formalities control it. Anyone who has something he wants to say joins in. People take sides and express opinions, accusing, denying, or defending persons involved. I witnessed one "talk" only, in 1952, which I mentioned before[1] and should mention again in this context. It occurred over a gift-giving episode at the time of !Nai's betrothal and involved persons in Bands 1 and 2 who were settled near together at the time. Khuan//a, the mother of !Gunda, !Nai's fiancé, had diverted a gift which people thought was making its way to Gao Medicine, the present husband of !Nai's mother. Instead of giving it to him at the time when an exchange of gifts was in order, she gave it to one of her relatives. !Nai's mother's sister, !U, sitting at her own scherm, began "the talk" by letting it be known what she thought of Khuan//a, in a voice loud enough to be heard in the two werfs, a startling contrast to the usual low flow of talk. Di!ai, !Nai's mother, sitting with her shoulder pressed against her sister's, joined in. People in the werfs went to sit at each other's scherms, forming little groups who agreed and supported each other. From where they sat, but not all at once and not in an excited babble, they made their remarks clearly, with quite long pauses between. Some expressed themselves in agreement with !U as she recounted Khuan//a's faults and deviations, past and present. Khuan//a's family and friends, who had moved to sit near her, denied the accusations from time to time, but did not talk as much or as loudly as !U. Khuan//a muttered or was silent. !U said she disapproved of her sister's daughter marrying the son of such a woman, but would reconsider her position if Khuan//a gave the expected gift to Gao Medicine. The talk lasted about twenty minutes. At that point Khuan//a got up and walked away and the "talk" subsided to !U's mutterings and others' low conversation. In a few days Khuan//a gave Gao Medicine a present, not the gift in question, but one which satisfied Gao, and, as they said, "they all started again in peace."

There is a third form of verbal expression which might be called a "shout" rather than a "talk," but as far as I know the !Kung have no special name for it. It is a verbal explosion. Fate receives the heat of the remarks in a "shout."

We were present on two such occasions, one in 1952, the other in 1953. Both were in response to the burning of scherms. In both instances little children, whose mothers had taken their eyes off them though they were only a few feet away, had picked up burning sticks from the fire, had dropped them on the soft, dry bedding grass in the scherms and, at the first burst of flame, had sensibly run outside unscathed. On the first occasion, the two children, who were about three years old, were frightened and were soothed and comforted by their mothers and other relatives. They were not scolded. On the second occasion, Khuan//a, the two-year-old granddaughter of Old ≠ Toma and !Gam, had set fire to her grandparents' scherm. She was not apparently frightened at all and was found placidly chewing her grandfather's well-toasted sandal. She was not scolded either. What was especially interesting was the behaviour of the Bushmen. On both occasions they rushed to the burning scherms, shouting all at once, in extremely loud, excited voices, volcanic eruptions of words. The men made most of the noise, but the women were also talking excitedly. No one tried to do anything, nor could they, for the scherms burned like the fiery furnace. I asked the interpreters to stand close to one person at a time and try to hear what he said. People were telling where they had been when the fire started, why they had not got there sooner. They shouted that mothers should not take their eyes off their children, that the children might have been burned. They lamented the objects which had been destroyed—all in the greatest din I have ever heard humans produce out of themselves. It went on for about eight or nine minutes in bursts, then tapered off for another ten. While Old ≠ Toma's scherm was burning, he and his wife, !Gam, the great maker of beads, sat on one side weeping. After the shouting had subsided, a dozen or more people set about looking for Old ≠ Toma's knife blade and arrow points and picking up what beads they could find for !Gam in the cooling ashes. The two instances of "shouts" provided examples of the vehemence which vocal expression can have and vividly illustrated the !Kung way of venting emotion in words.

There is still another kind of talk, not conversation, which I consider to be an outlet for tension and anxiety. We happened to hear it only in relation to anxiety about food and do not know if other concerns sometimes find expression in this way. It occurs in varying degrees of intensity. It is a repeating of something over and over and over again. For instance, whether it is actually so or not, someone may be reiterating that he has no food or that no one has given him food. The remarks are made in the presence of other individuals, but the other individuals do not respond in the manner of a discussion or conversation. In an extreme instance we saw a woman visitor go into a kind of semi-trance and say over and over for perhaps half an hour or so in ≠ Toma's presence that he had not given her as much meat as was her due. It was not said like an accusation. It was said as though he were not there. I had the eerie feeling that I was present in someone else's dream. ≠ Toma did not argue or oppose her. He continued doing whatever he was doing and let her go on.

All these ways of talking, I believe, aid the !Kung in maintaining their peaceful social relations by keeping everyone in touch with what others are thinking and feeling, releasing tensions, and keeping pressures from building up until they burst out in aggressive acts.

## NOTE

1. Lorna Marshall, "Marriage Among !Kung Bushmen," *Africa,* vol. xxix, no. 4 (Oct. 1959), pp 352–3.

# 17 | MARRIAGE BY KIDNAPPING AMONG THE YÖRÜK OF SOUTHEASTERN TURKEY

## Daniel G. Bates

*Marriage is usually thought of as an important means of forming alliances between families or groups. Still, it may engender conflict, as we see in the case of the Yörük, nomadic pastoralists of Turkey. A number of men may wish to marry the same woman, some households may not be able to raise the money needed for the bride price, and some young men may simply fall in love with women whom their parents deem inappropriate. From the woman's point of view, the solution to these problems found by some young men is often very disturbing: she may be abducted by a man whom she has no wish to marry. (Such kidnapping is called kız kaçirma.) Her family, too, will be outraged, and conflict may break out even among close relatives. Alternatively, women who are apprehensive about the marriages that their parents plan to arrange may induce men to elope with them. Although this procedure enables them to marry*

*the men they choose, it also ruptures social relations among families. Under-
standing the ways in which people break the rules and what is then done about
it may be as important as understanding the rules themselves in seeking to
explain how a society operates. Why do people preserve rules that they systematically break? This study concludes with the suggestion that the rules do
have important functions for the Yörük.*

. . . Among the Yörük of southeastern Turkey kidnapping and elopement are important means by which wives are acquired. Together they
can be seen as a special mode of marriage, distinct from the normative
one. The analysis will show that this mode of acquiring a spouse is
significant at a number of structural levels. It works to adjust the marriage system to the realities of individual choice, and to resolve the
question of which of the contenders qualified by kinship for a girl's hand
should receive it. Also, it mitigates the unequal effects of high cash bride
price on families of different categories of wealth. Furthermore, quite
apart from the motivations of the individuals concerned, this mode of
marriage contributes to an alternative system of marriage. That is,
kidnapping and elopement disperse affinal relationships and patterns of
social alignment in a society whose ideology of marriage and social
relations would concentrate them. . . .

Symbolic of the normative strategy by which a man takes a wife
among the Yörük is the money paid by agreement with the family of
the bride-to-be. Bride price (*başlïk*) is the money paid by the groom's
family, usually his father, to the girl's guardian, normally her father. It
is the culmination of inter-family negotiations. Quite apart from the
effects of the often large payment of cash, the tendering of and acceptance of başlïk money signifies the beginning of a social alliance between
the two families. It represents, from the boy's point of view, the successful conclusion of his efforts to find a bride in the approved manner.
Further, it marks his transition to social maturity and adult status. From
the vantage point of his father, it means that apart from the acquisition
of new in-laws, he has gained a valuable increment in the domestic
labor force, as well as the social recognition that comes with having a
multiple-family household. Without pursuing the question, it is the case
that domestic labor is an important determinant of familial wealth in
sheep. The acquisition of a bride for a son is a major step in expanding
the tent's supply of productive labor, and bride price might be seen as
compensation to the family which has lost an adult member.

The bride price payment itself is a substantial outlay for a family in
any category of wealth. It averages 5,368.00 T.L. ($1.00 = 12.00 T.L.)
for the 304 marriages recorded in the study, and the mean sum paid in
the five preceding years is close to 7,000.00 T.L. It usually necessitates
the sale of breeding stock as current rates of bride price represent two
to three years of milk or wool sales, the primary sources of cash income.

What is significant for the present analysis is that bride price requires
that a family coordinate its sons' marriage strategies with projections of
capital requirements and other economic factors. There is, for every

family, an optimal time in which animals can be sold; a point described not only by herd size and seasonal fluctuations, but also by market conditions. Moreover, it is rare that two sons, however close they may be in age, will marry in successive years. The usual pattern is for sons of median income families to marry with no less than two to three year intervals between bride price payments, and very often longer time is given for the herds to recuperate.

It is not the case that fathers often refuse altogether to provide başlĭk for sons eligible for marriage. On the contrary, the bringing of a new bride into the household is a source of prestige, and the outward sign of the social maturity of its head. The bride, her husband and later their children, should they remain that long, are important contributors to the household labor force. The problem is more one of timing, than a question of willingness on the part of the father to make the economic sacrifice.

Whereas the family of the would-be groom has latitude to speed-up or delay the search for a bride, it is difficult for the family of a marriage-able girl to avoid committing her once serious offers are made. Average age at marriage for girls is at 16.5 years of age or younger, since age estimates for women tend to over-represent actual age. Also, as we shall see, the risk of kidnapping itself encourages early marriages.

Eloping with or abducting a bride is extraneous to the processes of acquiring one by intra-family agreement, inter-family negotiation and a formal contract. In such situations başlĭk is again paid, after the fact, but is viewed as an indemnity. It is paid as an alternative to violence, and is exacted with bitterness on the part of the girl's father or brothers. It does not in itself symbolize the resumption of normal relations between the two households, let alone the beginning of the special affinal relationship.

From the perspective of the girl's family, elopement and kidnapping are equivalent to attacks on the household. They often will react with violence if they are able to apprehend the boy, and several deaths were determined in genealogies to have been caused during kidnapping attempts. If the girl is under 18 years of age, which for legal purposes can usually be claimed, the eloper or abductor is legally accountable for the crimes of statutory or actual rape. The girl's family almost invariably begins criminal proceedings in local court within 24 hours of the outrage.

Although Yörük do not often verbally differentiate elopement from forcible kidnapping these, of course, are distinguishable strategies in practice. In elopement, the boy strikes an agreement through a female intermediary for the girl to run off with him. It is likely that the couple will have had previous contact only in larger social gatherings or through the visits of the boy to her household on family business. The intermediaries are usually women well known in both houses and the sense of perfidy felt by the girl's parents and brothers further exacerbates the resultant discord. Sometimes the intermediaries are female affines from the girl's natal tent, often her brother's wife. In one documented instance, it was a resentful step-mother who had herself been abducted by force. In arrangements of elopement the girl, of course, is able to play a much more active role in choosing a mate than the normative system would allow.

In cases of actual abduction, approximately half of all kaçirma marriages, the man will enlist a number of male friends to assist him. These usually are from outside his own household, and are generally younger and single. Immediately upon seizing the girl, they take her to an isolated place and the prospective husband rapes her. This ensures that she will be disinclined to escape. Once her virginity is lost, any other prospects for a suitable marriage are greatly diminished. Most kidnapped brides accept their abductor and choose to remain with him because the alternative of returning home is not an attractive one.

## KAÇIRMA AND ITS IMMEDIATE CAUSES

So far the discussion has established the presence of structurally different modes of marriage; there remains now the problem of determining the causes and consequences of kidnapping and elopement for Yörük society. The problem can be approached on two levels. First, in demanding explanation, is the question of what features of Yörük society generate such a high rate of disapproved, socially disruptive behavior in an area as closely regulated as is marriage. At this level of analysis it is necessary to examine the motivations of those who participate in this mode of marriage. Second is the problem of analyzing the general significance of the phenomena for Yörük social and economic adaptations and interpreting it in terms of Yörük social structure.

The two main responses of Yörük informants to the query of why one would elope or kidnap are that the boy "fell in love" . . . or that he was impatient and could not wait for his family to find him a bride in the prescribed manner. As for the first reason, romantic love is a paramount theme in Yörük oral narrative . . . but is explicitly denied a role in the arranging of marriages. Elopement then, is often a solution to a problem that needs no further clarification here. The second category of explanation regarding impatience is a statement about an important set of constraints imposed by the normative system on the individual. Each person in a sibling set must marry in order of birth, and then the fact of high bride price dictates long-term economic planning for its accumulation. This is often contrary to the immediate self-interest of the single male since the society also restricts full adult status to those who are married. Sons therefore may wish to force their father's hands.

When men who have kidnapped are questioned they usually stress their disinclination to wait for their father to make the arrangements. Bride price is frequently brought up as featuring in decisions to kidnap or elope. It is likely a major immediate cause of motivation for kidnapping. Thirty-five of the 73 (or 48 percent) kidnap marriages involved a bride price payment of less than 1,000.00 T.L. which is nominal, while 11 (15 percent) entailed a payment well above the median. Twelve (16 percent) of the kidnap matches occurred with no indemnity, while relatively fewer of the arranged marriages took place without the transfer of bride wealth (7 percent or 20 out of 263). These latter were, in fact, all instances where daughters were exchanged thus obviating the bride price payment for both parties.

Sons in families with limited capital and no marriageable sisters are confronted with the likely prospect of late marriage. Kaçirma is a solution for the poor in that if the boy's father has little or no capital, the family of the girl can do little to secure an indemnity. Thus, those at the lower end of the wealth spectrum seem to reduce their effective bride price requirements through kidnapping, even though this is not a deliberate strategy on the part of the boy's parents. A significantly disproportionate number of the kidnap marriages where little or no bride price was paid are found among families who were in the lower rankings by wealth (30 out of 35).

Conversely, if he elopes or kidnaps, the son of a family of median or above holdings in animals is placing his own advantage before a more favorable economic course that his father would pursue. He acquires a bride, and a certain amount of bravado status among the young men of the tribe, but forces his father's hand with respect to making an immediate payment of bride price. Wealthy men are more apt to pay large indemnities.

In this way kidnapping can be interpreted as reducing the unequal impact that high cash payments of bride price would have on families in different categories of wealth. Even though the average bride price paid for all kidnap marriages is virtually the same as for normative ones, there are relatively more cases where none or only a nominal payment was made. These cases occur in the lower category of herd size.

Kaçirma is also related to the fact that the ideology of marriage often creates several contenders for the same girl. Generally it is clear which of a girl's several FBs has a son of marriageable age. However, what does happen with considerable regularity is that lacking a true FBS of an appropriate age, a man will negotiate a marriage for his daughter with a more distant agnate or consanguine. If he ignores the claims or advice of more closely related agnates, animosity may result. This was observed in the field and was noted as the source of several disputes. As a result a boy may attempt to abduct or elope with a girl whom he had hoped to marry in the normative fashion, one who is in fact a close kinswoman. His father, it should be noted, will not likely be a partner in this since he is responsible for the indemnity and because of the social disruption within the descent group entailed by kidnapping.

It appears, then, that the immediate causes and contexts of kidnapping and elopement are rooted in the rigidity of the normative system of arranged matches and in the requirements of large cash bride price payments. Elopement gives the girl freedom of choice otherwise denied her in this area, and the boy by either kidnapping or elopement is able to by-pass the often deliberate and time consuming plans of his household. One apparent immediate function of the practice is to facilitate the marriage of poorer men faced with raising cash payments in a market economy, thus leveling potential distinctions by wealth in this vital area of behavior. This redistributive aspect of kaçïrma is amplified by the higher indemnities paid by wealthy families whose sons pursue this mode of marriage.

## STRUCTURAL IMPLICATIONS OF KAÇÏRMA

The concentrating effect of the preferences for father's brother's daughter marriage has been noted. What one might not expect is that kidnap and elopement marriages exhibit the same order of preferences for the categories of close kin; that is, FBD is favored over other cousins and all other kinsmen display similar rates of marriage. Over 26 percent of kaçïrma marriages take place with true or classificatory FBD, with 14 percent with true or classificatory MBD. Despite the parallel preference for kinsmen in the two marriage strategies, there are significantly more marriages in the non-kin categories which has the *net effect* of dispersing marriages beyond the circle of consanguinal mates favored strongly in practice in arranged marriages. Moreover, those FBD kidnap or elopement marriages which seemingly reflect the normative ideology in terms of kinship, as do the cases of cousin kidnapping, nevertheless have quite different structural implications. These points will be taken up in the succeeding paragraphs.

In comparing kidnap and the culturally approved marriages, the one striking difference is the relatively greater number of kidnap marriages with non-consanguinal kin outside the lineage (see Table 1). Furthermore, it is clear that a significant amount of all extra-lineage, non-kin marriages occur that way (30.7 percent). Also, over half of all non-close consanguinal marriages (55.7 percent regardless of lineality) arise from kidnapping (see Table 1).

TABLE 1.  KAÇÏRMA AND EXOGAMY: 382 CASES AMONG THE YÖRÜK OF SOUTHEASTERN TURKEY

| Relation of Wife to Husband | Arranged | | Kidnap | | Total |
|---|---|---|---|---|---|
| | f | (%) | f | (%) | |
| All consanguinal kin, and lineage mates | 215 | (70.3) | 36 | (47.4) | 251 |
| All non-kin, outside lineage or tribe | 91 | (29.7) | 40 | (52.6) | 131 |
| TOTAL | 306 | (100.0) | 76 | (100.0) | 382 |

Chi-Square $x^2 = 14.3$; d.f. = 1; p. = .001

Note: Actual rates of lineage exogamy are somewhat higher than indicated here since consanguinal kin of all types are lumped together.

The dispersal effects of kidnapping can be shown to be statistically significant (see Table 1). If one assumed that kidnap marriages with non-kin occurred in place of arranged marriages with kin, one can say that over 30 percent (40 of 131) of all such "out marriages" were caused by kaçirma. Even if this assumption is only approximated in reality, kidnapping would generate a noticeable number of new extra-lineage kinship ties. This is of some importance in itself given that the normative ideology of the Yörük, like most Near Eastern tribes, gives marriage small scope for such alliance-functions. Preferred matches occur within the lower-level units of political segmentation.

Although the net effect of kidnapping is to disperse kin ties in a structural framework which concentrates affinal and cognatic relationships within pre-existing circles of close consanguinity, it is reasonable to question the extent to which such ties are usable in social transactions. Further, it is necessary to examine the effects of both kidnappings that occur within and outside the lineage, and to see these in the context of the Yörük political environment.

Kidnapping and elopement could broaden the *effective* kinship nexus of a family, provided that relations are normalized or if the children of such a marriage are able to interact normally with all of their cognatic relatives. The first condition is met with enough regularity so that a sizable number of long-married kaçirma couples were observed interacting closely with her kinsmen. This outcome, however, cannot be predicted at the onset of events, and the desire to gain affines does not motivate men to kidnap. The second condition is satisfied entirely. Children are not affected in any obvious way by the mode of marriage of their parents.

Immediately following a kidnapping or elopement, relations between the households involved are extremely poor, and remain so for a long period. Even though a bride price settlement may be paid shortly after the incident, there will be very little social or economic contact. The risk of violence is great under these circumstances and has been known to flare up even at reconciliation meetings several years later. The primary threat of violence emanates from two sources: the brothers of the girl and from the household into which she likely would have been married should such a normative arrangement have been in the planning stages. If physical confrontation is avoided during the initial days following the event, the families will usually follow a pattern of complete mutual avoidance. This is a recognized method of preventing the near-certain escalation of conflict. Also limiting potential violence is the fact that the affair is regarded as deviant behavior and all direct participants are morally somewhat suspect. This encourages the girl's agnatic kinsmen not to become closely involved in any direct action against the groom's family, as they would do in other cases of personal assault. If physical violence is prevented and if an indemnity is paid, time may lead to a true reconciliation. Such a conclusion is not predictable in any given instance, and furthermore will not occur soon enough to benefit the boy's father who paid the bride price. In cases where the girl is kidnapped by an already married or older man, it is unlikely that normalization of relations will take place at all.

On balance, ties of affinity created in this way are tenuous at best, and the alliance significance of kaçĭrma might seem to lie more in how the practice deflects inter-lineage cooperation and restricts social movement through avoidance. A conclusion of this nature, albeit negative, would nevertheless be ascribing considerable structural significance to kidnapping in as much as it would be then serving to isolate minimal named descent groups. However, this is not the interpretation which best fits the information at hand. The concluding discussion will show that kidnap-created ties of kinship can be activated to carry integrative social burdens, and that the dispersal of kin ties is ultimately important in much the same way that inter-group marriage is in any society where kinship is relevant in the political economy. It increases the options available to households plotting survival strategies in a complex system of land use.

The Yörük, as stated before, operate in the context of firm state political control and in a market economy. Grazing rights must be negotiated for seasonal usage since all pasturage of consequence is owned by non-Yörük villagers. The social unit which contracts for grazing rights for the spring highland pastures *(yayla)* and for winter lowland fallow grain fields *(kĭşlak)* is the camp group. This consists of families who contract to share the cost of rental prorated by the number of mature sheep owned per household. These groups vary in size from two to twenty tents, and are generally formed around a core of male agnates. Further, it is common for the tents of a group to sell their milk —the source of cash for rental fees—to a cheese-maker from the same lineage segment. Some of these men have recently acquired considerable economic power and provide *de facto* leadership functions although they hold no customary office. . . . The need for pasture rental money and the sale of milk to agnates tends to regularize camp group composition. At the same time it contributes to the stabilization of the wealth of a few households in an otherwise extremely fluid political economy. This encourages other members of the descent group to camp near them because of their superior ability to negotiate for good grazing.

Despite such selective forces, no tent is required to camp with any specific group in order to rent pastures, and indeed this would be impossible. There is great fluctuation in the number and distribution of grazing tracts available each year. No segment of the population— however defined—returns year after year to the same pasture tract in the summer or winter areas. Camp groups have to adjust to this variability in the resource base by regularly altering their composition. The optimal strategy for any Yörük tent is to camp with a sufficient number of other families to fully graze (but not over-graze) the land rented in a single tract. Without going into how a family pursues such a course, there is continual movement of tents among fluid camp groups as they adjust to the grasslands available each season. Also, the effective cost of grazing is not fixed, but will vary from pasture to pasture according to a number of variables: amount of water, closeness to roads, safety, altitude, etc. For example, some families will camp in areas where the risk of conflict with villagers is greater but the cash cost of grazing is lower. During a month-long period prior to renting for the subsequent season, there is intense negotiation not only between Yörük and village representatives, but also among Yörük men as tents attempt to join others or to put together camp groups. Almost always in this process, tents will join groups in which they have at least one kinsman or close affine. Usually (and ideally) these will be close agnates and the overall patrilineal coloration of the groups is clear.

However, on occasion every tent camps with groups in which the only kinsmen are affines or cognatic relatives outside the descent group. Sometimes this is dictated by the amount and configuration of pasturage available, but more often it is in order to lower grazing costs. Conflict within the descent group is likewise significant in decisions to camp apart from agnates. Of the eleven tents of a medium sized lineage closely observed in the field, eight camped for extended periods with groups in which the most direct ties among men were affinal or extra-lineage cognatic ones. In four of these cases there were also more distant agnates in the group joined, but the decision to camp was generated by interaction with the nearer kinsmen. In the remaining four cases, the only kin-type ties were affinal or cognatic. These decisions involved both economic and social objectives, the latter stemming from disagreements with male agnates. In one tent's decision to camp regularly with affines outside the head of household's descent group, these ties were originally created by the forced abduction of the wife. Here normal affinal relations had gradually been developed in the twenty years that elapsed. The major reason why this tent chose (during my investigation) to camp with the wife's mother's brother was disagreement over the marriage of a classificatory father's brother's daughter of the head of house which took place without his being consulted. Since he had a marriageable—but rather dim—son, he felt that his rights had been ignored. He later received a portion of the bride price as compensation, but still camped apart from male agnates for several seasons. Ironically, the ultimate cause of the altercation was the kidnapping of another girl in the descent group by a close agnate, an event which upset tentative plans for the boy's marriage. This kidnapping, which occurred while the ethnographer was travelling with the girl's tent, entailed considerable bitter disagreement within the descent group, and resulted in a number of social and residential realignments. . . .

The point of this is that affinal and cognatic ties beyond the descent group are utilized in camping and acquiring pasture, in spite of the ideology which stresses the patrilineal composition of residential groupings. In a number of instances observed in the field, the cognatic linkages used to join camp groups, for social visiting or mutual assistance were created by kidnap marriages in the previous generation. Although it is problematic whether or not a kaçîrma marriage will lead to useful affinal ties, and the object of kidnapping is not such an expectation, it is the case that children born of such matches will be able to interact normally with matrilateral kin. In particular the relationship of a man to his mother's brother is expected to be a warm and mutually supportive one.

It is paradoxical that one factor which serves to further disperse *actual* patterns of interaction is the high (relative to other kin types) incidence of kidnapping that takes place within the descent group. This generates conflict precisely within the circle of kinsmen where mutuality of interest and cooperation is most heavily stressed in ideology. This contradiction derives logically from the cultural model of marriage which emphasizes descent group endogamy through a preference for father's brother's daughter matches. As families realign socially in response to social disruption—such as that caused by marriage-by-capture—they often activate ties with distant kinsmen. Many of these, of course, stem ultimately from kidnap-created marriages since of all the marriages that take place outside the named descent group, one-third are formed by kaçîrma.

## CONCLUDING REMARKS

. . . First, it is clear that any adequate consideration of the Yörük system of marriage and structure will have to take into account the existence of different modes of marriage. If one were to do simply an analysis of how Yörük marriages statistically conformed by kin-type to the ideology of marriage, one would derive a limited picture of the actual system. Ideology calls for closely endogamous marriages and stresses the primacy of patrilineal ties in innumerable ways. On the face of it, the high frequency of marriages within the sub-tribal, named descent groups would indicate that the ideology is approximated in behavior. Yörük informants would heartily endorse such a conclusion. The Yörük cultural model of their own marriage system defines kaçîrma as an aberration. Native interpretation of actual marriage practices tends to regard kaçîrma as infrequent and random with respect to who kidnaps whom. Analysis shows, contrary to this, that it is quite common in all descent groups and that it is non-random: 26 percent of the women kidnapped or eloped with are true or classificatory father's brother's daughter to the man. Although relatively more kidnap marriages are outside the descent group, the emphasis on partilateral parallel cousin is clearly like that of the normative model. However, when the normative ideology is "acted out" in a kidnap marriage, the social consequences are quite different. Rather than strengthening ties among agnates, kidnapping here disperses actual patterns of interaction. Kidnapping, in general, tends to impel both patterns of social interaction and lines of kinship outward from named patrilineal descent groups.

Second, the high incidence of kidnapping in Yörük society is unrelated to any possible appreciation the Yörük might have regarding the utility of dispersed lines of kinship. Instead it is generated by such features of the culture as high bride price, the common inability of individuals to choose their own mates, the conflicting claims of agnates, and the fact that a man must be married to enjoy adult status.

The fact that the Yörük ideology of marriage—or what might be called their conscious cultural model—is not isomorphic with behavioral reality is hardly surprizing. What is more interesting is the interplay between ideology and patterns of behavior, in which kidnapping is something more than a distorted reflection of the cultural model. The kaçirma mode of marriage in Yörük society displays a dynamic order of its own and functions in an alternative system of marriage. Moreover, although it overtly contradicts the ideal model in a number of ways, it is not unrelated to the normative system.

Sahlins (1965), writing of the ideology of unilineal descent, suggests that the strength of the ideology may be inversely proportionate to actual practices affecting local group composition (1965:104–107). He suggests that the ideology thus disguises or allows quite divergent behavior, the recognition of which in the ideology would be disruptive. To some degree, the Yörük materials support this position in that actual patterns of social, economic and political interaction are less focused on named descent groups than the ideology would imply. However, the relationship between the Yörük model of normative marriage and actual modes of marriage is more complex. At one level, one can say that marriages do closely adhere to the ideology which calls for matches endogamous to the named lineages. However, given the high incidence of kidnapping, it appears that the strength of the ideology and its expression in marriage is the weak point in the system. The strong expression of patrilineal ideology and the concomitant (in the view of the Yörük) preference for closely endogamous marriage establish severe limitations on the internal cohesion that descent groups can achieve in practice. . . . Male agnates expect more from each other and correspondingly are the more bitterly disappointed, as must happen when support is sometimes not forthcoming. Some of the most important expectations center around marriage and, as we have seen, this is an area of considerable disagreement within the descent group and one which limits its effectiveness as a political unit. Brothers, direct lineal descendants and the sons of brothers will almost invariably submerge any internal conflict in response to physical assault from the outside. It is never certain if second or third degree male agnates would do so. If homicide is involved there will be a wider display of solidarity, but it is rare that any individual more distantly related to the victim than first cousin will take vengeance action. There is no evidence at all that groups larger than a few families form on the basis of descent for concerted political or economic action. The largest such groups are the ephemeral camp groups of fluid composition.

The question that immediately comes to mind, is why the society perseveres in maintaining a cultural model of marriage and descent group solidarity which is patently contradicted by regular and even rather predictable modes of behavior. . . . It seems clear that the strong ideology of patrilineal descent, associated as it is with the historical traditions of the culture, serves important functions in the contemporary economy and political milieu.

One of the ways in which the Yörük have adapted to a modern market economy is through rather elaborate and extensive arrangements for credit transfers of cash and animals. This almost always involves kinsmen, and most commonly agnates. The extension of credit terms to agnates is strongly supported by the ideology which calls for cooperation among relatives by descent. Since credit and interest are adjustments to market conditions, and since capital is continually being deployed in profit-oriented transaction, debts to kinsmen are ultimately collected in full when it suits the creditor's purposes to do so. In short, the market encourages rational economic decisions involving kin and non-kin alike. The ideology of descent mitigates the effects of this in a political economy where there is considerable seasonal and long-term variability in the wealth of households. It gives families who would otherwise be forced to settle because of loss of capital in livestock an opportunity to purchase more, paying high rates of interest, and thereby maintain themselves in the pastoral system. By strictly market criteria, many such families would be unacceptable credit risks. The ideology of unilineal descent sets some of the non-economic ends to which capital can be directed and is thus useful as another mechanism for redistribution.

Kaçirma can restrict the size of the descent-defined contingent on "good terms" at any given time and may, in fact, cut across lines of credit already established. However, since it is treated as idiosyncratic and deviant behavior, it does not threaten the ideological basis for descent group cooperation.

## REFERENCES

Aswad, Barbara Carlene Black, 1971, "Property Control and Social Strategies: Settlers on a Middle Eastern Plain," Anthropological Paper No. 44. Ann Arbor: University of Michigan Museum of Anthropology.

Bates, Daniel G., 1972, "Differential Access to Pasture in a Nomadic Society: The Yörük of Southeastern Turkey," *Journal of Asian and African Studies*, 7:48–59.

———, 1973, "Nomads and Farmers: A Study of the Yörük of Southeastern Turkey," Anthropological Paper No. 52. Ann Arbor: University of Michigan Museum of Anthropology.

Murphy, Robert F., and Leonard Kasdan, 1959, "The Structure of Parallel Cousin Marriage," *American Anthropologist*, 61:17–29.

Sahlins, Marshall, 1965, "On the Ideology and Composition of Descent Groups," *Man*, 97:104–107.

# 18 | POLITICAL CONFLICT AND REVOLUTION IN AN AFRICAN TOWN

## Elliott P. Skinner

*A multiplicity of different ethnic groups characterizes the social composition of most new African towns. In this study of the capital city of Upper Volta Elliott Skinner considers the problems and conflicts that arise when, with the end of colonial administration, inhabitants were confronted with the tasks of cooperation essential to running an urban center. Forming new laws and proposing city ordinances became difficult, for example, because of the divergent customs and organizations of constituent groups of the town. Pressures for rapid change exacerbated an already difficult situation, to the point where outright revolution occurred. This study is particularly interesting because it presents an example of conflict and revolution as responses to pressures arising from rapid social change.*

The urban centers of contemporary Africa are the crucibles for experimentation with new patterns of political life. Whereas in most rural areas, even during the colonial epoch, there was but a single administrative hierarchy with the chief at the apex, or with the colonial administrator above the chief, the situation in the urban center is different. Here there is often a multiplicity of political groupings and structures attempting to serve variegated occupational, economic, social, and ethnic constituencies. In the same social field there may be traditional rulers claiming the allegiance of their subjects; headmen of migrant groups pursuing the interests of their fellow countrymen; municipal authorities claiming to represent all the people of their town or commune; and the officials of the national government insisting that they have over-all control of all the groups within any unit of their nation-state. . . .

The problems of government in urban Africa are exacerbated by the presence of a multiplicity of socio-political groups, often claiming to represent different constituencies or the same constituency, and often seeking contradictory goals (Walsh 1969:1). There is usually also a lack of consensus about the nature, number, legitimacy, and interrelationship of these groups; and about the nature, applicability, and effectiveness of the political structures and techniques they employ.

One often finds that the town-based traditional African rulers who had survived the colonial epoch and were foresighted enough to side with the nationalists during the decolonization process, believing that they or their political organizations should play a dominant or an important role in governing the town. Second, the elders or chiefs of migrant-strangers, while seldom aspiring to political dominance or even autonomy in the political affairs of the town (although this happened in Luluabourg in Zaire), frequently discover that they and their people are politicized in having to react to the competing and conflicting pressures of urban political groups (Skinner 1963:312–313; Schildkraut 1970:251–69). Third, the newly appointed or elected municipal officials often find themselves in an unenviable position. While they claim it their right and duty to regulate or to provide such functions as: municipal water-supply, school-construction, intra-urban transportation, land use and house taxes, the resolution of small-scale conflict, and the recruitment of personnel for local administrative positions, their authority is frequently questioned and challenged.

In many cases, the equally new government of the nation-state attempts to perform the same function as the municipality. Its reasons for so doing are both administrative and political. Many new national governments, taking over from authoritarian colonial regimes, attempt to control all administrative decisions in their states including those made by the recently inaugurated municipal governments. One reason for this is that these officials are seldom sure what functions were performed at the various levels of government, or by which political subsystems, or political structures. Further, and perhaps of greater importance, is the desire of the national political systems to legitimize themselves, and to integrate their nation-states.

The result of these conflicting claims is the absence of a "clear-cut" political system within the towns. This being the case, the demands made upon the political authorities can not be well articulated—to use the concepts of the political scientists; the political institutions and structures used are often in conflict; and the processes governing decisions, compliance, and implementation are still inchoate (Werlin 1968: 46). Thus, there is often confusion about the nature of the regime operative in the town and differential support for the authorities whose task it is to convert the demands made upon the political system into outputs—or, in other words, to make policies and to have their decisions respected. The result is the lack of legitimacy, and this makes the government or the governments (in the case where the national government is in the town) vulnerable.

The challenge for people living in the contemporary African towns is to devise political organizations based on the realities of African urban centers with their many ethnic groups, multiple political cultures, and large numbers of indigent rural migrants in search of jobs and a better life. This might entail a willingness to abandon municipal governmental forms inherited from Western nations and a readiness to synthesize new ones. Failure to do this may indeed result in confusion and conflict as the following data from Ouagadougou indicate.

The governmental institutions in Ouagadougou in 1960 reflected the town's political history. The Mossi under Mogho Naba Oubri conquered the aboriginal Ninisi sometime during the thirteenth century and forced their earth priests (the *tengso-badamba*) to pay allegiance to Mossi rule (Skinner 1964:7–12). About two centuries later, Mogho Naba Niandeffo (c.a. 1470–1511) made Ouagadougou the capital or headquarters of the Oubri dynasty. The Mogho Naba built his palace compound in this town of some 5000 inhabitants and his provincial administrators established and controlled their own wards or *quartiers* in the area. The Chief Steward of the palace, the Baloum Naba, mediated between resident Mossi and later-arriving strangers.

The Mogho Naba and his chiefs lost full control over Ouagadougou after French conquest in 1896. The conquerors soon established a series of governmental institutions of their own in the town. These included a military command in 1897, a circle command in 1904, a territorial or colony government with a Lieutenant-Governor in 1919, and a quasi-municipal government, known as a *commune-mixte*, with an *administrateur-maire* in 1926.

During most of the colonial period, the French governed the African inhabitants of Ouagadougou through the traditional Mossi chiefs. These chiefs and their stranger counterparts adjudicated the minor problems of their people, recruited men for forced labor and the army, collected taxes, and furnished goods and services to the French administrators. So effective was this system of Indirect Rule in Ouagadougou, that there was little or no disorder in the town during the many administrative changes in the structure of the Upper Volta colony (Skinner 1970:-102–103).

The birth of the French Union after World War II affected the socio-cultural, and specifically the governmental institutions in Ouagadougou. In 1947 the town became host to the government of a recreated Upper Volta colony and witnessed both the birth of political parties, and the struggle between the chiefs and politicians for control of the new Territorial Assembly. The boundaries of the town were expanded to thirty-five square-kilometers; immigrants increased its population to 20,000; the French Parliament granted funds to improve its physical appearance; and new European commercial enterprises opened for business. In 1955 Ouagadougou was made a *commune de plein exercise,* and given its own municipal government, whereupon, in November, 1956, the town's people elected a Mossi politician to be their first mayor. Finally, on August 5, 1960, Ouagadougou emerged as the capital of the Independent Republic of Upper Volta. After independence, the large number of foreign Africans in the colonial administration were induced to return to their own countries and thousands of Mossi migrated to the town. Today, Ouagadougou has a population of some 110,000 of whom more than seventy-five percent are Mossi.

At independence the traditional Mossi political organization had no official or legitimate status in Ouagadougou. Indeed, the chiefs, municipal officials, and state officials all affirmed that the traditional political organization had been deprived of all of its functions. However, the fact was that both the municipal and the national governments used the chiefs in governing the town. First of all, the municipal government permitted the chiefs to retain control of the land within their wards until the municipality was able to assume control. Thus, the chiefs still had the right to distribute land to persons who needed it, including civil servants and politicians as well as migrant cultivators. In return for land, the ordinary people gave presents to the chiefs; civil servants and politicians not only gave presents but also became indebted to the chiefs. Second, the municipal government asked the chiefs to aid the census takers, since, without this help, many inhabitants would avoid the census and, later, the tax collectors. Third the municipality ignored the fact that the chiefs functioned as judges and conciliators between disputants, many of whom did not trust the official organs of government.

Surprisingly, local branches of the violently anti-chief political party also used the services of chiefs. They held meetings in the chiefs' compounds and expected the chiefs to mobilize the local people to welcome and parade for the President and visiting dignitaries.

The chiefs were called upon to perform these functions for both the municipality and the nation-state, because these two political organizations lacked the techniques and personnel for communicating with and serving not yet fully urbanized people. The municipality had found it easier for the chiefs to control the undeveloped areas of the town. Similarly, it preferred to take the chance that the chiefs would conceal a certain number of tax payers rather than fail badly in one of its primary tasks, that of taking a population census. The municipal courts, too, recognized that the chiefs, rather than distrusted officials, had more success reconciling litigants in lawsuits. The political party, for its part, found it more convenient to use the chiefs and their houses for mobilizing its members, than to build local meeting halls and assign less prestigeful persons to this task.

Because both the municipal and national governments used the chiefs as agents, many inhabitants of Ouagadougou believed that the chiefs had *de facto* if not *de jure* power, and by an interesting "feedback" effect, began to ask the chiefs' help in fulfilling municipal obligations. For example, those persons who were obliged to procure such government documents as an *acte de naissance, carte d'identité* and *carnet familiale,* but feared insults and delay from the bureaucrats in the Town Hall, asked the chiefs to intercede with these bureaucrats and thereby expedite matters.

Given all of these factors, why then did almost everyone insist that the chiefs were "finished"? It seems that this fiction functioned to avoid conflicts and problems between the chiefs and the more powerful municipal councillors and politicians. Moreover, it was by playing the appropriate and often unobtrusive roles in the primary areas of government, that some chiefs were chosen to play more important roles in the formally recognized governmental systems in the town.

The Municipal Council was the governmental organization constitutionally authorized to govern the town, or *commune,* of Ouagadougou. According to the French law of April 5, 1884, later adopted for Ouagadougou, "the aim of the *Commune* was to organize elementary social life, and the Mayor and Municipal Councillors were expected to look after the common interests, protect the public weal, regulate the communal life, and defend rights and liberty." Furthermore, the Municipal Council was expected to act as an intermediary between the people and the State, and to provide such services as: prepare and revise electoral lists, recruit military personnel, obtain demographic data, establish civil status, collect taxes and contributions, and provide services for the people of the *commune.*

The Municipal Council, elected in Ouagadougou in 1960, had a rather high percentage of civil servants, twenty-five out of forty-six members. Of these twenty-five councillors, fifteen came from traditional noble families. The second largest group in the Council consisted of ten notables (chiefs and Moslem leaders). These included traditional provincial governors (such as the Ouidi Naba, the Larhalle Naba, the Baloum Naba) and ordinary ward chiefs such as the Zogona Naba, and the chief of the Hausa strangers, the Zanguettin Naba. The Ouidi Naba and the Larhalle Naba also served as President of the Municipal Court and Adjunct-Mayor, respectively. There were six merchants and five war veterans on the Council, but no representatives of the tradesmen, a group of growing importance in the town.

During the early 1960s, the Municipal Councillors faced many problems meeting the demands of their constituents, many of whom were migrant cultivators adapting to urban living and needing such services as housing, schools, police, medical care, official papers, and jobs. Their other constituents, the town's large civil servant population, the politicians, and the new foreign ambassadorial populations, needed lights, fuel, running water, paved roads, sewage disposal, recreational parks, and modern markets. What made the tasks of the councillors difficult was that many of their constituents had different needs and different priorities. Thus, when the municipality banned cereal cultivation in the farmers' backyard plots to control mosquitoes, while permitting civil servants to raise leafy vegetables and Europeans to display ornamental shrubs, people complained of class and cultural discrimination. Again, when the municipality prohibited the construction of mud-brick houses, a measure designed to live down Ouagadougou's former sobriquet of Bancoville—a town built entirely of mud-brick called "banco" —and also to get higher taxes on concrete structures, the poor people complained that they were being expelled from town to make room for wealthier people.

On the other hand, some of the ordinances proposed by the Municipal Councillors could not be adopted because of the different social structures of the town's population. A councillor proposed a tax on each "household head" for the purpose of improving garbage collection, but the Council could not make up its mind what a household head was. Was he the head of each nuclear family? Or the head of an extended family in one household or in several households? Or the owner of the house-lot in front of which garbage is deposited? Or the head of each family living in the tiny rooms in multiple-room compounds? Finally, in confusion, the bill was tabled.

Many of the Municipal Council's difficulties stemmed from the lack of communication with the people and from the absence of mediating political structures through which new ideas could be articulated and communicated. The Municipality had no local offices in the wards. People with problems had to chance meeting the Councillors on the streets, visit them on their jobs, or wait for them at their homes—a not too satisfactory arrangement for those Councillors who disliked having their midday siestas interrupted. In contrast, whenever a Councillor wished to communicate with his constituents, he had less trouble because he could summon the people to the chief's compound without much difficulty.

The Municipal Council met officially and publicly only twice a year except for extraordinary sessions. However, these few meetings were meaningless for the majority of the town's people who were accustomed to making sudden demands on the chiefs whenever they had pressing problems. Yet, only if the Council met more frequently would the townspeople have become used to visiting the Town Hall to press their complaints and make their demands.

The difficulties of the Municipal Council of Ouagadougou were exacerbated by its need for money to develop new institutions of government. The tax-gathering machinery of the municipality was inadequate to collect even the ordinary taxes. Collecting taxes in the marketplace and from itinerant traders was a battle of wits between inexperienced young men and sharp-eyed men and women who quickly disappeared when the tax collector showed up. Collecting taxes from the more formal French businesses in town was even more difficult; it is a well-known national trait of Frenchmen to keep faulty tax records.

Ouagadougou's status as capital of the Upper Volta Republic created grave problems for the municipal government; for Ouagadougou, like the other municipalities in Black Africa discussed by Réné Dumont in his very critical book, *L'Afrique Noire est mal partie,* had to use many of its scarce resources for ceremonial purposes. Numerous roads in Ouagadougou were indeed paved in honor of those Presidents who attended the *Conférence des Chefs d'Etat et de Gouvernement de L'Union Africaine et Malagache* in March, 1963. And the Municipal government annually spent hundreds of thousands of C.F.A. in order to display a profusion of flags whenever the President of the Republic made an official trip or when foreign dignitaries visited the town. As was widely admitted, the desire for municipal and national prestige stimulated the installation of traffic lights and stop signs in Ouagadougou. The presence of these modern symbols would not have posed great problems if municipal police, to fulfill their traffic-ticket quota, did not haul unknowing rural visitors and careless urban citizens who violated traffic laws, to the *Commissariat de Police* where their fines or confiscated vehicles contributed to the income of the municipality. However, Réné Dumont (1962:67) was only partly correct when he alleged that it was civic pride that caused the "mayor of Ouagadougou to pass an ordinance forbidding the use of *deux-chevaux* as taxis."

Being host to the national government created severe political as well as financial problems for the municipal government, although the two things are interrelated. In the first place, the municipality's large number of employees, its rather substantial budget, and the leadership capabilities and efficiency of its mayors, made it a formidable political rival to the national government. Moreover, when visitors or resident Europeans praised the municipality for its services and for its improvements, the National Government felt threatened.

The dilemma and frustration of the national government was due both to its need to use the political structures of the municipality and of the chiefs to mobilize the citizens of Ouagadougou and its fear of doing so. For example, in December, 1964, the youth section of the political party in Larhalle ward was instructed by radio to meet at the home of the Larhalle Naba to prepare for the Independence Day celebrations. (Until relieved, in January, 1965, this traditional chief was also the mayor's chief assistant and technical councillor to the President.) In the middle of the session, a man stepped forward, interrupted the proceedings, identified himself as a Municipal Councillor, and complained that he had not been notified that this meeting was taking place in his ward. The young party members, especially one young man from the President's office, suggested that the Councillor should leave since he was elderly and the meeting was for the youth of the party. The Councillor replied that, as Municipal Councillor, he was the father of the people in the ward and was responsible to the Mayor for their activities. This brought hoots of laughter and protest from the party workers, and the Councillor stalked away mumbling to himself. This incident revealed that both the municipal and national officials saw themselves competing for leadership; it also showed that the councillor did not know where his power and functions began and where they ended. The situation was further complicated by the councillor in question being related to the chief at whose house the meeting was being held. This incident shows quite plainly that at least this councillor did not know which role he preferred and where the legitimate political boundaries of the various political structures lay.

The officials of the national government sometimes expressed the fear that the municipal authorities would use the prestige of their office to seek power on the national level. For example, when the municipality first proposed seeking foreign aid by becoming the "twin" city of Bordeaux, the national government concurred. But when it appeared that the mayor of Ouagadougou was becoming too chummy with his wartime friend, Bordeaux's mayor, M. Chaban-Delmas, close relations between the two towns were discouraged. Apparently the President feared that the heads of the two municipalities might use their collective influence with the French Government to ease him out of power.

Open conflict between the municipality of Ouagadougou and the government of the Republic of Haute-Volta broke out in August, 1964, over the construction of a canal in the town. At the request of the municipality and with the support of local Europeans, money for building a canal was included in a grant request of the national government to France. The French granted the request but the national government did not release the money, and, when flooding occurred during the rainy season, many people complained. The mayor, partly to protect himself and possibly to embarrass the President, who was having serious political troubles, released a statement to Radio Haute-Volta indicating that the municipality was not at fault for not building the canal, but "that the blame lay elsewhere." The President of the Republic was in France on one of his customary visits, and could not reply. As soon as he returned, however, he summoned members of the national party to Ouagadougou, and, during the course of the meeting, he castigated the mayor and declared that from 1965 onward the budget of the municipality of Ouagadougou would be subsumed under the budget of the National Government. The President sought to deprive the Municipal Council of its most important functions, thereby crippling it.

By the end of 1964, it was clear that the National Government not only distrusted the Municipal government but was determined to punish its officials. The opportunity came in 1965 when, by manipulating the nominating processes of the single party in the country, the President purged the Mayor and those municipal councillors who threatened him. Some twenty to forty-two per cent of the town's voters abstained during the municipal election of December 5, 1965, but the party claimed a victory of 98.97% of the votes cast. Nevertheless, less than a month later, the people of Ouagadougou, led by civil servants and labor leaders protesting salary cuts, increased taxes, and general austerity, rebelled against the Yameogo government. They called a general strike, rioted, stormed and sacked the National Assembly, and demanded that the army take power. The army "assumed its responsibility" and forced the President to resign.

The people of Ouagadougou have the dubious distinction of being the first group of urban African civilians to bring down a national government. They got rid of a political regime which did not know how to find a *modus vivendi* with an urban political subsystem trying to deal with their growing and pressing needs. The fall of the national government also resulted in the dissolution of the Municipal Council which had been elected on December 5, 1965. By Presidential Order, no elections were held for a new Municipal Council; instead, a Special Delegation was provisionally constituted to supervise the communal affairs of Ouagadougou. It is not known what provisions have been made in the new Upper Volta constitution just adopted for municipal government, but, unless there are drastic structural changes in the system, future municipal governments in Ouagadougou face serious trouble.

## CONCLUSION

The nature of the political conflict in Ouagadougou demonstrates quite clearly that the political system of this urban community could not contain the contradictory and competing groups without revolutionary changes. The conflicting elements in this urban system had been present and evolving during the colonial epoch, but, because of European dominance, there could be "peace in the feud." It is possible that, given time and relatively slow change, the autonomous subsystems could have developed connecting links so that conflict would have been minimal or avoided when independence came. The problem is that the subsystems in the town did not have time to adapt to each other. True, the Mossi traditional authorities did create links with the colonial regime so that cooperation was possible between the two. However, there was insufficient time for the municipal government to have established viable mediating structures or links with either the traditional system or with the retreating colonial regime. And when the new national government was established in the town, the resulting "formidable mass of confusion" did lead to "social chaos." In this case the relatively autonomous subsystems did not succeed in distributing the effects of the changes they were subjected to over the whole social field and the whole system broke down.

The recent reports of coups, countercoups, and rebellions in Africa have delighted those who were pessimistic about the ability of Africans to govern themselves. The social scientist, hopefully immune from racist sentiments, must look afresh at the data of the colonial period for explanations of these events. One suspects that much of the "stability" observed in colonial Africa was more a function of the political control of the dominant colonial system than of the equilibrium between the social groups and systems found there. Now that European political domination is over, the African systems are unable to contain their conflicting elements because of the absence of mediating structures or conflict-reducing mechanisms. There is no doubt that these structures and mechanisms will develop with time, but the nature of emerging social and political systems will be quite different from what they were during the pre-colonial and colonial epochs. Whether "autonomous" or any type of municipal governments will survive in the African nation-states is a moot point. If they do, then it will be because they have succeeded in relating to the declining traditional political organizations and to the increasingly dominant national state systems. The result may be that future municipal governments in Africa, may be as different from their European progenitors, as are the American systems which were equally derived from European sources.

## REFERENCES

BALANDIER, GEORGES, 1951, "La Situation Coloniale: Approche Theorique," *Cahiers Internationaux de Sociologie,* 11:44–79.

DUMONT, RÉNÉ, 1962, *L'Afrique Noire est mal partie.* Paris: Editions du Seuil.

EPSTEIN, A. L., 1958, *Politics in an Urban African Community.* Manchester University Press.

FALLERS, LLOYD, 1955, "The Predicament of the Modern African Chief," *American Anthropologist,* 57:290–305.

FRIED, MORTON H., 1967, *The Evolution of Political Society.* New York: Random House.

GLUCKMAN, MAX, 1963, *Custom and Conflict in Africa.* Oxford: Basil Blackwell.

MITCHELL, J. CLYDE, 1957, *The Kalela Dance,* Rhodes-Livingstone Paper, No. 27.

RADCLIFFE-BROWN, A. R., 1952, *Structure and Function in Primitive Society.* London: Oxford University Press.

SCHILDKRAUT, ENID, 1970, "Strangers and Local Government in Kumasi," *Journal of Modern African Studies,* 8(2):251–69.

SKINNER, ELLIOTT P., 1960, "Labour Migration and Its Relationship to Socio-Cultural Change in Mossi Society," *Africa,* 30(4):375–401.

———,1963, "Strangers in West African Societies," *Africa,* 33(4):307–320.

———,1964, *The Mossi of the Upper Volta.* Stanford: Stanford University Press.

———,1970, "The Changing Status of the 'Emperor of the Mossi' under Colonial Rule and since Independence," in *West African Chiefs: Their Changing Status under Colonial Rule and Independence,* Michael Crowder (ed.). Ile-Ife: University of Ife Press, pp. 98–123.

VAN DEN BERGHE, PIERRE, 1965, *South Africa: A Study in Conflict.* Berkeley and Los Angeles: University of California Press.

WALSH, ANN-MARIE, 1969, "Urban Administration and Planning," *African Urban Notes,* 55(4):1–34. East Lansing: Center for African Studies, Michigan State University.

WERLIN, HERBERT H., 1968, Conference on the Government of African Cities. Institute of African Government, Department of Political Science, Lincoln University, Pennsylvania.

# 19 AN ANALYSIS OF THE MEMPHIS GARBAGE STRIKE OF 1968

## Thomas W. Collins

*Urban conflict arising from racial discrimination in the United States is illustrated in this account of a strike. The incident demonstrates some of the complexities involved in analyzing social conflict in an urban context, for the relevant social distinctions include ethnic, racial, class, and occupational differences. We learn how such differences came into play in the process of changing relations of power and political participation in a complex society. This instance differs from those considered earlier in Part Five in that the relations among the groups concerned, both before and after confrontation, were of a kind perhaps peculiar to urban civilizations characterized by division of labor, rather than to tribal societies.*

On February 12, 1968, the city of Memphis Sanitation employees went on strike for higher wages and improved working conditions. Labor protests by public service employees had become quite common in the nation by the late 1960's but the Memphis strike was not just another labor dispute. In fact, it was highly unique, since it occurred in a metropolitan area with a long tradition of anti-union bias. Furthermore, the strikers were mostly black with poor education and little or no training. They were part of a regional subculture which had relegated them to the lowest rank in the political economy. The ramifications of their actions were enormous and extended well beyond their stated objectives in the walk-out. Indeed, it was a direct challenge to an entrenched life-style and value system. The purpose of this paper is to offer an analysis of the strike, the background factors leading to the initial confrontation, and the effects it had on the city. Special effort will be made to present this analysis from the point of view of the strikers, a view that has, thus far, been largely ignored.[1]

To understand the events leading to the strike, it is necessary to consider some important historical and environmental characteristics of Memphis. For example, its location on the Mississippi River and in the highly productive agricultural region of the Delta has molded the economy into a commercial and marketing center with only modest amounts of industrialization. Demographically, Memphis has traditionally been a way-station for migrants moving from the Delta to northern urban centers (euphemistically known as the Delta flow). The greater part of this migration consisted of economically impoverished families possessing only agricultural skills. Since the economy is non-industrial, the city has been able to absorb this labor, if only in menial service-type employment. Most of the migrants remained in Memphis only long enough to improve their resources and to gain essential techniques for survival in an urban environment. Therefore, the city has historically enjoyed a surplus of healthy labor, willing to work for low wages and yet, demanding very little in the way of public services. When the migrants reached a high level of dissatisfaction, they normally moved further north rather than attempting to change their local situation.

These demographic factors produced a rare sociopolitical structure, rare at least, in terms of 20th century United States. One sector is an affluent, service-consuming elite whose capital foundation rests in land and commercial activity. The second sector is larger and is primarily engaged in producing services for the elite sector. Vertical mobility between the two is minimal, nearly caste-like. Access to decision over the distribution of public resources has been retained by the elite. In fact, public power rested in the hands of one monolithic political ma-

chine for most of the first half of this century. Under the leadership of
E. H. Crump, the machine effectively precluded any development of
countervailing groups in city politics until well into the late 1950's.

## PROFILE OF SANITATION WORKERS

Predictably, the sanitation workers are migrants, thoroughly socialized
in the economic hardships of depressed Delta counties. For example,
Fayette County, Tennessee, where most of the informants in this study
originated, is the third poorest county in the United States. Over 44
percent of the population survive on an income below that of the mean,
$3,834. Unemployment among blacks, who make up 61% of the popu-
lation, runs 68% and higher. Housing and education is especially poor;
nearly 80% of the residences are substandard, i.e., without adequate
plumbing facilities. The median educational attainment is 8.6 years. All
the men interviewed from Fayette had either worked as share-croppers
or in some phase of agro-business.

In nearly every case, the employees belong to informal mutual aid
groups structured on the extended families. Developed as a means of
survival in the rural environment, these networks continue to furnish
vital support for migrants in the city. Resources, such as garden vegetables and fresh meat, produced in the county, sustain members in the
city while limited amounts of cash and used consumer goods flow back
to the county stem of the family. In some instances, these networks
remain viable for years, providing workers with their major social outlet
(i.e., visiting) and information on available employment. Over two-
thirds (67%) of those surveyed indicated they had learned of their
sanitation job opening through friends or relatives. On the other hand,
none of the men had sought the aid of formal agencies such as the State
Employment Office.

Shop foremen in the Sanitation Division have tended to encourage
these informal communication links as a regular recruitment technique. Foremen frequently asked prospective employees if they were
"a country boy" or, "who sent you?" The Division favored these men
over those reared in Memphis because, as one foreman explained,
"They work harder and are more stable." Given this hiring arrangement, it is quite common to find several men from the same family
network together on a truck crew or other such assignment.

## WORK CONDITIONS PROMPTING A LABOR DISPUTE

When the migrant first arrives in Memphis, his major concern is to
secure a job. Any job is important and relatively better than that which
could be obtained in the country. The work attitude was expressed in
a response to a question about types of employment. One worker
tersely remarked, "there is no worst job. I would take anything." However, the economically deprived employee has his outer limits of toler-
ance to depressing work conditions. The sanitation men reached these

limits by the beginning of the 1960's. The wage was $1.30 an hour with little or no job benefits. Only the truck drivers, who were mainly white, received vacations with pay. If an employee was injured on the job and could still work, he was offered a menial task around the office; otherwise he was let go. If one was killed, and a few were, his family received the equivalent of a month's salary plus burial expenses.

The job itself was little better than the wage and benefits. Each man was issued a tub for which he was responsible. Trash was collected from the back of the yard of each private residence and hauled to the truck waiting in the street. If the tub leaked, fluid from the trash would run down on the employee since he had to carry heavy loads on either his shoulder or his head. One retired worker described his situation, "In those days, I would sometimes get put off the bus 'cause I smelled so bad. I'd even have maggots in my pant cuffs at night. Some people called us the vultures 'cause we raided the garbage." A truck crew had responsibility for a neighborhood area. As a driver put it, "that meant if anything was thrown in the yard or in the street we had to pick it up. If a tree blew over in a private yard we had to go in with an ax and chop it up, then drag it out to the street and load it on the truck. If some guy was remodeling his house and threw bricks around the yard, we had to pick them up and carry them out on our heads. We had no guide lines as to what we had to do, we did everything." It should be noted here that Memphis was awarded the "Nations's Cleanest City" honor during many years of the 1950's.

Since the wages were so low, the employees had to "recycle" anything that was salvageable from their collections and apparently very little was missed including the coupons from discarded breakfast cereal boxes. "Ragging" was considered a reasonable income supplement by the management and the general public. In fact, during the strike a Memphis resident was reported to have questioned why the sanitation men were demanding a raise when they could keep anything found in the trash. People would sometimes leave used items on top of the trash container for the men, and if they kept the yard "picked up" they could expect a gift at the end of the year. Such paternalistic attitudes reflect the regional traditional values. John Dollard, in his study of a southern community in 1939, discussed a similar practice, "The Negroes seem to inherit the castoff clothes, automobiles, food, and social customs of the whites, and are marked by a general sort of second-handedness."[2]

Further injustices were inflicted on the workers by foremen. Several informants have reported that workers could be fired or suspended at the mere whim of a supervisor. For example, one reported, "My dad-in-law never took a drink in his life. But he was fired for being drunk on the job because some foreman said he saw him walking across the street with his head bobbing around. You never knew from one day to the next if you was going to get fired." Another worker said, "Once I picked up the trash from a house. After I left, the owner filled up the can again, and then called the bossman. He said the garbage had not been picked up. All I could say was that I'd picked up that house. I got three days off, no questions asked." A few of the informants related that some foremen and truck drivers demanded "kick-backs" from new employees during the six month probationary period. Perhaps the conditions were best assessed by a black minister shortly after the strike when he compared the city procedure to a slave system:

"... The slave out on the field, he had no recourse to justice except if he went to the master and the master could give it to him if he wanted to, at his own dictates; his whim. Well no man wants to stand that any longer and when he is denied, a strike will come."[3]

Working conditions during the 1960's became increasingly more repressive as the city attempted to economize with tax dollars. Previously, men had been permitted to sit out a few hours of a rain storm on their route to draw a full day's pay. The city became more rigid in 1963 about such matters and began to send the men home with the short pay. The impact of this hardship must be considered in view of the fact that Memphis receives an average of 60 inches of rain a year. In the months from January through March it will often rain for days at a time. Employees often had to work under hazardous conditions. For example, men had to ride on the back of a truck, fireman style, which would sometimes reach a speed of 45 miles an hour between routes. For the sake of economy, men had to use equipment that was frequently obsolete and dangerous. When two workers were killed in a truck accident in 1964, the employees complained bitterly that the deaths could have been avoided by the installation of proper safety devices. In short, there were a number of grievances which led inexorably to a final confrontation between sanitation workers and the city. But even under such insufferable conditions, many employees still had to be convinced that striking was worth the risk of losing a salary. The activists had to labor hard to convince marginal men that something could be done to improve their condition.

## CITY ATTITUDE TOWARD LABOR

Union activity is not unfamiliar to Memphis. The American Federation of Labor has represented the skilled workers in the city for most of this century. Indeed, preferential treatment was received by the AFL affiliated Memphis Trade and Labor Council in exchange for its political support of the Crump machine during the early 1930's. However, in 1936 this relationship was broken when the Council attempted to unionize city employees. In response to the union activity, the city fired fourteen employees of the fire department and blacklisted them.[4] The blacklist was so thorough it was impossible for them to gain other employment in the city for several months. During the same year, public school teachers and custodians formed a union which was also crushed. Crump's political lieutenants on the School Board forced the members to capitulate when served with an ultimatum: either give up the union or face dismissal.[5] City police were dealt a similar offer when they attempted to organize in 1943.[6] Thus, the city had established a policy of economic reprisals against employees in public service who attempted to carry on any union activity.

The Crump machine had other ways, too, to deal with organizers who were not directly employed by the city. When professionals were sent to the city by the CIO in the early 1940's to organize local plants, Crump's tactics shifted to the use of character assassination and the threat of terror. Organizers were labeled "communists" and "outside agitators engaging in un-American activity." When intimidation was not effective, union people were assaulted and often severely beaten by street toughs. Few assailants were ever apprehended in these affairs. Crump made his policy a matter of public record in 1943 when he announced: "I am opposed to the CIO. Their ruthless methods are destructive and retarding to the growth of communities wherein they are active . . . if the CIO could entrench itself in Memphis, this city would go back ten years."[7] In spite of this opposition, the CIO did manage to unionize a few plants in Memphis during the 1940's. However, in the prevailing atmosphere, the city remained well out of the influence of national union organization.

The death of Crump and the subsequent disintegration of his political machine in 1954 did not soften the local attitude toward labor. Union ideology was and is the direct antithesis of values expressed by local political and business leaders, the media, and the general public. It is, therefore, understandable that it took twenty years for city employees to form another union. Surprisingly, it was the low-skilled workers of the Sanitation Division who were first to make the challenge. This fact in itself speaks of how deeply these workers felt oppression.

In 1964, the sanitation employees chartered Local 1733 and affiliated with the American Federation of State, County and Municipal Employees (AFSCME), an international union with a reputation for effectively organizing marginal occupational groups in the nation. Much of their national activity has centered on women and minorities who have been largely ignored by the major labor organizations. Needless to say, a radical organization of this type was not well received by the citizens and community leaders of Memphis. City administrators unquestionably had wide support in the effort to limit the effectiveness of Local 1733.

## DIRECT CONFRONTATION

Prior to the major confrontation of 1968, the sanitation workers attempted two strikes, the first in 1963 to protest general working conditions. Since there was little support for the strikers, either among the employees or in the black community, the action lasted only a few hours. Strike leader T. O. Jones recalls, "Even the black community was against us. Some ministers came down and literally got down on their knees and begged us to go back to work. We didn't have much chance." For their efforts, a few men were dismissed and others were reassigned to less desirable jobs. But these leaders were not to be denied. They continued their efforts until they finally secured a charter for Local 1733. It is noteworthy that the union leaders were similar in background and skill to other employees with the exception of their outside exposure. All of them had either served in the military or had worked in some northern city which in part explains their higher degree of militancy.

In 1965, another strike was attempted to secure recognition for the union local but again it was poorly organized and lacked support in the wider community. Word was leaked of their plans, and before the men had hit the street, the city was ready with a court injunction. The legal action was weak (based on a vague Tennessee Supreme Court ruling regarding government employees) but it was enough to intimidate the sanitation workers to return to work.

The black middle-class in Memphis was not willing at this time to make a commitment to any direct confrontation, out of consideration of what they felt to be good relations with city government. According to historian David Tucker, the black middle class had been gaining a number of concessions in their efforts to desegregate the city.[8] Memphis public libraries, recreation facilities, and public accommodations had been opened to blacks. In 1965 they had helped elect a white mayor who was thought to favor further desegregation, particularly in industry and public schools. These expectations, however, proved to be false. Actually, little progress was made. Frustrations began to mount in the late 1960's. When a tough-minded mayor, Henry Loeb, was elected to office in 1967 without the support of any segment of the black electorate, the mood of the blacks changed to one of greater militancy with an emphasis on direct confrontation. The black middle-class organizations were waiting for an issue when the sanitation employees walked out on strike February 12, 1968. This time the employees were not ready to back down. They had organizational support, a militant union, and a city mayor who was capable of unifying the blacks.

The incident which sparked the walk-out actually occurred in another division of the Public Work Department. Thirty-five black employees had been sent home because of rain while several white employees, with identical work assignments, were permitted to remain and draw a full day's pay. The sanitation workers chose to strike in protest of the action. As predicted, the new strong-willed mayor took a firm stand in opposition to the employees. In the Crump tradition, he announced that Memphis was not New York and he would not yield to any union. A former City mayor reported that, "Loeb talked to the men like they might have expected to be talked to if they were still on a plantation working as sharecroppers." But the workers were just as adamant. As one put it, "Things were so bad back then that I made up my mind I wasn't coming back if we didn't win. The abuses were too much for us."

Once the administrators learned they could not force the men back on the job by intimidation, they set out to break the strike by hiring scab laborers, both white and black, to make collections on a limited basis. The fact that non-union black laborers would take jobs under the ominous threat of violence further relates how desperate rural men can be for employment. Employees who did not walk off their jobs at the beginning of the strike later joined the picket lines. A reluctant striker stated, "Henry Loeb's police couldn't protect me at home. I wanted to work, but I was afraid of the other men."

Actually, the greatest amount of violence in the strike came from the city, not the workers. Taking a cue from the late Mayor Crump's tactics, the city made a show of police force whenever possible. During the first protest march (one of many), the police reacted by macing (tear gasing) the strikers and black ministers indiscriminately. Additional gas was used in a black church where marchers had taken refuge from the attack. The police action stunned the black community and probably did more to unify it than any one incident in the history of Memphis. A minister in the march stated, "Police don't invade a black church. I mean, this is our sanctuary and they broke the law." This time people were not to be intimidated by their traditional adversary, the Memphis Police Department. Thus the dispute that began as a labor problem quickly turned into a major racial confrontation for the entire city.

Offered wide support, the strikers, with the influential black ministers, were able to escalate the pressure on city hall by calling for a boycott of white-owned downtown stores and selected companies. The city had managed to limit strike effectiveness by collecting trash but it could not cope with the economic pressures of a boycott. Also, a few white groups were formed to intercede in behalf of the strikers but such support was not widespread. On the contrary, there were cases where whites were voted out of their church membership for voicing an opinion of conciliation. Nor did the two daily newspapers print anything favorable to the black strikers (the papers were also boycotted). In the end, it was the boycott that finally brought the city around. The lost income of the downtown merchants during the two-month strike has not been made public, but it must have been staggering. This finally forced the mayor to make a settlement.

There was some question whether Dr. Martin Luther King should have been invited into the conflict in March. The boycott was working and opposition to the mayor was mounting. Also, it was understood that no protection could be expected for King since the police were clearly on the side of the city. Nevertheless, the ministers sent for the civil rights leader. His murder on April 4th brought nationwide focus on the city. Administrators had no choice but to make their peace with the strikers and the black community.

The city agreed to most of the union demands: recognition of the Local by establishing a dues check-off system; 10 cents an hour wage increase; merit promotion (a seniority system); and a realistic grievance procedure. For the first time in their lives, the men of the Public Works Department had job security. The occupation was the same and vertical mobility was still lacking, but the success in the strike was viewed as a beginning. They had challenged the system and won.

## ATTITUDES SINCE THE STRIKE

In the six years since the settlement, union members have demonstrated a surprising lack of willingness to push the city administration on hard bread and butter issues, i.e., wage increases and other benefits. Most members, thus far, appear content just to have a union. There is general consensus on the effectiveness of the union in terms of job security and grievance procedure. One worker summed up his feelings, "The Man can't run us out from down here anymore. If you stay straight, you have a job for life." Generally, the men react strongly to any attitude or action by foremen which can be interpreted as paternalism or vindictiveness. Men who submit to such treatment are sanctioned through the use of gossip or labeled an "Uncle Tom." Union stewards who are said to be soft on the city are quickly replaced. There are still a few employees who have been so thoroughly socialized in the traditions of rural southern life that it is difficult for them to lend their full support to the union. It is widely believed that these workers "will be shaped into line soon."

Job dissatisfaction is most often expressed by the younger men, particularly those who have been reared in the city or who have lived in Memphis long enough to change their network groups. Those with large families find it impossible to live on the base wage of $2.60 an hour. At least one-fourth of the men hold second jobs that extend their work week to 70 hours or more. A few are forced into "hustling" on weekends. Thus far, the union or the city has not been able to increase job mobility. A man cannot expect to be promoted to even the position of truck driver or crew chief until he has accumulated at least six years seniority. After 15 years, it is possible to be promoted to foreman, but the city has demonstrated a reluctance to offer this position to many black employees. Hence, the frustration tends to run high among those who are at the bottom of the seniority system.

In the past, men could quit their jobs and seek vertical mobility by moving north to industrial centers but this option is no longer open. A number of workers have expressed the belief that the cost of living is so high in the North that it is virtually impossible to improve their living situation. Therefore the ranks of sanitation employees are expanding with men who are willing to take a more militant stance to improve their current economic position. In future contract negotiations, the union leadership will be forced to assume a much harder line to keep these men satisfied.

Moreover, the strength of black blue-collar unionism has been steadily expanding since the 1968 strike. AFSCME has organized the Memphis City Hospital service staff and its membership now numbers over 5,000. Also, there are more blacks in formerly all-white unions in the city. In any future conflict it would appear impossible for these unions to ignore strike activity by AFSCME as they did in 1968. Thus the sanitation workers are in a position of power capable of making demands on the city political system quite independent of the black middle-class.

City administrators appear aware of this development. Therefore, they tend to take a more congenial approach in contract negotiations and grievance decisions. Although they have been slow to open up more available supervisory positions to blacks, administrators have attempted to introduce some training programs and upgrade existing positions. More employees are encouraged to apply for job openings outside the Sanitation Division in an attempt to increase their vertical mobility within the City structure. Foremen who have demonstrated a consistent unwillingness or inability to handle men in a biracial situation have been transferred. In some cases, however, the city is limited in the amount of change which can be made. If, for example, city administrators were to attempt to mechanize collections and hence pay higher salaries through increased productivity, it would reduce the number of jobs in the division. Moreover, the type of manpower training programs necessary to advance many of these employees to skilled-level jobs, is beyond the financial ability of any single municipal government. Therefore continuing innovation to upgrade the types of jobs available in the Sanitation Division will be somewhat restricted.

In summary, the sanitation strike was the single most important event in Memphis since the death of political boss Crump. Most notably, power relationships have changed. Not only have blacks improved their situation, but blue-collar blacks have become a factor in the decision-making process where before they existed only as a large minority to be ignored. For the employees who laid their jobs on the line, the actual increase in salary has been minimal, but their bargaining power is expanding with each contract negotiation. Furthermore, one cannot understate the value of the new status these men have achieved. As one worker succinctly put it, "That union makes me feel like a man."

## NOTES

1. Most of the data presented in this paper was collected over a twelve month period (December, 1972 through January, 1973), and utilized several traditional ethnographic methods, such as indepth interviewing and a structured survey. Additional data was obtained from the taped interviews stored in the Mississippi Valley Collection of the John Brister Library, Memphis State University. The latter interviews were collected by the Multi-Media Sanitation Strike Project.
2. John Dollard, *Caste and Class in a Southern Town* (New York: Doubleday, 1957, 3rd edition), p. 102.
3. Mississippi Valley Collections—Taped interview on File No. 41.
4. *Memphis Press-Scimitar,* February 14, 1936, p. 1.
5. *Ibid.,* May 20, 1936, p. 1.
6. *Ibid.,* October 15, 1943, pp. 1–2.
7. *Ibid.,* January 1, 1949, p. 1.
8. David Tucker, *Memphis Since Crump* (Ms, Memphis State University) ND.

# Part VI

## Turning to the Supernatural

Matters related to ritual and religion have often been treated as separate and apart from the ordinary and practical matters of life. But anthropologists have long been aware of the integration of beliefs and behavior concerning the supernatural world with everyday practical activities. This awareness is derived in part from the "holistic" perspective of anthropology itself.

Two insights emerge from this perspective. First, classifying some things as "religious" and others as "secular" is a product of a special kind of society—of an ethnocentric way of viewing the world. Societies that have highly specialized religious practititioners may well view the religious and the secular as two separate entities. Second, classifying the world in this way may obscure both secular aspects of religious activities and ritual and religious aspects of secular activities, even in such a specialized society. When belief in the influence of the supernatural enters into secular affairs, we are apt to consider it and practices associated with it as "superstition," rather than as religion. On the other hand, we frequently ignore secular aspects of religious activities. Some recent works by ecological anthropologists, like Roy A. Rappaport's *Pigs for the Ancestors*, have, however, drawn attention to the ecological functions of rituals.

The selection of articles in Part Six reflects in particular many anthropologists' concern with the role of the supernatural in people's adaptations to the real and recurring problems they face in life. Witchcraft, for example, can be viewed as a widespread response to social tensions, occurring in a broad range of types of societies. An important theme in several of the following papers is the role played by religion in human adjustment to social change.

Although religion and ritual are sometimes viewed as highly conservative elements of culture, they may in fact be components of radical social transformation. In particular, disaffected minorities, the weak and powerless, and even the upwardly mobile may find in religious movements the organizing capacity necessary to assist them in changing (as well as in explaining) their places in the larger social structure. Although their forms of religion must deviate from dominant forms in order to serve their special purposes, these people also tend to draw heavily upon cultural precedents. The amalgam of old and new in such movements helps to legitimize them in the eyes of their adherents, to help them to reinterpret their changing world as change takes place.

Religious movements have played extremely important roles in history. One outstanding example is that of Christianity, which arose among a people defeated and oppressed by an imperial power. The subsequent course of the movement was classic, defining the essential characteristics of its success: a visionary leader, emphasis on a return to fundamentals, bypassing of the dominant religious structure, and triumph in the face of persecution. In fact, persecution of members of such movements sometimes contributes to their success, for an external perception of them as a threat confirms their righteousness and power in their members' eyes.

Many religious movements have also failed, including a number of native American religious movements that flourished briefly but then died out.

Religious movements may or may not succeed in helping their adherents to better their social positions. Should they succeed, however, their own nature changes by necessity: They become "establishment."

# 20 | WITCHCRAFT PRACTICES AND PSYCHOCULTURAL THERAPY WITH URBAN U.S. FAMILIESMadeleine Leininger

## Madeleine Leininger

*Madeleine Leininger, a medical anthropologist, examines an old phenomenon recently raised to public prominence: manifestations and accusations of witch-*

*craft in the United States. She describes the circumstances in which manifestations occur and the methods used to help witchcraft victims. She also suggests that witchcraft in industrial and nonindustrial societies alike is an individual, or even an in-group, response to social tension. She finds that witchcraft is increasingly prevalent in American urban society, for a number of reasons, including competition among ethnic groups, heightened drug use, and the spread of belief in astrology. What is particularly fascinating about Leininger's study is the responses of individuals who, under social tension, first seem to seek out members of their own groups—often within their families—to serve as "scapegoats." Then, in a later phase, the "scapegoats" become identified by groups or families as the objects of witchcraft practices by outsiders. In each instance both the actual victim and the "medium" through whom the malevolent intentions of the witch are transmitted are females in all reported instances, in contrast to the practice among the Zande (Evans-Pritchard, 1937), where both sexes are involved as both witches and victims.*

Witchcraft, a psychocultural and social interactional phenomenon, continues to hold the interest of cultural anthropologists, humanists, and many lay persons. Until recently in this country, witchcraft has been a fairly taboo topic and has not been discussed in an open manner in public educational and service institutions. For many health professionals, witchcraft is a new and intriguing subject and they have a limited understanding of its nature and dynamic process. Many persons in our society characterize witchcraft as demon possession, superstition, antireligious, nonscientific, and as a mystical power over human and supernatural phenomena. Some persons find the idea of witchcraft very frightening, others find it amusing, and still others remain sufficiently intrigued to explore the phenomenon with an open-minded attitude.

In recent years, adolescents, religious groups, and individuals interested in mysticism, astrology, and transcendental media have shown increased interest in witchcraft. As a consequence, magazine and newspaper articles, television and radio programs, and film productions have provided information about witchcraft. In addition, educational institutions have offered special courses, group discussions, and public sessions on witchcraft. Thus witchcraft has become a more common and open topic of public discourse than it was a decade ago. Furthermore, witchcraft has generated sufficient interest in several settings to become a topic for systematic investigation.

In this paper, witchcraft refers to the psychocultural and sociological process by which an individual and group(s) subtly and skillfully influence the behavior of others primarily in a harmful way, but there is also evidence of *positive* secondary consequences which may alleviate life stresses for the persons involved in witchcraft. In general, witchcraft is viewed as a malevolent phenomenon and as a situational misfortune to cope with psychocultural problems and social stresses. Witchcraft practices have been generally characterized as involving mysterious actions, the use of impersonal powers, reliance upon supernatural beliefs, and the use of symbolic modes of communication to affect the behavior of others in a harmful way. From a structural-functional analysis, however, social scientists have also identified some *positive* functions or consequences related to witchcraft practices.

For several decades, Kluckhohn (1944), Nadel (1952), Evans-Pritchard (1937), and other anthropologists have studied witchcraft behavior in Western and non-Western societies and have presented theoretical interpretations and descriptive accounts of witchcraft from cultural, psychological, and social viewpoints. Anthropological findings and explanations of witchcraft have been the primary source for understanding witchcraft, especially in non-Western societies. There is, however, an urgent need to study and understand the prevalence of witchcraft in modern American society, giving fresh thought to the psychocultural forces and changing social structure features which influence the development of witchcraft. Accordingly, efforts should be made to use these insights to help anxiety-ridden witchcraft victims and their families and to make known the means by which therapists can help them. The purpose of this paper is, therefore, to make a modest contribution toward these latter efforts.

Contrary to popular belief, witchcraft is *not* a unique behavior phenomenon restricted to primitive, nontechnological, or non-Western societies. Forms and processes of witchcraft continue to be found in highly developed and technological cultures such as that of the United States. Moreover, witchcraft practices and victims have been reported recently in almost every part of the United States in mental health clinics, general hospitals, community health agencies, educational institutions, and in social gatherings.[1] Unfortunately, statistical data on precise witchcraft occurrences are not available; however, the author received reports of nearly 200 witchcraft cases in a three-year period through her work with and interest in witchcraft victims. Since witchcraft is generally a highly secretive ingroup experience, and because victims fear that witchcraft may not be accepted by professional health workers, it often goes undetected and unreported.

The author contends that there may be several significant reasons for the increased interest in and prevalence of witchcraft. First, the very rapid movement in this country over a short period of time to reduce inequities and to provide equal rights and opportunities for all ethnic, cultural, and social groups has produced tensions and a fertile climate for witchcraft accusations. Signs of unrest and distrust and challenges between and among different groups who may have never interacted with one another until recently are evident.

Second, there has been a heightened interest and involvement in extrasensory perceptual experiences, transcendental media, and other forms of special psychic experiences, particularly by adolescents. These youths have also been actively involved in the use of a wide variety of drugs and other stimuli in an attempt to obtain special psychophysiological "release experiences" to assuage current societal problems and stresses.

Third, there is evidence of an increased use of secretive and highly symbolic forms of communication in order to relate differently and intimately with humans, superhumans, animals, and nature. The use of special modes, mediums, and seemingly strange forms of communication provides the climate for witchcraft practices which are secretive, mystical, and symbolic in form and function.

Fourth, in recent years there has been a marked increase in a belief in astrology as a guide for one's actions and thought patterns. Many people today will not leave their homes or begin a day's work without checking their horoscope reading. This reading often provides a perceptual set and a psychosocial guide for one's thinking and actions. Witchcraft behavior is frequently linked with horoscope readings and astrological predictions, especially with predictions of what forces may cause a witchcraft victim harm.

Fifth, there is also an increase in the use of magical explanations by people who are nonscientifically disposed to explain unusual and unknown scientific findings. Undoubtedly, these magical explanations have arisen because of the tremendous gap in understanding highly scientific and technological data and they are used to cognitively bridge two different perceptual worlds, namely, the highly scientific and the nonscientific. Supernatural and mystical explanations are important means to reduce conceptual incongruencies and to understand complex phenomena and the many unknowns in our society.

Sixth, many youths today are actively seeking and testing what is "real" and "not real," and in so doing, they may test witchcraft spells and incantations with their peers. The youth are faced with trying to understand divergent cultural norms and conflicts in value systems, and witchcraft practices are used to test such value orientations and to make life more congruent with one's interests and identity.

Finally, witchcraft practices may be increasing in our society in order to cope with problems related to acculturational stresses which may be exceedingly troublesome for some individuals and groups. The necessity for rapid and sudden adjustments to groups with different life styles is producing obvious psychocultural stresses on various groups. Witchcraft behavior, as discussed in this paper, reveals the psychocultural struggle of certain groups to adjust to rural-urban acculturational situations.

## THEORETICAL FRAMEWORK AND EMPIRICAL PHASES

Using a theoretical framework which was inductively developed through direct participant-observation experiences with witchcraft victims, the author focused primarily upon Spanish-speaking (Spanish and Mexican-Americans) families and a few Anglo-American students attending college in a large university setting in the United States. In the process of providing therapy to four of the Spanish-speaking families and two Anglo-American families as well as observing and studying 40 additional Spanish-speaking families (the latter without being involved in therapy), the author developed the following theoretical formulation which was used as a guide for helping the bewitched victim and his family.

Witchcraft behavior reflects the process by which some individuals and groups experience psychocultural and social stresses which arise within a designated primary group (to be referred to as the ingroup). Later, these stresses are perceptually and cognitively displaced to a secondary group (to be referred to as the outgroup) which the primary group has known for some time. . . . Throughout this paper, the terms "ingroup" and "outgroup" are used in a general sense to represent all the cases studied. Furthermore, the term, ingroup or primary, refers to the initial locus of the family stresses and the term, outgroup or second- ary, to the group receiving the displaced stresses of the ingroup.

## PHASE ONE: THE PREWITCHCRAFT STRESS PERIOD

Phase one of the prewitchcraft period was characterized by the in- tended victim and his family (primary ingroup) experiencing intense interpersonal conflicts which arose from identifiable social, economic, and acculturational problems. One of the early signs of prewitchcraft stress was a decrease in the traditionally shared verbal communication among family members and a general distrust of each other's behavior. As the communication problems increased and the interpersonal stresses became more evident, the family members began to distort and misinterpret one another's behavior.

Since the majority of families had shifted from a rural to an urban way of life, economic stresses related to maintaining an adequate income to live in the city were often a basis of quarrels and subtle antagonisms among the family members.

But most importantly, the families were in conflict with and/or am- bivalent about "new" cultural values encroaching upon their tradi- tional values. Generally, some of the younger family members, in an annoying and semi-hostile manner, would "try on" the new values to which they had been recently exposed. Sometimes the "new" ways of acting were openly challenged or verbally suppressed when the behav- ior appeared completely out of harmony with past behavior modes.

Scapegoating behavior was clearly evident in the ingroup with one family member serving as the victim. This victim was frequently blamed for matters which were generally unresolved problems or con- flicts which the total family needed to face. Many unresolved family problems could be identified, and most of them were related to discrep- ancies in "new" and "old" cultural values and family practices. Because of the intense and largely covert interpersonal tensions and communi- cation problems along with the economic concerns and conflicting val- ues, no family member was able to assume a group leadership role to discuss these problems openly. Instead, the intrafamily tensions in- creased with the scapegoat victim being harrassed more and more by all family members. The family accusations became formalized, the tension mounted, and later (phase three) the scapegoat victim became legitimately the witchcraft victim. By the time phase three occurred, the victim had been emotionally and socially conditioned to take the bewitched victim role.

## PHASE TWO: DISPLACEMENT TO THE OUTGROUP

Phase two was characterized by the family ingroup members becoming increasingly angry with and distrustful of one another and finally displacing their feelings and problems to a known outgroup. The ingroup members continued to openly accuse each other of not helping and of not being concerned about one another's most urgent needs, e.g., food, sleep, clothing, and money. Although all ingroup members tended to blame each other for their problems, the scapegoat member continued to receive the greatest share of blame. There was evidence that family members denied their feelings about one another, especially when directly confronted about them. As the ingroup members became increasingly angry with one another, they withdrew to their bedrooms or left the house. Their silent periods reflected passive hostility to one another. In general, the ingroup members were afraid to express their pent-up feelings openly to one another, except for some periodic blasts of anger at the scapegoat family member.

Soon the primary ingroup began to cognitively displace its problems and feelings to a secondary outgroup. In all cases studied, the ingroup knew the outgroup, whose members were distant kinsmen—for example, "second or third cousins." In some cases, the outgroup was a social group whom the ingroup had known for at least six months, and in most cases, the ingroups and outgroups had been socially and economically dependent upon one another prior to the displacement phenomenon.

After the displacement of feelings and problems to the outgroup occurred, the ingroup and outgroup markedly decreased their contact with each other. Gradually, they showed increased fear and open anger toward one another and accusatory statements were secretively passed between the two groups. The intense fear and anger between each group led to avoidance behavior, and soon the groups began to talk cautiously and secretively about one another. The "terrible" ways and "horrible" witches in the outgroup were commonly discussed by the ingroup for a number of months and during the third phase.

## PHASE THREE: IDENTIFICATION OF THE BEWITCHED VICTIM, THE WITCHES, AND THE WITCH MEDIUMS

The third phase was characterized by intense ingroup-outgroup antagonisms and by identification of the bewitched victim, the witches, and the witch mediums. At this time, the scapegoat victim in the ingroup was clearly victimized and identified as the bewitched person. In all cases studied, the bewitched member was a female who was conditioned to assume the role because she had been the scapegoat family member, as described in phase one. The bewitched person became increasingly ill (emotionally and physically) as the witches in the out-group were perceived to be affecting her in a covertly destructive manner. As the witchcraft accusations increased, the victim felt more and more frightened, helpless, and controlled by the outgroup witches. She would remain silent and angry and would often stay in bed for hours with the door closed or locked. The witchcraft accusations and the perceived malevolent acts were talked about by both groups in a cautious, angry manner, but without direct verbal exchanges. As the malevolent acts were perceived to increase, the ingroup noted that the bewitched victim became more acutely ill; as the acts decreased, the victim got better. The bewitched victim was sometimes brought to a hospital or to a mental health clinic for relief of her symptoms during the intense period of witchcraft accusations between the two groups.

During the third phase, *witchcraft mediums* who had the power to transmit covert messages from the outgroup witches into the body or mind of the bewitched victim were also identified. As these frightening auditory and visual messages were relayed to the bewitched victim, she became extremely tense or openly aggressive to those near her. The witch mediums (usually one or two) were found in the ingroup and were thought to have been "chosen" by the outgroup witch to transmit her malevolent directives to the bewitched victim. That the witch medium was in the ingroup and near the bewitched person was terrify-ing to the medium himself as well as to the victim. It was almost an untenable situation since neither the medium nor the victim thought they could change their roles—they, too, were helpless in influencing the witches to be less destructive and horrible. In all cases studied, the witch medium was usually a female who was terribly distraught that she had been "picked" as the medium because it pinpointed her as the immediate person causing harm to the victim. Often the witch medium was the mother or an older sister of the victim. Thus one can envision the tense daughter-mother relationships that existed, accompanied with feelings of intense fear, helplessness, and hostility. Occasionally, the witch medium would use her indirect power upon their ingroup family members to threaten and control their behavior when family relationships seemed out of control. All family members greatly feared the power of the witch mediums as well as the witches and thought that they themselves might become bewitched at any moment.

## PSYCHOCULTURAL APPROACH AND THERAPY

The author attempted psychocultural therapy with six families (four Spanish-speaking and two Anglo-American families) in their homes. She saw each family about three hours each week (two sessions) and for a period of four to eight months of therapy. The therapy with the four Spanish-speaking families will be described in this first section, followed by a brief account of one of the two Anglo-American families.

In working with all cases, the author was identified as a professional nurse who had come into the home to help and study the sick member of the family. The Spanish-speaking families identified her as a *medicas* —a person who combined indigenous practitioner skills with professional practices; whereas the Anglo-American families saw her as someone providing help in a "crisis situation." In working with the families I used a similar psychocultural nursing therapy approach, employing psychotherapy methods and cultural data such as kinship ties, ethnohealth beliefs, economic aspects, social concerns, and religious beliefs. The families seemed responsive to this comprehensive and multidimensional approach.

## The Spanish-Speaking Families

As the author began working with the six Spanish-speaking families, she learned that two of the young females (20 and 25 years of age) had been in psychiatric hospitals for varying periods of time, one for seven months and another for one year. In each case, the victims' conditions had been diagnosed as "paranoid schizophrenia" and they had been dismissed with a "guarded prognosis."[2] Their families felt that the hospital's professional staff had not helped their daughters and commented: "She is worse than before she went to the hospital. They did not seem to understand our situation. It was hard to tell them about it." One of the Spanish-speaking patients had made a serious suicidal attempt three months before the author began working with her. A number of the psychiatric staff were baffled about the patient's "secretive behavior" and the meaning of her communication referents.

The Spanish-speaking families seemed desperate for help since the bewitched victim in each family had not improved and the indigenous curers had "given up on the victim." Thus the climate for helping them seemed favorable. Fortunately, the author had known two of these families through her study of an urban Spanish-speaking community and its health care system (Leininger 1969)—and it was important to these families that they knew the author.

At the start of therapy with the four Spanish-speaking families, the author focused upon their family ties and past relationships and took their genealogies. The latter seemed to be extremely important to the families, enabling them to tell about each family member and what had happened to them in recent months as well as to their family and friends. Furthermore, the genealogies were the key means for discovering the male and female witches as well as the witch mediums. When the families spoke about the witches, they whispered their names and always spoke of them with intense fear because of their great power and malevolent ways.

After the initial warm-up sessions using the genealogies and other relevant sociocultural data, the family members gradually became more at ease in talking about their family concerns and the sick members in the family. In a short time, they discussed the anger, fear, and distrust which existed among them. The author listened attentively to each family member's concerns, fears, and conflicts with no attempt to modify their behavior. It was felt that this approach was important in this initial phase of the therapy so that the members could openly express their feelings to an outsider who was actively interested in them, but who was not trying to suppress their feelings. Family members made direct and hostile accusations to one another, but especially to the bewitched victim. Initially, the victim was completely overwhelmed at these accusations and occasionally cried or left the room. Gradually, the author interceded in behalf of the victim and offered her emotional and social support by protecting and defending her feelings. When this occurred, the victim's ego became stronger and more confident. She would talk in a more coherent manner and would try to handle the accusations that she felt were unfair. For example, one victim stated: "You (family) 'caused' me to become ill. You have picked on me too long in this family. I did not do everything you said I did. Whenever I tried something different, I was pounced upon. I don't know why you always pick upon me."

During the course of the family "talk-out" sessions, the members discussed their past and current problems in adjusting to different "kinds of people and new ways in the city." There was evidence of conflict between their traditional cultural norms and the different sets of norms they were being exposed to in the urban community. Several common themes became evident in the family therapy sessions and will be highlighted and summarized below.

First, there had been unresolved family problems related to value changes and their ambivalence about changing traditional family relationships. For example, in one Mexican-American family the daughter was very angry with her mother for not permitting her to be more independent and "to be like other teenagers in the city." From a cultural viewpoint, this mother believed in maintaining close surveillance on her daughter, but after the family moved to the city, the daughter wanted to try some of the urban norms and to "live a different life." The mother, however, was extremely reluctant to let her daughter be so free and felt she needed even greater surveillance and protection than when they had lived in the rural area.

Second, the ingroup families were feeling the impact of the diverse ideologies of the different people encountered in their work and school settings and they were experiencing ambivalence about changing their own values. The families talked about how much they valued the warm, friendly, and generous attitudes which they had maintained traditionally with their extended family kinsmen. Lately, they felt these values were changing and that even their distant kinsmen (the outgroup) were becoming "cold, impersonal, and ungenerous people like the rest of these city people." The ingroup family members gave several examples of how their outgroup kinsmen or friends (toward whom they now felt hostile and frightened) had become extremely selfish and inconsiderate. In fact, the ingroup members were highly critical of the outgroup's behavior and were unwilling to forgive or forget such inconsiderate behavior. They said the outgroup had been stingy in giving gifts, loaning money, and helping them with occasional family celebrations. It was, therefore, no wonder that the outgroup became the ingroup's target for the displacement of its angry, distrustful, and suspicious feelings.

Third, a series of traditional cultural norms had been broken in each of the family ingroups, and the witchcraft victim was blamed for breaking them. And since the victim was perceived in each family to have violated the norm most flagrantly, she was vulnerable to most of the witchcraft accusations. In addition, the ingroup had become emotionally tense with one another because of a "cultural awkwardness" in changing their life style from one set of norms to another. They did not seem to know how to act as they "tried out" new or different behaviors in the family context and they were uncomfortable with the new ways.

Fourth, as the ingroup families spoke about their angry and antagonistic feelings toward the outgroup, they were oblivious to the dynamics of their own internal family relationships and their displacement of family problems and hostilities to the outgroup. None of the families studied were aware of this important aspect of their behavior until the author helped them to see such relationships. In time, some of their anger, which had been displaced to the outgroup, subsided as the author focused therapy upon ingroup behavior and explored ways to resolve family conflicts.

In the process of working with the families, the specific incidents, problems, and feelings of the ingroup that seemed to have precipitated the cycle of events were dealt with. As a consequence, it was observed that as feelings of anger and hostility shifted from the ingroup to the outgroup, the ingroup members became more comfortable with one another and gradually began to work on their own problems. It was also apparent that as the ingroup dealt with their problems as a group, family unity and solidarity increased. It was, however, a difficult task for the therapist to help the ingroup see the relationship between their own behavior and the displacement of problems to the outgroup. This goal was not achieved until after the ingroup learned to trust each other and work as a family unit again.

During the therapy, the victim challenged the family members who called her "sick" for she felt *all* the family members were involved in similar stresses and were also "sick." As she made these counterchallenges, the author encouraged her to express other feelings and reassured her that other family members would not be allowed to harm her.

The families also talked about the economic pressures they had experienced and how they had to work long hours to meet the monthly costs of urban living. They had expected their outgroup friends to help them economically, however, the outgroup was also feeling economic pressures and was unable to provide the gifts, food, or help that they had earlier. Hence, the ingroup began to realize that their expectations of the outgroup were probably unrealistic and that they would have to deal with their own problems as best they could.

The author talked with some outgroup members who were accused of acting malevolently toward the group. Interestingly, the outgroup members were aware of their culturally defined role in witchcraft and that there were witches among them who were causing harm to the ingroup victim and his family. They were, however, very cautious in talking with the author as they were uncertain about her role since they had never experienced an "outside professional" person who wanted to help them with "their witchcraft." Two outgroup "witches" said that they were acting protectively in order to control the behavior of the ingroup whom they greatly feared—and so, they did not mind being accused of being witches since they felt they were protecting their families.

Occasionally, members of the ingroup would meet or see a member of the outgroup at the store, church, or school. There was always great fear of each other and efforts were made to avoid direct contacts—even if it meant walking or driving several blocks away from the person. In one instance, a male "witch" from the outgroup boarded a bus driven by a member of the victim's ingroup. The "witch" started to enter the front of the bus, quickly recognized the ingroup member driving the bus, and then entered the bus at the rear. He sent another person to the front to pay his fare. Later, the driver said he had been extremely frightened to have the "witch" riding "his bus" and wanted to leave his job. The author was able to help this ingroup member retain his job, and in time, he gradually changed his feelings, but only after his sister (the bewitched victim) showed signs of health improvement. In general, the ingroup and outgroup members were not able to confront one another about their actions and feelings. The author chose not to work with the outgroup members but rather to help the ingroup members modify their behavior so that they themselves could deal with the outgroup in time—which did occur in the majority of families.

With two of the Spanish-speaking families, a large black cat was the symbol which indicated that the family and home were bewitched. For example, in one of these families the ingroup believed that the black cat had been sent by the outgroup witches who desired to cause them evil. They contended that the outgroup had broken the window and dropped the cat in their basement. Initially, they were terrified of removing the cat because they feared it would cause the victim's death or provoke outright family revenge toward them. Instead, they kept the cat well cared for and fed each day. Finally, as their group unity increased, they decided to release the cat from the basement, after which the victim's husband repaired the window. The decision to remove the cat was a major one and caused great fear; however, once they felt "strong enough" to remove the cat, the ingroup became greatly relieved and more relaxed in their home. Symbolically, it meant that the outgroup was no longer living in their basement since the cat was the symbol of oppressive witchcraft practices from the outgroup which brought harm to the bewitched victim and the family. Removal of the cat was a significant factor in achieving a positive direction in the family therapy. The ingroup used the author to support them in their decision because in the past they had had to wait until the outgroup "released" the cat from their house. Having the cat in the house clearly sustained the illness associated with witchcraft behavior.

Since the goals of the therapy for both the Spanish-speaking and the Anglo-American families were similar, with only slight modification according to symbolic referents, they are presented now. The therapy or treatment goals were based upon empirical cultural, psychological, economic, and social data which were conceptualized into a theoretical framework as described earlier. The author attempted to: (1) provide expressive therapy for the ingroup members by focusing upon their social tensions and daily living problems, (2) provide an emotional supportive relationship using cultural referents for an extremely harrassed bewitched victim, (3) assist the group to cope with acculturation changes and the concomitant shift in value orientations, and (4) help the family to function again as a viable and cohesive social group under the duress of cultural changes.

### Anglo-American Families

Turning briefly to the two Anglo-American families I worked with for approximately six months, I found similar dynamics in operation as noted above with the Spanish-speaking families. Although there was some variation in the linguistic expression and symbolic cultural forms, the same ingroup-outgroup theoretical model was used and similar therapy goals were applied. While both Anglo-American cases were similar, only one of the families will be discussed.

Reo, a fictitious name, was a 21-year-old college student who had lived in a small midwestern rural community. According to Reo and her family, she had been "hexed" by two college students (referred to as the "hex-witches") at the end of her first year of college in a large urban community. The family had taken Reo to a psychiatric clinic because "she was acting strangely toward us and her classmates." During the interview with the clinic staff she said she had been "hexed" by some classmates who were distant friends, but with whom she had quarreled prior to being bewitched. Since then, Reo felt that these two "witches" were acting unfriendly toward her and influencing her behavior "from a distance." With her closest classmates and family she felt she was being accused of things she did not do. (Scapegoat behavior toward Reo was evident within her family and close ingroup classmates and was based upon social tensions and interpersonal antagonisms.)

Reo said that previously her "close classmates" and family had been good, dependable persons, but lately they seemed to be suspicious, unfriendly, cold, and even fearful of her. She told the clinic staff that one friend, who was now a terrible "hex-witch," was forcing her roommate and also her sister to influence her (Reo's) thoughts and actions by using "McLuhan's medium techniques" and by making her feel strange and sick. The clinic staff were baffled by "the hexing" phenomenon, but diagnosed her case as "paranoid schizophrenia with a guarded prognosis." She was sent home after two weeks of hospitalization (largely on a medication regime) with some mild tranquilizers and was told to return "if things got worse for her and the family." Things did seem to get worse and they returned to the outpatient clinic where the author agreed to provide therapy in the home.

There was no difficulty in working with this Anglo-American family because they viewed the author as another "Anglo" and as a professional nurse who had worked with other families with similar difficulties. The family members desperately wanted help because they were very frightened of what Reo might do to herself or to them and commented that "we believe she is being influenced by that college group (outgroup), but we don't know what to do about it and what she might do."

After Reo was "hexed," she attended some of her classes, but gradually withdrew from them as she became more emotionally disturbed and experienced periodic episodes of nausea and vomiting. Reo also feared she would encounter the hex-witches on the campus and she was most fearful of them and what they might do to her—ranging from being haunted mentally to being killed by the witches.

As I worked with Reo and her family in their home, using indirect interview therapy techniques similar to those used with the Spanish-speaking families, Reo explained how she had been initially victimized by a large black spider. She said her distant college "hex-witches" had put the spider on her dormitory door, after which "she knew they were going to cause her harm." She also told how this college outgroup had once been kind to her, but had become harsh and unkind. She said that they used to have snacks with her, but suddenly became angry and hostile toward her after they "hexed" her. Reo felt her older sister was also involved in making her ill since her sister also knew this college outgroup. Reo thought the latter were sending messages through her sister.

The changes taking place in Reo's family life were similar to those taking place in the Spanish-speaking families. Reo's family also had moved from a rural to an urban community about three years before, and they were encountering acculturational stresses and conflicts in rural-urban value systems. They were able to identify some of the differences they were experiencing between rural and city life, but were unable to cope with their ambivalence about "which ways would be better for them." They found rural life with its many warm and friendly neighbors a real asset in contrast with their cold and busy city neighbors whom they really did not know. Nor could they depend upon their city neighbors in times of crisis like they did with their rural counterparts. They had had many ambivalent feelings about sending Reo to college and they "just knew something would happen to her there and that is why the oldest daughter did not go to college." They had two other daughters who would soon be ready for college (the reason they had moved to an urban community), and they did not know how to handle this problem.

Also, all adult family members were employed in semiskilled and unskilled jobs in the city. They often left the house at 7 A.M. and returned at 6 P.M., and had little time to discuss their family problems and be together as a group as they had been previously in the rural community. Economic problems were evident and they were deeply concerned about how to make a living in the city. There was no question that many of the initial problems which were related to witchcraft had begun with ingroup family problems and interpersonal tensions. Even before Reo was "hexed" at college, the family relationships had become tense with the family members growing increasingly irritable, impatient, and suspicious of one another. They were not fully aware of what was happening to their family relationships, except that "it was not going well." Reo was the family scapegoat member who received their accusations. Moreover, Reo revealed in the family therapy sessions that she had decided to go to college to "get away from all this family bickering and the unfair accusations placed upon me—I just could not take it any longer." The displacement phenomenon to the college outgroup occurred after the family social tensions had become unbearable and the family members were unable to talk with one another without quarreling or physically fighting.

Fortunately, the author was able to talk with Reo's college outgroup who also spoke about the noticeable change in Reo's behavior. They said they had become frightened of her and decided to "leave her at a distance" since they "could no longer understand her." They did feel that they sent "wave lengths" to her and were influencing her behavior unfavorably by the use of "transcendental power communication modes." Later they asked about Reo's health and wondered if they could "use their power to help her get well." They had been very angry with her because "she did not treat us fairly and was unkind, scary and uncharitable to us." They also admitted that they had placed the black spider on her door because "we wanted to scare her."

In working with Reo and her family, the same approach and goals described above were used over a period of four months. Most of the time was spent talking about: changes in rural-urban values and what to do about them; perceptions and anxieties about college life; and how to cope with social, economic, interpersonal family problems in the future in a city way of life with different cultural norms. The family also was extremely sensitive and, hence, secretive about sharing their "family problems with the whole hospital staff or psychiatric group" as they were sure the staff "would not believe" their daughter was hexed, and did not know "how to help her." Because Reo's behavior became worse, they had decided to try the clinic but were disappointed that she did not improve while in the hospital.

Perhaps because they desperately wanted help, this family responded quite readily to family therapy. They liked that therapy was given in their home. The author also worked with Reo on other hostilities and offered her emotional support as she talked about her role as a scapegoat member of the family. Family antagonisms gradually subsided and the family was still functioning as a group one year after the author left them. Reo subsequently completed a college degree and another daughter has enrolled in college.

## GENERAL OBSERVATIONS AND FUNCTIONAL ANALYSIS OF WITCHCRAFT DYNAMICS

The author observed that as the initial tensions and conflicts mounted in the family ingroup, there seemed to be *no* traditional institutionalized norms and practices which the family could rely on to cope with its problems. Moreover, the family contacts to obtain help from outside groups were limited because of the differing cultural norms involved. In general, the family members felt socially and culturally alienated and alone with their problems with no way to deal with them or resolve them.

Although most of the ingroup families had been living in an urban community for at least two years, it was apparent that their traditional values had been challenged only recently by their own family members and by outsiders. The exposure to a number of individuals and groups through work, school, and church seemed to increase their insecurity about themselves as a social group and about the values that they held. Interestingly, each family member was trying to resolve his value conflicts by himself and was afraid to talk openly about them with other family members. In time, the unresolved cultural value differences and social tensions increased so that the family members were unable to converse with one another in an acceptable manner.

The displacement of anger and the maintenance of stresses between the ingroup and the outgroup were dynamic features of the witchcraft practices and had several important social, cultural, and psychological functions which can be summarized here.

First, the displacement of angry feelings from the ingroup to the outgroup helped the ingroup become socially and psychologically more comfortable with one another and kept them united during the heightened ingroup conflict period.

Second, the identified witches in the outgroup (who were perceived to be highly destructive and powerful) were important in explaining the sick victim's behavior to the ingroup. While this temporarily served to relieve the ingroup family members by focusing their group problems on one family member, it also disguised the family's critical problems which ultimately had to be dealt with in the family therapy sessions. Concomitantly, the witches functioned as a powerful external threat to the ingroup and brought them together from fear in order to prevent the witches from generating more "deadly power" upon the sick victim.

Third, the scapegoating behavior exerted upon an ingroup member not only localized the emotional and social conflicts of the family in one member, but it also prepared and conditioned the victim and the others for the roles they would play in the witchcraft practices. Most importantly, the bewitched victim knew the role she would be expected to play, and she served as a barometer for determining the strength and nature of the ingroup-outgroup relationships by the degree of her illness.

Fourth, witchcraft practices were clues to cultural, social, economic, and psychological stresses which were extremely difficult for the ingroup to handle and required a nonfamily member to be helpful and objective. Reports of other victims who had not been helped in this way revealed either a prolonged illness in the hospital or increased social pathology in the family.

Fifth, symbolic referents such as cats and lizards served the important function of legitimizing the witchcraft phenomenon and of alerting the victim and the family to difficulties with an outgroup.

## SUMMARY

In this paper, the author has presented a theoretical framework, based upon empirical data, regarding witchcraft behavior and its functions in selected urban families in the United States. Through an intensive study and the provision of psychocultural therapy to four Spanish-speaking and two Anglo-American families, the author was able to help the bewitched victims and their families.

An analysis of the six families, plus other families who did not receive therapy, disclosed that ingroup tensions and problems (which were largely a consequence of acculturation and the ensuing economic, social, and psychocultural stresses) were displaced in time to a known outgroup whose witches acted upon the scapegoat or bewitched victim in the ingroup. Witchcraft practices in these families were important psychocultural and social mechanisms to cope with ingroup problems generated by external societal concerns.

The theoretical model with three major phases served as an important guide in providing psychocultural nursing therapy to the six families. The therapy was largely supportive and expressive in form involving the use of cultural value orientations adapted to the current life and environmental situation of the families. Although witchcraft behavior has been described in the anthropological literature since the early part of this century, there have been no known reports of professional groups attempting to relieve bewitched victims and their families through psychocultural therapy. However, with the reported increase of interest in witchcraft in this country and the increase of bewitched victims seeking help, it seems important that professional staff (and especially mental health personnel) become more knowledgeable of the witchcraft phenomenon and explore ways to relieve victims and their families of such stress.

NOTES

1. The majority of the witchcraft cases were reported to the author by anthropologists who were doing field work in local communities, and by a few who were employed at a medical center or hospital.
2. This diagnosis and prognosis statement was commonly found with many witchcraft victims studied, and generally with no indication on the patient's record of his suffering from bewitchment phenomena.

REFERENCES

EVANS-PRITCHARD, E. E., 1937, *Witchcraft, Oracles and Magic Among the Azande.* Oxford: Clarenton Press.
KLUCKHOHN, C., 1944, *Navajo Witchcraft.* Boston: Beacon Press.
NADEL, S. F., 1952, "Witchcraft in Four African Societies: An Essay in Comparison," *American Anthropologist,* 54:18.
LEININGER, M., 1969, *Study of the Health-Illness System of Spanish-Americans in an Urban Community,* unpublished report.

# 21 | WITCHCRAFT EXPLAINS UNFORTUNATE EVENTS

## E. E. Evans-Pritchard

*In a now classic paper E. E. Evans-Pritchard describes the logic of Zande witchcraft in East Africa and shows how this practice helps people to understand particular misfortunes. The idea of misfortune, or "bad luck," in our own culture is very similar to the Zande notion of witchcraft, except that the Zande see its origins in the unique power of particular people—witches. Witchcraft is intertwined with all aspects of Zande life; a boy who is injured on the hunt, a potter whose bowl breaks in the firing process, and the owner of a hut that catches fire all blame these events on witches. Those most frequently accused of being witches are those who arouse the envy and enmity of their neighbors. As one cannot accuse one's own family members of witchcraft (a hereditary trait), even conflict within the household can be accounted for by the malevolent intentions of an outsider. In many respects witchcraft helps people to respond to problems and tragedy; it answers the question "Why me?" It also encourages people to avoid public ostentation or public striving for success.*

It is an inevitable conclusion from Zande descriptions of witchcraft that it is not an objective reality. The physiological condition which is said to be the seat of witchcraft, and which I believe to be nothing more than food passing through the small intestine, is an objective condition, but the qualities they attribute to it and the rest of their beliefs about it are mystical. Witches, as Azande conceive them, cannot exist.

The concept of witchcraft nevertheless provides them with a natural philosophy by which the relations between men and unfortunate events are explained and with a ready and stereotyped means of reacting to such events. Witchcraft beliefs also embrace a system of values which regulate human conduct.

Witchcraft is ubiquitous. It plays its part in every activity of Zande life; in agricultural, fishing, and hunting pursuits; in domestic life of homesteads as well as in communal life of district and court; it is an important theme of mental life in which it forms the background of a vast panorama of oracles and magic; its influence is plainly stamped on law and morals, etiquette and religion; it is prominent in technology and language; there is no niche or corner of Zande culture into which it does not twist itself. If blight seizes the groundnut crop it is witchcraft; if the bush is vainly scoured for game it is witchcraft; if women laboriously bail water out of a pool and are rewarded by but a few small fish it is witchcraft; if termites do not rise when their swarming is due and a cold useless night is spent in waiting for their flight it is witchcraft; if a wife is sulky and unresponsive to her husband it is witchcraft; if a prince is cold and distant with his subject it is witchcraft; if a magical rite fails to achieve its purpose it is witchcraft; if, in fact, any failure or misfortune falls upon any one at any time and in relation to any of the manifold activities of his life it may be due to witchcraft. Those acquainted either at firsthand or through reading with the life of an African people will realize that there is no end to possible misfortunes, in routine tasks and leisure hours alike, arising not only from miscalculation, incompetence, and laziness, but also from causes over which the African, with his meager scientific knowledge, has no control. The Zande attributes all these misfortunes to witchcraft unless there is strong evidence, and subsequent oracular confirmation, that sorcery or one of those evil agents which I mentioned in the preceding section has been at work, or unless they are clearly to be attributed to incompetence, breach of a taboo, or failure to observe a moral rule.

When a Zande speaks of witchcraft he does not speak of it as we speak of the weird witchcraft of our own history. Witchcraft is to him a commonplace happening and he seldom passes a day without mentioning it. Where we talk about the crops, hunting, and our neighbors' ailments the Zande introduces into these topics of conversation the subject of witchcraft. To say that witchcraft has blighted the groundnut crop, that witchcraft has scared away game, and that witchcraft has made so-and-so ill is equivalent to saying in terms of our own culture that the groundnut crop has failed owing to blight, that game is scarce this season, and that so-and-so has caught influenza. Witchcraft participates in all misfortunes and is the idiom in which Azande speak about them and in which they explain them. Witchcraft is a classification of misfortunes which while differing from each other in other respects have this single common character, their harmfulness to man.

Unless the reader appreciates that witchcraft is quite a normal factor in the life of Azande, one to which almost any and every happening may be referred, he will entirely misunderstand their behavior towards it. To us witchcraft is something which haunted and disgusted our credulous forefathers. But the Zande expects to come across witchcraft at any time of the day or night. He would be just as surprised if he were not brought into daily contact with it as we would be if confronted by its appearance. To him there is nothing miraculous about it. It is expected that a man's hunting will be injured by witches, and he has at his disposal means of dealing with them. When misfortunes occur he does not become awe-struck at the play of supernatural forces. He is not terrified at the presence of an occult enemy. He is, on the other hand, extremely annoyed. Some one, out of spite, has ruined his groundnuts or spoiled his hunting or given his wife a chill, and surely this is cause for anger! He has done no one harm, so what right has anyone to interfere in his affairs? It is an impertinence, an insult, a dirty, offensive trick! It is the aggressiveness and not the eeriness of these actions which Azande emphasize when speaking of them, and it is anger and not awe which we observe in their response to them.

Witchcraft is not less anticipated than adultery. It is so intertwined with everyday happenings that it is part of a Zande's ordinary world. There is nothing remarkable about a witch—you may be one yourself, and certainly many of your closest neighbors are witches. Nor is there anything awe-inspiring about witchcraft. We do not become psychologically transformed when we hear that someone is ill—we expect people to be ill—and it is the same with Azande. They expect people to be ill, i.e., to be bewitched, and it is not a matter for surprise or wonderment.

But is not Zande belief in witchcraft a belief in mystical causation of phenomena and events to the complete exclusion of all natural causes? The relations of mystical to common-sense thought are very complicated. . . . Here I wish to state the problem in a preliminary manner and in terms of actual situations.

I found it strange at first to live among Azande and listen to naïve explanations of misfortunes which, to our minds, have apparent causes, but after a while I learned the idiom of their thought and applied notions of witchcraft as spontaneously as themselves in situations where the concept was relevant. A boy knocked his foot against a small stump of wood in the center of a bush path, a frequent happening in Africa, and suffered pain and inconvenience in consequence. Owing to its position on his toe it was impossible to keep the cut free from dirt and it began to fester. He declared that witchcraft had made him knock his foot against the stump. I always argued with Azande and criticized their statements, and I did so on this occasion. I told the boy that he had knocked his foot against the stump of wood because he had been careless, and that witchcraft had not placed it in the path, for it had grown there naturally. He agreed that witchcraft had nothing to do with the stump of wood being in his path but added that he had kept his eyes open for stumps, as indeed every Zande does most carefully, and that if he had not been bewitched he would have seen the stump. As a conclusive argument for his view he remarked that all cuts do not take days to heal but, on the contrary, close quickly, for that is the nature of cuts. Why, then, had his sore festered and remained open if there were no witchcraft behind it? This, as I discovered before long, was to be regarded as the Zande explanation of sickness. Thus, to give a further example, I had been feeling unfit for several days, and I consulted Zande friends whether my consumption of bananas could have had anything to do with my indisposition and I was at once informed that bananas do not cause sickness, however many are eaten, unless one is bewitched. . . . I shall record here a few examples of witchcraft being offered as an explanation for happenings other than illness.

Shortly after my arrival in Zandeland we were passing through a government settlement and noticed that a hut had been burnt to the ground on the previous night. Its owner was overcome with grief as it had contained the beer he was preparing for a mortuary feast. He told us that he had gone the previous night to examine his beer. He had lit a handful of straw and raised it above his head so that light would be cast on the pots, and in so doing he had ignited the thatch. He, and my companions also, were convinced that the disaster was caused by witchcraft.

One of my chief informants, Kisanga, was a skilled wood carver, one of the finest carvers in the whole kingdom of Gbudwe. Occasionally the bowls and stools which he carved split during the work, as one may well imagine in such a climate. Though the hardest woods be selected they sometimes split in process of carving or on completion of the utensil even if the craftsman is careful and well acquainted with the technical rules of his craft. When this happened to the bowls and stools of this particular craftsman he attributed the misfortune to witchcraft and used to harangue me about the spite and jealousy of his neighbors. When I used to reply that I thought he was mistaken and that people were well disposed towards him he used to hold the split bowl or stool toward me as concrete evidence of his assertions. If people were not bewitching his work, how would I account for that? Likewise a potter will attribute the cracking of his pots during firing to witchcraft. An experienced potter need have no fear that his pots will crack as a result of error. He selects the proper clay, kneads it thoroughly till he has extracted all grit and pebbles, and builds it up slowly and carefully. On the night before digging out his clay he abstains from sexual intercourse. So he should have nothing to fear. Yet pots sometimes break, even when they are the handiwork of expert potters, and this can only be accounted for by witchcraft. "It is broken—there is witchcraft," says the potter simply. Many similar situations in which witchcraft is cited as an agent are instanced. . . .

In speaking to Azande about witchcraft and in observing their reactions to situations of misfortune it was obvious that they did not attempt to account for the existence of phenomena, or even the action of phenomena, by mystical causation alone. What they explained by witchcraft were the particular conditions in a chain of causation which related an individual to natural happenings in such a way that he sustained injury. The boy who knocked his foot against a stump of wood did not account for the stump by reference to witchcraft, nor did he suggest that whenever anybody knocks his foot against a stump it is necessarily due to witchcraft, nor yet again did he account for the cut by saying that it was caused by witchcraft, for he knew quite well that it was caused by the stump of wood. What he attributed to witchcraft was that on this particular occasion, when exercising his usual care, he struck his foot against a stump of wood, whereas on a hundred other occasions he did not do so, and that on this particular occasion the cut, which he expected to result from the knock, festered whereas he had had dozens of cuts which had not festered. Surely these peculiar conditions demand an explanation. Again, if one eats a number of bananas this does not in itself cause sickness. Why should it do so? Plenty of people eat bananas but are not sick in consequence, and I myself had often done so in the past. Therefore my indisposition could not possibly be attributed to bananas alone. If bananas alone had caused my sickness, then it was necessary to account for the fact that they had caused me sickness on this single occasion and not on dozens of previous occasions, and that they had made only me ill and not other people who were eating them. Again, every year hundreds of Azande go and inspect their beer by night and they always take with them a handful of straw in order to illuminate the hut in which it is fermenting. Why then should this particular man on this single occasion have ignited the thatch of his hut? I present the Zande's explicit line of reasoning—not my own. Again, my friend the wood carver had made scores of bowls and stools without mishap and he knew all there was to know about the selection of wood, use of tools, and conditions of carving. His bowls and stools did not split like the products of craftsmen who were unskilled in their work, so why on rare occasions should his bowls and stools split when they did not split usually and when he had exercised all his usual knowledge and care? He knew the answer well enough and so, in his opinion, did his envious, backbiting neighbors. In the same way, a potter wants to know why his pots should break on an occasion when he uses the same material and technique as on other occasions; or rather he already knows, for the reason is known in advance, as it were. If the pots break it is due to witchcraft.

We must understand, therefore, that we shall give a false account of Zande philosophy if we say that they believe witchcraft to be the sole cause of phenomena. This proposition is not contained in Zande patterns of thought, which only assert that witchcraft brings a man into relation with events in such a way that he sustains injury.

My old friend Ongosi was many years ago injured by an elephant while out hunting, and his prince, Basongoda, consulted the oracles to discover who had bewitched him. We must distinguish here between the elephant and its prowess, on the one hand, and the fact that a particular elephant injured a particular man, on the other hand. The Supreme Being, not witchcraft, created elephants and gave them tusks and a trunk and huge legs so that they are able to pierce men and fling them sky high and reduce them to pulp by kneeling on them. But whenever men and elephants come across one another in the bush these dreadful things do not happen. They are rare events. Why, then, should this particular man on this one occasion in a life crowded with similar situations in which he and his friends emerged scatheless have been gored by this particular beast? Why he and not someone else? Why on this occasion and not on other occasions? Why by this elephant and not by other elephants? It is the particular and variable conditions of an event and not the general and universal conditions that witchcraft explains. Fire is hot, but it is not hot owing to witchcraft, for that is its nature. It is a universal quality of fire to burn, but it is not a universal quality of fire to burn *you*. This may never happen; or once in a lifetime, and then only if you have been bewitched.

In Zandeland sometimes an old granary collapses. There is nothing remarkable in this. Every Zande knows that termites eat the supports in course of time and that even the hardest woods decay after years of service. Now a granary is the summerhouse of a Zande homestead and people sit beneath it in the heat of the day and chat or play the African hole game or work at some craft. Consequently it may happen that there are people sitting beneath the granary when it collapses and they are injured, for it is a heavy structure made of beams and clay and may be stored with eleusine as well. Now why should these particular people have been sitting under this particular granary at the particular moment when it collapsed? That it should collapse is easily intelligible, but why should it have collapsed at the particular moment when these particular people were sitting beneath it? Through years it might have collapsed, so why should it fall just when certain people sought its kindly shelter? We say that the granary collapsed because its supports were eaten away by termites. That is the cause that explains the collapse of the granary. We also say that people were sitting under it at the time because it was in the heat of the day and they thought that it would be a comfortable place to talk and work. This is the cause of people being under the granary at the time it collapsed. To our minds the only relationship between these two independently caused facts is their coincidence in time and space. We have no explanation of why the two chains of causation intersected at a certain time and in a certain place, for there is no interdependence between them.

Zande philosophy can supply the missing link. The Zande knows that the supports were undermined by termites and that people were sitting beneath the granary in order to escape the heat and glare of the sun. But he knows besides why these two events occurred at a precisely similar moment in time and space. It was due to the action of witchcraft. If there had been no witchcraft people would have been sitting under the granary and it would not have fallen on them, or it would have collapsed but the people would not have been sheltering under it at the time. Witchcraft explains the coincidence of these two happenings.

# 22 | CARGO CULTS
Peter M. Worsley

*It is not always possible to distinguish religious behavior from political action, let alone to separate beliefs about the social order from divine precepts. In our own society, for example, local church or synagogue congregations sometimes become involved in political movements, for we judge the propriety of our social order in terms of our views of what humankind ought to be, an essentially religious perspective.*

*Peter Worsley has examined the role of organized religion in one society's response to the impact of its political subjugation by a technologically more advanced society. In Melanesia the arrival of European colonial administrators, merchants, and missionaries had a dramatic effect on the traditional social order. Worsley shows that the spread of religious cults announcing the end of the world was one means by which local people adapted to their new circumstances. The so-called cargo cults are more than syntheses of Christian and native beliefs. The development of the cults in various societies follows a similar sequence: a set of beliefs spread, people begin to organize in reference to them, and gradually these beliefs and the cult itself take on an explicitly anti-European orientation. They finally become the vehicle for political opposition to foreign rule and social dominance.*

*Cargo cults illustrate a process that has taken place many times and in many different regions of the world. Such developments are generally called "millenarian movements." Frequently they have nativist elements (an emphasis on a return to "native," as opposed to foreign, traditions) and rely upon the visions of charismatic leaders. Several such movements have arisen among native North Americans. But perhaps the best known example is that of Christianity, which rose 2000 years ago in an oppressed colony of the Roman Empire.*

Patrols of the Australian Government venturing into the "uncontrolled" central highlands of New Guinea in 1946 found the primitive people there swept up in a wave of religious excitement. Prophecy was being fulfilled: The arrival of the Whites was the sign that the end of the world was at hand. The natives proceeded to butcher all of their pigs—animals that were not only a principal source of subsistence but also symbols of social status and ritual preeminence in their culture. They killed these valued animals in expression of the belief that after three days of darkness "Great Pigs" would appear from the sky. Food, firewood and other necessities had to be stock-piled to see the people through to the arrival of the Great Pigs. Mock wireless antennae of bamboo and rope had been erected to receive in advance the news of the millennium. Many believed that with the great event they would exchange their black skins for white ones.

This bizarre episode is by no means the single event of its kind in the murky history of the collision of European civilization with the indigenous cultures of the southwest Pacific. For more than 100 years traders and missionaries have been reporting similar disturbances among the peoples of Melanesia, the group of Negro-inhabited islands (including New Guinea, Fiji, the Solomons and the New Hebrides) lying between Australia and the open Pacific Ocean. Though their technologies were based largely upon stone and wood, these peoples had highly developed cultures, as measured by the standards of maritime and agricultural ingenuity, the complexity of their varied social organizations and the elaboration of religious belief and ritual. They were nonetheless ill prepared for the shock of the encounter with the Whites, a people so radically different from themselves and so infinitely more powerful. The sudden transition from the society of the ceremonial stone ax to the society of sailing ships and now of airplanes has not been easy to make.

After four centuries of Western expansion, the densely populated central highlands of New Guinea remain one of the few regions where the people still carry on their primitive existence in complete independence of the world outside. Yet as the agents of the Australian Government penetrate into ever more remote mountain valleys, they find these backwaters of antiquity already deeply disturbed by contact with the ideas and artifacts of European civilization. For "cargo"—Pidgin English for trade goods—has long flowed along the indigenous channels of communication from the seacoast into the wilderness. With it has traveled the frightening knowledge of the white man's magical power. No small element in the white man's magic is the hopeful message sent abroad by his missionaries: the news that a Messiah will come and that the present order of Creation will end.

The people of the central highlands of New Guinea are only the latest to be gripped in the recurrent religious frenzy of the "cargo cults." However variously embellished with details from native myth and Christian belief, these cults all advance the same central theme: the world is about to end in a terrible cataclysm. Thereafter God, the ancestors or some local culture hero will appear and inaugurate a blissful paradise on earth. Death, old age, illness and evil will be unknown. The riches of the white man will accrue to the Melanesians.

Although the news of such a movement in one area has doubtless often inspired similar movements in other areas, the evidence indicates that these cults have arisen independently in many places as parallel responses to the same enormous social stress and strain. Among the movements best known to students of Melanesia are the "Taro Cult" of New Guinea, the "Vailala Madness" of Papua, the "Naked Cult" of Espiritu Santo, the "John Frum Movement" of the New Hebrides and the "Tuka Cult" of the Fiji Islands.

At times the cults have been so well organized and fanatically persistent that they have brought the work of government to a standstill. The outbreaks have often taken the authorities completely by surprise and have confronted them with mass opposition of an alarming kind. In the 1930s, for example, villagers in the vicinity of Wewak, New Guinea, were stirred by a succession of "Black King" movements. The prophets announced that the Europeans would soon leave the island, abandoning their property to the natives, and urged their followers to cease paying taxes, since the government station was about to disappear into the sea in a great earthquake. To the tiny community of Whites in charge of the region, such talk was dangerous. The authorities jailed four of the prophets and exiled three others. In yet another movement, that sprang up in declared opposition to the local Christian mission, the cult leader took Satan as his god.

Troops on both sides in World War II found their arrival in Melanesia heralded as a sign of the Apocalypse. The G.I.'s who landed in the New Hebrides, moving up for the bloody fighting on Guadalcanal, found the natives furiously at work preparing airfields, roads and docks for the magic ships and planes that they believed were coming from "Rusefel" (Roosevelt), the friendly king of America.

The Japanese also encountered millenarian visionaries during their southward march to Guadalcanal. Indeed, one of the strangest minor military actions of World War II occurred in Dutch New Guinea, when Japanese forces had to be turned against the local Papuan inhabitants of the Geelvink Bay region. The Japanese had at first been received with great joy, not because their "Greater East Asia Co-Prosperity Sphere" propaganda had made any great impact upon the Papuans, but because the natives regarded them as harbingers of the new world that was dawning, the flight of the Dutch having already given the first sign. Mansren, creator of the islands and their peoples, would now return, bringing with him the ancestral dead. All this had been known, the cult leaders declared, to the crafty Dutch, who had torn out the first page of the Bible where these truths were inscribed. When Mansren returned, the existing world order would be entirely overturned. White men would turn black like Papuans, Papuans would become Whites; root crops would grow in trees, and coconuts and fruits would grow like tubers. Some of the islanders now began to draw together into large "towns"; others took Biblical names such as "Jericho" and "Galilee" for their villages. Soon they adopted military uniforms and began drilling. The Japanese, by now highly unpopular, tried to disarm and disperse the Papuans; resistance inevitably developed. The climax of this tragedy came when several canoe-loads of fanatics sailed out to attack Japanese warships, believing themselves to be invulnerable by virtue of the holy water with which they had sprinkled themselves. But the bullets of the Japanese did not turn to water, and the attackers were mowed down by machine-gun fire.

Behind this incident lay a long history. As long ago as 1857 missionaries in the Geelvink Bay region had made note of the story of Mansren.

It is typical of many Melanesian myths that became confounded with Christian doctrine to form the ideological basis of the movements. The legend tells how long ago there lived an old man named Manamakeri ("he who itches"), whose body was covered with sores. Manamakeri was extremely fond of palm wine, and used to climb a huge tree every day to tap the liquid from the flowers. He soon found that someone was getting there before him and removing the liquid. Eventually he trapped the thief, who turned out to be none other than the Morning Star. In return for his freedom, the Star gave the old man a wand that would produce as much fish as he liked, a magic tree and a magic staff. If he drew in the sand and stamped his foot, the drawing would become real. Manamakeri, aged as he was, now magically impregnated a young maiden; the child of this union was a miracle-child who spoke as soon as he was born. But the maiden's parents were horrified, and banished her, the child and the old man. The trio sailed off in a canoe created by Mansren ("The Lord"), as the old man now became known. On this journey Mansren rejuvenated himself by stepping into a fire and flaking off his scaly skin, which changed into valuables. He then sailed around Geelvink Bay, creating islands where he stopped, and peopling them with the ancestors of the present-day Papuans.

The Mansren myth is plainly a creation myth full of symbolic ideas relating to fertility and rebirth. Comparative evidence—especially the shedding of his scaly skin—confirms the suspicion that the old man is, in fact, the Snake in another guise. Psychoanalytic writers argue that the snake occupies such a prominent part in mythology the world over because it stands for the penis, another fertility symbol. This may be so, but its symbolic significance is surely more complex than this. It is the "rebirth" of the hero, whether Mansren or the Snake, that exercises such universal fascination over men's minds.

The 19th-century missionaries thought that the Mansren story would make the introduction of Christianity easier, since the concept of "resurrection," not to mention that of the "virgin birth" and the "second coming," was already there. By 1867, however, the first cult organized around the Mansren legend was reported.

Though such myths were widespread in Melanesia, and may have sparked occasional movements even in the pre-White era, they took on a new significance in the late 19th century, once the European powers had finished parceling out the Melanesian region among themselves. In many coastal areas the long history of "blackbirding"—the seizure of islanders for work on the plantations of Australia and Fiji—had built up a reservoir of hostility to Europeans. In other areas, however, the arrival of the Whites was accepted, even welcomed, for it meant access to bully beef and cigarettes, shirts and paraffin lamps, whisky and bicycles. It also meant access to the knowledge behind these material goods, for the Europeans brought missions and schools as well as cargo.

Practically the only teaching the natives received about European life came from the missions, which emphasized the central significance of religion in European society. The Melanesians already believed that man's activities—whether gardening, sailing canoes or bearing children —needed magical assistance. Ritual without human effort was not enough. But neither was human effort on its own. This outlook was reinforced by mission teaching.

The initial enthusiasm for European rule, however, was speedily dispelled. The rapid growth of the plantation economy removed the bulk of the able-bodied men from the villages, leaving women, children and old men to carry on as best they could. The splendid vision of the equality of all Christians began to seem a pious deception in face of the realities of the color bar, the multiplicity of rival Christian missions and the open irreligion of many Whites.

For a long time the natives accepted the European mission as the means by which the "cargo" would eventually be made available to them. But they found that acceptance of Christianity did not bring the cargo any nearer. They grew disillusioned. The story now began to be put about that it was not the Whites who made the cargo, but the dead ancestors. To people completely ignorant of factory production, this made good sense. White men did not work; they merely wrote secret signs on scraps of paper, for which they were given shiploads of goods. On the other hand, the Melanesians labored week after week for pitiful wages. Plainly the goods must be made for Melanesians somewhere, perhaps in the Land of the Dead. The Whites, who possessed the secret of the cargo, were intercepting it and keeping it from the hands of the islanders, to whom it was really consigned. In the Madang district of New Guinea, after some 40 years' experience of the missions, the natives went in a body one day with a petition demanding that the cargo secret should now be revealed to them, for they had been very patient.

So strong is this belief in the existence of a "secret" that the cargo cults generally contain some ritual in imitation of the mysterious European customs which are held to be the clue to the white man's extraordinary power over goods and men. The believers sit around tables with bottles of flowers in front of them, dressed in European clothes, waiting for the cargo ship or airplane to materialize; other cultists feature magic pieces of paper and cabalistic writing. Many of them deliberately turn their backs on the past by destroying secret ritual objects, or exposing them to the gaze of uninitiated youths and women, for whom formerly even a glimpse of the sacred objects would have meant the severest penalties, even death. The belief that they were the chosen people is further reinforced by their reading of the Bible, for the lives and customs of the people in the Old Testament resemble their own lives rather than those of the Europeans. In the New Testament they find the Apocalypse, with its prophecies of destruction and resurrection, particularly attractive.

Missions that stress the imminence of the Second Coming, like those of the Seventh Day Adventists, are often accused of stimulating millenarian cults among the islanders. In reality, however, the Melanesians themselves rework the doctrines the missionaries teach them, selecting from the Bible what they themselves find particularly congenial in it. Such movements have occurred in areas where missions of quite different types have been dominant, from Roman Catholic to Seventh Day Adventist. The reasons for the emergence of these cults, of course, lie far deeper in the life-experience of the people.

The economy of most of the islands is very backward. Native agriculture produces little for the world market, and even the European plantations and mines export only a few primary products and raw materials: copra, rubber, gold. Melanesians are quite unable to understand why copra, for example, fetches 30 pounds sterling per ton one month and but 3 pounds a few months later. With no notion of the workings of world-commodity markets, the natives see only the sudden closing of plantations, reduced wages and unemployment, and are inclined to attribute their insecurity to the whim or evil in the nature of individual planters.

Such shocks have not been confined to the economic order. Governments, too, have come and gone, especially during the two world wars: German, Dutch, British and French administrations melted overnight. Then came the Japanese, only to be ousted in turn largely by the previously unknown Americans. And among these Americans the Melanesians saw Negroes like themselves, living lives of luxury on equal terms with white G.I.'s. The sight of these Negroes seemed like a fulfillment of the old prophecies to many cargo cult leaders. Nor must we forget the sheer scale of this invasion. Around a million U. S. troops passed through the Admiralty Islands, completely swamping the inhabitants. It was a world of meaningless and chaotic changes, in which anything was possible. New ideas were imported and given local twists. Thus in the Loyalty Islands people expected the French Communist Party to bring the millennium. There is no real evidence, however, of any Communist influence in these movements, despite the rather hysterical belief among Solomon Island planters that the name of the local "Masinga Rule" movement was derived from the word "Marxian"! In reality the name comes from a Solomon Island tongue, and means "brotherhood."

Europeans who have witnessed outbreaks inspired by the cargo cults are usually at a loss to understand what they behold. The islanders throw away their money, break their most sacred taboos, abandon their gardens and destroy their precious livestock; they indulge in sexual license or, alternatively, rigidly separate men from women in huge communal establishments. Sometimes they spend days sitting gazing at the horizon for a glimpse of the long-awaited ship or airplane; sometimes they dance, pray and sing in mass congregations, becoming possessed and "speaking with tongues."

Observers have not hesitated to use such words as "madness," "mania," and "irrationality" to characterize the cults. But the cults reflect quite logical and rational attempts to make sense out of a social order that appears senseless and chaotic. Given the ignorance of the Melanesians about the wider European society, its economic organization and its highly developed technology, their reactions form a consistent and understandable pattern. They wrap up all their yearning and hope in an amalgam that combines the best counsel they can find in Christianity and their native belief. If the world is soon to end, gardening or fishing is unnecessary; everything will be provided. If the Melanesians are to be part of a much wider order, the taboos that prescribe their social conduct must now be lifted or broken in a newly prescribed way.

Of course the cargo never comes. The cults nonetheless live on. If the millennium does not arrive on schedule, then perhaps there is some failure in the magic, some error in the ritual. New breakaway groups organize around "purer" faith and ritual. The cult rarely disappears, so long as the social situation which brings it into being persists.

At this point it should be observed that cults of this general kind are not peculiar to Melanesia. Men who feel themselves oppressed and deceived have always been ready to pour their hopes and fears, their aspirations and frustrations, into dreams of a millennium to come or of a golden age to return. All parts of the world have had their counterparts of the cargo cults, from the American Indian ghost dance to the communist-millenarist "reign of the saints" in Münster during the Reformation, from medieval European apocalyptic cults to African "witch-finding" movements and Chinese Buddhist heresies. In some situations men have been content to wait and pray; in others they have sought to hasten the day by using their strong right arms to do the Lord's work. And always the cults serve to bring together scattered groups, notably the peasants and urban plebeians of agrarian societies and the peoples of "stateless" societies where the cult unites separate (and often hostile) villages, clans and tribes into a wider religious political unity.

Once the people begin to develop secular political organizations, however, the sects tend to lose their importance as vehicles of protest. They begin to relegate the Second Coming to the distant future or to the next world. In Melanesia ordinary political bodies, trade unions and native councils are becoming the normal media through which the islanders express their aspirations. In recent years continued economic prosperity and political stability have taken some of the edge off their despair. It now seems unlikely that any major movement along cargo-cult lines will recur in areas when the transition to secular politics has been made, even if the insecurity of prewar times returned. I would predict that the embryonic nationalism represented by cargo cults is likely in future to take forms familiar in the history of other countries that have moved from subsistence agriculture to participation in the world economy.

# 23 | RELIGIOUS MASS MOVEMENTS AND SOCIAL CHANGE IN BRAZIL

## Emilio Willems

*Peter Worsley's paper on cargo cults shows how religious movements may serve as significant devices for political mobilization in tribal societies affected by colonial contact and rule. But it is not only in tribal societies that religious movements are important features of sociopolitical change. In this study by Emilio Willems the role of Protestant Pentecostal and Spiritualist sects in the process of culture change in Brazil is highlighted. Willems examines the history and characteristics of Pentecostal and Spiritualist sects and the ways in which they contrast with the dominant organized religion, Roman Catholicism. In an effort to understand the sects' growing success in attracting adherents, he examines the ways in which they serve the social and psychological needs of their members, suggesting that there is an important relation "between the general process of culture change and the role and functions" of these religious mass movements. In order to fulfill their functions and to be acceptable to the people they serve, these movements must have religious, as well as social and therapeutic, content. This necessity is related to the traditional context in which they develop.*

The role of religious movements in the process of culture change in Latin America is almost entirely unexplored. Attention has been focused on such phenomena as economic underdevelopment, political radicalism, illiteracy, technological backwardness, rural-urban migrations, and the growth of shanty towns, rather than on religious movements whose links with the main stream of cultural transformations seem less obvious. Reports presumably dealing with "whole cultures" have chosen to ignore movements involving millions of people, as well as the emergence of organizational patterns which constitute, in some ways at least, a revolutionary break with the past.

The stereotype of a thoroughly Roman Catholic Latin America may have deflected the attention of some students from the rise of non-Catholic religions and the attendant changes of the traditional social structure. It is true, of course, that non-Catholic religious movements are only in their incipient stages in some countries; but they have reached the proportions of mass movements in others.

Nowhere, however, have they found more diversified expressions or attracted more people than in Brazil. The three largest and functionally the most significant non-Catholic movements of contemporary Brazil are Pentecostalism, Spiritualism, and Umbanda. The two major Pentecostal sects, the Assembly of God and the Christian Congregation, were founded in 1910 as an outgrowth of Protestant proselytism. Since the Pentecostals have shown a biblical reluctance in counting their followers, almost no figures on their early development are available, but for about two decades their proselytic effort seems to have caused little concern to the established Protestant churches. A survey published in 1932[1] stated that only 9.5 percent of the Brazilian Protestants, excluding the communities of German origin, belonged to Pentecostal bodies. The movement has gained momentum especially since World War II, and according to the Evangelical Federation of Brazil, the Christian Congregation counted, in 1958, a total of 500,000 members, including minors. At the same time, the total membership of the Assembly of God was reported to be 1,000,000. Thus out of a total of 2,697,273 Brazilian Protestants, 1,500,000 or 55 percent belonged to the two principal Pentecostal bodies. Should the total of 4,071,643 Brazilian Protestants reported for 1961 be correct, the Pentecostal movement would have by now well over 2,000,000 followers.[2]

The beginnings of organized Spiritualism were traced back to 1873 when the Society for Spiritualist Studies of the Confucius Group was established in Rio de Janeiro. There are no reliable figures on the dissemination of the new faith, but it did not reach proportions of a mass movement until 1920. Umbanda, however, is much more recent. If the source quoted by Bastide is accurate, its formal detachment from the Macumba took place by 1930, but it did not acquire its present characteristics of widespread religious movement until well after World War II.[3]

The reliability and significance of membership figures concerning Spiritualism and Umbanda are difficult to ascertain. According to Camargo, the number of Spiritualists grew from 463,400 in 1940 to 824,553 in 1950.[4] Official figures are lower, as the following table shows.

GROWTH OF
SPIRITUALISM IN BRAZIL

| Year | Total |
| --- | --- |
| 1953 | 488,017 |
| 1958 | 636,449 |
| 1959 | 673,318 |
| 1960 | 680,511 |

Source: Anuário Estatístico.

Both Camargo and Kloppenburg recognize that the relatively low degree of institutionalization of Spiritualism and Umbanda makes statistical accuracy virtually impossible. The State Department of Statistics in São Paulo enumerates only those Spiritualists who are affiliated with some center. Most Spiritualists, however, meet only in private homes and are thus not covered by statistical inquiries.[5] The Umbanda is neither recognized as a separate denomination by the census authorities, nor do the

> Kardecist Spiritualists . . . permit or tolerate that the Umbanda Spiritualists . . . declare themselves as "Spiritualists." Therefore, in official classifications, the enormous proportion of Umbandistas and Philo-Spiritualists appears under the common denominator "Catholic" . . .[6]

Sheer numbers seem to justify the classification of Pentecostalists, Spiritualists and Umbandistas as mass movements, but there is the added fact that all three are concerned with the transformation of the surrounding society. Some aspects of the proposed changes are mystical or utopian, others are practical and are actually being carried out; but, as we shall see further on, the mere existence of these movements constitutes evidence of a major change of the traditional social structure. No matter how different they may seem at first glance, all three movements share at least five major characteristics: they are concerned with similar forms of supernaturalism; they were originated by cultural diffusion, their beliefs are compatible with certain traditions of Brazilian folk Catholicism and messianism; they are organized in sectarian structures; and they perform, competitively, similar or identical functions.

It is assumed that the rapid expansion of the three movements may be explained in terms of their functional adaptation to a changing society and culture. Thus the description of the first four characteristics is intended to lead to an analysis of those specific needs and wants of several million Brazilians these movements appear to fill.

## SUPERNATURALISM

The main concern of the three movements is with spirit possession. The belief in the descent of supernatural beings and their temporary incarnation in human beings occurs in a large number of widely different societies, and in spite of formal and functional variations the anthropologist easily recognizes a common denominator in such beliefs and their manifestations. Following the biblical model, the Pentecostals believe that, under certain conditions, they may be possessed by the Holy Spirit. Although reports on on the possession of isolated individuals are commonplace, most cases occur during collective cult performances whenever the eagerly sought emotional lift has reached a high pitch. The audience is shaken by laughter, weeping, shouting, or chanting; some individuals talk in tongues or have visions of "celestial beauty"; some fall down in ecstasy and feel removed to heaven or paradise. God or the angels speak to them, and many return from their trance "full of the spirit of worship, prayer, and love."[7] Thus the charismatic gifts of the Holy Spirit are bestowed upon the faithful through the act of *tomada,* or seizure.

Brazilian spiritualism, in its most sophisticated version, follows the teachings of Allan Kardec. The sessions are attended by groups of faithful who number from five to one hundred.[8] One or several of the participants are mediums who, at the ritual request of the session leader, receive disembodied spirits of various types. "Spirits of the Light" utter advice about a variety of personal problems; promises of help alternate with mild reprehensions which are sometimes administered with "a surprising sense of humor." Unexpected spirits may visit upon a medium, often with the malicious intention of confusing and shocking the participants.[9] The more "enlightened" spirits may offer so-called "passes" through the body of a medium, whose hands, touching head, shoulders and arms of the patient, are believed to communicate "beneficial fluids" facilitating the solution of physical, psychological or moral problems. The therapeutic powers of a medium possessed by a spirit are comparable to those of a Pentecostalist who performs miraculous cures or is cured himself by temporarily partaking of the powers of the Holy Spirit.

Umbanda is to be considered a successful attempt to combine the Macumba, or Brazilian version of voodoo, with some of the basic teachings of Spiritualism.[10] "In the African tradition the *orixá,* who is a god, seizes the *Filha do Santo* (daughter of the Saint) whereas the *cavalo* (medium) of the Umbanda is possessed by a disembodied spirit."[11] Each *orixá* commands a vast number of spirits, and the medium, while in trance, becomes the bearer of the spirit's wisdom. The *orixás* are identified with certain Catholic saints. This of course is in contrast to the doctrine of Spiritualism. Thus Umbanda is the outcome of a three-way syncretism associating African, Catholic and Spiritualist elements in one loosely knit body of doctrine which makes allowance for unlimited local variations. To the extent that Umbanda centers engage in purely magical practices, including sorcery, they are called Quimbanda.

## THE ROLE OF CULTURAL DIFFUSION

None of the three movements originated in Brazil. In spite of an overly indigenous or nativistic approach in doctrine, ritual, and behavior, particularly among the adherents of the Umbanda, there is nothing autochthonous about any of its aspects. African cult forms, variously named Macumba, Candomblé or Xangô, antedated Umbanda syncretism by more than a hundred years. They have been accurately defined as adaptations of African elements transferred to Brazil by slaves. Direct lineal affiliation with these Afro-Catholic phenomena seems restricted, however, to certain urban areas of northeastern and eastern Brazil. In São Paulo, Camargo failed to discover any indication of a cultural continuity between Macumba and Umbanda. Thus the latter is to be considered the result of secondary diffusion, not only in São Paulo, but in other parts of Brazil. Perhaps the most puzzling aspect of Umbanda is its

Indian component which is also part and parcel of the Macumba inheritance. Since both Macumba and Umbanda are urban phenomena, it seems extremely unlikely that these "influences" result from contacts with any identifiable Indian culture, not to mention the watered down and highly distorted versions of such indigenous grafts. Again, their presence is attributable to diffusion, probably through the channels provided by the popularization of Brazilian Indianism, a literary movement of the nineteenth century.

The introduction of Spiritualism to Brazil has been traced to the middle of the past century,[12] when Europe was in the grip of a Spiritualist wave whose backwash was powerful enough to reach the Americas. Yet in contrast to most areas of diffusion where it was hardly more than a fad, Spiritualism almost immediately took roots in Brazil, and by 1873 it assumed at least some of the aspects of an organized religion.[13] Amalgamation of Spiritualists and African elements in the Umbanda is relatively recent. To shed some light upon its meaning we shall attempt to interpret it in terms of certain processes of social change.

The largest of the three mass movements, Pentecostalism, can clearly be traced to the proselytic endeavors of two foreign missionaries, Daniel Berg, a Swede who founded the Assembly of God in 1910, and Luis Francescon, an Italo-American who became a Presbyterian in Chicago. A few years later, he was, as he put it, "sealed with the gift of the Holy Spirit," and repeatedly received messages from the Lord who suggested that he dedicate his life to missionary work. Under "divine guidance" he went to São Paulo whose large Italian population proved receptive to his preachings. At first his Christian Congregation, founded in 1910, was a sect for Italian immigrants, and all services were conducted in Italian. By 1930, however, it was quite obvious that the Italians were rapidly being assimilated by Brazilian society, and among the native-born generations there were very few who wished to be reminded of the cultural heritage of their parents and grandparents. Thus guided by opportunity and divine revelation, as are all decisions in this sect, the elders decided in 1935 to drop the Italian language. This well-timed adjustment to a changing cultural situation not only assured survival of the sect but laid the foundations for an increasingly rapid expansion outside São Paulo City and the state of São Paulo.

Recent diffusion of Pentecostalism has been accompanied by a heavy proliferation of new sects, some of which can be traced to the proselytic efforts of American missionaries.

## COMPATIBILITY OF THE THREE MOVEMENTS WITH BRAZILIAN FOLK RELIGION

On the surface, the emergence of the three religious movements may be regarded as a break with the Roman Catholic traditions of the country. At the level of Brazilian folk religion, however, their incompatibility with existing beliefs and practices seems open to considerable doubt. In fact, it is our contention that at least part of the surprising vitality of these movements stems from their affinity with certain folk traditions. Folk Catholicism, unlike church-controlled religion, is flexible and unorthodox. In spite of occasional outbreaks of fanaticism, it is basically tolerant and receptive to innovations. The miracle is probably the most frequent source of change within the framework of folk Catholicism. Christ or the Virgin appears to a person; the locale of the vision rapidly becomes a center of miracles and worship and the visionary a thaumaturge or new saint. Folk Catholicism stresses the belief in mystical experiences, in possessions, and in charismatic leadership. A rich historical tradition of messianic movements established numerous precedents for the second coming of Christ taught by many sects.[14] True enough, the Pentecostal sects do not ordinarily announce the second coming of Christ at some future date. Their message contains the far more appealing prospect of an immediate coming of the deity. The repentant believer may expect the descent of the Holy Spirit *here and now* rather than in a distant future. And he comes to the individual rather than dispersively to a group of people. Communion with or seizure by the Spirit is an everyday experience which may be observed whenever the members of a congregation gather for religious services. There is nearly always somebody who has visions, speaks in tongues or prophesies. In fact, we never encountered a practicing Pentecostalist who had not been "baptized" by the Holy Spirit. It would seem that converts who fail to have such an experience withdraw from the congregation after a certain time.

Thaumaturgy or the working of miracles is another powerful tradition of folk Catholicism which the Pentecostal sects incorporated in their body of belief and ritual. There are two ways in which miracles are performed. Seizure by the Spirit is often accompanied by a miracle, in the sense that the person who has been seized by the Spirit finds himself suddenly cured of some "incurable" ailment. Another person, preferably the pastor, who has previously been seized by the Spirit, performs the miracle by touching the patient's head with his hands, or by uttering a prayer over him. Finally, an almost medieval belief in evil spirits, witches and demons of European, Indian or African extraction has been reduced, by the Pentecostals, to possession by the devil. There are a variety of ways in folk Catholicism in which evil spirits including Satan may intervene in human affairs, possession being only one of these. The Pentecostalists admit in their preachings and writings that the devil sometimes seizes a member of the congregation and speaks and acts through his body. Prayer, rather than any specific exorcistic ritual, seems to be the defense against such occurrences.

The cult of the Holy Spirit, as practiced by the Pentecostals, has, of course, a precedent in the *Festa do Divino Espirito Sante,* part of the Iberian heritage and one of [the] high points of the annual round of religious festivals.[15] The rural migrant who joins a Pentecostal sect thus finds himself on familiar ground. Here, an element of his own cultural background is brought back to him in a new and most exciting form.

In contrast to Pentecostalism, Umbanda is, in fact, a folk religion. To the Afro-Catholic tradition of the Macumba were added some of the essentials of Spiritualism to make it more palatable to the slowly rising urban masses and their yearning for middle-class symbols.

Umbanda, as well as Spiritualism, share with the Brazilian folk religion belief in spirits, both good and evil, and the possibility of communicating with or of being possessed by them. And the performances of the mediums, especially their healing powers, suggest considerable affinity with the role of thaumaturgy in folk Catholicism. One could conceivably interpret the continuity of the three movements with Brazilian folk traditions in terms of a pervasive mysticism which seems to constitute a common ground for understanding and emotional involvement.

## STRUCTURE

The statement was made initially that the emergence of the three movements generated organizational patterns implying a revolutionary break with the past. To substantiate this assertion, it ought to be emphasized that the Pentecostal sects, Umbanda, and the Spiritualists recruit the bulk of their adherents among the lower social strata. Such organizational spontaneity, however, is out of line with the feudal traditions of Brazilian society.

Within these traditions, the upper classes, supported by the Catholic Church, were supposed to provide, paternalistically, for the material and spiritual needs of the lower classes which were not believed to have the ability to engage in concerted action of their own. On the whole, the lower classes lived up to this expectation which conveniently helped maintain the status quo. Occasionally they demonstrated a surprising and uncalled-for capacity for rallying around a messianic leader and his promises of a better world, but such rebellious endeavors were consistently suppressed whenever they appeared.

The Pentecostal sects emerged as "by-products" of the revivalistically oriented Protestant churches. I have presented evidence elsewhere that the rapid growth of these sects is related, in space and in time, to major socio-cultural changes of the last three or four decades. The fact that the occurrence of Spiritualism and Umbanda seems confined to urban centers, particularly to the metropolitan areas of Rio de Janeiro and São Paulo, suggests that these movements are even more closely related to cultural change than is Pentecostalism, which has numerous rural ramifications. At any rate, the rapid development of all three movements seems to proclaim the coming of age of social strata formerly known for their lack of organizational spontancity. The movements have proved their ability to develop a supernaturalism adapted to their needs and to defy openly, by their mere existence as distinct and antagonistic social aggregates, the traditional social order. Yet the attitude of defiance finds an even stronger expression in the internal organization of the three movements.

Most Brazilian Pentecostal sects are characterized by a precarious equilibrium between egalitarianism and charismatic leadership. In the sharpest possible contrast to the Catholic church and the rigid class structure of Brazilian society, the structure of the sects is characterized by the absence of an ecclesiastical hierarchy and by a radical reduction of the social distance between clergy and laity. In principle, the ministry is open to anybody who has scored some success as a missionary, and everybody is expected and encouraged to participate in the proselytizing activities of the sect. There is little or no emphasis on theological training, but to have received the gifts of the Spirit, especially his healing powers, ranks high among the qualifications of an aspirant to the ministry. Possession by the Spirit, however, is considered a grace rather than a privilege.

No sect has carried social egalitarianism further than the Christian Congregation. Its position *sui generis* within the Pentecostal movement is characterized by the fact that it minimizes the distinction between laity and clergy almost to the point of obliteration. There are neither bishops nor pastors. The spiritual leadership of the sect is entrusted to a self-perpetuating board of elders "invested with the gifts of the Spirit," meaning that they must have been baptized by the Holy Spirit.

Unlike other sects we had opportunity to investigate, the Christian Congregation repudiates the idea of a pastoral mandate instituted by ordination and based on the assumption of implicit validity. Much to the contrary, the functionaries of the sect, regardless of rank and merit, must seek divine validation for each individual act they are called to perform. In fact, only the Holy Spirit has the power to make decisions, and the sect's functionaries are mere executors of his revealed will. Thus the Spirit stands for group consensus, and reference to his decisions prevents dissent within the sect.

In the Assembly of God and in most smaller Pentecostal sects, however, there is a structural inconsistency causing the sort of strain and stress which produces cleavages and schisms. On the one hand, the sectarian character of these groups emphasizes, surely as a reaction against the Catholic tradition, egalitarianism and the primacy of the laity, especially in all aspects concerning missionary work. On the other hand, the successful leader, who has received more than an ordinary share of graces from the Holy Spirit, is easily held in awe by the faithful. His voice is respected as the voice of God, and if he can add to his other endowments the reputation of a miracle worker—a successful healer, perhaps—there is no limit to the reverence he is accorded by his followers.

Two opposing principles are thus operative in the Pentecostal sects; one is "democratic" and the other "authoritarian." They clash as soon as rival leaders with similar divine endowments arise and accuse the ones in power of misusing their authority or, as they sometimes put it, of "antidemocratic behavior." If the rival is able to sway enough followers, the split occurs and a new sect is born. There is now the Pentecostal Church Brazil for Christ, the Pentecostal Church of Biblical Revival, the Pentecostal Church Miracle of Jesus, and seven or eight other sects which are almost continuously subdividing or changing their names. The Pentecostals tend to interpret this as an indication of growth rather than of disintegration, and one informant invoked the image of cellular fission which, in fact, defines the process metaphorically. The mother sect, in spite of losing part of its membership, is ordinarily not weakened in the long run and usually continues to grow.

The Pentecostal movement could and did take advantage of certain organizational precedents set by the Protestant churches, but neither Spiritualism nor Umbanda were equipped to absorb the sudden influx of many thousands of new adherents. There was, of course, a proliferation of local centers; but if either movement was to become a sect or church, the development of a large number of small, disconnected cult centers was certainly not the way to achieve that objective. Some means of unification or centralization had to be devised to insure doctrinal and structural coherence.

This proved to be less a problem to the Spiritualists than to the Umbanda. Allan Kardec's interpretation of the Gospel and his numerous other writings provided a body of doctrine in which the Spiritualists found a common denominator. Furthermore, the Brazilian medium, Francisco Candido Xavier, receiving authoritative messages from reputable spirits, validated that doctrine by reinterpreting it in terms which were particularly meaningful and appealing to Brazilians.

> Whereas in Europe the Spiritualist idea was only object of observations and laboratory research, or of great and sterile discussions in the field of philosophy, and this in spite of the moral excellency of Kardec's codification, Spiritualism penetrated Brazil with all its characteristics of a Christian revival lifting the souls to a new dawn of the faith. Here, all its institutions rested on love and charity. Even scientific associations which, now and then, appear to cultivate it (Spiritualism) under the label of metapsychology, are absorbed by the Christian program, under the invisible and indirect orientation of the Lord.[16]

The book from which these lines were taken bears the significant title, *Brazil, Heart of the World, Fatherland of the Gospel.* It suggests the pride the national apostle and reinterpreter of European Spiritualism took in converting into a true religion what had been an intellectual hobby in its area of origin.

The foundations were thus laid for a structure which was to congregate thousands of local centers into federations. In 1951 there were already twenty-one federations in different states of Brazil;[17] but they were neither streamlined nor unified, and some of them competed for membership. Most regional federations joined the Brazilian Spiritualist Federation, but some did not. Spiritualist youth organizations began to emerge in 1932, and in 1949 the Youth Department of the Brazilian Spiritualist Federation was established. Its main objective is indoctrination. In São Paulo City, the two largest regional federations maintain a center of social assistance and evangelization which is sought by approximately ten thousand persons every week.[18] Spiritualism's rapid expansion is largely because [of] its effort to solve social problems by providing institutional assistance. The relative position of the Spiritualist movement in this respect may be gleaned from the following comparative table.[19]

INSTITUTIONS IN BRAZIL, 1958

|  | Catholic | Protestant | Spiritualists |
| --- | --- | --- | --- |
| Hospitals | 45 | 3 | 25 |
| Clinics | 178 | 56 | 168 |
| Asylums | 56 | 24 | 64 |
| Shelters | 50 | 15 | 104 |
| Schools | 1,008 | 618 | 435 |
| Others | 659 | 318 | 919 |
| Total | 1,995 | 1,034 | 1,715 |

The structural problems facing the Umbanda are compounded by "its internal dynamics which leads to instability of conceptions and a tendency toward syncretism of all conceivable shades."[20] There is no doctrinal or ritual unity; each *terreiro* (cult center) has its own system, and each leader thinks he has the monopoly on the absolute truth. The fiercely defended ritual peculiarities of each *terreiro* seems even more significant if the proliferation of these cult centers is taken into account. In the major areas of Umbanda development—the state of Guanabara and Rio de Janeiro—thirty thousand centers were reported some years ago.[21]

Umbanda is usually referred to as an "African" religion, meaning that, in addition to the presence of African elements in belief and ritual, its membership is composed of colored Brazilians. Although Negro membership looms disproportionally large, Umbanda has attracted too many individuals of non-African background to be classified as a "Negro religion." In São Paulo at least "the whites attend, in large proportions, the *terreiros* and even descendants of Italians, Syrians, and Japanese seek in its practices the magic effectiveness which had not been unknown to them in their countries of origin."[22]

The nature of the leadership prevalent in the Umbanda centers does not easily reconcile itself to the transfer of power to federative associations. In the Umbanda, Bastide writes,

the leader of the session who speaks to the mediums, questions the spirits, drives them away, or commands them, assumes the role of a thaumaturge; in the new sect he takes the place which the *pagé* occupied in Amerindian society, or on the African continent. No longer are the disembodied spirits dominant; it is the magician who becomes the master of the spirits.[23]

Unlike his Spiritualist counterpart, the Umbanda leader appears to be a modern version of the shaman who competes with other shamans for control of the spirit world and those who believe in his powers. He is unlikely to surrender a fraction of his power to a federation, and if he does it is usually external pressure or the impossibility of providing certain expected services which induces him to agree on an uneasy and precarious alliance with his competitors.

To understand the structural differences between Umbanda and Pentecostalism, one has to compare the ways in which they have been growing. Like its predecessor, the Macumba, Umbanda has developed by the proliferation of local centers which achieved autonomy long before any central organization existed.

Pentecostalism, however, started with the foundation of sects by schism or secession from established churches. The new sects then set about to win converts by organized missionizing. Successful missionaries would found new congregations which were, in the beginning at least, dependent upon the central organization of the sect. Thus whatever authority or power is located in the individual congregation obviously derived from the sect, whose leaders tend to maintain structural ties with the local congregations.

With its emphasis on local uniqueness, charismatic leadership, and structural priority, the Umbanda proceeded in exactly the opposite way: integration has been possible only to the extent that local leaders have been willing to delegate at least some power to a broader organization.

## FUNCTIONS

### Healing

To substantiate our contention that the growth of the three movements is explicable in terms of their structural and functional adaptability to the culture of the lower social strata, it must be made clear, in the first place, that the term "lower strata" is intended to cover, not just the working class, but also the many who have achieved a rather precarious position in the lower ranks of the middle class. They all are beset by a variety of problems caused by the turbulent fashion in which culture change has been taking place during the last three decades. The identification of the three movements with the lower strata does not, by any means, imply identical composition of their membership nor the absence of variations in the social composition of local subdivisions of each movement.

The extent to which the three sects concern themselves with the alleviation of what may broadly be subsumed under the rubric, "physical and mental troubles," clearly indicates one of the areas where certain otherwise unsatisfied needs of the lower strata are met. The traditions of folk medicine with its countless magic components are, of course, very much alive. A steady flow of rural migrants from different regions carries a store of therapeutical magic to the city where a kind of "cross-fertilization" of the medical lore belonging to various subcultures takes place. It is against this background that the people's receptivity to the therapeutics of the Pentecostals, Spiritualists, and Umbandistas should be weighed.

The general inclination to accept, or at least to try out, the prescriptions of a prescientific medicine should be considered with the fact that the masses cannot afford the services of scientific medicine, and the free medical care provided by public and private institutions is highly limited. The constant influx of thousands of rural migrants, many of whom are in need of medical assistance, tends to make even generously planned institutional facilities inadequate within a few years. It is not surprising, therefore, that the prospect of having one's maladies cured constitutes the most powerful attraction of the three movements.

Among the Pentecostals, any leader who demonstrates unusual skill as a miracle healer is likely to draw large crowds. One of the most successful healers, an American missionary of the International Church of the Four-Square Gospel, gained many followers in São Paulo, and when his sect sponsored the National Crusade of Evangelization in 1956, many Protestant groups joined this interdenominational movement. The revival tent was (and still is) used extensively for spontaneous gatherings of the crusade which invaded many regions of Brazil. It seems that the revivalistic atmosphere of the crusade caused many defections among the established churches, and a number of new Pentecostal sects primarily concerned with the mediation of divine healing emerged.

The most conspicuous of new sects is probably the Pentecostal Church Brazil for Christ under Manuel de Mello, a markedly personalistic movement of considerable fluidity. Located in downtown São Paulo, the headquarters of this sect are constantly besieged by a ragged crowd waiting patiently in line for a prayer or a few words of solace from the thaumaturge. The aspect of the crowd leaves no doubt about the recent rural origin of its components.

The therapeutic functions of Pentecostalism are not limited to individual healing performances; they seem to play a significant role in the broader context of conversion and the radical change of personal habits. Many of our informants associated sickness with vice and conversion with health. The recurrent leitmotif of many life histories volunteered by converts ran like this: "Before my conversion I lived in vice and sin. I was always sick and no doctor could cure me. When I finally accepted the Spirit, my ailment miraculously disappeared and I have enjoyed excellent health ever since." The idea of "rebirth" which is so often associated with religious conversion thus appears to contain a physiological component.

In the Spiritualist and Umbandista centers, equal emphasis is put on healing. Camargo found that more than 60 percent of those who approach either sect are seeking relief from some ailment.[24] In fact, both sects use the therapeutic prospect as a proselytic device.

While the Pentecostal etiology of diseases emphasizes vice or sin as a probable determinant of diseases, Umbanda stresses the notion that nonfulfillment of sacred obligations may arouse the wrath of an *orixá* (African God), who punishes by inflicting illness upon the negligent. An alternative explanation ascribes physiological or mental troubles to acts of black magic. In either case, magical procedures are prescribed to placate the *orixá* or to undo the effects of sorcery.

The more sophisticated etiology of the Kardecists recognizes the possibility of disembodied spirits causing the symptoms of physical or mental maladies. Such "fluidic" actions are inspired by vengeance, mischief, or simple ignorance on the part of certain spirits. But an illness may also be interpreted as a Karmic tribulation, by means of which a person redeems himself of faults committed in a previous life. A third alternative recognizes inadequate development of mediumistic capabilities as a possible cause of mental perturbation or actual sickness. Negligence or ignorance prevents a person from developing his mediumistic potential; he becomes the victim of forces which he is unable to control, or even to identify.[25] Spiritualism, of course, provides therapeutical resources against such sufferings, but along with the supernatural approach the techniques of homeopathic medicine are available.

### Reconstruction of the Personal Community

Since the lower strata of the metropolitan areas of Brazil are predominantly composed of migrants from rural regions or preindustrial towns, it may be assumed that their endeavor to find a niche in urban society involves adaptive changes of considerable magnitude. Back in his home town or village, the migrant was a member of a highly integrated group of kinsfolk and neighbors who constituted, in the terminology of Jules Henry, his "personal community," or "the group of people on whom he can rely for support and approval."[26]

Usually a man was born into his personal community; he took its structural implications for granted and was consequently unable to anticipate the problems arising from being deprived of its benefits. Although some migrants succeed in rebuilding at least a simulacrum of the lost personal community by joining relatives or people from the same town, most of them suffer from severe cultural shock, leading to such forms of anomic behavior as are reflected in the life histories of numerous sect members.

The migrant reacts to the novel situation by seeking, mostly by trial and error, a group of people in whose midst he may find emotional affinity and recognition as a person. Among the various alternatives he may choose, the three religious movements rank among the most accessible ones, especially since they compete with each other for new members and actually use proselytic techniques designed to solve personal problems in need of immediate attention. In any of the three movements, particularly in the Pentecostal sects, a person encounters the opportunity to rebuild his personal community.

The typical Pentecostal congregation is a highly cohesive primary group which tends to absorb the newcomer to an extent unmatched by most established churches. No matter how humble, unskilled or uneducated, the individual convert immediately feels that he is needed and relied upon; he is respectfully addressed as "brother," his services are requested by people who speak his own language and share his tastes, worries, and interests, who work with him at the same tasks and share with him the certainty of belonging to the "People of God," as the Pentecostals often call themselves. Whether he belongs to a construction team erecting a new temple or to a group of singing and guitar playing missionaries walking the streets, hospitals, and prisons in search of new converts, the Pentecostalist soon realizes that he belongs, that he is understood, needed and recognized as an equal among equals.

In the mediumistic sects, the participant encounters similar opportunities to rebuild his personal community. But there is one significant difference. Each center, or *terreiro*, is believed to benefit from the regular presence of particular spirits knowledgeable in the affairs of each member, his aspirations, afflictions and hopes, and willing to assist, encourage, admonish or censure him and thus to assume functions which are typically performed by the more influential members of one's personal community. Since the mediumistic religions emphasize the oneness of the "natural" and "supernatural," it seems to make sense to include the spirits among the prominent members of one's personal community.

## Symbolic Subversion of the Traditional Power Structure

It was previously pointed out that sects seem to rid themselves of those structural elements of Brazilian society which have acted as a source of frustration. By asserting their organizational spontaneity, they have rejected the paternalistic tutelage of the upper strata. They emphasize social equality and thus negate the traditional class structure. "The festive character of the Umbanda means confraternization. In its midst there are neither classes nor castes."[27] They chose a theology which dispenses with the salvation monopoly of the Roman Catholic Church and its priestly hierarchy, which is perceived—rightly or wrongly—as a rampart of the traditional society. Their religious beliefs put the supernatural within the immediate reach of anybody who embraces the new faith.[28]

Yet direct and personal access to the supernatural, either through possession or through contact with those possessed, and vicarious participation in the benefits bestowed upon these by a spirit sets the members of the sects apart from ordinary humanity. The Pentecostalists especially like to think of themselves as the "Chosen People" or the "People of God." Possession by the Holy Spirit is interpreted as a legitimization of such privileged status. The sect members are, without exception, actual or potential recipients of the "Powers of the Spirit." The first seizure of "baptism by the Spirit," which a Pentecostalist seeks as anxiously as a Plains Indian seeks his vision, puts a seal of divine approval on the individual. By renouncing "the world" through repentance and adoption of an ascetic way of life one merits these extraordinary powers, which obviously contrast to the situation of powerlessness in which the Pentecostalists find themselves, individually and as members of a social class. The prevalent criteria of class differentiation, such as wealth, family background, education, and occupation, are ignored and often deprecated as manifestations of sinful *mundanismo,* or worldliness. Since the Pentecostalists as a class are not allowed by the "world" to attain distinction in any of these aspects, their validity is altogether denied. In a sense, this is subversion of the traditional or emerging social order in the language of religious symbolism.

Exactly what are these "powers of the Spirit" which confer special status on the Pentecostalists? In addition to thaumaturgy, spiritual illumination, persuasion, prophesying and glossolalia are the most treasured graces accessible to the convert. Illumination, variously called *discernimento* (discernment) or *alta percepção interior* (high internal perception), enables the Pentecostalist to recognize and understand the truth, and the power of *persuasão* transforms him into a fearless and convincing missionary who finds himself under an almost irresistible compulsion to disseminate the Word of God.

The social significance of the powers of the Spirit thus relates to the internal structure of the Pentecostal sects as well as to their position in the society at large.

The unequal distribution of these powers among the members of a sect opens up avenues of social mobility ordinarily denied to the Pentecostalists as members of an underprivileged class. The larger the share of such powers, the more likely it seems that the recipient will make his way to the top of the sectarian structure.

Bestowal of the powers of the Spirit upon the members of the Pentecostal sects acts as a compensatory mechanism for the frustrations inflicted by being deprived of actual power within Brazilian society. Or, to repeat the interpretation by Walter Goldschmidt:

> The appeal of the emotional religion and the asceticism for the disfranchised is this: It denies the existence of this world with its woes. *It denies the values in terms of which they are the underprivileged and sets up in their stead a putative society* in the kingdom of God, where, because of their special endowments (which we call emotionalism) they are the elite. It is the society of the saved. Millenarism is of the essence, for it is thus that the putative society is created; asceticism is the denial of the world in which they have been denied; and emotional participation is public acclamation of their personal acceptance into this world of super-reality.[29]

Similarly, the mediumistic abilities of the Spiritualists and Umbandistas confer a sense of power and achievement on both the mediums and those who are allowed to enter into personal communication with the spirit world through their mediums. A compensatory mechanism is put into motion when "meek public employees and humble domestic servants are suddenly transformed in[to] vehicles of illuminated spirits, bearers of sublime message."[30] It has been pointed out that Spiritualists have indeed a moral obligation to develop their mediumistic capabilities or face the supernatural sanctions threatening those who have been remiss of their duty to acquire firsthand contact with the spirit world. Such emphasis tends to make available spirit possession to the largest possible number of adherents.

The Spiritualists invoke spirits, often the spirits of famous departed that are believed to have reached superior levels of perfection. Contact with such reputable spirits, particularly the personal interest which these take in one's affairs, contributes to ego enhancement.

While the Kardecists unequivocally seek the association of spirits that during their lifetime had achieved distinction and high status, Umbanda doctrine embodies contradictory elements suggesting a more devious approach to the spirit world and its structural interpretation. As pointed out before, Macumba rid itself of its socially most undesirable associations with low-ranking African cult elements to the extent that it became Umbanda, i.e., by adopting certain elements of Spiritualism.

> Spiritualism becomes the idiom into which the phenomena of mystic trance are translated, and this idiom, accepted by the savants, studied by metapsychology, gives the African the assurance that his experience is no longer an experience of barbarians, or primitives, but that this experience has human rather than racial value.[31]

Thus the integration of Spiritualist principles gained increased social recognition for Umbanda and doubtlessly enhanced the self-image of its colored membership. The fact that some Brazilians of higher social strata were attracted by its rituals meant, of course, protection from its enemies and implicit transfer of power to the leaders of major *terreiros* who were no longer at the mercy of police officers and local politicians eager to capitalize on the reactions of the sect's opponents. And

> adherence of the white civil servant, business man, or industrialist to Umbanda assumes, in the eyes of the Negro, the meaning of a reversal of values; no longer is the Caboclo, the savage, nor the African the slave, subject to all kinds of whims of the whites; they have become the gods of the new religion and the former master bends his head humbly to them.[32]

To lend more credibility to this interpretation, it ought to be added that spirits of slaves as well as those of former masters often appear in sessions attended by colored people. Invariably, the audience learns that the spirits of the slaves have already reached the higher levels of perfection, while their masters are still tormented by the illusion of being incarnated. They carry heavy chains and need all the charity and patience of mediums and guides to take their first steps on the narrow path of spiritual ascent.[33]

The adherents of the Umbanda are derided by the Kardecists for invoking the "inferior" spirits of "Caboclos" and "old Negroes." But the Caboclos and old Negroes stand for the Indian and African ancestors of the Umbandistas, and the vindication of high status for such spirits seems quite consistent with the desire to subvert the traditional social order and its value system. Since this subversion cannot be carried out in reality, it is transferred to the spirit world, where the Indians and the Africans occupy higher levels of spiritual perfection, and the class of the "masters" is relegated to the lower levels. In a broader sense, Umbanda may be interpreted as a manifestation of Brazilian nationalism, inasmuch as it emphasizes and thus validates the Indian and African heritage of the lower social strata.[34]

The emphasis placed upon the therapeutical and social functions of the three religious movements is not intended to reduce their religious significance to the point of obliteration. Much on the contrary, the extraordinary degree to which the lifeways of these people are pervaded by religious representations and norms—quite in accord with the sacredness of their cultural tradition—provides the atmosphere of mystical belief in which the spirits associate with man in an effort to build a better society, without the inequities and maladies that afflict its actual counterpart. In a more secularized frame of mind, the sects would probably cease to perform the functions which now constitute their main attractions. The success story of the three movements makes sense only when related to the context of sacred folk traditions caught in the turmoil of profound and rapid cultural change.

## SUMMARY

There are now between four and five million people involved in what may be considered the largest religious mass movement in the history of Brazil, perhaps of Latin America. In the first place, there is the rapid growth of Protestantism; but within Protestantism the characteristics of a mass movement proper apply primarily to the Pentecostal sects, whose combined membership is now in the neighborhood of two million.

The second largest movement comprises the various sect-like organizations which embraced the creed and practice of Spiritualism. Partially overlapping with Spiritualism there are some large cult groups, for example the Umbanda, whose doctrinal contents feed upon African elements which have been perpetuated by institutions such as Macumba, Candomblé, and Xangô.

The concomitance of these movements with sociocultural change is, of course, more than mere coincidence. This [paper] is intended to examine the relationships between the general process of culture change and the role and functions of these movements.

## NOTES

1. Erasmo Braga and Kenneth G. Grubb, *The Republic of Brazil: A Survey of the Religious Situation* (London, New York, and Toronto: World Dominion Press, 1932), p. 71.
2. Prudencio Damboriena, *El protestantismo en América Latina* (Friburgo y Bogotá, Oficina Internacional de Investigaciones Sociales de FERES, 1963), I, 16.
3. Roger Bastide, *Les religions africaines au Brésil* (Paris: Presses Universitaires de France, 1960), p. 443.
4. Candido Procopio Ferreira de Camargo, *Kardecismo e Umbanda* (São Paulo: Livraria Pioneira Editôra, 1961), p. 176.
5. *Ibid.*, p. 17.
6. Buenaventura Kloppenburg, *"Introducción Histórica"* in Candido Procopio de Camargo, *Aspectos sociológicos del espirtismo en São Paulo* (Friburgo y Bogotá: Oficina Internacional de Investigaciones Sociales de FERES, 1961), p. 19.
7. W. C. Hoover, *Historia del Avivamiento Pentecostal en Chile* (Valparaiso: Imprenta Excelsior, 1948), p. 33.
8. Camargo, *op. cit.*, p. 18.
9. The spirits of Catholic priests belong to this category.
10. Roger Bastide, *Les religions africaines au Brésil* (Paris: Presses Universitaires de France, 1960), pp. 443 ff.
11. Camargo, *op. cit.*, p. 36.
12. Zêus Wantuil, *Las mesas giratórias y el Espiritismo* (Rio de Janeiro, 1958), p. 57.
13. Kloppenburg, *op. cit.*, p. 12.
14. For studies of Brazilian messianism see Maria Isaura Pereira de Queiroz, *La guerre sainte au Brésil: Le mouvement messianique du Contestado* (São Paulo: Universidade de São Paulo, Faculdáde de Filosofia, Ciências e Letras. Boletim No. 187, 1957), p. 1958.
15. Emilio Willems, "Acculturative Aspects of the Feast of the Holy Ghost in Brazil," *American Anthropologist* (1953), 400–408.
16. Francisco Cândido Xavier, *Brasil, coracão do mundo, pátria do Evangelho* (Rio de Janeiro: Federacão Espírita Brasileira, 1938), pp. 177–178.
17. Kloppenburg, *op. cit.*, p. 16.
18. Camargo, *op. cit.*, p. 28.
19. *Ibid.*, p. 137.
20. *Ibid.*, p. 33.
21. Bastide, *op. cit.*, p. 443.
22. Camargo, *op. cit.*, p. 35.
23. Bastide, *op. cit.*, p. 438.
24. Camargo, *op. cit.*, p. 94.
25. *Ibid.*, p. 100 ff.
26. Jules Henry, "The Personal Community and Its Invariant Properties," *American Anthropologist*, LX (1958), 827.
27. Emanuel Zespo, *Codificacão da lei de Umbanda* (2nd. ed.; Rio de Janeiro: Editôra Espiritualista Ltda., 1950), p. 147.
28. Some of these traits the sects share with the established Protestant churches.
29. Walter R. Goldschmidt, "Class Denominationalism in Rural California Churches," *American Journal of Sociology*, XLIX (1944), 354.
30. Camargo, *op. cit.*, p. 125.
31. Bastide, *op. cit.*, p. 432.
32. Bastide, *op. cit.*, pp. 467–468.

33. Camargo, *op. cit.*, p. 125.
34. Bastide, *op. cit.*, p. 468.

## REFERENCES

ANUÁRIO ESTATÍSTICO DO BRAZIL, 1958, Rio de Janeiro, Brasil: Conselho Nacional de Estatística.

BASTIDE, ROGER, 1960, *Les religions africaines au Brésil.* Paris: Presses Universitaires de France.

BRAGA, ERASMO, and KENNETH G. GRUBB, 1932, *The Republic of Brazil: A Survey of the Religious Situation.* London, New York and Toronto: World Dominion Press.

CAMARGO, CANDIDO PROCOPIO FERREIRA DE, 1961, *Kardecismo e Umbanda.* São Paulo, Livraria Pioneira Editôra.

DAMBORIENA, PRUDENCIO, 1963, *El protestantismo en América Latina,* Vol. I. Friburgo y Bogotá: Oficina Internacional de Investigaciones Sociales de FERES.

GOLDSCHMIDT, WALTER R., 1944, "Class Denominationalism in Rural California Churches," *American Journal of Sociology,* XLIX: 348–355.

HENRY, JULES, 1958, "The Personal Community and Its Invariant Properties," *American Anthropologist,* LX: 827–831.

HOOVER, W. C., 1948, *Historia del Avivamiento Pentecostal en Chile.* Valparaiso: Imprenta Excelsior.

KLOPPENBURG, BUENAVENTURA, 1961, *"Introducción Histórica,"* in Candido Procopio de Camargo, *Aspectos sociológicos del espiritismo en São Paulo.* Friburgo y Bogotá: Oficina Internacional de Investigaciones Sociales de FERES.

QUEIROZ, MARIA ISAURA PEREIRA DE, 1957, *La guerre sainte au Brésil: Le mouvement messianique du Contestado.* São Paulo: Universidade de São Paulo, Faculdade de Filosofia, Ciências e Letras, Boletim No. 187.

WANTUIL, ZEUS, 1958, *Las mesas giratórias y el Espiritismo.* Rio de Janeiro.

WILLEMS, EMILIO, 1953, "Acculturative Aspects of the Feast of the Holy Ghost in Brazil," *American Anthropologist, 400–408.*

XAVIER, FRANCISCO CANDIDO, 1938, *Brasil, coracão do mundo, pátria do Evangelho.* Rio de Janeiro, Federacão Espírita Brasileira.

ZESPO, EMANUEL, 1960, *Codificacão da lei de Umbanda,* 2nd ed. Rio de Janeiro: Editôra Espiritualista Ltda.

# Part VII
## Perspectives and Retrospectives

Anthropologists, perhaps to a greater extent than other scientists, are prone to considerable self-examination in the context of their research. The nature of field experience often forces the ethnographer to confront emotional and ethical issues that other social scientists may manage more easily to evade. As the fieldworker becomes deeply involved in the lives of the people he or she has intended to study objectively, it is difficult to escape questions about the appropriate role of the researcher. Upon observing injustice, ought one to intervene? But such intervention would violate an important aspect of objective analysis; having interfered with normal processes, how does one know what one has studied? Having lived among and imposed upon others, is not one partly responsible for their welfare? Finally, what are the responsibilities of the anthropologist to his or her own society? Is he or she obliged to study it as well? To change it? These questions have long disturbed anthropologists.

There are other reasons why fieldwork encourages serious reflection. Many ways of life that have persisted for millennia are now disappearing. As human beings we are all the poorer for this loss of cultural diversity. It enriches us to see and appreciate different ways of handling fundamental problems. Some of the societies that are being dramatically changed have achieved means of using their resources and technology that are energetically efficient while minimizing risks to their environment. For example, some East African pastoralists seem to have managed their herds more effectively than those who conduct modern ranching operations in the same area (see Part Two, especially Baker's paper on the Karamoja). We should learn what we can while we can still observe technologically less complex societies as functioning entities.

The responsibilities of anthropologists and other scientists who work with people are considerable. We must carry out our work in ways that do not impose on others' rights to privacy and security. We also have responsibilities to fulfill once we return to our own communities. Foremost among them is the responsibility of communicating our findings promptly and in ways that make them accessible to the public. It is a basic obligation to those who grant funds and to those who bear the burden of being investigated. In addition, the researcher has an obligation to address problems facing his or her own society and to relate the findings of his or her discipline to their solution.

# 24 | THE END OF FIELDWORK
## John Middleton

*An anthropologist looks back on his fieldwork experience with a critical eye. In this selection John Middleton evaluates the techniques that he used for gathering information in the light of what he he has gained. He looks at his own role among the people he studied, the emotions he experienced, and the changes in his position over time. What emerges from these reflections is pertinent to much of anthropological field research: in an effort to become more objective about cultures—his or her own and those of others—the anthropologist must undergo an entirely subjective experience. Participant observation involves deep absorption in the everyday lives of other people.*

### THE STUDY OF CULTURAL VARIATION

During the time I was there I worked in four parts of Lugbaraland, as well as visiting other areas of the country. . . . After about nine months [in south-central Lugbaraland] I decided that I should work elsewhere and moved to northern Lugbaraland for a few weeks, then to western Lugbara on the Congo border, then briefly to the eastern part of the country, and then back to the same part of northern Lugbara that I had already visited. I spent most of the second year there, with a couple of weeks in southern Uganda, in Lugbara settlement of cotton farmers in Buganda and Bunyoro.

The three other areas in Lugbaraland itself were basically very similar to that in which I had already spent many months. But, partly because I had taken care to spend those months in one area, so that I knew it very well (as well, I suppose, as I know any place on earth), the differences in detail were immediately obvious to me. The area of western Lugbara, on the Congo border, was A'dumi. I was very unhappy there. The main reason was that I was again in the position of a newly arrived stranger, without friends or "kin"; but in addition this was an area of much intermingling of small groups of different clan affiliations, which had taken refuge there after having moved from the harsher colonial regime over the border in the Congo. There was considerable competition for land and power, and it was an area notorious for its sorcery. For a time I thought that my discovery of the importance of sorcery and of the persistent malice and hostility that lay behind it were due to my own sense of frustration and longing for the relatively ordered life I had left behind me in my earlier place of work. But at least I was soon aware of this possibility and realized that it did not explain what I found, although it certainly was the cause for my sour remarks about the people there in my diary of the period.

After a short stay of four weeks, I spent some weeks among the eastern Lugbara of Omugo. This was an area much affected by Islam and the scene of some of the early hostility to the colonial administration that culminated in the Rembe-inspired revolt of 1919 at Udupi. . . . Here my dissatisfaction that had been so obvious during my stay at A'dumi died down, as I was able again to see the importance of the marked differences in cultural detail from the area I knew so well from my first year. Unfortunately I found that I could understand very little of the local dialect, so that my progress was very slow and the results as far as filling pages of notes very disappointing. The differences from the first area were also marked enough for me to realize that I could not build on what I had learnt there. But whereas A'dumi had struck me as an area of some disintegration from what I assumed to be a more "traditional" system, it was very clear that Omugo, Udupi, Aringa, and the other parts of eastern and northeastern Lugbaraland could in no way be regarded in that light. They were simply very different from what I had experienced during the previous year. This made me reconsider my view of A'dumi, and I returned there for a week to see whether I had merely been misled in what I had learnt there. That week, although short, enabled me to view A'dumi more dispassionately and to put my experience there in proper perspective. These weeks also taught me something that I was not fully to appreciate until much later, when I spent a short time in Metu, among the western Madi: that the cultural variations within Lugbara were as great as between them and the Madi, their related neighbors to the east.

I spent the remainder of my fieldwork period in one place in north-central Lugbara, called Maraca. . . . I chose this for several reasons. It was the center of a densely populated region, near the heartland of the country close to Mounts Eti and Liru; it was said to be very "traditional" in many ways, yet had been the scene of the first colonial administrative center established by the Belgians in 1900. Also I had very friendly relations with the county chief who lived a few miles from where I did, at a place he called Ovujo, "the house of idleness"; with the local sub-county chief, he who introduced me to the men who told me about the prophet Rembe; and with my cook's father, who lived a little way from where I established myself. I had stayed there for short periods during the previous year. I knew, therefore, that here I had kin ready-made, as it were, and was able to gain a great amount of valuable data which provided me with the bulk of the worthwhile information I collected during the total research period. Much of the work described in previous chapters was done in Maraca, although I have not explicitly mentioned the changes in locale in them. I was able to come to this area with both a considerable knowledge of Lugbara culture in general, with a knowledge of what I was looking for, and with a fresh eye. I saw everything as though for the first time, but with some knowledge of its likely significance and its relevance to my own work. Here I also took on another helper, Oraa, a local man of some age but a younger full-brother of an Elder: he was therefore near the sources of local power and knowledge but was not himself concerned to exercise it. He was ideal as introducer and also as informant.

There is no need to relate what I did in Maraca in detail. . . . But there is one point that should be made. By this time I was aware of the general pattern of Lugbara culture and social organization, so that I no longer regarded items of behavior as isolated but could expect, and grasp when I saw them, the relations between them. In other words, I was able by this time to comprehend the totality of everyday social behavior much as did the Lugbara themselves. If I observed farming, for example, I was aware of the general cosmological background to it; if I heard a discussion about witchcraft I could place it within the wider system of notions of sin, sacrifice, lineage segmentation, conflict for authority, and so on. In brief, I was aware not only of the interrelationships between one item of behavior and another but also of the bounds of Lugbara culture. Before this I had always been aware that there could be a vast range of behavior of which I knew nothing; but now, although of course I continued to collect new details of culture until the last day of my stay, I knew what was the totality of cultural detail and variation that I was likely to find. This was not, however, a time when all I had left to do was to fill in a few gaps of detail; I had rather to continue to seek out those relations between items of behavior and belief that I had not realized existed, and—perhaps more important since after all everything is ultimately related in one way or another to everything else—to weigh the significance of each relationship in the totality of Lugbara culture.

## INTERVIEWS AND OTHER MUNDANE MATTERS

Although I do not wish to discuss field "techniques" as such, I should say something about how I carried out interviews with informants. I have read in accounts of fieldwork methodology about the various ways of structuring interviews, with the implication that this is necessary for any successful gathering of data. I do not believe that this is true. It is clear from my own experience among the Lugbara that I found myself in four kinds of interview situations. The first was that in which I would be sitting among a mass of people who were engaged in drinking beer or performing a ceremony or ritual where my presence was to them merely peripheral and of little importance. On these occasions I would participate as far as I could in whatever was going on, which usually meant drinking, eating, and making as much sense as I could out of the hubbub of conversation around me. I suppose this merits the term "interview-situation." I know that on many occasions I very much wanted to interrupt what was going on with questions, but I never did. The main point of my being there was to observe the whole process and flow of activity in a given situation and I tried to be as inconspicuous as I could and to observe as much as I could for later questioning. If you like, these were preparatory interviews in which I would mark in my notebook and in my own mind points that I could discuss more privately later. They were also important in that my mere presence as an observer and participant was witness to my role of merely being an observer. On these occasions I showed myself to be above board, to be interested in the everyday life around me, and as far as I was able to behave as an ordinary person. It was rare on these occasions that there was not some stranger present whom I would notice asking puzzled but discreet questions about me. He would be told that I was the man who was learning Lugbara culture and history so that I could tell people in Europe about it. The questioner would accept this information with a nod (as my reputation spread quickly) and often with a smile and a handshake for me. . . . From the point of view of filling out my notes these occasions yielded little, but from that of understanding the life around me they were invaluable.

The second type of interview situation was that in which I would sit with two or three people, perhaps a man, his wife, and children, or a couple of men working in a field, and would discuss matters of interest with some care and with myself asking fairly carefully thought out questions. By that I do not mean that I thought out the phrases that I would use, but that I would try to ask my questions in a particular sequence in order to fill in points on which I wanted particular information. On many occasions these discussions became inconsequential as the people themselves would grow interested and excited, either because I was talking about something that was important to be told to me or important to be hidden from me. I would always try not to guide the conversation too much since I found after the first few months that if I did so either the people would grow bored or it would not occur to them to fill in the gaps in my own knowledge that would have been of interest to me had I known about them. These interviews were important for two reasons: from them I could fill in gaps of information and could ask for more detailed accounts than would be possible to obtain

in general discussions with large numbers of people present; and because again they enabled me to make friends and to see the main lines
of Lugbara culture open out before me. At these times I always wrote
in a notebook and would transcribe my notes the same evening if I
could possibly do so, with the date and identity of the informants. I
could also take photographs much more easily at these times than when
in a large mass of people, when there was always likely to be someone
who did not like the idea.

The third type of interview was probably the most profitable as far
as filling up my notebooks was concerned. These were long discussions
with one person. I found that at any one time I would have one or two
cronies who would play for a period of a week or two the role of
inseparable confidant. Their motives were many and mixed. At times
they were people who would gain prestige by being with me. Sometimes they would get a great deal of beer from me; sometimes they
thought they could pay off old grudges by gossiping about their enemies. I think that this kind of interview situation is universal in anthropological fieldwork, and although it is very valuable it is not always
easy to deal with. The Lugbara, although they lack marked differences
of wealth or status, are extremely competitive and jealous people. So
that bosom friendships of this kind can be somewhat harmful unless
very carefully handled. At the same time the Lugbara are friendly
people and I was not willing to snub a man who was merely trying to
be helpful because of the risk of being involved in personal quarrels. My
childhood had been spent largely near a small town near London, but
with regular and extended holidays among farm people of a small and
remote hamlet. In that village I, as a kinsman of a locally important
farmer, had been in a situation not unlike that in which I found myself
among the Lugbara. I was a stranger, and though a fairly wealthy one
was yet a young man who did not show obvious signs of snobbishness
and wished to be friendly with everybody. In other words I am saying
that I tended in Lugbaraland to play by ear and to let things come as
they might. Looking back I think now that I should perhaps have taken
greater care not to have let myself be involved in various obscure
interpersonal quarrels and jealousies. On the other hand the mere fact
that I was told about these quarrels and jealousies was extremely valuable and indeed essential, especially when I began to analyze the cycle
of lineage segmentation and the concomitant rites of sacrifice. All that
I can really say here is that I behaved in exactly the same way as would
anyone involved in the everyday life of any small village or neighborhood. I respected confidences and tried not to give offense, and tried
to preserve an Olympian detachment from local quarrels and a sense
of understanding and compassion. I come here to what is probably the
single most difficult problem that faces an anthropologist: living among
people who are themselves living out their everyday lives as does everyone in any society anywhere, but at the same time trying hard to remain
outside these local relationships and to be an impartial observer of
them. I admit that living with people such as the Lugbara, whose cul-

ture is in many ways so different from my own, many events that caused them to feel anger, guilt, or shame, were not events that caused me to feel the same sentiments nor even to imagine myself feeling them in those situations. There were also many situations when by observation or from gossip I learned of various actions that I found objectionable, but I would later have to talk with their perpetrators as though I cared nothing about their doings and when I knew that by doing precisely nothing would cause those people who had told me about the actions to feel that I was two-faced or cowardly in not regarding the people concerned in the way that they did themselves. These are matters on which one can advise a would-be fieldworker only by suggesting to him that he observe common sense and good manners and maintain a sense of decency and of understanding the weaknesses of other people. If this sounds smug and pretentious then I can answer only that I know no other advice.

The last type of interview situation was the somewhat different one of interviewing a person while filling in a questionnaire. I used questionnaires on several occasions. The first comprised four surveys that I made in different parts of the country to obtain some basic demographic information, with emphasis on the patterns of marriage within the group and with its neighbors. In each case I took a major section as the relevant group (some five to eight hundred people), and obtained data from every household in the section's territory. I had the questionnaire duplicated, in Lugbara, a single form covering all the members of a single homestead. I found that it would take me almost a morning to complete one form, so that I obviously had to have help. I asked the local mission-run secondary schools for assistance, and found a few schoolboys from each of the actual groups I wished to survey who were willing to help me in their school vacations. These were the only people who I actually paid in cash, by the day, for helping me. After spending a few days showing them what was required, we would visit every compound covered by the survey to introduce ourselves, and my assistants returned later to fill in the forms. They were of much value to me, and I wish that I had been able to do more of this work. I should add here that this was done toward the end of my stay, when I knew exactly what I wanted and when I could use questionnaires not to elicit fresh cultural details but rather to provide quantitative demonstration of processes of which I already knew the outlines. The work took a couple of months in each area.

As I have said, this was a slow process and I left most of the donkeywork to my helpers. However, from the few questionnaires that I did myself I found that if I spent an hour in filling in the replies to the actual questions on the paper I would spend at least another hour and a half in discussing them. I found that it was usually impossible to answer the questions in the order set out on the paper but that I had instead to fill them in in the order in which they occurred spontaneously in the course of conversation. I found also, and this is perhaps important, that information gained by questionnaire could be of a very superficial and public nature and I always took great care to administer them in public with as many people standing around listening, giving advice, and volunteering information of their own, as cared to attend. On one occasion I remember clearly administering half a dozen questionnaires to half a dozen people at the same time, trying to go down the list of questions going from one informant to another before passing on to the next question. The noise of argument must have carried a good quarter of a mile, but at least it was obvious that I was not hiding anything; despite the grievous departure from strict canons of technique in administering a questionnaire, such a way of doing it was certainly better in the Lugbara situation than sitting carefully and cold-bloodedly with a single person at a time. One must remember that as far as Lugbara of that time were concerned, virtually no one in the audience could read the marks I wrote on the pieces of paper, so that the more publicity given to what I was doing the better it was.

In passing I must admit that I can still only wonder at the kindness and patience of the many people with whom I spoke, often about matters of considerable intimacy, and that the degree of trust shown in me was really astonishing. I think that it is important and indeed wish to stress the fact that all depends upon one's own approach to one's informants. I have heard of anthropologists who have had chiefs and others in power punish people who refused to give information, and I have heard of others who will pay people or even get them drunk to get them to divulge secret information on matters that they would normally prefer not to discuss with strangers. I have also known anthropologists who have acquired confidential information and then use it in later interviews to elicit still further confidential information from other informants. It seems to me that such behavior is intolerable. I am not saying that I made no mistakes with informants but at least I did not break confidences or publish confidential information. The Lugbara accepted me as a guest and a friend and I tried to behave properly in these roles.

## THE ROLE OF FIELDWORKER

By the end of two years in the field I had acquired a status in Lugbara eyes that appeared to be a reasonably stable one. I have mentioned early in this book something of the rather ill-defined roles that I had been given at the beginning of my stay. I had essentially been given, first, the status of a human being; then the incipient or uncertain semi-status of an immature social being, a stranger; then a more clearly definable and acceptable full status of a social or socialized being. I had, as I have mentioned, begun the development into a fully mature social being that is gone through, much more gradually and carefully, by a growing child and by a stranger who enters a Lugbara community from outside.

In the beginning the role I played was associated—with one exception—with technical activities: I was concerned with farming, hut-building, making spears and drums, and the like. The symbolic content of what I did and learned was minimal, and whatever such content there was was at the time almost beyond my comprehension. The exception, of course, was that at first I was given the role of European and so a man of power and nontraditional authority: this role became increasingly anomalous as I was given a more socialized total status in Lugbara society, and eventually the contradiction had to be resolved.

The change in role in the first year was expressed mainly in being allotted a status defined in terms of quasi-kinship. I hope that I have explained the nature of this enough to make it meaningful. Its acquisition was preceded by the various events that marked a change in my status from "thing" to "person": eating, drinking, dancing, and so on, and with events that marked the gradual loss of my "European" status, such as the invitation to drink *waragi* at the site of an illicit still.

The status of European, insofar as it was possible for it to be dropped —after all, it was not possible for me to drop it completely, since I *was* a European and not a Lugbara in any final analysis—was removed from me after about eight months. I was not all that aware of this process at the time it took place, but I saw later what it represented. The first development was not a single event but a series of occasions at which I took part in various activities at which European administrators and missionaries as well as Lugbara—both "New People" and ordinary persons—participated. They included various government holidays, with parades at the district headquarters in Arua; religious festivals and school celebrations, held at the two missions, and odd meetings and conversations with European officials. I noticed more and more that on these occasions, some formal, others not, I was increasingly placed on the Lugbara side. Whatever the situation, it was not unexpectedly always regarded by the Lugbara as one for the expression of the then basic axis of conflict in the region—Lugbara versus the others, or less commonly, Africans versus the others. I was counted more and more as being on the Lugbara side, perhaps as a Fifth Column agent of the Lugbara pretending to be on the other side but in reality "our child," "the child of Nyio" and similar phrases. I need not enlarge on this point, and perhaps I am exaggerating the significance of these incidents, but I noticed that when later discussing them I was increasingly included among the "we" rather than among "those Europeans."

Another occasion was to me both important and frightening. I was called about midnight to go to the hut of a young married woman, whose family I by then knew quite well, who was in childbirth. It was a breech birth and she was very weak from pneumonia. After many hours' labor, her mother, an old lady with whom I had often joked using the obscenities of a Lugbara joking relationship (since by some roundabout way I was reckoned as her husband's sister's son), suggested that I be called in. By this time it was known that my closest friend among the local Europeans was the doctor, so that it was assumed that I had unlimited medical expertise. When I reached the hut the woman was very weak. Obviously I was medically unskilled and other than suggesting that fewer old women and less herbal smoke in the hut might help, there was not much that I could do. If she were to die, presumably I would be to blame, since men should not be present at a birth, yet I clearly had to do something. I remembered what little medical knowledge I did possess and tried to assist. The baby was finally born and lived, as did the mother. The following day her mother came to visit me, with her sisters and other members of both the wife's and the husband's lineages, and talked for some time. One statement made was "now we know you are not a European, but a good person, and we are glad you are here as sister's son." The mother added that although she had wanted to call me earlier than she had, she had been frightened lest I pollute the homestead and endanger the birth; but she had been overcome by the argument that as I was not a Lugbara this could not apply to the situation. She had been wrong in that regard and yet paradoxically here was I, not a European, but a proper, trustworthy, person; being a "sister's son" helped, since sisters' sons could perform certain actions for someone that were too intimate to be done by a person's patrilineal kin. She was puzzled, realizing that her argument was, in the terms of her own culture, paradoxical. Until the previous day I had been a European, or at least more a European than a Lugbara; the scale had now tilted slightly and I could be regarded as more a Lugbara than a European.

Somewhat cynically one might well ask what is the point of discussing all this about the fieldworkers' changing role. The anthropologist is not undergoing a course in psychoanalysis, although the experience of being a field anthropologist may almost certainly be as intensive as being under analysis—it is not guided but in many respects remarkably similar (I write as someone who has not experienced analysis, so any indignant analyst can contentedly shoot me down here). The anthropologist is engaged in an arduous task of trying to understand and interpret a culture other than his own, and must retain this as being his only task for a period of two years. His behavior in the role he is given by his hosts is determined—or should be determined—by this single aim. Ultimately I am here leading to the question of how and when does one know that one has a reasonable idea of the culture and organization that one is studying. With this problem goes another that is present throughout one's field research and that is implicit in all that I have written so far: this is how does one estimate the accuracy, relevance, and completeness of the information given by informants. Clearly there are times when one is deliberately misled but it is much more common for one to be given incomplete information through no bad intention or fault of informants. The criterion for knowing that one has understood a culture and the cultural behavior that one witnesses might be said to be that one can predict what is likely to be the answer given to questions about them. The word predict here raises many epistemological questions that cannot be discussed in a book of this size; but something should be said of them since it seems to me that they are important. One cannot predict human behavior in the way that an astronomer can predict the appearance of a comet. The Lugbara cannot do that for their own behavior nor we for ours. However, it is not so much a matter of prediction of the future as of understanding the completeness and complementarity of the set of roles played before one in a given social situation. For example, the sacrificial rites that I have mentioned earlier were dramas played out for a certain end, with the actors being those taking part, the dead ancestors, Divine Spirit, and myself. Perhaps it would be better to call them scenes in a long drawn out drama than individual dramas themselves: none could fully be understood in isolation from the others. Each of these scenes had an expected number of actors whose roles were in a certain pattern of relationships and were composed of certain expected items of behavior. If one of these were missing or were misplayed the Lugbara would realize this and would state that the ritual concerned would be ineffective and should therefore be performed on another occasion. My competence at analysis of the situation was made clear only when I could myself realize that a particular role was missing, miscast, misplayed, or in some other way out of its proper place in the whole constellation of roles whose correct performance made up the scene before me.

I come here to an important point when one is studying nontraditional or innovative social behavior. When the prophets and the Christian evangelists initiated their ritual performances in response to situations of radical conflict, ambiguity, and change, the response to them by ordinary Lugbara was precisely that of bewilderment, uncertainty, irritation, and even anger because they could not comprehend a total and expected pattern in the scene before them. It was only at the very end of my stay that I was able to interpret in this way the Lugbara reaction to such figures and to realize that I did in fact understand something of Lugbara ritual performances. The same applied of course to many other situations, such as the behavior of many administrators and missionaries to that of many "New People" and, of course, to my own behavior. I first noticed this when I heard some Lugbara telling other Lugbara of the events that had occurred when several of us had visited southern Uganda. Their description of what we had seen and done were couched in terms that were very different from my own and which I saw at first as a distortion of our experiences. During that visit we had been to one or two Lugbara settlements of labor migrants, and the men with me could not place properly the behavior of those migrants because the scenes they were playing were as it were part of a different drama to that with which they were familiar in their homeland. It was after this that I began what I found to be extremely fruitful discussions in which I compared the accounts given to me by close informants of events and situations that we together had witnessed to my own description of the same events and situations that I had written down immediately on my return from them. The more I learned about Lugbara the closer were our various accounts of these same events, except on the few occasions when we had traveled into non-Lugbara situations, some of which I could interpret correctly by my own cultural traditions and others in which we were all ignorant of the expected dramatic structure of what we saw (such as a visit to the Kuku of the Sudan). In brief, what I am trying to say is that one cannot predict the events of a given situation but one can see the structure or pattern within the scene that is part of a total drama; and one then knows that one understands as much of another culture as one can hope to understand.

I had been warned by my teacher, Professor Evans-Pritchard, that there is a time when one thinks one is wasting one's time and is a failure. He was correct. In my case it was about nine months after I first entered Lugbaraland. I seemed to have no understanding of the language, I seemed to have no friends or confidants, I seemed to know nothing of the people or their culture. This sense of failure and of frustration would seem to affect us all sooner or later, I am told by colleagues. It was in my case compounded of several elements, most of them connected with my own somewhat romantic and optimistic expectations about my role among the Lugbara.

I had been trained to be a research anthropologist, and this stay among the Lugbara whom I wished to study was in a sense, as I saw it at that time, the culmination of a long period of apprenticeship: the apprentice, although hardly a master, was at least thrown on his own resources as a craftsman. I do not clearly remember exactly what I hoped to achieve even within a few months, but when very little seemed to have been achieved I felt lonely and despondent. I think that probably I had written too many initial field notes. My diary was another matter and when I look at it now I realize its value; but my first half-year's field notes are virtually useless except on a few matters such as technology, and these lack any sociological understanding.

I see also now how much of my sense of frustration, and much else of what I felt and did, were due to my own uncertainty as to my role among the Lugbara. It would be expected that one would have this sense of uncertainty during the period when one is being given a mature status by one's hosts: and indeed I experienced it at this precise time. It was clear to me, whether I liked always to admit it or not, that I was never completely accepted as one of themselves by the people among whom I worked—as I have mentioned before, a stranger can never be accepted, despite the self-deception of many sentimental travellers in Africa. I was always ultimately under the protection of the central government, whether they had wished to leave me alone or to deport me. The visitor longs to be accepted by his hosts, both emotionally and otherwise. I found for myself that there are likely to be three ways in which a fieldworker—or at least an anthropological fieldworker, whose position is very different from that of an economist, sociologist, teacher, historian, technician, or others—tries, consciously or not, to attain this affective link. I am assuming here, of course, that he is a fieldworker, that is, an objective observer; a full participant in the life of his hosts, even from his point of view if not from theirs, is no longer an observer in the anthropological sense. Perhaps this is both the easiest and emotionally the only satisfying course to take, but it makes research impossible and its findings unreliable. The three ways easily open to observer are to assist his hosts in such ways as providing them with medicine; to act as their spokesman vis-à-vis the central government or other external agency that his hosts find it difficult to deal with; and to build up a series of mutual friendship obligations that in some way fall short of complete participant equality. It is clear that these three courses (with full participation as the fourth) differ in the degree to which the fieldworker regards his hosts as objects. As Lévi-Strauss has written, one can only observe people as objects, whether we or they like it or not. But we are also people, and find the objective role as an emotionally unsatisfying one. One problem is obvious: that if we play the roles I have mentioned above, since they are all to one degree or other asymmetrical, they become frustrating. Probably the first response of most people is to accuse the other party of being selfish, or greedy, or in some other way showing that they lack the purity of one's own motives. If one gives several hours a week to dressing dirty and unsightly wounds and sores, one becomes annoyed when one's patients do not follow medical routine; if one gives a patient drugs one gets angry if he gives or sells them to others. If one puts in a word to the agent of the central government on behalf of people who are badly represented there, one may grow resentful if one's advice in the matter to the people one is representing is not taken, or if they try to presume on one's powers and demand more help than one can give while still retaining the role of impartial observer. If one has a friend—and I acquired a handful of close friends about whose behavior I could not remain impartial or objective—one expects him not to abuse that friendship, even if the abuse is in our cultural terms and not in his.

I am not saying that one should not grow angry, resentful, or frustrated at these responses. I am saying merely that at times I did, and from conversations with anthropological colleagues I have found that they did the same. I am saying merely that the role of the anthropological fieldworker is one of paradox, ambiguity, and uncertainty, and these are increased with the greater degree of difference in cultural expectations between his hosts and himself. There is not much that one can do about his hosts' behavior, but there is quite a lot one can do about his own. In my view, the most important thing is to know exactly what is one's own role as an observer, however one's hosts may regard it or their own. As I have said at the beginning of this book, my teacher told me that the most important part of a fieldworker's abilities is to have good manners, since these imply a knowledge of one's own status and values in interpersonal relations. To have this knowledge is, of course, to avoid condescension and patronizing, faults that are found, I fear, most particularly among those fieldworkers who assume, for one reason or another, that they have some special innate sympathy for and intuitive understanding of the people among whom they are living. Most of these merely think that they have these desirable qualities and their behavior is usually, in my experience, one that generates ambiguity and misunderstanding. Let me give two trivial examples. Lugbara always insisted that I should behave as a "European," or rather as a European without power over them, although I behaved as a pleasant and power-less human being who happened to have been born "across Lake Albert." If I did not dress in a fairly formal and clean manner they did not approve, saying that I was behaving "like a Greek" (the nearest thing in their particular experience to a "poor white") and was regarding them as unworthy of respect and good manners. And whenever I in-vited acquaintances to my hut to drink or to eat they expected at least some of the beer to be "European" and served in glasses and at least some of the food to be served on a plate and eaten with fork or spoon. No one likes a slummer, whether in New York or in tne Appalachians: why should people in an African city or village be expected to be any different? I am not saying, of course, that the observer should behave like a caricature of an Anglo-Indian colonel: that is as far on the other side; and one could argue that that kind of behavior is due also to uncertainty and often to fear, especially one expressed in collective and ethnic terms.

I am saying that the role of the anthropological fieldworker is not an easy one, and that the chief difficulty is usually one that arises from the paradox in his role, that he must be both objective and yet be a partici-pant to the greatest degree that he can while still retaining objectivity. This is not advice for people who must cope with neighbors, or teach them, or administer them or have any other kind of role. Others with somewhat similar difficulties, of which the most obvious is probably the psychoanalyst, meet them differently. But there is here an essential difference that the analyst is an objective observer only with regard to individuals for ritually defined periods, whereas the anthropologist has the far harder task of being unable and unwilling to set aside ritually defined interview periods. There are, as we all know, many anthropolo-gists who have done precisely this: they set certain times aside for clearly defined interviews, and live outside the fieldwork situation at other times. Except in the case engaged in ethnological reconstruction, as among certain American Indian groups, for example, I cannot see the value of doing this. It is a denial of the role of fieldworker.

## WRITING UP THE FIELD MATERIAL

Finally I should say something about the writing-up of the data I had collected on my return to England from Uganda. After all, a man who has spent two years or twenty years on ethnographic field research but does not write up his findings for public use might just as well never have been to the field as far as the discipline of anthropology is con-cerned. As we all know there are some anthropologists who find it virtually impossible to set down their findings on paper. I assume that they find the paradox of being an anthropological fieldworker so diffi-cult that they cannot readjust to their own culture.

I found on my return to England considerable difficulty in leaving one culture for another, even though the second had been my own. My first recollection is of noticing various minutiae of behavior in England of which I had previously been unaware. For example, I noticed how English women—but not English men—looked quickly at one another's clothing in passing in the streets. Coming as I had done from a virtually naked people I could perhaps hardly fail to see the social significance placed on wearing the clothes suitable to one's social position and aspirations. Again I soon noticed how English women would appear ashamed of being pregnant, whereas among the Lugbara to be pregnant is a source of pride and a cause for congratulation by patting the woman's stomach—something that I only just stopped myself doing on more than one occasion in England. I noticed what seemed to me to be the loudness and ill-manners of the children although what of course I was really seeing was the difference between Lugbara culture, in which children know their status as incipient adults, and English culture in which children have a subculture and an indeterminate status. I think that all anthropologists have similar experiences when returning from the field. This sense of strangeness and of awareness did not last for more than a few weeks, but it made clear to me my sense of uncertainty as to my proper role of a person who had lived in more than one culture and tried to observe more than one set of social values.

Looking back to my behavior after my return I see now that my uncertainty as to my role was expressed, as it is in most cases, by an excitement and a garrulousness concerning the Lugbara, whom I discussed avidly with anyone whom I met and was willing to listen to me. They were "my people," the object of an intense personal experience which I was willing to interpret to others although not totally willing to share with them. My own sense of uncertainty was lessened by the fact that I returned to a department in which all members had themselves done fieldwork or were planning to do it, and many of whom had only just returned from the field. This latter group was in the eyes of its own members set apart, and there can be no doubt that the excitement and fascination we felt for our common work was both helpful to us in a psychological sense and fruitful for us with regard to thinking about and interpreting our field experience and material.

I had one academic year in which to write a doctoral dissertation on my fieldwork, and I had chosen for the title of my thesis the very general one of "The social organization of the Lugbara of Uganda," which could of course cover virtually anything. I was fortunate at having no work other than to write the dissertation, although I did also have the immediate obligation of writing a report on labor migration. I was told that the dissertation would act as my formal report to those institutions that had sponsored my fieldwork. I spent those nine months mainly in writing the dissertation, which involved presenting some of the material I had collected so as to give an orderly picture of the society. This was not quite so easy as it may sound, since the various notions as to pattern and structure that I had held in my mind at the end of my actual field period soon proved not to be fully adequate when

I attempted to put them down on paper. When I could no longer see the wood for the trees I was lucky in being able to turn to my labor migration report, in which the trees themselves were of major importance. By writing up the material for the thesis I was being made to objectivize my experiences and thus to resolve again the paradox of the anthropologist that I have mentioned above. I need not go into details of the thesis itself, which is from my viewpoint today a very inadequate presentation of Lugbara society. I think that there is often far too much pressure placed upon younger anthropologists to have a doctoral dissertation published immediately as a hard-cover monograph. I would say that a thesis is one thing and a book is another; the former is something to be got rid of as soon as possible, whereas the latter is a much more important work which is the real *raison d'être* of one's being privileged to be an anthropologist at all. By the summer of 1953, therefore, I had written a report on labor migration for the Government of Uganda, and had submitted and had accepted the dissertation.

I was at this point extremely fortunate—more so than I realized at the time—to be able to return to Lugbaraland for a period of three months during the summer. I did this in the company of three other people, so I was able to finish my fieldwork among the Lugbara both while working with a team and also after I had had a long period of writing and thinking about the former material that I had collected. There is no need in discussing this work, since for my part I spent most of the time in filling in gaps of information that had become apparent to me during the time I was writing the dissertation. The people with me were three students, all of my own academic standing: one was a soil chemist, one a botanist, and the third a geographer. All were excellent at the work they did and between us we were able to collect a great deal of valuable data regarding Lugbara ecology and agriculture. I found that my style of work was hardly possible in the company of other people, since we were simply too many to be accepted easily by the Lugbara at any one time. We were able efficiently to measure fields and to discover details of ecology that I found extremely important and meaningful when added to my former information about such matters as patterns of settlement and processes of group segmentation. But it was not possible to set up the close personal ties that had been so important for me during my own previous work. One man may be accepted as a quasi-kinsman, but three more were too many. All I need say here is that if the four of us had gone to Lugbaraland in the way in which I had gone myself three years previously we could not have acquired any very close knowledge of the workings of Lugbara society. We might have been very efficient at collecting quantifiable data, but any close and intimate knowledge of Lugbara culture and its values would not have been possible for us to collect, due simply to the inhibiting factor of our being so many strangers that Lugbara could not easily have absorbed us as "kinsmen." I think that this would not hold true of a husband and wife team, for the simple reason that a husband and wife could easily be accepted into the kinship system. But this was not possible for four unrelated men and I do not think the Lugbara found it easy or possible to regard us as being in any sense brothers to one another, which might have resolved that particular problem. However, I shall not continue this particular discussion, because although we worked as a team our situation was unusual, in that one of us had already spent two years in the area. We were therefore not in the position of a newly arrived team and our particular experience is of little value to other people in a more usual situation.

What is worth saying about this final visit is that it was perhaps the most immediately productive of any three-month period I had spent there. First, because I knew at that time exactly what were the points that I was investigating, and that with my two-year former experience the very fact that I was forced by my company to behave somewhat distantly and objectively removed many of the personal difficulties as well as many of the personal delights of my main fieldwork tour. In later years I was able to do fieldwork in Zanzibar and in Nigeria, and much the same is true of those researches. I was in an objective sense a far more competent fieldworker, for the very reason that my tie with the people whom I was studying was much less emotionally laden than that I had had with the Lugbara. I was able on these later occasions not to put myself into the position of paradox that I had been in among the Lugbara. This was not merely because these were second and third field projects but also because they were shorter and directed to specific research projects: in Zanzibar the study of land tenure and in Lagos that of immigrant associations. I was able to control any sense of uncertainty and frustration to a far greater degree but my work was more superficial, more objective, and with much less understanding and less sympathy and affection. I was not involved in anything in the same sense as among the Lugbara. I do not mean to say that I could not have been if I had had longer and less clearly defined projects: I am merely reporting my own experience. But these several years later I do not remember the people of either Zanzibar or Lagos as I do the Lugbara.

# 25 | A FIELD EXPERIENCE IN RETROSPECT

## Elliot Liebow

*For John Middleton the problem of maintaining objectivity was a critical issue. Is it easier—or more difficult—to be objective when one is studying a people much closer to home? In this selection Elliot Liebow recounts some of his experiences in fieldwork in a subculture of his own society. We learn that many of the problems of doing ethnographic fieldwork are the same whether the work takes place among Eskimos, Africans, Arabs, or urban slum dwellers: establishing rapport, learning the language (or local idiom), overcoming suspicion, examining one's own prejudices and emotional reactions. The experience of fieldwork appears to bring about changes in the perspectives of the researcher that go far beyond the limited material sought in the research itself.*

Robert read the book slowly and with feeling, pausing only occasionally to take a swig of gin and chase it quickly with some beer. Lonny listened quietly and watched with blinking eyes as Robert changed his voice for each of the characters, assuming a falsetto for Snow White. But my own interest started to wander, probably because I had already read the book and seen the movie.

Suddenly Robert raised his voice and startled me back into attention. I looked at Lonny—placid, eye-blinking Lonny—and at Ronald—a handkerchief around his head and a gold earring stuck in his left ear making him look like a storybook pirate—and wondered what the hell I was doing there with these two guys, drinking gin and beer and listening to *Snow White and the Seven Dwarfs.*

I thought back to the events leading up to this situation. From this perspective, everything looked normal and reasonable. I retrieved my can of beer, sat back and listened to the rest of the story. Robert gave it a damn fine reading.

—Field Note, April 1962

## BACKGROUND

When I came to the Child Rearing Study Project on January 1, 1962, this NIMH-supported study of "Child Rearing Practices Among Low Income Families in the District of Columbia" was well into its third year. My job was to collect field material on low-income adult males to complement the data already secured through family interviews.

From the very beginning I felt comfortable with the prospect of working with lower-class Negroes. I was born and raised in Washington, D.C. My father and mother were both Jewish immigrants from Eastern Europe—my mother from Latvia, my father from Russia. My father was a grocer and we lived in rooms above or behind the various stores which he operated. All were in predominantly Negro neighborhoods.

School and playground were white, but all of our customers and most of the neighbors were Negroes. Among them and their children I had many acquaintances, several playmates and a few friends. The color line, retraced daily at school and playground and home, was always there; but so were my day-by-day contacts with Negro men, women and children in the store, on the street, and occasionally in their houses; watching a crap game in Sam's place; witnessing the Devil being exorcised from a woman writhing on the floor of a storefront church from my seat in the back row; shooting crap for pennies in a dark hallway; sitting with Benton on the curb, poking aimlessly at debris, waiting for something interesting to happen. It was not until I was seventeen and enlisted in the Marine Corps that I began to move in an almost exclusively white world.

## PREPARING FOR THE FIELD

I spent the first week in familiarizing myself with the project and with the work that had already been done. I had several informal discussions with Dr. Hylan Lewis, the director of the project, and gradually gained a feeling for the kind of material that was wanted. Importantly, he laid down no hard-and-fast ground rules on the assumption that the job could best be done if I were free to feel my way around for a few weeks and discover for myself the techniques that were most congenial to me. His one prescription was that the work be securely anchored in the purposes of the project, remembering, too, that "Everything is grist for our mill." As I think back on this now, I see a clear connection between his instructions and his fondness for the quotation, "The scientific method is doing one's darndest with his brains, no holds barred."

Having partially digested the project literature, I told the director that I was ready to get started. He suggested a neighborhood that might be "a good place to get your feet wet." His instructions were: "Go out there and make like an anthropologist."

"Out there" was not at all like the Indian village of Winisk on Hudson Bay in which I had done field work. I was not at all sure how one "makes like an anthropologist" in this kind of "out there." Somewhat wistfully, perhaps, I thought how much neater things would be if anthropologists, as they had done in the early thirties, limited themselves to the study of "wholes," a tribe, a village, or some other social unit with distinct boundaries and small enough to be encompassed in its entirety by direct observation.

When I thought about just what I was going to do, I kept in mind the job Richard Slobodin had done for the Child Rearing Study in the summer of 1960.[1] As part of the effort to get at community as well as family influences in child rearing, the director had assigned Slobodin to "make like an anthropologist" in a one-block enclave in northwest Washington. It seemed to me that I could use his work as a model and, in the course of a year, produce several such studies, each covering a strategic part of the world of the low-income male. I thought of doing a neighborhood study, then moving on say, to a construction laborers' union, then a bootleg joint, and perhaps rounding these out with a series of genealogies and life histories. I was going to give myself about a month or so of poking around town, getting the feel of things before committing myself to any firm plan of action.

## IN THE FIELD

In taking up the director's suggestion that this would be "a good place to get your feet wet," I went in so deep that I was completely submerged and my plan to do three or four separate studies, each with its own neat, clean boundaries, dropped forever out of sight. My initial excursions into the street—to poke around, get the feel of things, and to lay out the lines of my field work—seldom carried me more than a block or two from the corner where I started. From the very first weeks or even days, I found myself in the middle of things; the principle lines of my field work were laid out, almost without my being aware of it. For the next year or so, and intermittently thereafter, my base of operations was the corner Carry-out across the street from my starting point.

The first time out, I had gone less than one short block when I noticed a commotion up the street. A man—Detective Wesley, I learned later —was dragging a kicking, screaming woman to a police call box. A small crowd had gathered on each of the four corners to watch. I approached two men and asked what the woman had done. Both were uncertain. The younger of the two said that he had heard two stories and proceeded to tell me both of them, concluding with the observation that he had known Detective Wesley for six or seven years and that he was "nobody to fool with."

I said that sometimes being a cop seems to do something to a man. This led to a discussion of policemen and each of us contributed personal experiences or anecdotes on the subject. After ten or fifteen minutes of this, the older man said goodbye and walked off. The younger man stayed on. Across the street from where we were standing was the Downtown Cafe. I suggested that we go in and have some coffee and he agreed. As we walked across the street he asked if I was a policeman. I told him no and explained that I was working on a study of family life in the city. There was no more discussion about who I was or why I was there. We sat at the bar for several hours talking over coffee.

I had not accomplished what I set out to do, but this was only the first day. And, anyway, when I wrote up this experience that evening, I felt that it presented a fairly good picture of this young man and that most of the material was to the point. Tomorrow, I decided, I would go back to my original plan—nothing had been lost.

But tomorrow never came. At nine the next morning, I headed down the same street. Four men were standing in a group in front of the Carry-out.

Three were winos, in their forties—all marked with old scars on face and neck, dressed shabbily, but sober. The fourth was a man of thirty-two or thirty-three, who looked as if he had just stepped out of a slick magazine advertisement. . . . One of the winos had a month-old puppy stuck in the front of his overcoat. Only the dog's head was exposed.

The group approached me and one of the older men said, "Isn't he a nice puppy?" I said yes, and began patting the dog. "He just bought him," one man said. "I wanted the female, too, to breed them," said the man holding the dog, "but that woman, she sold the female to her friend."

The puppy was whining. "Maybe it's hungry," said the older man, "let's get him some hamburger." "No man, he'll get worms from that stuff," said one of the others. I suggested milk and we all went into the Carry-out. I asked the waitress for a half pint of milk. The man asked for a saucer. "You can't feed him here," the waitress said, "the Health Department would close us up." She gave us a paper plate and the milk (paid for by me). We took the dog into a hallway next door. Everyone was pleased at how eagerly the puppy drank.

A man who had been in the Carry-out joined us in the hallway. "That's a shepherd, isn't he? Just what I want for my little boy." I said, "I wish I could get one for my little girl, but she's allergic to all animals, dust, and lots of things." "It's better that way," said one of the winos. "She'll outgrow it. But man, if you don't have that until you're full grown—man, look out." "Yes, that's right," the newcomer agreed. "I know a woman who got allergies after she was grown and she got bronica asthma with it."

The dog finished the milk. The owner put him back in his overcoat and I shook hands all around with the winos. We split up three ways. The winos went up the street, the well-dressed man down the street, and the new-comer—who turned out to be Tally Jackson—and I went into the Carry-out.

For more than four hours Tally and I lounged around in the Carry-out, talking, drinking coffee, watching people come in and go out, watching other hangers-on as they bantered with the waitresses, horsed around among themselves, or danced to the jukebox. Everyone knew Tally and some frequently sought out his attention. Tally sometimes participated in the banter but we were generally left undisturbed when we were talking. When I left at two o'clock, Tally and I were addressing each other by first names ("Elliot" was strange to him and we settled for "Ellix") and I was able to address the two waitresses by their first names without feeling uncomfortable. I had also learned to identify several other men by their first names or nicknames, had gotten hints on personal relationships, and had a biographical sketch (part of it untrue I learned later) of Tally.

Back on the street, I ended up at the Downtown Cafe, this time by way of the morning's now very drunk owner of the puppy, who was standing near the entrance. The puppy was our bond and we talked about him with an enthusiasm that perhaps neither of us felt. Later, the well-dressed man who had also been part of the puppy episode came in and joined me at the bar. Then, still drinking beer at the bar stool, I met two other men in quick succession. The first man had to leave shortly for his night-shift busboy job at the restaurant. The other was a surly man in his middle thirties who initiated the contact by taking the stool next to me and asking what kind of work I did, adding that he had seen me around the day before, watching Detective Wesley drag that woman across the street.

I told him briefly what my job was.

"Well, if you hang around here you'll see it all. Anything can happen and it does happen here. It can get rough and you can get your head knocked in. You'll be okay though, if you know one or two of the right people."

"That's good to know," I told him, guessing (and hoping) that he was one of the "right people." He left me with the impression that he was being friendly and, in a left-handed sort of way, was offering me his protection.

By the end of the second day I had met nine men, learned the names of several more, and spent many hours in close public association with several men, at least two of whom were well known. And perhaps most important of all, in my own mind I had partly sloughed off that feeling of being a stranger and achieved that minimum sense of "belonging" which alone permits an ease of manner and mind so essential in building personal relationships.

Over the next three or four weeks, I made several excursions into other neighborhoods and followed up at the Downtown Cafe and the Carry-out shop on an irregular basis, getting to know some of the people better and many others for the first time. Frequently I ate breakfast and lunch at the Carry-out and began putting occasional dimes in the jukebox and in the pinball machine. Ted Moore, who worked at a liquor store nearby and whom I had first met in the Carry-out while he was waiting for the store to open, regularly alternated with me in buying coffee and doughnuts in the morning. At the Downtown Cafe the man who told me that I'd be okay if I knew "one or two of the right people" publicly identified me as his friend. ("Sure I know him," he told another man in my presence. "We had a long talk the other day. He's my friend and he's okay, man, he's okay. At first I thought he was a cop, but he's no cop. He's okay.")

All in all, I felt I was making steady progress. There was still plenty of suspicion and mistrust, however. At least two men who hung around the Carry-out—one of them the local numbers man—had seen me dozens of times in close quarters, but they kept their distance and I kept mine. Once, accidentally, I caught the numbers man's eye as I walked in. We held the stare for three or four seconds and I nodded slightly but he wouldn't let go. I went on about my business, determined that I wasn't going to be stared down next time and that he'd get no more nods from me unless he nodded first. As it turned out, I didn't have long to wait.

One mid-February day, I walked into the Carry-out.

. . . Tally was having a cup of coffee. "Look here," he said. "Where is this place?" Tally took out a sheet of paper from an envelope and handed it to me. It was a summons to appear as a witness for the defense in the case of the United States versus Lonny Reginald Small. A faint stamp indicated that Tally was to report to the United States District Court for the District of Columbia at 3rd and Pennsylvania Avenue, Northwest, at ten o'clock this morning. I read off the address. It was then 9:40. I suggested that Tally take a cab, but when Tally said he didn't have the money I offered to drive him down. He quickly accepted. On the way, Tally explained that Lonny was a friend of his. Lonny was being tried for murdering his wife last summer. "Lonny is a nice guy," he said. "He's one hundred percent."

Thus began a three-week odyssey into the world of Lonny Small, a young man of twenty-six who, according to the jury's subsequent verdict of "not guilty," had choked his wife to death accidentally. Upon his acquittal, Lonny was rearrested in the courthouse for a violation of probation (on a previous grand larceny conviction) in another jurisdiction. He waived extradition, was given a hearing, was released on an appearance bond, and after another hearing he was again placed on probation.

Almost imperceptibly, my association with Tally, and through him with Lonny, was projecting me into the role of a principal actor in Lonny's life. By being with Tally through the trial, I found that first Tally, then Lonny, were looking to me for leadership and, as in the question of waiving extradition, for decision making. Court officials, apparently taking their cues from Lonny, began looking to me as his spokesman.

The follow-up of Lonny, which took most of my time for at least the next two weeks, carried me into dozens of places and into contact with scores of people. Throughout this period I stayed in close touch with the project director, getting clearance for and weighing the possible consequences of my growing involvement with the authorities. I went to three different jails during this time, sat through one murder trial and two hearings in judges' chambers, testifying at one of them. I went to bondsmen's offices, to the United States Employment Service, to the Blessed Martin de Porres Hostel (for homeless men) and into several private homes. I met policemen, judges, lawyers, bondsmen, probation officers, and one of Lonny's former employers. I talked with his friends and at least one enemy, his mother-in-law, whose daughter he had killed. I met in council several times with various members of this extended family (who accepted me, through Tally, as Lonny's friend, no questions asked) in their houses, and drove around with them to the houses of other members of the family trying to raise money for Lonny's bond.

Meanwhile, back at the Carry-out, where Tally and I were meeting regularly at night and where I tried to stop in during the day whenever possible, people I had never seen, or others I had seen but never spoken to, began coming up to me and asking, "Is Lonny out yet?" or "Did you raise his bail yet?" or simply, "How's it going?" Bumdoodle, the numbers man, one of those who had not known Lonny, was especially solicitous of Lonny's welfare. He, too, began calling me by my first name and, although I kept no record of it, I think it was at this time that he dropped all subterfuge in taking numbers in my presence and soon began taking bets from me.

By the middle of March, Tally and I were close friends ("up tight") and I was to let him know if I wanted or needed "anything, anytime." By April, the number of men whom I had come to know fairly well and their acceptance of me had reached the point at which I was free to go to the rooms or apartments where they lived or hung out, at almost any time, needing neither an excuse nor an explanation for doing so. Like other friends, I was there to pass the time, to hang around, to find out "what's happening."

I switched my day around to coincide with the day worker's leisure hours: from four in the afternoon until late at night, according to what was going on. Alone, or with one, two or half a dozen others, I went to poolrooms, to bars, or to somebody's room or apartment. Much of the time we just hung around the Carry-out, playing the pinball machine or standing on the corner watching the world go by. Regularly at five, I met my five "drinking buddies" when they came off from work and we went into a hallway for an hour or so of good drinking and easy talk.

Friday afternoon to Sunday night was especially exciting and productive. I'd go to Nancy's "place" (apartment) where, at almost any hour, one could get liquor, listen to music, or engage in conversation. Or perhaps seven or eight of us would buy some beer and whiskey and go up to Tonk's apartment near the Carry-out where he lived with his wife. Occasionally, I'd pair up with one or two men and go to a party, a movie, or a crap game, which might be in almost any part of town. Sunday afternoon was an especially good time to pick up news or happenings of the preceding forty-eight hours. People were generally rested up from the night before, relaxed, and ready to fill one another in on events which involved the police, breakups of husband-wife relations and bed-and-board arrangements, drink-stimulated brawls, sex adventures, and parties they had witnessed, heard about, or participated in over Friday and Saturday.

By April most people seemed to be taking it for granted that I belonged in the area. At least two men did not trust me or like me, but by then I was too strongly entrenched for them to challenge successfully my right to be there, even had they chosen to do so. New people moved into the area and I found myself being regarded as an old-timer, sometimes being asked to corroborate events which predated my arrival.

Throughout this period, my field observations were focused on individuals: what they said, what they did, and the contexts in which they said them or did them. I sought them out and was sought out by them.

My field notes contain a record of what I saw when I looked at Tally, Richard, Sea Cat and the others. I have only a small notion—and one that I myself consider suspect—of what they saw when they looked at me.

Some things, however, are very clear. They saw, first of all, a white man. In my opinion, this brute fact of color, as they understood it in their experience and as I understood it in mine, irrevocably and absolutely relegated me to the status of outsider. I am not certain, but I have a hunch that they were more continuously aware of the color difference than I was. When four of us sat around a kitchen table, for example, I saw three Negroes; each of them saw two Negroes and a white man.

Sometimes, when the word "nigger" was being used easily and conversationally or when, standing on the corner with several men, one would have a few words with a white passerby and call him a "white mother-fucker," I used to play with the idea that maybe I wasn't as much of an outsider as I thought. Other events, and later readings of the field materials, have disabused me of this particular touch of vanity.

Whenever the fact of my being white was openly introduced, it pointed up the distance between me and the other person, even when the intent of introducing it was, I believe, to narrow that distance.

> . . .All of us left Tally's room together. Tally grabbed my arm and pulled me aside near the storefront church and said, "I want to talk to you." With no further introduction, he looked me straight in the eye and started talking.
>
> "I'm a liar. I been lying to you all along now and I want to set it straight, even if it means we can't be friends no more. I only lied to you about one thing. Everything else I told you is gospel truth but I did lie about one thing and that makes me a liar. I know that some white people think that if you catch a man in a lie one time you can't never trust him after that. And even if you feel that way about it I still got to tell you. You remember when you first come around here, I told you. . . . Well, that was a lie. . . . I didn't think nothing of it at first, but then you and me started going around together and when we started getting real tight, my conscience started whomping me. I kept looking for a place to tell you but it never seemed right. Then tonight . . . I knew this was the right time. I knew you were going to find out and I didn't want you to find out from somebody else. . . ."

Once I was with Richard in his hometown. It was his first visit in five years. We arrived in the middle of the night and had to leave before daybreak because Richard was wanted by the local police. We were in his grandmother's house. Besides Richard, there were his grandmother, his aunt, and two unrelated men, both long-time friends of Richard.

The group was discussing the possibility of Richard's coming home to stay and weighing the probable consequences. In the middle of the discussion, Richard interrupted and nodded at me. "Now Ellix here is white, as you can see, but he's one of my best friends. Him and me are real tight. You can say anything you want, right to his face. He's real nice." "Well," said his Aunt Pearl, "I always did say there are some nice white people."

Whether or not there is more to these citations than "Some of my best friends are . . ." or "Yes, but you're different," the wall between us remained, or better, the chain-link fence, since despite the barriers we were able to look at each other, walk alongside each other, talk and occasionally touch fingers. When two people stand up close to the fence on either side, without touching it, they can look through the interstices and forget that they are looking through a fence.

The disadvantage of being white was offset in part by the fact that, as an outsider, I was not a competitor. Thus, in the matter of skin color, I saw myself nowhere in the spectrum of black- to light-skinned (or "bright"); I was completely out of it, with no vested interest. It could be that this made it possible for some people to speak freely to me about skin color.

> "You know, I'm the darkest one in my family. All my aunts, uncles, everybody is light-skinned and they were all down on me, except my grandmother. . . . She'd do anything for me, maybe because she saw everyone else against me. . . . All the time I was coming up, I kept hoping somebody would have a baby darker than me."

Looking at me, however, the people I came to know in the area probably saw more than a "white male adult." They saw or knew many other things as well, any one of which relegated me to outside status. Those with whom I was in regular contact knew, for example, that I was with them because it was my job to be with them, and they knew, according to their individual comprehension and my ability to communicate, just what my job was. They knew that I lived outside the area. They knew that I was a college graduate, or at least they associated an advanced education with the work I was doing. Moreover, it was apparent, certainly to me, that I was not fluent in their language. Thus, I was an outsider not only because of race, but also because of occupation, education, residence, and speech. The fact that I was Jewish came up only twice. Once, a man who worked but did not live in the area threw some Yiddish expressions at me because "I thought you looked Jewish." The other time was when I met a soldier in a local bootleg joint. We had been talking for some ten minutes or so when he asked me whether I was "Eyetalian." I told him I was Jewish. "That's just as good," he said. "I'm glad you're not white."

The fact that I was married and a father, and that I was bigger than average size—6'1", 185 pounds—probably didn't matter much, except as they entered incidentally into my personal relationship with one or another individual. Since the people I spent most of my time with ranged in age from twenty to the middle forties, I would guess that my age (thirty-seven) was not significant in itself.

On several different counts I was an outsider[2] but I also was a participant in a full sense of the word. The people I was observing knew that I was observing them, yet they allowed me to participate in their activities and take part in their lives to a degree that continues to surprise me. Some "exploited" me, not as an outsider but rather as one who, as a rule, had more resources than they did. When one of them came up with the resources—money or a car, for example—he too was "exploited" in the same way. I usually tried to limit money or other favors to what I thought each would have gotten from another friend had he the same resources as I. I tried to meet requests as best I could without becoming conspicuous. I was not always on the giving end and learned somewhat too slowly to accept food or let myself be treated to drinks even though I knew this would work a hardship on the giver.

When in the field, I participated as fully and as whole-mindedly as I could, limited only by my own sense of personal and professional propriety and by what I assumed to be the boundaries of acceptable behavior as seen by those I was with.

Occasionally, when I wanted to record a physical description of say, a neighborhood, an apartment, or a social event, I tried to be an observer only. In practice, I found it impossible to keep all traces of participation out of a straight observer role.

One Saturday night, with my observer role clearly in mind, I went to a dance at the Capitol Arena where more than a thousand people were jammed together. I was the only white male, this was my first time at such an event, the music was so foreign to me that I picked out the wrong beat, and I was unable to identify several of the band instruments. I was, willy-nilly, an observer. But here are a few lines excerpted from the field observation:

> It was very hot, it was very noisy, it was very smelly, and it was all very exciting. It was impossible to remain simply an observer in a place like this, even for someone as phlegmatic as I. It was only a few minutes after Jackie Wilson started singing that I discovered that the noise wasn't nearly loud enough, the heat wasn't nearly hot enough, and the odor from more than a thousand closely packed people was not really strong enough at all. Like everyone else, I wanted more of everything.

Almost from the beginning, I adopted the dress and something of the speech of the people with whom I was in most frequent contact, as best I could without looking silly or feeling uncomfortable. I came close in dress (in warm weather, tee or sport shirt and khakis or other slacks) with almost no effort at all. My vocabulary and diction changed, but not radically. Cursing and using ungrammatical constructions at times—though they came easily—did not make any of my adaptations confusable with the speech of the street. Thus, while remaining conspicuous in speech and perhaps in dress, I had dulled some of the characteristics of my background. I probably made myself more accessible to others, and certainly more acceptable to myself. This last point was forcefully brought home to me one evening when, on my way to a professional meeting, I stopped off at the Carry-out in a suit and tie. My loss of ease made me clearly aware that the change in dress, speech, and general carriage was as important for its effect on me as it was for its effect on others.

In retrospect, it seems as if the degree to which one becomes a participant is as much a matter of perceiving oneself as a participant as it is of being accepted as a participant by others.


## NOTES

1. Richard Slobodin, " 'Upton Square': A Field Report and Commentary."
2. From the outset, I had decided I would never shoot crap, pool, or play cards for money, or bet money in any way (numbers excepted, since playing numbers is safely impersonal), and would meticulously avoid the slightest suspicion of a personal involvement with any woman. These self-imposed restrictions to some extent underline my marginality. My explanation that I couldn't afford to chance a fight or bad feelings because of my job was usually accepted and I was generally excused from participating in these activities rather than excluded from them.

# 26 | THE STRUCTURE OF PERMANENCE: THE RELEVANCE OF SELF-SUBSISTENCE COMMUNITIES FOR WORLD ECOSYSTEM MANAGEMENT

## William C. Clarke

*This selection by William Clarke exemplifies one important new direction that researchers in anthropology and the social sciences are taking: a concern for the quality of life incorporating insights gained in research. Here the author, drawing on his extensive fieldwork among the Bomagai-Angoiang farmers of New Guinea, asks what we can learn from them about the improvement of our own situation. Clarke has developed a model of how we might create a more appropriate technological and agricultural basis for contemporary society, one that would offer greater stability and less risk than does our present management of resources. Ethnologists, geographers, planners, and workers from other social and natural sciences should pool their knowledge and learn from one another. Equally important, we must learn from the experiences of people around the world and from those societies that still pursue ways of making a living designed for "permanence," rather than for change. Clarke does not mean that we must view the world of "primitives" as a kind of paradise lost or that we should consider returning to earlier patterns of survival. Rather, we should use contemporary knowledge in all spheres to construct something new, stable, and satisfying.*

*From an economic point of view, the central concept of wisdom is permanence. We must study the economics of permanence. Nothing makes economic sense unless its continuance for a long time can be projected without running into absurdities. . . . The economics of permanence implies a profound reorientation of science and technology, which have to open their doors to wisdom and, in fact, have to incorporate wisdom into their very structure.—E. F. Schumacher, 1974, pp. 26–27*

Readers of this essay will be familiar with the accelerating deterioration of the human environment that marks our world today. I will, therefore, not repeat in any detail what is contained in an also accelerating number of books and papers on the ecological crises associated with too many people or too much technology or both. Instead I will shuttle between a small, technologically simple community in Papua New Guinea and the whole endangered ecosphere, looking as I go at the lessons that the whole might learn from a tiny part. My effort is motivated by two tenets. The first is that studies of small communities and micro-regions can reveal something about larger regions and world-wide socio-economic processes. I do not mean by this, as has been argued by some geographers in the past, that combining many studies of micro-regions will somehow produce a synthetic understanding of larger regions; rather, it is my belief that the intimate understanding available from the study of even one small system may make the larger more comprehensible. My second tenet is that geographers and anthropologists, who more than other scientists have studied human ecology at the micro-scale, should try more to apply their findings to the world's ecological crises. This means less of an "objective" role for human ecologists. As Anderson has written with regard to human ecology as practiced by anthropologists

> The myth of "value-free" social science is now thoroughly dead, and we must take responsibility for our actions. In anthropology, this will mean on the one hand an expansion of applied anthropology from its present rather *ad hoc* shape to a synthesizing discipline at least as powerful as economic development theory, and on the other a concern by human ecologists with applied anthropology and with the wider context of the world crisis. It will mean a broader focus of research. (Anderson, 1974, p. 266)

. . . Because the Bomagai-Angoiang have little to offer in the way of explicit statements as to what gives their ecosystem the property of resilient permanence, we must look directly at the system's structure and function in order to derive principles of permanence. Seven such principles are briefly discussed in the following paragraphs.

One, the Bomagai-Angoiang strategy of agriculture is "palaeotechnic" rather than "neotechnic," in the sense that it is not dependent on an energy subsidy or extra-system nutrient sources. As described in detail in Clarke (1971), the Bomagai-Angoiang are classic shifting cultivators who utilize forest to inhibit weeds and erosion, to maintain soil structure and fertility at levels adequate for intermittent crop production, and to provide materials and supplementary sources of food. . . . Locally captured solar radiation provides the energy for the trophic structure; and all nutrients are internal to the system except for a small, natural input and output associated with rainfall and the outflow of streams. The inherent permanence of such a system contrasts clearly with the precarious security of neotechnic systems with their breached nutrient cycles and their requirement for artificial extra-system inputs from an ever-dwindling reserve. Papers by Manners (1974) and Groth (1975) provide recent details on this as well as other neotechnic dangers discussed below.

Two, Bomagai-Angoiang agricultural behaviour is not self-poisoning. As is now widely acknowledged for the ecosphere, hyper-pollution provides a limit to growth even if energy supply does not. The plant-soil complex is unable to use, hold or recycle fully the massive inputs of fertilizer associated with neotechnic agriculture. The resulting outflow, together with the intentional biotoxins applied to control crop pests, diseases and weeds, is a poisonous or eutrophic component in ecosystems that include neotechnic agricultures. Bomagai-Angoiang agriculture has no comparable toxic flow, and the waste products of their agriculture are promptly assimilated back into the local organic complex.

Three, net energy yields of Bomagai-Angoiang agriculture are strongly positive. For Tsembaga agriculture, Rappaport (1971, p. 127) estimated normal ratios of garden yield to labour input at from 18–20 to one. That is, for every calorie of energy they invested, the Tsembaga received 18–20 calories of food energy—a return similar to that of the Bomagai-Angoiang. Hodder (1973, pp. 97–98) has summarized several other examples of the relatively high energy returns of palaeotechnic shifting cultivation. Steinhart and Steinhart (1974) expand the comparison from shifting cultivation through more intensive palaeotechnic agricultures to the most intensive neotechnic food-supply systems of the U.S.A., which require 5–10 calories of fuel-supplied energy to obtain one food calorie; that is, a negative energy yield. It is further reported (Pimentel et al., 1973) that food-related energy use is continuing to increase in the U.S.A., whose style of "productive" agriculture is presented as a model for regions that have a lower yield per hectare or per farmer hour but still have a positive yield of energy. Making the situation even more threatening in both energetic and environmental terms is the diminishing return associated with increasing neotechnic inputs. Doubling yields often requires many times as great an increase in inputs of fertilizer, energy, pesticides and other technological inputs (Groth, 1975; Hewitt and Hare, 1973, p. 30). Such a relationship is only one facet of the general decline in efficiency levels that comes with economic development and increasing energy consumption per capita (Jackson, 1975). Although they now have a high value productivity, the high input systems cannot be permanently maintained because of Odum's law (Odum, 1973) that net energy is the only energy with true value to society. Until recently, of course, the Bomagai-Angoiang thought of their agricultural system only in terms of an energy budget, not a cash-return budget, and had no choice but to accept Odum's law if they were to survive into the following year.

Four, Bomagai-Angoiang agriculture utilizes the products of bound time but only within the scale of a human life and only within the absorptive capacity of the existing ecosystem. All ecologists know that a mature natural ecosystem such as a tropical forest uses its photosynthetic product largely for maintenance (e.g. Golley, 1972, p. 79). But the complex organization and sizeable biomass of the forest are the result of an accumulation of negentropy through time, the time required for plant succession to move toward maturity. The Bomagai-Angoiang make use of this time-binding process when they fell the forest . . . and incorporate the effects of plant succession into their gardens. . . . It is this process that makes their agriculture less labour demanding than an intensive palaeotechnic system such as wet rice cultivation, which lacks fossil-fuel technology and whose space is too densely populated to permit palaeotechnic time-binding. This is to say, neotechnic fossil-fuel technology is time-binding on a geologic scale; it makes possible the dedication of immature neotechnic ecosystems to output rather than to maintenance. The concentration of the unabsorbable products of time also causes the ecosystemic distortions that we know as environmental problems. The palaeotechnic Bomagai-Angoiang, on the other hand, proceed more closely along the lines of natural ecosystems and use time-bound products and conditions on a small scale as an aid to self-maintenance within a matrix of maturity. Such a process ensures permanence in comparison with the neotechnic operation. As Margalef (1968, p. 29) put it in writing on the concept of succession, "The structures that endure through time are those most able to influence the future with the least expense of energy."

Five, the energy moving through the Bomagai-Angoiang ecosystem is fairly evenly spread among the human population. Within the acephalous Bomagai-Angoiang community, control of resources is widely dispersed, and their palaeotechnic method of production is predominantly land- or labour-dependent. They have few alternatives to the use of their labour, but in many respects individuals are autonomous. Little energy is required to preserve social or economic coherence because the socio-economic structure is lateral rather than hierarchical. In less egalitarian societies, which have created specialized channels for high energy flows from outside the system and which have shifted their purpose from production for maintenance to consumption, there is a loss of autonomy at both the individual and national levels as the coherence of systems and subsystems increases. Rappaport, in a paper that has stimulated my chain of thought here, elaborates on the relationship.

> With loss of local self-sufficiency there is also loss of local regulatory autonomy, and the homeostatic capacity lost from the local system is not adequately replaced by increasingly remote centralized regulators responding to increasingly aggregated and simplified variables through operations increasingly subject to cybernetic impedances and time aberrations. Moreover, the responses of the distant regulators are often to factors extraneous to some of the local systems affected by them. For instance, changes in oil prices threaten to cause starvation in India by reducing the production of Japanese fertilizer upon which Indian agriculture depends. The coherence of the world system increases to dangerous levels as the self-sufficiency of local systems is reduced and their autonomy destroyed and replaced by more centralized agencies whose operations are inadequate to the regulation of the complex systems over which they preside. Hypercoherence is, of course, encouraged by advances in high energy technologies of production, transport, processing and communication, but money also abets it by

imposing upon the diversity of the world the specious simplicity of a single metric which forces all things into apparent commensurability. (Rappaport, 1947)

Flannery (1972) in a paper on the cultural evolution of civilizations has evoked hypercoherence as one of the universal "pathologies" that can lead to the collapse and devolution of civilizations. Approaching from the direction of present-day economic development, Brookfield reaches a related conclusion

> As society and economy are enlarged in the course of development, as communities trade autarky for access to a wider range of goods and services, new and coarser patterns of resource evaluation and selection replace the older, finer patterns. Specialization replaces diversity; economic risk is added to natural risk. (Brookfield, 1975, p. 208)

Six, especially before European contact, the Bomagai-Angoiang looked on their resources as productive capital to be preserved. They saw secondary forest regrowth as a "garden mother," that is, as something out of which would issue later sustenance. In their garden management they practiced a selective weeding that gave tree seedlings a head start in plant succession, for they knew the benefits that came from rapid regrowth of forest. . . . They preserved for their children a habitat and set of resources only slightly modified from what they had inherited themselves and they foresaw their children carrying on the same tradition. Except for what was probably a gradual shift toward grassland,[1] the Bomagai-Angoiang bore immediately or within their shallow time-binding operations the whole cost of production rather than passing it on to ". . . those conveniently voiceless unfortunates, the future generations . . ." (Anderson, 1974, p. 268). Of course, short-term profit at the expense of the future had little meaning to the Bomagai-Angoiang because they had no backflow of money to stimulate output. Once their basic needs for food and shelter were satisfied, wants having to do with prestige, social relations, and entertainment were constricted by the limited variety and productive capacity of their palaeotechnic life. What they wanted they could make or get by local trade without borrowing from their descendants' resources.

Seven, Bomagai-Angoiang subsistence is based on poly-culture and diversity. Their gardens and household plantings contain over three dozen species of food-producing plants, and many of the species contain a number of varieties. Wild forest and planted orchards provide other foods as well as a habitat for wild animals. As is typical of forest-dwelling shifting cultivators, the Bomagai-Angoiang plant their many crops in an intricately mixed, several-layered arrangement; segregated stands of a single species are unknown. . . . The gardens too are separated from each other within a spontaneous mixture of primary forest and secondary vegetation in various stages of regrowth. The advantages of such poly-cultural diversity as an agricultural strategy are well known: protection against the epidemic spread of crop diseases and pests; fuller utilization of solar radiation and soil nutrients; a variety of foods, provid-

ing better nutrition and a more interesting diet than that obtained from a single staple; and a phased harvest of different crops over several months or longer. In ecosystemic terms, diversity is another way of saying maturity, which—according to many authorities—implies stability and resistance to perturbation. Economic disadvantages listed for poly-cultural agriculture are that its destandardized variety prevents or makes less effective the use of machinery and some other neotechnic inputs and that it is unsuitable for cash cropping. Consequently, reduction of diversity generally accompanies economic development (Janzen, 1973). In the case of peoples as remote from modern transport as the Bomagai-Angoiang, the use of machinery is an unlikely effect of Western influence, but cash cropping can penetrate. Indeed, its introduction to such peoples is encouraged as a way to tie their previously self-sufficient system to the putative benefits of the economically developed world. Because cash moves into the ecosystem in return for only one or two particular crops, these often come to dominate the agricultural system. Poly-cultural diversity is replaced by a trend toward the mono-culture that brings the cash necessary to meet at least in part the demand for extra-system goods and for foods produced elsewhere with an energy subsidy. The resilience imparted by local diversity gives way to an extenuated structure that is liable to breakage at several points.
. . .

It is the argument of this essay that the principles of permanence manifest in the Bomagai-Angoiang's ecosystem can contribute towards solutions of present-day ecological problems, but obviously not on the level of direct imitation. Even if practically possible, few persons now caught up in the neotechnic world would want to become palaeotechnic shifting cultivators; and when palaeotechnic man learns of the neotechnic world, he generally wants to join—a warning to us not to romanticize the palaeotechnic. As poets or philosophers we commend the intimate links between man, place and artifact in the palaeotechnic world; as ecologists we admire the resilient permanence of some of its ecosystems. But it has its own set of debilitating and disabling diseases, its discomforts, its high infant mortality, its often far from ideal nutrition, its own kinds of environmental problems, and its comparatively limited opportunities. There is no reason why palaeotechnic man should hold to these in the face of neotechnic promises of a better life. The admired permanence of some palaeotechnic systems of production results from lack of power, not from the ethnical moderation of the systems' managers.

But we, as observers from the neotechnic world, always come back to that permanence, that longevity: palaeotechnic agricultural systems such as the Bomagai-Angoiang's have gone on for 10,000 years or more, neotechnic agriculture is showing signs of a breakdown after not many decades. What is the essence of palaeotechnic permanence? Is there some sort of structural difference between permanent and impermanent systems of production? We must try to find such knowledge and apply it to our future if we want to survive with dignity. Because (Beer,

1972, p. 184): "If we do not, the future will happen to us. We shall not like it."

What I see now as the essential structural difference between the two sorts of systems is represented in Figure 1. Model ecosystem a summarizes the seven principles of permanence; ecosystem b shows the processes and results of their violation. In ecosystem a the grid lines represent the only significant input of energy—an almost even income and fairly even utilization of solar radiation throughout the system. Solar energy is extra-terrestrial in origin, free, abundant but not concentrated. It is a gentle rain everywhere in the system. Because of its characteristics, there is no control necessary to import or distribute solar energy and so there is no inequality created by its use. The points in model a represent organisms or nodes of energy capture and consumption; these could be plants, animals, man or his economic activities. In accord with the even availability of energy, these nodes are fairly evenly distributed. They and the ecosystem's subsystems—represented by the cubes formed by the intersecting grid lines—are relatively autonomous, which gives the opportunity for the build up of a diversified local organization to utilize fully the local energy rain. Because the energy topography of the whole system is smooth, pooled accumulations of waste from energy use—pollution, that is—are unlikely. Some transformations of energy may be concentrated (as in the transport and subsequent burning of fuel wood) but not beyond the capacity of the system to absorb and disperse. Because there is no energy subsidy, the system must be adapted to survive on solar income, which can be considered as permanently available.

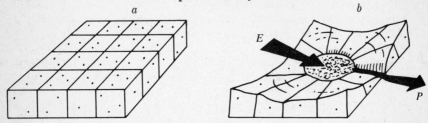

FIGURE 1. Representation of energy distribution in two ecosystems. a.Model of an ecosystem with a homogeneous distribution of energy. b.Model of an ecosystem showing the distortion and pollution (P) resulting from a large, concentrated input of energy (E) from terrestrial sources.

In model b a terrestrial source of neotechnic energy has been tapped and imported into the ecosystem. The result of this input is distortion and simplification. The grid lines of solar-energy use converge toward the centre of distribution of the terrestrial energy as local people together with their energy-consuming activities are attracted to the energy concentration—consider migration to cities. Put in other words, the energy topography is distorted downward toward the point of terrestrial energy input, resulting in an erosion or slippage of local energy and people toward the centre of the basin. What economists call "growth poles" can also be seen as "energy sinks." Brookfield, writing more from the point of view of economics or economic geography, clearly describes the process represented by model b

> The essential fact of development has been the creation of a worldwide interconnected system, which has facilitated much higher levels of adaptation and far more complex systems of allocation and redistribution. Any redistributive system must have nodes, which can be viewed in social, economic or geographical space. The holders of these nodes have become dependent on the network and its flows, but have compensated this dependence by acquiring control over the allocation of scarce resources and production—that is, power. Among the scarce goods have been innovations of many kinds, which have been integrated into the system by entrepreneurs with such a distribution as to increase control, wealth and power in certain nodes. These "growth poles" have become the locus of an increasing measure of control, leading to the progressive marginalization of the rest of the network. Adaptation to scarcity has thus taken the form of alleviating scarcity for some at the cost of increasing its relative impact on others. (Brookfield, 1975, p. 206)

Put in an evolutionary framework, it is clear that the process of gaining control of concentrated terrestrial energy can be seen as adaptive for particular individuals, corporations, peoples and nations. They have been able to consume energy and expand at the expense of others. As Rappaport (1974) points out, White's "basic law of cultural evolution" that "culture evolves as the amount of energy harnessed per capita per year is increased" does accord in a general way with mankind's experience—and with the history of who dominates whom. But man's experience is short in evolutionary terms, and the span of neotechnic evolution, which has so enchanted most economists, is far shorter. Some biologists and ecological anthropologists are now questioning the belief that success in competition for energy necessarily indicates the most successful mechanism of adaptation. Survival may also depend on other attributes that use little energy (Vayda and McCay, 1975). Eventually, this view will be forced on neotechnic man in the face of the high costs that more and more accompany the much praised low prices that neotechnic production has been able to bring. Economists such as Mishan (1969) have already demonstrated the harmful gap between low prices and the high cost of economic development.

To summarize the costs illustrated in model b.

a. Simplification. The energy input, which is associated with profit maximization, encourages simplification. Diversified adaptive processes and knowledge as well as actual genetic resources drain out of the ecosystem as cash flow stimulates mono-culture and other forms of standardization.
b. Accelerated entropy. Degrading energy and materials is a necessary part of life, but with neotechnic processes man carries it to extremes.

Scarce, concentrated energy and materials are used at such a rate that the structure of the system is warped. If the high flow of energy is cut off, the system must contain more entropy than before and will be less able to utilize the abundant solar energy for which scarce terrestrial energy was temporarily substituted.

c. Social distortions. Along with the loss of autonomy and equality already mentioned come other social distortions such as alienation, which includes the sense of loss of control and purpose that unites individuals to their society. There is now a recognition of the need to redistribute the benefits and power that have come with high energy technology or that high energy technology has caused to be restricted to certain segments of society—witness the concern for social justice and rural improvement. But attempts to bring about redistribution require further energy inputs because the flow must be uphill against the gravity of the distorted energy topography— hence one reason for the common argument that we must use more resources to achieve a more equable world.

d. Hyper-pollution. Waste from the concentrated use of neotechnic energy and materials accumulates in a pool of pollution, which poisons both the local system and larger parts of the ecosphere. As with social distortions, so it is frequently argued with regard to hyper-pollution that we need still more energy in order to dispose of the pollution. This is like advising a fat man to lose weight by eating more so that he will have more energy to exercise more in order to lose weight.

My main purpose in this essay has been to explore the structure of permanence in the hope that I could make a contribution toward creating an image to help guide neotechnic man toward a less precarious way of life. The exploration was based on the contrast of a relatively stable ecosystem inhabited by a small community of Papua New Guinean gardeners with the unstable ecosystem inhabited by neotechnic man. I argued that the first exhibited relative but not static permanence, whereas the second exhibits a trend toward breakdown because of the distorting stresses that neotechnic energy use puts on the structure of permanence. I have implied that the most valuable contribution that human ecologists may now be able to make to mankind's welfare will come from attempts to abstract from their studies of small communities principles that can be related to larger systems of human life. I used above the phrase "an image to help guide neotechnic man" because I believe there is a need for a sort of utopian purpose. By this I mean not a detailed design for an unworkably happy society but only some general goals that could be used as compass directions in a move to restructure our ideas on the relations between man and environment. The going itself is not enough—as it seems to be in societies obsessed with progress. There must be a goal, a possible and desirable destination. But at this stage to press for anything more specific than a set of principles or a general goal would be self-defeating because its implementation would require too great a diversion of energy for control and for countering resistance to changes in power relationships. Besides, I think Bateson's (1972) cautions against actions that are too purposeful must be taken seriously. As Slobodkin has written of Bateson's work

> . . . Bateson develops the distinction between "purposeful" action (in the sense of solving a discrete problem) and "ecological" action (in the sense of dealing with problems in their full context). Thus instead of the solution to one problem becoming a more difficult problem than the one it was meant to solve, the entire self-regulating system in its full ramification is considered. If this is done, many problems drastically change their character. (Slobodkin, 1974, p. 70)

This is to say that the first step has to do with our minds rather than with manipulation of the external world, for—as Hardin (1968) has so eloquently argued with regard to the population problem—there is no technical solution. The application of more energy will not help. A new world must begin with a new mind; if the image is strong enough, our successors will be able to work out the details as they go.

Certain necessities are already clear and have been discussed in many recent works, such as those by Taylor (1972), Odum (1969), Goldsmith *et al.* (1972) and Groth (1975). Most of the proposals point at least to some degree toward what Taylor (1972, p. 209) called "the paraprimitive society," by which he meant not an impossible return to the pure primitive but ". . . a society which tries to combine the advantages of primitive group structure with those of technology." A few of the specific necessities for the paraprimitive society are stated here.

One, a lower material standard of living than that of industrial nations. Of course, less neotechnic production means a higher standard of living in terms of unpolluted food, air and water.

Two, a slower rate of technological change, which implies a lowered energy need as well as offering several other advantages.

Three, decentralization of power and production and formation of smaller communities. Opinions vary as to optimum size of communities (Taylor, 1972, p. 212), but most authorities would agree with Rappaport (1971, p. 131) that small autonomous systems are more sensitive to ecological problems than larger, more complex organizations.

Four, changed education to develop a changed relation between man–man and man–nature. The central theme for this changed education is expressed differently by different authors but always revolves around the change from an exploitative I–It (subject–object) relationship to an I–Thou reciprocal relationship—that is, a change from man in unilinear control of nature to man within an ecosystem.

Five, limitation of population growth.

Six, moves in the direction of palaeotechnic agriculture; for example: less intensive agricultural technology, poly-culture, more diversified cropping patterns, substitution of land for artificial fertilizer, more organic fertilizer, acceptance of lower yields per unit of land, more of a live-and-let-live relationship with insects. . . .

Seven, maintenance and deliberate creation of varied environments. Margalef (1968, p. 50) believes that the best solution to the dilemma of exploitation in opposition to conservation is ". . . a balanced mosaic, or rather a honeycomb, of exploited and protected areas." Odum (1969, p. 268) argues for a similar compartmentalization ". . . so that growth-type, steady-state, and intermediate type ecosystems can be linked with urban and industrial areas for mutual benefit." In other words, few ecologists believe that man should or successfully can "seize control of nature." We must disintensify, leave a few untended corners. Golley writes in this regard

> We are a part of cybernetic systems (ecosystems) just like any other living population. Since, by definition, cybernetic systems operate by error control, we can expect that we will err in our interactions with other parts of the biosphere. If this is true, then it is illogical, indeed it is suicidal, to think that we can bring the biosphere under our control and provide the management to maintain biosphere stability. Man has always relied on the nonhuman parts of the biosphere to repair mistakes in ecosystem management and to provide control of human numbers. If we wish to live in a biosphere similar to that present today or present in the past, we must limit our control of the biosphere, so that sufficient unmanaged habitats and areas exist to provide the plants, animals, and microorganisms necessary in repair processes. We must preserve the repair processes to bring the system back to an equilibrium and permit us to start over again. (Golley, 1972, p. 89)

In conclusion, I return to my earlier remark that it is ironic that the Bomagai-Angoiang and similar palaeotechnic groups believe they have nothing to teach the neotechnic world. In studying their long-lived ecosystems, human ecologists have seen all the principles of permanence discussed or implied in this paper. Now that all over the world communities like the Bomagai-Angoiang are disappearing as "victims of progress" (Bodley, 1975), the task remaining is to apply these principles and to build into the neotechnic-dominated ecosphere a structure of permanence. If we do not, we will all—neotechnic and palaeotechnic alike—become victims of progress.

## NOTE

1. Clarke (1966) outlines the increased labour input that comes in New Guinea with a shift from forest- to grass-dominated spontaneous vegetation.

# REFERENCES

ANDERSON, E., 1974, "The Life and Culture of Ecotopia," in *Reinventing Anthropology*, D. Hymes (ed.). New York: Vintage Books, pp. 264–283.

BATESON, G., 1972, *Steps to an Ecology of Mind.* New York: Ballantine Books.

BEER, S., 1972, "Management in Cybernetic Terms," in *Scientific Thought.* Paris: UNESCO, pp. 167–185.

BODLEY, J., 1975, *Victims of Progress.* Menlo Park, California: Cummings.

BROOKFIELD, H., 1973, "Full Circle in Chimbu: A Study of Trends and Cycles," in *The Pacific in Transition: Geographical Perspectives on Adaptation and Change*, H. Brookfield (ed.). London: Edward Arnold, pp. 127–160.

———, 1975, *Interdependent Development.* London: Methuen.

BUCHBINDER, G., 1973, "Maring Microadaptation: A Study of Demographic, Nutritional, Genetic and Phenotypic Variation in a Highland New Guinea Population," Ph. D. Dissertation, Columbia University.

CLARKE, W., 1966, "From Extensive to Intensive Shifting Cultivation: A Succession from New Guinea," *Ethnology*, 5: 347–359.

———, 1971, *Place and People: An Ecology of a New Guinean Community.* Berkeley and Los Angeles: University of California Press.

DICKINSON, J., 1972 "Alternatives to Monoculture in the Humid Tropics of Latin America," *Prof. Geog.*, 24: 217–222.

FLANNERY, K., 1972, "The Cultural Evolution of Civilizations," *Ann. Rev. Ecol. Systematics*, 3: 399–426.

GOLDSMITH, E., *et al.*, 1972, "A Blueprint for Survival," *Ecologist*, 2, no. 1: 1–43.

GOLLEY, F. B., 1972, "Energy Flux in Ecosystems," in *Ecosystem Structure and Function*, J. A. Wiens (ed.). Eugene: Oregon State University Press, pp. 69–90.

GROTH, E., 1975, "Increasing the Harvest," *Environment*, 17, no. 1: 28–39.

HALL, A. D., and R. E. FAGEN, 1956, "Definition of System," *Gen. Syst. Yearbook*, 1: 18–28. Reprinted in W. Buckley (ed.), 1968, *Modern Systems Research for the Behavioral Scientist.* Chicago: Aldine.

HARDIN, G., 1968, "The Tragedy of the Commons," *Science*, 162: 1243–1248.

HEWITT, K., and K. HARE, 1973, *Man and Environment: Conceptual Frameworks*, Commission of College Geography, Resource Paper No. 20. Washington, D.C.: Association of American Geographers.

HIDE, R., 1974, "On the Dynamics of Some New Guinea Highland Pig Cycles," unpublished Ms.

HODDER, B.W., 1973, *Economic Development in the Tropics*, 2nd ed. London: Methuen.

JACKSON, R. T., 1975, "In Praise of Burundi, Paraguay *et al.*" *Area*, 7: 83–86.

JANZEN, D. H., 1973, "Tropical Agroecosystems," *Science*, 182: 1212–1219.

LEIGHLY, J., ed., 1963, *Land and Life: A Selection from the Writings of Carol Ortwin Sauer.* Berkeley and Los Angeles: University of California Press.

MCARTHUR, M., 1974, "Pigs for the Ancestors: A Review Article," *Oceania*, 45: 87–123.

MANNERS, I.R., 1974, "The Environmental Impact of Modern Agricultural Technologies," *Perspectives on Environment*, Manners and M. W. Mikesell (eds.). Washington, D.C.: Association of American Geographers, pp. 181–212.

MARGALEF, R., 1968, *Perspectives in Ecological Theory.* Chicago: University of Chicago Press.

MISHAN, E., 1969, *The Costs of Economic Growth.* Harmondsworth: Penguin Books.

ODUM, E. P., 1969, "The Strategy of Ecosystem Development," *Science*, 164: 262–270.

ODUM, H. T., 1973, "Energy, Ecology, and Economics," *Ambio*, 2: 220–227.

PIMENTEL, D., *et al.*, 1973, "Food Production and the Energy Crisis," *Science*, 182: 443–449.

RAPPAPORT, R., 1967, *Pigs for the Ancestors: Ritual in the Ecology of a New Guinean People*. New Haven: Yale University Press.

———, 1971, "The Flow of Energy in an Agricultural Society," *Scient. Am.*, 224, no. 3: 116–132.

———, 1974, "Energy and the Structure of Adaptation," presented at 140th Annual Meeting of the American Association for the Advancement of Science, San Francisco.

SCHUMACHER, E. F., 1974, *Small Is Beautiful: A Study of Economics as if People Mattered*. London: Abacus.

SLOBODKIN, L., 1974, "Mind, Bind, and Ecology: A Review of Gregory Bateson's Collected Essays," *Hum. Ecol.*, 2: 67–74.

STEINHART, J. S., and C.E. STEINHART, 1974, "Energy Use in the U.S. Food System," *Science*, 184: 307–316.

TAYLOR, G., 1974, *Rethink*. Harmondsworth: Penguin Books.

VAYDA, A.P. , 1971, "Phases of the Process of War and Peace among the Marings of New Guinea," *Oceania*, 42: 1–24.

VAYDA, A. P., and B. J. McCAY, 1975, "New Directions in Ecology and Ecological Anthropology," *Ann. Rev. Anthrop.*, 4:293–306.

WADDELL, E., 1972, *The Mound Builders: Agricultural Practices, Environment, and Society in the Central Highlands of New Guinea*. Seattle: University of Washington Press.

# ABOUT THE AUTHORS

DANIEL G. BATES was born in Long Beach, California. He studied at Robert College in Istanbul, Turkey, and the University of Freiburg in Germany and received both his B.A. in 1964 and his Ph.D. in 1971 from the University of Michigan. Since 1971 he has taught at Hunter College of the City University of New York, where he is Associate Professor and Chair of the Department of Anthropology. He is also a member of the Doctoral Faculty in Anthropology at the Graduate Center of the City University. Professor Bates has done extensive fieldwork in Southeastern Turkey and among the Goklan Turkmen of Northeastern Iran. He is the author of a monograph, *Nomands and Farmers: The Yoruk of Southeastern Turkey* and has published articles in edited collections and in such journals as *American Anthropologist, Anthropological Quarterly, Journal of American Antiquity,* and *Journal of Asian and African Studies.* With Susan Lees, he is coeditor of the journal, *Human Ecology.*

SUSAN H. LEES was born in Chicago, Illinois. She received her B.A. from the University of Chicago in 1965 and her M.A. and Ph.D. from the University of Michigan in 1966 and 1970, respectively. She has published a monograph, *Sociopolitical Aspects of Canal Irrigation in the Valley of Oazaca,* and numerous articles concerning the social and ecological implications of rural development. She has done field research in Latin America and Israel, and has been engaged in applied, as well as theoretical anthropology. At present, she is Associate Professor in the Department of Anthropology at Hunter College, C.U.N.Y. and co-editor of *Human Ecology,* and interdisciplinary journal, with Daniel Bates.

# A NOTE ON THE TYPE

The text of this book is set in Gael, a CRT/Videocomp version of Caledonia, a linotype face designed by W.A. Dwiggins. It belongs to the family of printing types called "modern face" by printers - a term used to mark the change in style of type-letters that occurred about 1800. Caledonia borders on the general design of Scotch Modern, but is more freely drawn than that letter.

Composed by Com Com, Allentown, Pa.

Printed and bound by R.R. Donnelley & Sons Company, Crawfordsville, Ind.